Communism and the

Yugoslav National Question

EAST CENTRAL EUROPEAN STUDIES

OF COLUMBIA UNIVERSITY

Communism and the Yugoslav National Question

PAUL SHOUP

1968

COLUMBIA UNIVERSITY PRESS

New York and London

EAST CENTRAL EUROPEAN STUDIES
OF COLUMBIA UNIVERSITY

The East Central European Studies comprise scholarly books prepared at Columbia University and published under the auspices of the Institute on East Central Europe of Columbia University. The faculty of the Institute on East Central Europe, while not assuming responsibility for the material presented or the conclusions reached by the authors, believe that these studies contribute substantially to knowledge of the area and should serve to stimulate further inquiry and research.

The Communist Party of Bulgaria: Origins and Development, 1883–1936
Joseph Rothschild

Yugoslavia in Crisis, 1934–1941   J. B. Hoptner

The First Partition of Poland   Herbert H. Kaplan

Czechoslovak National Income and Product, 1947–1948 and 1955–1956
Thad Paul Alton and Associates

Polish-Soviet Relations, 1932–1939   Bohdan B. Budorowycz

Hungarian National Income and Product in 1955
Thad Paul Alton and Associates

Politics of Socialist Agriculture in Poland: 1945–1960
Andrzej Korbonski

Polish National Income and Product in 1954, 1955, and 1956
Thad Paul Alton and Associates

Comintern and Peasant in East Europe, 1919–1930
George D. Jackson, Jr.

Piłsudski's Coup d'Etat   Joseph Rothschild

Communism and the Yugoslav National Question   Paul Shoup

To Professor Philip E. Mosely

WHO INTRODUCED THE AUTHOR TO EASTERN EUROPE

AND WHO HAS WORKED UNTIRINGLY TO PROMOTE

COOPERATION BETWEEN

THE YUGOSLAV AND AMERICAN PEOPLES

Preface

THE AUTHOR wishes to acknowledge the assistance given him from many quarters, in particular from all those Yugoslavs who shared with him their knowledge of the events described in this volume. A particular debt of gratitude is owed to the faculty and staff of the Law Faculty of the University of Belgrade for their cooperation in the task of gathering materials for this study.

Publication of this work has been made possible through the support of the American Philosophical Society, the Russian Institute of Columbia University, and the University of Virginia.

In the account that follows, all proper names are rendered in the original Serbo-Croatian, Slovenian, or Macedonian, transliterated from the Cyrillic to Serbo-Croatian equivalents in the case of Macedonian. Place names are given in their English form if an accepted English usage exists; otherwise they are given in Serbo-Croatian. Russian, Bulgarian, and other proper names from other Slavic tongues are transliterated according to the Library of Congress system, with a few modifications.

PAUL SHOUP

University of Virginia
September, 1967

Contents

Communism and the

Yugoslav National Question

Abbreviations

ASNOM	Macedonian Anti-Fascist Council of National Liberation
AVNOJ	Anti-Fascist Council of National Liberation of Yugoslavia
CP	Communist Party
CPY	Communist Party of Yugoslavia
FJUS	Federation of South Slavs
IMRO	Internal Macedonian Revolutionary Organization
IVZ	Islamic Religious Community
MPR	Macedonian People's Republic
NOF	National Liberation Front
SNOF	Slavo-Macedonian National Liberation Front
ZAVNOH	Croatian Anti-Fascist Council of National Liberation

Introduction

THE YUGOSLAV national question is a problem which has for years posed a challenge to scholars of East Central Europe by virtue of its complexity, the absence of reliable information, and the vehemence with which rival national groups have attacked each other for real or imagined violations of national rights.

Yugoslav and Western scholars have made valuable contributions to our understanding of various incidents connected with the national question. An authoritative history of the problem has yet to be written, however. The problem is simply too immense.

This study of the Communists and the national question seeks a middle road, eschewing the task of describing national relations in Yugoslavia in their entirety, while focusing on one major period in the development of the national question, that freshest in people's minds and most relevant to the study of contemporary East Central Europe.

Not all the issues raised in the pages to follow are of recent origin, however. The history of Communist involvement in the national question extends back in time to World War I, and even earlier, to the formative period of the socialist movement in the Balkans at the turn of the century. No account of communism and the national question would be complete without reference to these events.

As a terminal point, the study has chosen the dismissal of Aleksander Ranković from his positions of power in the Yugoslav Communist Party in the summer of 1966—a relatively recent event, and yet significant because it marked the end of one stage in the development of the national question. National relations since that time are, by and large, described in an abbreviated form.

A certain ambiguity accompanies the term "national question" when speaking about Yugoslavia. In fact, the phrase encompasses at least two distinct, if interrelated, problems. One is domestic in character, and concerns relations among national groups, or national groups and minorities, in a multinational state. The other problem concerns the role of nationalism in influencing the conduct of foreign policy, and is frequently brought up in connection with the behavior of the Yugoslav Communist regime in its dealings with other states, above all, the Soviet Union.

It might be considered desirable, in order to avoid confusing the two issues, to speak of the "nationalities" question in the pages to follow. This account nevertheless has chosen to adhere to prevailing usage in Yugoslavia and Eastern Europe generally, and draws no sharp dividing line between the internal and international aspects of the national question. Those issues, domestic or international, which illuminate Communist attitudes toward, and relations with, the Yugoslav nationalities have been included for discussion, while those which do not have to a large extent been omitted.

A certain amount of essential information on the nature of the Yugoslav national question is important for an understanding of the material presented in the chapters to follow. Thus, although the history of the national problem does not lend itself easily to summation, a few observations on national relations in Yugoslavia are in order before taking up the complex issues posed by Communist policy and the national question.

It has been noted that the most elementary facts concerning the Yugoslav national question may be the subject of considerable controversy. This observation can be easily verified by examining the debate that has surrounded the problem of the number of nationalities that together make up the Yugoslav state. At the time Yugoslavia was formed, many persons could be found supporting the position that all Yugoslavs were of one nationality (the Communists, among others, adhered to this view). This attitude was at first rejected by the Yugoslav government. In the early years of the nation's existence, three separate "tribes"—the Serbs, Croats, and Slovenes—were recognized as existing within the country's boundaries. The implementation of this view was evident in the official title given the country when it was formed after World War I: the Kingdom of the Serbs, Croats, and Slovenes. After 1929, when parliamentary government was suspended and a drive was launched to halt the fragmentation of the country into rival national groups, official policy sought to win acceptance for the idea of a Yugoslav nationality. Only one national group, the Yugoslavs, was therefore recognized by the government, and in accordance with this position the country was renamed Yugoslavia. After 1939, when it proved necessary to grant the Croats a large degree of autonomy, the notion that all Yugoslavs were of one nationality was officially abandoned.

Although these shifts in the position of the Yugoslav government contributed considerably to the uncertainty over the number of major national groups that deserved recognition, some agreement among the Yugoslavs prior to World War II concerning the status of the major nationalities was discernible. By and large it came to be the consensus that the Serbs, Croats, and Slovenes were distinct, if related, nationalities.

However, no such general accord existed concerning the remaining Slav groups in the Yugoslav population, nor in respect to the minorities. Prior to the end of World War II, controversy was most intense over the national identity of the Macedonians. The Yugoslav government said they were Serbs, while the Bulgarians claimed they were Bulgarian, and the Macedonians themselves were divided. Most Serbs felt that the Montenegrins were not a nationality in their own right, and some Montenegrins sided with the Serbs on this issue, while others supported the view that the Montenegrins were a full-fledged nationality distinct from the Serbs. Many Moslems of Slav extraction in Bosnia and Hercegovina felt that they deserved recognition as a national group rather than being treated, as was the case, as a religious community.

These controversies did not entirely subside when the Communists came to power. The solution pursued by the Communist Party, however, was calculated to limit controversy to an absolutely irreducible minimum. In place of the former three "tribes," or nationalities, five Slav nationalities (not counting Slav minorities) were recognized after World War II: Serbs, Croats, Slovenes, Macedonians, and Montenegrins. A brief word concerning the size of these groups and their distribution will help clarify the multinational character of present-day Yugoslavia.

Of the five nationalities, the Serbs are by far the largest and most widely distributed.[1] While the majority live in the Republic of Serbia,

[1] The exact figures on the national composition of the Yugoslav population can be found in Appendix A. No ethnic map has been published on the basis of these fig-

a sizable group (30 percent) live in other republics, where they constitute a Slav "minority" element. Taken together, the Serbs in Yugoslavia number approximately seven million. While this is not a majority of the population, it is considerably more than the next largest and most important group, the Croats.

The Croats number four million and are also found in relatively large numbers outside their own republic—in Bosnia, in Hercegovina, and in Vojvodina. The Dalmatian Croats, while situated within the territory of the Croatian Republic, are frequently considered as a group somewhat apart from other Croatians, not necessarily because of any sense of belonging to a Dalmatian nationality, but because peculiar historical influences and local geographic conditions have shaped a special way of life for the Dalmatians over the centuries.

The Slovenes are a compact national group of one and a half million. Up until World War II, Slovenian nationalism directed much of its efforts toward regaining the Slav irredenta situated across the Yugoslav boundary in Italy and Carinthian Austria. Today, the former of these irredentas has been largely liquidated by the acquisition of most of Istria by Yugoslavia. Meanwhile, the Slovenian minority in Carinthia has remained a bone of contention between the Yugoslavs and the Austrians.

The Macedonians number approximately one million, making them at present the fourth largest Slav group in Yugoslavia. To an even greater degree than in the case of the Slovenes, the Macedonian nationality has been plagued by the division of more or less Macedonian regions (their exact extent being highly disputed) among a number of states—in this case Yugoslavia, Bulgaria, and Greece.

---

ures, but the report on nationalities of Yugoslavia giving the results of the 1948 census contains five maps showing the distribution of each nationality by percent in the districts of Yugoslavia. See FNRJ, Savezni Zavod za Statistiku, *Konačni rezultati popisa stanovništva od 15 marta 1948 godine,* Vol. IX: *Stanovništvo po narodnosti,* pp. xx–xxv. For an ethnic map based on the prewar Yugoslav censuses of 1921 and 1931 (which did not distinguish among nationalities but did give religious affiliations), see Markert, ed., p. 32. A concise description of ethnic differences in Yugoslavia can be found in Kerner, ed., Chapter II. The most ambitious and influential attempt to differentiate among the Balkan Slavs on the basis of broad ethnic criteria, including such factors as temperament and character, was made by the Serb ethnographer Jovan Cvijić in his work *Balkansko poluostrvo i južnoslovenske zemlje,* Vol. II: *Psihičke osobine Južnih Slovena.*

The Montenegrins, closely related to the Serbs, are the smallest of the major Slav groups in Yugoslavia, totaling about 500,000. Their reputation as a proud and warlike nationality has given them fame beyond their numbers. Montenegrins can be found outside their own republic in the Autonomous Region of Kossovo-Metohija and in the larger cities of Serbia and Dalmatia. Although the Montenegrins have not had the problem of an irredenta in recent times, they have been engaged in numerous boundary disputes with neighboring Albania.

The status of the 700,000 Moslem Slavs is ambiguous. They have gained partial recognition as a nationality in the postwar period.[2] At the same time, they do not yet enjoy the privileges (such as possessing a republic) which have accompanied national recognition in the case of the other major Slav groups. Most of these Moslem Slavs are situated in the Republic of Bosnia and Hercegovina.

Minorities constitute approximately 10 percent of the Yugoslav population. There are almost one million Albanians and approximately 500,000 Hungarians within Yugoslavia's borders, as well as a smaller number of Slovaks, Czechs, Italians, Turks, Bulgarians, and Rumanians. There was once a large German minority as well, but practically all Germans were expelled from the country at the end of World War II.[3]

Differences in religion and culture run deep among the nationalities of Yugoslavia. The Serbs, Montenegrins, and Macedonians comprise a large Orthodox bloc, while the Croats and Slovenes are Catholic.[4] Nationality has commonly depended on one's religion in areas of mixed nationality where ethnic and linguistic differences are minimal, for example, in the case of the Serbs and Croats in Bosnia and Hercegovina. Conversion to Islam had a profound effect on the national attitudes and cultural values of the Moslem Slavs; so much so, in fact, that many have felt themselves to be more Turk than Slav. Cultural differences among the Yugoslav nationalities have generally patterned themselves

[2] See Chapter 5.

[3] Chapter 3 gives more information on the fate of the German minority.

[4] In the interwar period, the Serbs claimed that a number of Dalmatian Catholics were Serbs. The census of 1953, in which nationality was determined by the declaration of each individual, showed 8,812 Serbs who indicated they were Catholic. The extreme right of the Croatian national movement—Josip Frank and Ante Pavelić—spoke of "Orthodox Croats" in advancing their claims for a Greater Croatia. In 1953, 1,215 Croats said they were of Orthodox faith.

on religious divisions. For five centuries the Orthodox portions of the country lived under Turkish rule, while the Catholic areas of Yugoslavia in the north, governed by Austria, Hungary, and Venice, were developing a Central European or Latin pattern of culture. While Turkish rule did not disadvantage the Balkan Slavs to the degree that many persons have implied, it did deprive the Balkan peoples of contact with European culture at a time when their national kindred in the north were acquiring habits considered advantageous in the operation of modern society.

Nevertheless, the influence on the national question of contrasts in religion and culture among the peoples of Yugoslavia can be exaggerated. How greatly, and in what ways, the national characters of the Yugoslav peoples differ has never been accurately determined, and a case could be made that the Yugoslav nationalities have been divided by some characteristics, such as extreme national sensitivity, common to one and all alike. Far more important as a contributing factor to national rivalries over the years have been the widely differing historical experiences of the South Slavs. The Yugoslavs were never united in one state (the closest approximation was the short-lived kingdom of the Bosnian king Tvrtko in the fourteenth century). Following the growth of nationalism in Central Europe and the Balkans in the nineteenth century, most of the South Slav nationalities developed their own independent national movements—proud, uncompromising, and imbued with a unique sense of mission derived from the desire to recapture the real or imagined glories of short-lived medieval kingdoms of the past.

The rapid spread of nationalism among the South Slavs, and the negative aspects of this phenomenon, were already the object of criticism prior to World War I. In *The Southern Slav Question and the Hapsburg Monarchy* (1911) the elder Seton-Watson observed that "incredible as it must appear to any foreigner, there is no Anthology in existence which covers both Croat and Serb poets within the same covers. . . . The two are kept in air-tight compartments by what can only be described as childishly provincial bigotry." [5] But Seton-Watson was not immune to the emotions that he himself so rightly criticized. In defense of the Austro-Hungarian monarchy he suggested, in the same

[5] P. 130.

volume, that "the triumph of the pan-Serb idea would mean the triumph of Eastern over Western culture, and would be a fatal blow to progress and modern development." [6] This notion of the "Eastern" character of Serbian culture, already prevalent among the Croats at the time Seton-Watson wrote, has remained a thorn in Serb-Croat relations up to the present time.

In the early years of national awakening in Eastern Europe and the Balkans, relations among the South Slavs were also complicated by the fact that national movements varied greatly in respect to their maturity and the degree of independence they had won for their peoples. Serbia gained recognition by the Great Powers as a fully sovereign state at the Congress of Berlin in 1878, and by 1914, thanks to her successes in the Balkan Wars, had come into possession of areas in which the majority of the population were of Albanian or undetermined "Macedonian" nationality. Prior to World War I, Croatia and Slovenia attempted, but failed, to win autonomy within the Austro-Hungarian Empire. Montenegro prior to the creation of a Yugoslav state was independent, a close ally of Serbia, while in Macedonia a national movement known by its initials as IMRO (Internal Macedonian Revolutionary Organization) had seen its goal of autonomy for Macedonia shattered by the partition of the region among Serbia, Greece, and Bulgaria as a result of the Balkan Wars. Cooperation among these groups did develop along fruitful lines in some cases, and differences could be submerged, at least temporarily, in the face of a common enemy. But in the persecution of the inhabitants of Macedonia by the Serbs, to cite only one example, all the old issues of national exploitation and intimidation which had earlier inflamed the passions of the Slavs against the Turks were reborn, with disastrous results for relations among the Serbs and Macedonians in later years.

The union of the South Slav peoples into one state was, until World War I, more of an abstract ideal than a practical goal. The members of the Illyrian movement, active in Croatia and Slovenia prior to 1848, were the first group to take up the cause of unity among the South Slavs. In the latter half of the nineteenth century, support for a Yugoslav state developed among the Serbs in Croatia and spread to the Croatians.

[6] P. 337.

Although preoccupied with the task of winning autonomy within the Habsburg monarchy, most Croats were sympathetically inclined toward the concept of cooperation and eventual confederation of the South Slavs.[7] Serbian socialists supported the idea of a Balkan federation including Bulgaria and Greece. On the other hand, enthusiasm for a Yugoslav state did not characterize most Serbs. By far the great majority of Serbian parties and their supporters prior to World War I were caught up in the struggle over Bosnia-Hercegovina, and dreamt of the day when a Greater Serbia might be created by the annexation of Bosnia and Hercegovina to the existing Serbian nation.

The formation of a Yugoslav state was the direct result of the events of World War I. With the collapse of the Habsburg monarchy, the Slovenes and the Croats had little alternative but to ally themselves closely with Serbia. The dominant political figure in Serbia, Nikola Pašić, was at first reluctant to sacrifice the goal of a Greater Serbia for the purpose of creating a South Slav state. But under pressure from the Allies, and deprived of his principal ally, Russia, by the revolution in that country, Pašić was compelled in 1917 to agree to the formation of a Yugoslav state once hostilities had ceased.[8]

The coming into existence of Yugoslavia, which took place at the end of 1918, was welcomed by many persons who had been active in the Yugoslav movement, or who favored a Balkan federation, prior to World War I. The Yugoslav Committee in London, which brought these people together during the war, engaged in forceful and effective propaganda for the creation of the new state. Nevertheless, the union itself was by and large the product of necessity, hastily undertaken, and carried through without adequate consideration of the rights and obligations of the participating groups.

These difficulties might not have been of great importance for the new

[7] The Serb-Croat coalition, a political grouping which dominated Croatian politics from 1905 to 1918, demanded revision of the Agreement of 1868 with Hungary as the first step toward the satisfaction of the national rights of the peoples of Croatia. In the long run, the coalition urged the union of the South Slav peoples in an independent Yugoslav state.

[8] In the Corfu declaration of July, 1917, Pašić and the Yugoslav Committee in London agreed that the new state would be a constitutional monarchy under the Karadjordjević dynasty. A constitutional convention voting by a qualified majority was to determine the internal structure of the new state.

state if the Yugoslav idea had seized the imagination of the Yugoslav peoples and swept aside old national loyalties. Unfortunately, however, this did not occur. Yugoslav unity was not a goal which inspired genuine devotion and sacrifice among Yugoslavs. It should be noted in this connection that the rather pallid image projected by those favoring the Yugoslav idea was a serious handicap to efforts to break down the parochialism of the Yugoslavs and replace local national feelings with a genuine Yugoslav patriotism. Unlike the national movements of most South Slav nationalities, the Yugoslav movement could never point to an authentic national leader around whom loyalties could form, or appeal to a glorious tradition of struggle against a foreign occupier.

As a consequence of these facts, and as a result of the short-sighted policies of the Serbian-dominated governments which ruled the country, the national question grew steadily worse between the two world wars. The most serious dispute that arose was between the Serbs and Croats; the latter felt humiliated and exploited in the new state and demanded autonomy as a way of freeing themselves from the hegemony of the Serbs.[9] The Yugoslav government finally took steps to satisfy the Croatian demands in 1939,[10] but by this time mutual suspicions and fears had permanently poisoned relations between Croats and Serbs in Yugoslavia. Macedonia, where Bulgarian national feeling was strong among certain segments of the population, was in a state of repressed rebellion in the interwar period.[11] The minorities also felt estranged from the government in Belgrade, and their national grievances were played upon by irredentist elements from abroad.[12]

[9] For the Croatian viewpoint, see Vladko Maček, *In the Struggle for Freedom,* and Rudolf Bićanić, *Ekonomska podloga hrvatskog pitanja.*

[10] Under the Sporazum (agreement) of September, 1939, the Croatians received almost complete autonomy, including their own assembly and, perhaps more important still, a Croatian Ministry of the Interior. The central government retained responsibility for foreign affairs, religious affairs, defense, transport, and certain other fields. The Ban, or governor, was to be appointed by the king and was responsible to the Croatian assembly. A constitutional court was to be established which would judge the constitutionality of acts of the Banovina and settle all disputes between the Banovina of Croatia and the central government.

[11] For conditions in Macedonia, see Joseph Swire, *Bulgarian Conspiracy.*

[12] Information on the minorities in the interwar period can be found in Ewald Ammende, ed., *Die Nationalitaten in den Staaten Europas,* and Josef Chmelar, *Die nationalen Minderheiten in Mitteleuropa.*

Despite continual political agitation occasioned by fierce national rivalries, Yugoslavia experienced only sporadic outbursts of physical violence among her nationalities in the interwar period. World War II supplied the hitherto missing element of large-scale violence. Following the collapse of the country before the onslaught of the Axis powers in 1941, waves of terror and brutality swept across Yugoslavia. Croatian fascists, known as Ustaši, committed excesses against the Serbs in Croatia, Bosnia, and Hercegovina. Serbian Chetniks were guilty of atrocities committed against the Moslem population in Serbia, the Sandžak, and Bosnia-Hercegovina. Bulgarians, Hungarians, and Albanians massacred Serbs from Vojvodina, Kossovo-Metohija, and Macedonia. Finally, the Germans attempted to carry out the denationalization of Slovenian territory annexed to the Third Reich.[13]

As a consequence of these nationally inspired excesses, the formation of a viable Yugoslav state after the war was placed in gravest jeopardy. Deep divisions within the Yugoslav government-in-exile also gave little reason to expect that the national question could be successfully brought under control even if a Yugoslav state was reestablished with the assistance of the Allied powers.[14] When national strife was indeed curbed at the end of the war, it was not as the result of a reconciliation of national differences but because the Communists, by seizing power and carrying out revolutionary changes in Yugoslav society, drastically limited the scope given to expressions of national discontent.

Although numerous polemics have attempted to lay the blame for national conflict on one or another of the Yugoslav nationalities, it seems clear that the agitation and the violence in connection with the national question which preceded the Communist take-over were the result of strong nationalistic sentiments which could be found equally in all national groups. This does not mean that the Yugoslav nationalities were totally opposed to reconciling their differences within a Yugoslav state. On the contrary, in the interwar period outright separatism was confined largely to the national minorities, to elements in the Macedonian

---

[13] Official Yugoslav accounts of these atrocities are contained in DFJ, Državna komisija za utvrdjivanje zločina okupatora i njihovih pomagača, *Saopštenja o zločinima okupatora i njihovih pomagača.*

[14] For the Serbian view of exile politics, see David Martin, *Ally Betrayed;* for the Croatian view, P. D. Ostović, *The Truth about Yugoslavia.*

population, and to a minority among the Croats.[15] Most Croats leaned toward a solution of the national question based on a loose confederation of the Yugoslav peoples, while the Serbs favored unitary rule directed from Belgrade, the form of government which in fact prevailed until the Croats received their autonomy in 1939. Finally, there remained a small group committed to the Yugoslav ideal as a means of transcending narrow national rivalries. These pro-Yugoslavs could be found among the intellectuals (who, it should be noted, also supplied recruits for the extremist nationalist movements), among one segment of the Slovenian middle class, and in certain regions, especially Dalmatia and Serbian districts in Croatia and Vojvodina. Until World War II, therefore, the concept of a Yugoslav state remained the starting point for bringing about a cessation of national strife, although the idea of Yugoslav unity was not itself strong enough to effect a reconciliation of rival national groups.

In brief, the roots of national conflict in Yugoslavia lie largely in historical experiences which have created bitterness and suspicion among closely related nationalities. While different in many respects, and violently partisan in defending narrow national interests, these national groups also have many common features and have largely been committed to working out their problems within the framework of a common state.

While the national question has its roots in history, it is nevertheless an issue with far-reaching ramifications which touch on every aspect of Yugoslav life. In the chapters to follow it will become quite evident that relations among the Yugoslav nationalities involve complex political, economic, and social issues—problems too complex, indeed, to be encapsulated in introductory comments of this nature.

The role of economic nationalism in stimulating national rivalries has

15 In the elections of 1920 the Croatian States Rights Party (with a program of Croatian independence) obtained 10,880 votes and two mandates. It boycotted the constituent assembly. In the elections of 1923 the Party fell to 8,089 votes and won no mandates. In 1925 it ran three candidates (Ante Pavelić, Prebegand, and Aleksandar Horvat). None were elected and the Party obtained only 882 votes in Zagreb where its appeal was strongest. In alliance with the Croatian bloc of Ante Trumbić in 1927, Pavelić was elected from Zagreb. The States Rights Party was dissolved in 1929 and Pavelić left the country to continue his agitation for Croatian independence in exile while secretly organizing his Ustaši organization within Yugoslavia.

been a question of particularly great concern since the Communists came
to power. The existence of this problem does not lessen the importance
of historically derived attitudes in shaping the course of national relations. But, as the account to follow hopes to demonstrate, the Yugoslav
national question today is very much part of the contemporary drama
of nation-building and economic development now being played out in
many parts of the world. Whatever judgment one wishes to pass on the
Communists' efforts to cope with the national problem, therefore, it
must be borne in mind that the difficulties they face are not restricted
to Yugoslavia alone but are universal in character. By the same token,
the struggle of the Yugoslav peoples to find a just and lasting solution
to their differences has been part of a much larger drama that transcends
the problem of the fate of the Yugoslav peoples themselves. What has
been at stake—and what this account hopes to show is still at issue in
Communist Yugoslav—is whether closely related and intermixed peoples
can, regardless of past differences, find ways to live at peace with one
another while cooperating for the common good in matters of joint concern. Thus, in the last analysis, universal and basic issues form a thread
throughout the complex problems of national relations to be described
in the pages that follow.

1

The National Question and the Yugoslav Communist Party
1919-1941

THE COMMUNIST PARTY of Yugoslavia (CPY) was founded in 1919, a year after the act of union which created the Yugoslav state. It was a coincidence of history, but still significant in a symbolic sense, that the new state and the revolutionary party were born so close together. For the Yugoslav Communists were to become the first truly Yugoslav party in the history of the country. Tito, after he became the Party's secretary and ruler of Yugoslavia, was to become the first real Yugoslav national leader.

It is surprising to learn, in the light of these facts, that the movement which played such a major role in the struggle for the unity of the Yugoslav peoples was itself hopelessly divided on the national question for long periods of time prior to World War II.

During the period between 1919 and 1941, the Yugoslav Communist Party debated the national question almost as fiercely as the non-Communist parties. The factionalism which developed in the Party became legendary. In a fit of irritation, Palmiro Togliatti, addressing the Yugoslav Communists in the capacity of an emissary from the Communist International, once accused the Yugoslavs of being temperamentally unable to take a united position on the national question, or on any other issue, because of their disputatious Balkan temperament.[1]

The reasons for the disputes which divided the Party in the interwar period did not, of course, lie simply in the emotional nature of the South Slavs. Nor was the controversy within the Party over the national

[1] The speech has been reproduced in the Yugoslav collection of documents on the history of the Party in the interwar period, Istorijsko odelenje Centralnog komiteta KPJ, *Istorijski arhiv Komunističke partije Jugoslavije*, Vol. II: *Kongresi i zemaljske konferencije KPJ, 1919–1937*, pp. 463–64. Volumes in this series will subsequently be referred to as *Arhiv*.

question the product of nationalistic fervor, although this feeling was in evidence in the ranks of the Party from time to time. Unlike most non-Communist groups, the Communists were not involved in the defense of local interests or intent on defending national honor; rather their job was to pursue revolutionary aims. There was never complete agreement on how this objective was to be attained, however, and the task of the Communists was made infinitely more difficult by the atmosphere of continual tension and controversy prevailing in the country as the result of the national problem. Not surprisingly, there were strong differences of opinion over how to accomplish the revolutionary goals of the Party under such conditions. It is to these differences, in turn, that many of the bitter factional disputes in the Party in the interwar period can be traced.

The difficulties of adapting revolutionary strategy to the Yugoslav situation had roots in the theoretical problems which faced all Marxist socialists when dealing with the phenomenon of nationalism. Marx himself frequently expressed his views on the behavior of national groups in Europe (including the Balkan peoples, of whom he tended to be critical), but he failed to provide an adequate explanation for the persistence of nationalism in the face of his own predictions that the class struggle would inevitably come to overshadow national loyalties.

This inability to come to grips with nationalism characterized much of socialist ideology. Only among the socialists of the multinational empires of Eastern Europe and Russia was the attempt made to give a theoretical explanation of national rivalries from which some practical guidance could be drawn for the solution of national difficulties. The most important of these efforts was the plan of the Austrian socialists Renner and Bauer for extraterritorial autonomy of nationalities within the Austrian Empire, which was later supplemented by Otto Bauer's influential work, *The National Question and Social Democracy* (1907). A rival work, *Marxism and the National Question* (1913), was prepared by Stalin under Lenin's direction for the Russian Bolsheviks. Stalin attacked the Austrian plan and suggested instead that the socialists should adopt the slogan of self-determination in cases where national conflict existed within multinational states. The Austrian plan, although perhaps difficult to apply in practice, was a genuine effort to seek a solution of the nationalities question in the conditions that then prevailed in the

Austro-Hungarian Empire. The Bolshevik theory (which had little influence at the time outside of the ranks of Lenin's followers within the Russian Social Democratic Party) was more opportunistic and polemical in tone, and hoped to exploit Russia's national difficulties for political ends by offering the discontented national groups in the empire the vague, but appealing, right of self-determination.

These discussions within socialist ranks over the question of nationalism were not directly concerned with the problems of the Balkans. It was generally assumed that the decisive confrontation between the bourgeoisie and the proletariat would have to take place in the strongholds of capitalism—the great European powers—and that the Balkan states were of peripheral importance. Then, too, the primitive conditions of the region seemed ill-suited for the development of a working-class movement.

Socialism nevertheless found a receptive audience among the radical intelligentsia who succeeded, prior to World War I, in establishing small but vocal socialist parties in Bulgaria, Serbia, and the South Slav portions of the Austro-Hungarian Empire. The Social Democratic Party of Croatia and Slavonia and the Yugoslav [Slovenian] Socialist Party accepted the Austrian socialist view of the national problem and sought broad autonomy for the Slovenian and Croatian nationalities within the empire. At the Second Congress of the Social Democratic Party of Croatia and Slavonia held in 1896, a demand was made for full autonomy for Croatia-Slavonia and Dalmatia within the framework of the empire. In 1908 the Croatian socialists sharpened their position by calling for the solution of the national question within Austria-Hungary "on the basis of a democratic constitution, according to which each nation would be secured full governing, political, and educational freedom." [2] Both the Croatian and the Slovenian socialists supported the creation of a Yugoslav state in 1918, although the Croatian socialists were the more enthusiastic of the two groups for union.[3]

[2] Accounts of these meetings may be found in Strugar, pp. 112 and 118, and *Arhiv,* VI, 57 and 123.

[3] In a declaration issued in an assembly of the Croatian socialists on May 1, 1918, it was stated that "Slovenes, Croats, and Serbs are one and the same people, and that as a consequence they have all the attributes of one people, and especially in this respect . . . that they constitute an independent free state." Korać, III, 308. The declaration which the Slovenes issued at the time of the Yugoslav Socialist Confer-

In Macedonia, the socialists were caught up in national rivalries and never succeeded in forming a unified Macedonian socialist party. The first socialist group in Macedonia was formed by Vasil Glavinov in 1893, and was active in Macedonia until it merged with the Bulgarian "Narrow" socialist party just prior to the Balkan Wars, a number of its leaders being absorbed into the left wing of IMRO in the process. Glavinov fought against the interference of the Balkan powers in Macedonian affairs; [4] he attended the first Balkan conference of socialists in 1910 and presumably lent his support to the policy of a Balkan federation approved at this meeting. At the same time, Glavinov supported the merger of Macedonian socialists with the Bulgarian Narrows. Other socialist groups which appeared after the turn of the century favored the creation of an independent socialist movement in Macedonia. In 1909 the Serbian socialists entered the picture, setting up their own organization in Skoplje for the purpose of forging a united Macedonian socialist movement, but the differences between Glavinov on the one hand, and those who favored the creation of an independent socialist movement on the other, could not be satisfactorily reconciled,[5] and from this time on, hopes for unity among the Macedonian socialists faded in the turmoil of the Balkan Wars.

The national policy of the Serbian Social Democrats prior to World War I was a blend of internationalism, derived from the revolutionary teachings of Marxism, and a fierce national pride which originated in identification of their party with the national aspirations of Serbia and suspicion of the imperialist designs of the European powers against Serbia and the rest of the Balkans. The Serbian socialists were sincere and dedicated internationalists, as their opposition to Serbian territorial claims in Macedonia and Albania prior to World War I made clear.[6]

---

ence, held in October, 1918, to rally the socialists of the empire behind Yugoslavia, has been reproduced in part by Korać, III, 288–89. In this statement, the Slovenian socialists accepted union in much more guarded terms than were used by the Croatian socialists.

[4] *Arhiv,* VI, 23–35 and 226.

[5] The compromise resolution of the meeting of Macedonian Socialists convened in Salonica in 1910 to create a united party has been published in Zografski, *Za rabotničkoto dviženje,* pp. 242–43. For other accounts of socialism in Macedonia, see Marjanović, *Nastanak i razvitak radničkog pokreta u Jugoslovenskim zemljama;* Lapčević, *Istorija socijalizma u Srbiji;* Kofos, *Nationalism and Communism in Macedonia.*

[6] On the Albanian problem, see Tucović, *Srbija i Arbanija.*

Alone among the socialist parties in Europe, the Serbian Social Democrats voted against granting war credits to their government in 1914.[7]

But the fact that the Serbian socialists were strongly influenced by national feelings was revealed in their reaction to the annexation of Bosnia-Hercegovina in 1908. The Serbian Social Democratic Party bitterly attacked the "colonial" policies of the Austrian government and urged the Austrian socialists, without success, to join in a demand for the self-determination of Bosnia-Hercegovina.[8] The inspiration for this appeal to the principle of self-determination (which some Yugoslav Communists have interpreted as a Leninist view toward the national question) was to be found not in Marxist theory on the national question but in outraged Serbian pride and in the conviction that Austrian influence in Bosnia-Hercegovina would slow the progress of socialism in the Balkans. "The occupation of Bosnia-Hercegovina," wrote the Serbian socialist leader Dimitrije Tucović, "has completely prevented the natural development of the Balkan peoples and their amalgamation (*grupisanje*). If that had not happened, there would already have taken place in the Balkans that national amalgamation *without which there cannot be correct political and cultural development.*"[9]

The solution favored by the Serbian socialists for the national question in the Balkans was Balkan federation, an idea which had first found support among the Serbian socialists in the 1870s, and prior to World War I had been endorsed by most of the socialist groups on the peninsula. After the war, the idea was to become the victim of the intrigues of the international Communist movement, while many socialists had doubts concerning the practicality of such a federation even earlier. But Balkan federation was sincerely and earnestly advocated by the socialists as the alternative to fratricidal strife, and was given up only reluctantly as a result of the events of the Balkan Wars and World War I.

The idea of federation was looked upon with distrust by the Croatian socialists, however, and as a result became an issue which separated Yugoslav socialists of the north and south. There were also drawbacks to the plan as it was conceived by the Serbian socialists and others, for

---

[7] For the position of the Serbian Social Democratic Party during the war, see Walling, pp. 107–8, and Lapcević, *Rat i srpska socijalna demokratija*, pp. 128–34.

[8] Strugar, p. 26.

[9] Lapčević, *Rat i srpska socijalna demokratija*, p. 11.

little consideration was given to the method by which the federation was to be organized, especially the number and size of its participating units [10] (although it was envisaged that Macedonia would enter such a grouping as an autonomous member). The Serbian socialists were primarily concerned with the economic advantages of a Balkan union, and seem to have had little awareness of the need to provide a guarantee of the inviolability of national rights and to ensure the free expression of national cultures, problems which had so concerned Renner and Bauer in their plans for reorganization of the Austro-Hungarian Empire.

The Serbian Social Democratic Party adhered to the principle of Balkan federation through World War I. In an announcement appearing in the French *Humanité* in July, 1917, dealing with the Balkan question, the Committee of the Serbian Social Democratic Party in France supported the principles laid down at the Balkan Conference of 1910; [11] at the last congress of the Party in 1919 a decision was taken again stating the Party's approval of the idea of Balkan federation into which Macedonia would enter as an equal partner.[12]

But from the time of the Bulgarian attack on Serbia in 1915 until the end of World War I, more and more Serbian socialists began seeking other solutions to the national question. The idea that Serbia should be enlarged by the addition of those areas that were naturally Serbian came to be accepted by an important segment of the Party. This idea formed the basis for an impassioned plea for a greater Serbia made by Dušan Popović and Triša Kaclerović (both of the left wing of the Party) to the Stockholm conference of socialists in September, 1918. These opponents of Serbian nationalist ambitions in the past now called for a Serbia that should become "an Adriatic state, that is, should unite with Bosnia, Hercegovina, and Dalmatia," and urged that such a union was "the first necessary condition for the advance of socialism." [13]

The creation of Yugoslavia in 1918 provided the Serbian socialists with much of what they had hoped to achieve through Balkan federa-

[10] The resolution of the Balkan conference, for example, left this question quite vague. Besides references to Balkan "federation," or "confederation," published sources shed little light on the attitude of the socialists toward the position of the nationalities in a Balkan federation.

[11] Todorović, ed., pp. 235–36.

[12] Lapčević, *Rat i srpska socijalna demokratija*, p. 161.

[13] Korać, III, 309–10.

tion, and they were quick to recognize it. In November of 1918 the Serbian Social Democratic Party came out with a statement in which the creation of a Yugoslav state was supported as strongly as Balkan federation and unification of Serbia had been in their day. In words practically identical to those which the Croatian socialists had been using up to this time, the Serbian socialists adopted the proposition that "the Serbs, Croats, and Slovenes are one nation, for they have one language and identical remaining ethnic characteristics. They feel like one people and desire union." [14]

The year 1918 thus found the socialists united on the national question and quickly reorienting themselves to the idea of working within a South Slav state. In respect to other problems the socialists were not as successful in reaching agreement, however. A whole series of divergent opinions quickly developed between the "Social Patriots" on the one hand, who joined the temporary Yugoslav government, and the revolutionaries on the other. The chaos and confusion of this period naturally aided those with revolutionary views, whose ranks were augmented by Bolsheviks and indoctrinated soldiers returning from Russia (especially to Vojvodina and Croatia). The Croatian and Slovenian socialists were split, but the Serbian socialists went over to the Bolsheviks en masse, and with their overwhelming weight thrown on the scales a Communist Party (or Workers' Party, as it was known for a year) was formed in 1919. The Communists quickly asserted themselves as a major factor in Yugoslav politics until their activities were drastically curbed in 1920. The Party was finally outlawed completely in August of 1921.

In the turmoil of the immediate postwar years, little thought was given to the national question by the Communists. There was no resolution passed on the subject at either the First or the Second Congress of the Party, and the national problem was not at issue in any of the factional struggles of this period. Rather than seeking to exploit the national question for their own ends, the Communists vigorously supported the principle of centralism and the formation of a unitary state. One could see

[14] The statement continued: "It follows that their union in one national state is a great political, economic, and cultural need which is beyond any discussion. Thanks to national union the proletariat gets a broad field for agitation and organization and a more reliable basis for developing class war and, in the last analysis, for a showdown with its national bourgeoisie." Lapčević, *Rat i srpska socijalna demokratija,* p. 157.

evidence of this as early as 1918 among the Yugoslav Communists residing in Russia, whose section attached to the Bolshevik party adopted
an uncompromising demand to "do away with the divisions of the state,
and in their place establish one Yugoslav Socialist Soviet Republic." (An
earlier proposal had called for a "federal system and national rights" but
had been overriden by Filip Filipović, soon to become secretary of the
Yugoslav Communist Party.) [15] At the Vukovar congress of the Yugoslav Communist Party (June, 1920), the enthusiasm for centralism was
revealed in the proposal that Yugoslavia, as a "Soviet Republic," should
join with other Balkan peoples to form a Balkan-Danube federation,
which in turn would be an "integral part" of an international federation
of Soviet republics.[16] In this breath-taking vision, the individual nationalities of Yugoslavia were reduced to total insignificance.

For several years this attitude of aloofness from the national issue
served the Communists well. As a result of its support for a unitary state,
the Party gained favor in Serbia and Montenegro, and by its unceasing
attacks on the government, it attracted support in regions where national
unrest was growing. The non-Communist parties encouraged the voters
with national grievances to vote Communist by charging the Communists
with being "Egzarhista" (pro-Bulgarian) in Macedonia and "Frankov-
luci" (Croatian Nationalists) in Croatia. In the local elections of 1920
the Communists showed strength in many parts of the country, and in the
fall of 1920 they made a surprising showing in the elections for the constituent assembly, placing third and electing 59 deputies. In these elections the Party ran especially well in areas which were in opposition to
Belgrade, either because of growing national unrest (Croatia), economic
distress (Montenegro and Dalmatia), or both (Macedonia). In Montenegro and Macedonia the Communists received the greatest number of
votes of any party. Everywhere, however, the Party attracted a large
number of supporters, even in Serbia.[17]

15 *Četrdeset godina*, I, 43.

16 *Arhiv*, II, 35–36. The First Congress in 1919 had even less reference to anything connected with the national question. An editor's note to *Arhiv*, II, 473, says
that the practical action program called for "one national state with fullest self-
government in oblasts, okrugs, and opštinas."

17 In Macedonia, in the local elections of August, 1920, the Party won in Veles,
Prilep, Kumanovo, and Djakovica and lost, then won, in Skoplje. The Moslem vote
in Macedonia went to the Radicals, who had allied themselves with the Turkish

Events soon forced the Party to reconsider its attitude toward the national question. As a result of the repressive measures taken against the Communists in 1920 and 1921, their revolutionary hopes were dashed and the Party was thrown into confusion. New splits appeared in 1921 over whether the Party should seek concessions from the government to restore its legality. The optimism of the early years was eclipsed by a growing pessimism among a right-wing group in the Party led by the Party secretary, Sima Marković. Marković, a Serb and former anarcho-syndicalist, led the fight to legalize the Party. He now began to support a policy of constitutional concessions to meet the demands of the Croats with the hope that this would end national unrest and permit the Party to maintain its policy of aloofness from the national question.

The attitude of the Party toward the national question also came into conflict with the interests of the Communist International. Initially, the Comintern reacted in a confused fashion to the situation in the Balkans; Zinoviev's ringing declaration on the Balkans issued in the spring of 1920 was addressed to "The Communist Parties of Bulgaria, Rumania, *Serbia,* and Turkey." [18] For a period of three years, until May of 1922, there was no public criticism of the Yugoslav Party's national policy by the Communist International, and the CPY was permitted to pursue

---

and Albanian political leaders. In the elections for the constitutent assembly, the Communists proved themselves the strongest party in Macedonia, winning 38 percent of the vote (it should be noted, however, that only 55 percent of those registered bothered to vote). In Montenegro the CPY received more votes than any other party, obtaining 10,900 out of 28,650 cast, and sent four deputies (two of whom were born in Serbia) to the constituent assembly. According to Batrić Jovanović, p. 79, there were 30,000 members in the Party in Montenegro at the end of 1920! In the local elections in Croatia in the spring of 1920 the Party showed great strength in Belgrade, Zagreb, Osijek, and other cities, even though it was competing with a rival "Centrumaši" Communist group. In 1920, excluding Dalmatia, there were 15,500 persons in the Party in Croatia, according to Moma Marković and Ivan Lača, p. 21. Dalmatia had somewhat over 2,000 Party members at the time. In Ljubljana, the CPY fell behind the other main parties and received a handful more than the socialists in very light voting. Analyzing the Communist vote of 1920 for its national significance has attracted many authors. The basic data for the elections to the constituent assembly can be found in *Ustavotvorne skupštine, statistički pogled izbora narodnih poslanika.* For discussions, see D. A. Tomašić, "The New Class and Nationalism," *Journal of Croatian Studies,* I (1960), 53–74, and his *National Communism and Soviet Strategy;* R. V. Burks, *The Dynamics of Communism in Eastern Europe;* and Avakumović, pp. 42–48.

[18] *Kommunisticheskii Internatsional,* No. 9 (1920), pp. 1405–10. Italics added.

its policy of aloofness from the growing national dispute in Yugoslavia without interference from Moscow.[19] But it was clear that from its inception the Comintern had a view on the national question which was contrary to the position of the Yugoslav Communists. Reflecting the hostility of the Soviet Union to the Versailles settlement, the Comintern was openly critical of the formation of Yugoslavia, and saw in growing national rivalries the opportunity to strike a blow against the new state. The interest of the Comintern in encouraging national rivalries was also based on certain assumptions (evident in the Zinoviev declaration) concerning the desirability of exploiting the national question in the Balkans by persuading the mass of workers and peasants, especially the latter, to seek satisfaction of their national grievances by supporting the Communist movement. This policy was openly and vigorously pressed at meetings of an offshoot of the Comintern, the Balkan Communist Federation, which was under the influence of the Bulgarian Communists and was openly hostile to Yugoslavia.[20]

The Comintern strategy, apart from its hostility toward the Yugoslav state, was unacceptable to Sima Marković and his supporters for a number of reasons, all involving fundamental questions of the role of a Communist party in a multinational state with a largely peasant population. First of all, the attitude of the Comintern was in conflict with the opinion of the new right wing of the Party that it was impractical to organize for

[19] The Second Congress of the Third International set out the basic line on the national question in the Resolution on the National and Colonial Question. There was apparently no specific discussion of the Yugoslav national problem at the meeting, however. There are no records of criticism of the Yugoslav position at the Third Comintern Congress of 1921 (attended by Marković). The Comintern intervened in the affairs of the Party at the First Area (*zemaljska*) Conference of the CPY in June, 1922, but apparently not on the national question. The resolution of the Fourth Comintern Congress, which can be found in *Arhiv*, II, 417–20, makes no mention of the national question, and a report by Felix Kohn, the Polish Communist, on the congress and the Yugoslavs says that the quarrels within the Party, including those on the national question, were of a personal nature. *Fourth Congress of the Communist International*, pp. 282–83. Sometime in the spring of 1923 the ECCI (Executive Committee of the Communist International) sent out a letter with detailed criticisms of the Yugoslav Party, including the question of national policy (*infra.*).

[20] The policies of the Balkan Communist Federation have been described in detail by Joseph Rothschild, *The Communist Party of Bulgaria*. In the discussion of the Macedonian question that follows, the position of the Federation toward Yugoslavia and Macedonia will be examined in more detail.

the seizure of power under the conditions that then prevailed. In connection with this pessimistic appraisal of the revolutionary situation in Yugoslavia, it was inevitable that doubts should arise over the position of the Comintern that the peasant could be utilized as a revolutionary force, or the justification for proposing, as Topalović observed in his critique of the Comintern position at the Vukovar congress of the Party, that "revolution is easier in underdeveloped countries." [21] Secondly, the position of the Comintern suggested a complete reversal in the relationship between the class struggle and the national issue which had been asserted by socialist theory up to that time. While it was true that Serbian socialist thinking had from time to time displayed nationalistic overtones, it was axiomatic to the Yugoslav Communists brought up in the traditions of the Serbian Social Democratic Party and Austrian socialism that focusing on national issues tended to distract revolutionary forces from the class struggle, and that the attempt to temper national emotions with moderation and reason was an onerous but inescapable duty of socialists in the emotion-charged atmosphere of the Balkans. It was elementary Marxism to Marković and his supporters that one could not hope to strengthen class solidarity while encouraging centrifugal forces along national lines within the working-class movement.

Debate within the Party over the national question began to develop in 1922 between the Marković faction on the one hand and a left faction supporting the Communist International on the other. In the early rounds the right faction prevailed, but in May, 1923, the left gained partial control of the Party.[22] This development was paralleled by the open intervention of the Comintern in the affairs of the Yugoslav Party, and the quarrel over the national question was joined in earnest,

[21] *Akcioni program Komunističke partije Jugoslavije*, p. 8.

[22] Marković's reasoning was clearly evident in the program of the new front party—the Independent Workers' Party of Yugoslavia—established at the end of 1922. The program, which appeared early in 1923, spoke of unresolved "tribal disputes" due to economic differences between "various regional tribal centers." *Arhiv*, II, 279. In May of 1923 the Comintern sent a letter to the CPY which, among other things, criticized its stand on the national question and insisted that the Yugoslav Party come out for "absolute self-determination of nationalities even to the point of actual separation from the Yugoslav state." At a plenum of the ECCI held a month later, the Yugoslav delegation defended the Yugoslav position against the strictures of Zinoviev to "use the nationality factor against the bourgeois regime." Williams, pp. 32–35 and 59.

to continue until the defeat of the right-wing Marković faction in 1926. Throughout this period, Party pronouncements on the national question fluctuated back and forth, now revealing the strength of one faction, now another, and most often an uneasy compromise between the two.

What concessions Communists should be prepared to make to national feeling were subject to intense scrutiny as a result of this conflict within the Party. Although the positions of the left and right factions were to become increasingly dogmatic as time wore on, the subject of nationalism was opened to searching analysis in the first flush of the debate, and wide-ranging proposals were made for dealing with the national question. For many Communists, it was apparent, federalism had become an attractive approach, and proposals for a federal system were frequently discussed in the Party press during the course of 1923 in connection with the debate over the national question. Among those who favored the federal plan, however, there was considerable uncertainty over when and how such a system should be introduced. Djuro Cvijić, one of the spokesmen for the left position, argued that, once the revolutionary and national issues were clearly joined (as the Comintern was urging), it should be possible for the Party to support the idea of a federation of "workers' and peasants' governments" from every national region.[23] August Cesarec, also generally associated with the left, advocated consideration of some form of federalism blended with the leftist appeal to self-determination on the grounds that self-determination alone was a "dry" slogan not sufficiently attractive to the Yugoslavs.[24] Few supported the federal idea out of nationalist sentiments; when one participant in the debate proposed union with Radić and the creation of a republican federation of workers' and peasants' governments, arguing that the Serb-Croat quarrel was essentially between two separate nations or two capitalisms, rather than due to the "imperialism" of one side against the other,[25] he was roundly criticized by both the left *and* the right, who were, each for its own reasons, centralists at heart.

Sima Marković developed his position in the pages of the Party newspaper *Borba,* strongly attacking all proposals for federalism as both in-

[23] *Borba,* Feb. 15, 1923, p. 5. (References to *Borba* in connection with the debate of 1923 are based on copies of the original documents made available to the author by the Institute for the Study of the Workers' Movement, Zagreb.)

[24] *Ibid.,* Aug. 30, 1923, pp. 2–4.

[25] See the contribution of Mbt in *Borba,* Oct. 11, 1922, pp. 5–6.

consistent and tending to weaken the solidarity of the working class.[26] At the same time he defended the plan of autonomy for national regions. His reasoning was spelled out in detail during the height of the discussion over the national question within the Party in 1923 in two volumes, *The National Question in the Light of Marxism* and *The Constitutional Question and the Working Class of Yugoslavia.*[27]

These works occupy a unique position in the history of the national question, for they represent the only methodical analysis of the Marxist approach to nationalism to appear from the ranks of the European Communist parties under Comintern control in the interwar period, and they were the last full-length treatment of the subject by a member of the Yugoslav Party for over three decades. Basing his analysis primarily on the pre-World War I works of Stalin, Marković sought theoretical justification for his personal conviction that the national question was not one which the Party could exploit for revolutionary ends. In this vein Marković argued that nationalism originated with the bourgeoisie and that the reconciliation of national conflicts should be sought within a capitalist framework; if not, the class struggle would remain stillborn, overshadowed by the demagogic appeals of competing national groups. Marković took the position that Yugoslavia was no exception to this general rule; that the people of the country desired union; and that, for this reason, the solution of the national question lay in finding a form of state organization most likely to reconcile conflicting national interests. In words which were to become the focus of the controversy, he stated that the national question was for the present a "constitutional question." In his practical recommendations, Marković repeated his well-known opposition to federalism, urging revision of the constitution to provide "broad autonomy" for each of the Yugoslav peoples.[28] In respect to nationality, Marković professed indifference: "As far as our position is concerned," he wrote, "it is altogether the same whether the Serbs, Croats, and Slovenes are three 'tribes' of one nation or three nations." [29]

The debate of 1923 ended with a partial victory for the left; at the

[26] *Borba*, Dec. 6, 1923, pp. 5–6.

[27] *Nacionalno pitanje u svetlosti Marksizma* and *Ustavno pitanje i radnička klasa Jugoslavije.* Another work of Marković's in which he reveals certain of his attitudes toward the national question is *Der Kommunismus in Jugoslawien.*

[28] *Nacionalno pitanje u svetlosti Marksizma,* pp. 119–22.

[29] *Ibid.,* p. 103.

third regional conference held in December, 1923, the Party took a position on the nationalities question unacceptable to Marković and Života Milojković, a trade union leader in Serbia who stood behind Marković on the national issue. For the first time the CPY came out unequivocally against the Versailles settlement, and spoke of the "sovereignty" of the Yugoslav peoples and their right to form separate states. But the statement made important concessions to Marković as well, especially in the explicit recognition that the "unity of the Serbs, Croats, and Slovenes lies in the line of direct historical progress and the interests of the class struggle." [30]

The polemics over the national question continued in 1924, marked by growing pressure on the Yugoslav Party from the Comintern to exploit the national issue for revolutionary ends. At the Fifth Congress of the Comintern held in June, extensive reports on the national question in Europe bore down heavily on the theme of exploiting nationalism to spread Communist influence while pressing for the right of self-determination for all suppressed nationalities, even in some cases *before* the party made its bid for power. The congress resolution called for the "separating of Croatia, Slovenia, and Macedonia from Yugoslavia and the creation of independent republics"; the Yugoslav Party was urged to seek support for its national program among the peasants and to enter into agreement with the Croatian Peasant Party leader Stefan Radić in order to conduct a joint campaign against the government in Belgrade.[31] Later in the year, a "Platform of Agreement" over the national issue was worked out between warring factions in the Yugoslav Party under the supervision of a

[30] *Arhiv*, II, 66–67.

[31] *5th Congress of the Communist International*, pp. 189–90. The resolution of the congress on the national question in Central Europe and the Balkans can be found in *International Press Correspondence*, No. 64 (Sept. 5, 1924). A meeting of the Balkan Communist Federation was convened a month later, at which the general line of the Comintern was pressed even more sharply. This meeting also dealt with the Macedonian question and touched on the minority question for the first time by reopening the matter of the Bulgarian minority in the Tsaribrod district. See Rothschild, p. 232. The harshest attack against Yugoslavia at this time was launched by the Bulgarian Communist Kolarov, who criticized the Yugoslavs for not wishing to see the end of the Yugoslav state, and strongly pushed the notion that the national question was a peasant question (an idea Stalin was to make famous a year later). See *The Communist International*, N.S., No. 4 (July-August, 1924).

Comintern agent.[32] The agreement, however, represented a compromise in which the influence of the Marković position was still evident.[33]

The stubborn insistence of Marković in maintaining his position in defiance of the Comintern finally led to a confrontation between the Yugoslav Party secretary and the leaders of the Communist International in the spring of 1925. The occasion was the Fifth Plenum of the Executive Committee of the Comintern held in Moscow in March and April. Stalin himself chose to participate, making the meeting the high point of the controversy within Communist ranks in Yugoslavia and elsewhere in Europe over the feasibility of associating the Communist parties with national groups dissatisfied with the results of the Versailles settlement.[34]

Despite the dramatic character of the confrontation between Marković and Stalin, most of the arguments at the Fifth Plenum took a familiar form. Stalin attacked the view that the Yugoslav national question could be solved by constitutional reforms. In this he was supported by Zinoviev, who publicly criticized Marković in the pages of *Pravda* while the plenum was in progress for failing to recognize the presence of revolutionary and national unrest in the Balkans among the peasantry.[35]

Marković did inject a special note into the proceedings, however, by arguing that his position was really based on the writings of Stalin himself. Whatever the tactical wisdom of such a move (and Marković seems grievously to have misunderstood Stalin in taking such an approach), the result was to shift the arguments, if only briefly, from the question of existing conditions in the Balkans to the problem of the proper Marxist approach to the national question in general. Stalin felt constrained to reply to Marković on this point, arguing that the national question had entered into a fundamentally new stage. No longer was the struggle among

[32] For a brief account of the meeting by one who attended it, see the contribution of Todor Zografski in *Četrdeset godina* I, 172. A breakdown of the delegates attending the meeting by regions from which they came has been compiled in U.S. Department of State, "Macedonian Nationalism," p. 14.

[33] *Arhiv*, II, 331–36; *Četrdeset godina*, I, 171.

[34] The main debate took place in the Yugoslav Commission of the plenum of the ECCI. Marković (alias Simović, and referred to by Stalin as "Semich") then defended his position in the commission; no report of his speech on this occasion is available. Stalin spoke to the commission on March 30; this speech was reprinted in *Bolshevik* on April 15. Marković prepared an article defending his position; this piece, and Stalin's response to it, were published in *Bolshevik* on June 30.

[35] *Pravda*, April 1, 1925, p. 5.

the bourgeoisie the central issue (as Stalin himself had implied in his 1913 work on the national question). Following the Russian Revolution, Stalin argued, the national question had come to revolve around the conflict between the imperialists and the exploited masses in the colonies. Under this new set of circumstances, the oppressed class, which was also the group fighting for national independence, was the peasantry, not the bourgeoisie. For this reason, said Stalin, employing a phrase which was to be repeated frequently after this time, the national question was now a question of the peasants.[36]

The line of reasoning which Stalin employed to support this conclusion was a curious one, emphasizing as it did the problem of colonies and ignoring the peculiar conditions of national strife in the Balkans to which Zinoviev and others had repeatedly addressed themselves in justifying the Comintern's appeal to nationalism among the peasants. Taking Stalin's argument at its face value, the fact that Yugoslavia was a multinational state wracked by national controversy was not as important as the colonial status of the country and the fact that the peasants were being exploited by foreign imperialists.

One is forced to the conclusion that Stalin himself did not have any intention of applying his theory of colonialism directly to the Yugoslav situation (except in so far as it might serve as a convenient justification for the argument that the peasants of the dissident national groups were being exploited by Belgrade), but was thinking primarily in terms of an international crisis which might end in a new war in Europe. Under these circumstances—Stalin seemed to be saying—it was the duty of the Yugoslav Communists to exploit the old idea that the Balkan peoples were a colony of the European powers, and stand ready to demand a revision of the boundary settlements arrived at after World War I.

Although the theoretical argument leading up to this conclusion was obscure, to say the least, the strategy Stalin was recommending was not an unreasonable one from the point of view of the interests of the international Communist movement. Here Marković, perhaps intentionally, seemed to have missed the point. Marković insisted that he supported all "national revolutionary" movements against imperialism and that he favored self-determination and even revolutionary exploitation of the national issue. But his position remained focused on the national ques-

[36] *Bolshevik,* No. 7, April 15, 1925.

tion as it appeared to the Yugoslavs themselves, without regard for the interests of the international Communist movement or even the realities of international politics. Nothing was more revealing, in this respect, than Marković's argument that after all, in Serbia, where three kings alone had been overthrown in the last half of the nineteenth century, the constitutional question was an excellent starting point for revolutionary activity! [37]

In point of fact, Stalin did not begin his controversy with Marković with the intention of forcing the Yugoslav Communists to accept the breakup of Yugoslavia as inevitable. In this, as other points of strategy, Stalin followed existing Comintern policy, arguing that for Croatia self-determination was a right, not a duty, and even suggesting that the Soviet type of federal system might be introduced in Yugoslavia if the Communists ever came to power [38] (this had already been proposed in a general way at the Fifth Congress of the Comintern the preceding year). When Marković persisted, even after the Fifth Plenum, in holding to his position and challenging Stalin on theoretical grounds, Stalin's tone not surprisingly became harsher, and he warned Marković that, if war or revolution should break out in Europe, self-determination could become an urgent question. Pressing the point home, Stalin then reminded Marković that under no circumstances could the present borders of Yugoslavia be taken as the "starting point and legal basis for the solution of the national question." [39] All this was confusing, given the earlier reference by Stalin to a Soviet system of federalism in Yugoslavia. What was clear was that Stalin, while attacking Marković for being wedded to the status quo, was not yet ready to advocate the open dismemberment of Yugoslavia. That such a moment could come, however, was made clear in Stalin's warning.

Marković's debate with Stalin anticipated an even more famous dispute between the Soviet dictator and the Yugoslav Communist Party a little more than twenty years later. The parallel between Tito and Marković is not entirely inappropriate, for in both there was apparent a conviction, perhaps not openly stated but powerful nevertheless, that the interests of the Yugoslav Party and of the Yugoslav state had to be viewed as one if the revolutionary movement was to succeed, against the view of the

[37] *Ibid.,* No. 11–12, June 30, 1925.
[38] *Ibid.,* No. 7, April 15, 1925.
[39] *Ibid.,* No. 11–12, June 30, 1925.

Comintern that first allegiance was owed to the Soviet Union as the bastion of the Communist world in the struggle with capitalism. Beyond this, however, comparisons are dangerous. Marković was deeply influenced in his behavior by conditions in Yugoslavia and by Yugoslav history. Tito, it will become evident in a later chapter, was driven to defy Stalin on quite different grounds—from a desire to duplicate Soviet achievements without giving much thought to Yugoslavia's peculiar conditions. Marković's arguments were those of prewar social democracy; Tito, in his dispute with Stalin, reasoned as a well-trained product of the Comintern revolutionary school. Finally, Marković was defying Stalin from a position of weakness; Tito, from a position of strength.

In the meantime, the debate between the left and right factions of the Party had become centered on the issue of collaboration with non-Communist nationalist groups in Yugoslavia. This policy had been initiated upon the insistence of the Comintern in 1924 with the aim of associating the Party with the rising national unrest in Yugoslavia. The left, which cooperated with the Comintern in carrying out this policy, did not abandon its revolutionary slogans, but it was willing to make temporary alliances over the national issue that were unacceptable to the more conservative, and less flexible elements in the Party. As a result, new divisions arose, or old ones were deepened, within the Party, and the position of the Communists on the national question became more difficult to follow than ever.

Nowhere were the problems of making the transition from the Marković position to one of active association with nationally discontented elements more evident than in Macedonia, where the Party, largely under the control of Serbs,[40] had consistently resisted the idea of any special

[40] It is difficult to get any reliable data concerning the national views of the members of the Communist Party in Macedonia, just as it is close to impossible to get any accurate information concerning the nationality of the Slav population in that region as a whole. Several things can nevertheless be established in respect to the Macedonian situation. The bulk of the population, following World War I, was deeply hostile to the Belgrade government. Many had family ties in Bulgaria, or had participated in some way in the Bulgarian occupation from 1915 to 1918. In terms of membership, the Party was mixed. Some Party organizations were controlled by "Bulgarian Macedonians" (in Veles, for example). Other areas were just as clearly Serbian, and certain Serbian elements, such as the colonists, were an important source of recruitment for the rank and file of the Party. It is characteristic, in respect to this mixture of nationally oriented elements, that, when an organization

solution for the Macedonian problem outside the framework of Yugoslavia.[41] The pressure on this defense of the status quo had begun to mount in 1922, when the Balkan Communist Federation had come out strongly for an autonomous Macedonia in a Balkan federation.[42] Marković placed the Yugoslav Party in opposition to this plan, and instead proposed some form of autonomy for Macedonia within Yugoslavia.[43] The dispute between the Bulgarians and the Yugoslavs was temporarily glossed over when the third regional conference of the CPY adopted the Comintern position on the Macedonian problem.[44] But in 1924 the issue

---

broke up under police persecution, reports spoke of one part of the membership fleeing to Sofia, the other part to Belgrade. There is less room for doubt concerning the national orientation of the Party leadership in Macedonia, nor any question concerning the nationality of those who controlled the Party. The Serbs were clearly predominant. At first the Macedonian Party was not even permitted to form a regional (*oblast*) committee and remained directly under the control of the central Party leadership in Belgrade. Leading positions in the Party were occupied by Serbs drawn from the old Serbian Social Democratic Party, from "national workers" in Macedonia who had fought Bulgarian influences before the Balkan Wars, and from the new intelligentsia on which the Yugoslav government relied to administer the area. In one or another of these categories were the Serbian Party leaders Dušan Čekić, Milan Marković, Petar Djordjević, Kosta Stefanović, and Dragutin Tasić.

[41] In February, 1920, the slogan "Balkan Federation of Soviet Republics" first appeared in the pages of the Macedonian Party organ *Socijalistička Zora*, but without explanation. *Istoriski arhiv na Komunističkata partija na Makedonija*, I, 53–54. In April the subject was treated in *Socijalistička Zora* at more length; an article described the role of the Balkans as a colony of the imperialist powers, and sounded the slogan "Federation is the way out!" Such a federation, it was suggested, could not be formed by the bourgeoisie. This reasoning followed the Comintern line, but in addition the article called for a "Balkan Socialist Soviet Republic" without any mention of autonomy for Macedonia, and quite deliberately played up the crisis in Europe, adding that "all this goes for our Balkans as well." The implication was clearly that the Balkans were on the periphery of the coming revolution, not at its epicenter. *Istoriski arhiv na Komunističkata partija na Makedonija*, I, 25–27.

[42] At the conference of the Balkan Communist Federation in Moscow in December, 1922, a resolution was passed calling for autonomy for Macedonia, Thrace, and Croatia within a future federation of Soviet republics. Rothschild, p. 232. At the Berlin conference of the organization in December, 1923, these slogans were repeated.

[43] *5th Congress of the Communist International*, p. 191; Williams, p. 56.

[44] The conference came out in favor of "unity and autonomy" for Macedonia and spoke in support of a "voluntary union of independent Balkan republics." The statement thus bowed to the Comintern demand for autonomy for Macedonia; at the same time it was clear that it could be interpreted from the Marković point

of Macedonia became the focus of renewed controversy when the Comintern, looking for support among the nationalist separatist elements in the Balkans, hit upon the idea of an alliance with IMRO.

The first steps in the realization of this improbable combination were successful. In April, 1924, negotiations were completed [45] between agents of the Comintern, on the one hand, and the wing of IMRO consisting of the Protogerov-Aleksandrov group and the federalists led by Philip Atanasov and Todor Panitsa, on the other.[46] An agreement was reached calling for the liberation and reunification of Macedonia, the "democratization" of the Balkans, and the union of Balkan states into a Balkan federation. All the states of the Balkans were held responsible for denying the Macedonians their national rights, but Bulgaria was made to appear far less culpable than either Yugoslavia or Greece; the influence of the Balkan Communist Federation in the document, and behind it the Bulgarian Communist Party, was not difficult to discern.[47]

With the publication of this agreement, troubles began. Far from aiding the Party in Macedonia, the alliance with IMRO created the utmost imaginable confusion. The Bulgarian Communists, as part of this maneuver, succeeded in getting the Balkan Communist Federation to adopt resolutions in March and July of 1924 which were highly favorable to their interests, and which in fact omitted any criticism of the Bulgarian role in the Macedonian question.[48] The Greek Communist Party, outraged, at first refused to publish the resolution adopted at the March meeting of the Balkan Communist Federation, and the Yugoslav Communist Party also resisted the demand made in the Federation's resolutions for the

---

of view as well. The declaration did not speak of self-determination and the right of secession for the region, a set of demands that were being made for other national regions in Yugoslavia. *Arhiv,* II, 74–77.

[45] Tentative contacts were established in 1922. Rothschild, pp. 177–78.

[46] Negotiations were carried out in Vienna in March with Chaulev representing the Protogerov group, Vlahov the interests of the Communists, and Atanasov and Panitsa the Federalists. The agreement was then signed by Protogerov; whether the agreement had Aleksandrov's approval is still debated, but it appeared with his signature. Protogerov and Aleksandrov tried to prevent publication of the agreement, but it appeared in the first issue of *La Fédération Balkanique.*

[47] *La Fédération Balkanique,* No. 1 (July 15, 1924), pp. 11–16.

[48] *International Press Correspondence,* No. 31 (May 29, 1924), pp. 312–13, and Rothschild, p. 235.

union and autonomy of Macedonia.[49] When the IMRO declaration appeared, the CPY rejected the plan and forbade Party members to give it their support.[50] It is reported that at this point the Comintern summoned a special delegation from the CPY to Moscow and in May, 1924, forced them to accept the IMRO position.[51]

On the other hand, the Protogerov-Aleksandrov faction of IMRO, under pressure from the Bulgarian government, renounced the April agreement; a bitter struggle for power broke out within the organization, as a result of which practically all those in any way associated with the agreement met death by assassination. Dimitar Vlahov, who had acted as a front for the Communists in making the agreement, was one of the few exceptions. When cooperation with existing IMRO groups proved impossible, the Comintern set up its own organization in 1925, IMRO-United, under Vlahov's supervision. The group never gained any real influence within Macedonia, and after a time Vlahov found it necessary to expel from its ranks the remaining federalists with leftist leanings (Atanasov, and then Georgi Tsankov) for failing to adhere to the Communist line.

The experiment of cooperation with IMRO was the inspiration of Moscow and the Bulgarian Communist Party, from which the Yugoslav Communists stood to gain little, regardless of the course of events. What threatened, if the alliance with IMRO had proved successful, was a struggle between the Yugoslav and Bulgarian Communists for control of the Party organizations in Macedonia, for contacts between IMRO and the Communists took place on Bulgarian soil, and before the whole scheme collapsed plans were being laid for the joint penetration of Vardar Macedonia by the Bulgarian Communist Party and IMRO.[52]

[49] *5th Congress of the Communist International,* p. 191; *I kongres na Komunističkata partija na Makedonija,* p. 42; Rothschild, p. 232. The Greek Party finally bowed to Comintern pressure on the Macedonian issue in December, 1924, accepting the slogan of an independent and united Macedonia. Kofos, *Nationalism and Communism,* p. 78.

[50] U.S. Department of State, "Macedonian Nationalism," p. 20.

[51] *Ibid.*

[52] See the reminiscences of the Macedonian Communist Alekso Martulkov, p. 365, where he describes how, in June of 1924, Vasil Glavinov appeared in Sofia and informed him of a plan for united action in Macedonia between the CP and IMRO. Khristo Jankov was to be sent to the Solun district, Angel Pop Vasilev

Another experiment initiated by the Comintern had almost equally disastrous results. This was the attempt to reach agreement with Radić. Radić was hardly a more promising ally than IMRO, but the Comintern was set on exploiting the opportunity offered by that politician's restless search for backing abroad for the Croatian cause. In the spring of 1924 Radić paid a visit to Moscow and made his party a member of the Krestintern, or Peasant International. The Comintern and the Balkan Communist Federation now urged the Yugoslav Communists to develop cooperation with the Croatian Peasant Party. Serbian elements in the CPY found this policy extremely distasteful; Radić did nothing to ease the situation by attacking the Serbian Communists in the pages of Krestianskii Internatsional, calling them "centralists who stand for the same point of view as the Serb militarists," and rather tactlessly boasting that as a consequence "it is only natural that the Croatian workers and the majority of the members of the Yugoslav Communist Party came over and enlisted in our ranks, where they remain today." [53]

In a matter of months after visiting Moscow, Radić reversed his course completely and accepted a post in the government coalition in Belgrade. Although completely outwitted, the Comintern continued to uphold the principle of cooperation with the Croatian Peasant Party.[54] The action of Radić caused anguish among the ranks of the Yugoslav Communists, however, and led to an open break between Milojković (the trade union ally of Markovic) and the CPY in the fall of 1924.[55] Cooperation with national groups had proved a complete failure, and the Party was once more split over the national question.

---

to the Bitolj district, and Martulkov himself to the Skoplje district. He was given instructions to "establish ties between the Internal Organization [IMRO] and the Communist organization there."

[53] *Krestianskii Internatsional,* No. 3–5 (June-July, 1924), p. 53.

[54] *Ibid.,* No. 7–9 (Sept.-Oct. 1924), pp. 43–53.

[55] Milojković's views were set forth on various occasions, especially in a declaration published October 8, 1924, in the Party newspaper *Organizovani Radnik.* This declaration was in turn an answer to the "Theses" of the Central Committee of the Independent Workers' Party of Yugoslavia (IWPY) attacking the Milojković position. The declaration of October 8 read, in part: "The opposition [i.e., the Milojković group] asserts that the tasks of the Marxist proletariat are purely negative and that the proletariat in its national policy should not take the position of so-called practicism, because the danger threatens that the class struggle will be transformed into a bourgeois-nationalist policy." This portion of the declaration

At the Third Congress of the CPY in Vienna in June, 1926, temporary unity was restored between the left and the right factions, and Marković was finally compelled to accept the Comintern line on the national question in its entirety.[56]

The condition of the Party was nevertheless very little improved; one of the statements made at the Third Congress spoke of "depression, passivity, and despair" in the ranks of the CPY following the defection of the Croatian Peasant Party.[57] Marković was kept on as secretary in a combined party leadership, but after the congress bitter factional warfare again broke out, leading to intervention by the Comintern once more in the spring of 1928 and the election of an entirely new party leadership, neither of the left nor of the right, at the Fourth Congress held at Dresden in October (it was at this congress that Togliatti was prompted to make his deprecatory remarks concerning the Balkan character of the Yugoslav Party).

Now national policy took a sharp turn toward extremism. At the Fourth Congress every nationality—including the Albanian minority—was urged to seek immediate secession from the Yugoslav state.[58] At the same time, the Sixth Congress of the International laid down a rigid line of noncooperation with all bourgeois parties, and ordered the Communist movement to engage in revolutionary action in alliance with the peasants for the establishment of worker-peasant republics. This slammed the door on cooperation with all nationalist parties, at least officially.

---

was quoted by "Boshkovich" (Filip Filipović) in an article entitled "Polozhenie v Kompartii Iugoslavii," *Kommunisticheskii Internatsional,* No. 4 (April, 1925), p. 57. Milojković bitterly attacked cooperation with Radić, which he is supposed to have described as "spitting on the revolutionary honor of the proletarian avantguard." See *Arhiv,* II, 316; the remark is from the "Theses" of the Central Committee of the IWPY and is attributed to Milojković in No. 64 of *Organizovani Radnik.* The October 8 resolution of the opposition faction was signed, Filipović reported, by 34 comrades, almost all Serbs. See B. Boshkovich, "Sobitiia v Iugoslavii," *Kommunisticheskii Internatsional,* No. 2 (February, 1925), p. 162. According to this account, an enlarged plenum of Party organizations took place on November 25 and 26; of the 88 organizations that took part, 79 were for the "Theses" of the Central Committe of the IWPY, and only one against. The rest presumably did not commit themselves.

[56] *Arhiv,* II, 110. The Party Congress was held in Vienna, of course, because the Party was still legally outlawed in Yugoslavia.

[57] *Ibid.,* II, 95.

[58] *Ibid.,* II, 163.

These extremist revolutionary plans would have placed the Party in a difficult position under the best of circumstances. But at the same time conditions for Party work in Yugoslavia took a sudden turn for the worse with the advent of the dictatorship of King Aleksander in 1929. The Communists were ruthlessly hunted down and arrested. As a result of this persecution, and the completely unrealistic policies adopted by the Comintern, the Party collapsed, its leaders fled abroad, and Party membership dropped to several hundred in all of Yugoslavia.

After a decade of turmoil, the Party had completely failed to turn the national question to its own advantage. The responsibility for this debacle lay most clearly with the Comintern. But all three elements involved in the struggle to shape the Party's national policy—the right and left factions and the Comintern—were in some degree involved in the Party's failure. Conversely, each group had stood for certain approaches toward the national question which were to influence Communist policy in later years.

Although the Comintern had been consistent in its pursuit of Soviet interests, its policies were extremely difficult to justify in ideological terms. In theory, the need for the Communists to abandon their earlier aloofness toward the national question was supported by the assertion that in the Balkans the national question was a "revolutionary one." This position encompassed two related, if somewhat different, ideas: that exploited national groups would support the Communist party in its revolutionary activities, and that a "final" solution of the national question would only be achieved through self-determination resulting from the revolutionary seizure of power by the Communists and their allies. But time and again the Comintern urged collaboration with dissident national groups in Yugoslavia who had not the slightest interest in revolution, with the inevitable consequence that what groups were to be considered "revolutionary" tended to be defined in terms of national attitudes, rather than the significance of national protest being measured in terms of its association with revolutionary goals.

The miscalculation of the Comintern—and it was a fundamental one—lay in assuming that the nationalist movements would accept communism if they could be convinced that only a revolution would bring them satisfaction of their national demands. On the other hand, it was easy to overlook the fact that, behind the opportunism and self-delusion of the Comintern, there lay an attempt to formulate a new approach toward nationalism which would associate the search for national justice with the revolutionary traditions of Marxism and, conversely, inculcate some of the Marxist international outlook upon the national movements. The Comintern, and Stalin specifically, performed a great service by eliminating resistance to this approach within the Yugoslav Party. Therein, it might be added, lies the difficulty in evaluating Stalin's contribution to the solution of the national question in Yugoslavia. Today the Yugoslav Communists, while they are by and large critical of Stalin for his hostility toward the Yugoslav state, must admit that a "correct" position on the national question was only achieved under his guidance.

The right wing of the Yugoslav Communist Party has been accused of taking a pro-Serbian attitude toward the national question. On this controversial point, several facts are clear: the Party was indeed overwhelmingly under the influence and control of Serbian Communists, drawn mostly from the old Serbian Social Democratic Party, up until 1928.[59] In the case of Sima Marković and those who supported him, further, there can be no doubt of the existence of a predisposition to look at the problem of Yugoslavia from a Serbian point of view. This was evident in the attitude of the CPY toward Macedonia; one can also find, in reports to the Comintern in the early 1920s, such references as "the

[59] The persons who served in the post of secretary or president of the Party in this period, all Serbs, included Filip Filipović, first Party secretary, Pavle Pavlović, Sima Marković, Triša Kaclerović, Kosta Novaković and Mihailo Todorović. The first non-Serbian secretary was Jovan Mališić-Martinov, a Montenegrin, who was chosen for the post in 1928. Records for the Party's Politburo, or Executive Committee, and for its Central Council are spotty. But of 8 members of the Executive Committee in August, 1920, 5 are definitely Serbs, and the remaining three probably so. Of the 8 members of the Central Party Council elected at the First National Conference of July, 1922, 5 are probably Serbs, 1 is a Slovene, and 2 are unknown. Immediately after the meeting, two members were dismissed and one member added, changing the national composition of the body to 5 definitely Serbian or 6 probably Serbian and 1 unknown. After the victory of the "left" faction in May, 1923, a more varied national composition is evident, including supporters of the left view from Zagreb. Numbered among them were Djuro Djaković and Djuro Cvijić, both Serbs from Croatia, Kaclerović, a Serb, and others so far not identified. The 1928 Dresden Congress chose a ruling body, a partial listing of which indicates 4 Serbs (1 of these, Djuro Djaković, from Croatia), 2 Montenegrins, 1 Croat (Djuro Salaj), and 1 unknown, probably a Serb.

newly annexed provinces," [60] when speaking of the Austro-Hungarian regions of Yugoslavia.

When revolutionary hopes were high, these early leaders of the Party spoke enthusiastically of a system of hierarchical socialist republics in the Balkans; one senses, in this zeal of the Belgrade Communists for centralism and uniformity, the outlines of a new type of revolutionary nationalism tinged with ethnic overtones of a kind which was eventually to develop, in pronounced form, in the Soviet Union.

The rapid evolution of this view to the position that the national question must be viewed as a "constitutional" one was consistent with the earlier tendency to downgrade the national question and continued to show the influence of a Serbian point of view. At the same time, a subtle change was taking place in the alchemy of revolutionary attitudes. Revolutionary centralism lost its attraction to those doubtful of imminent revolution but reappeared in the position of the left wing, whose policy of encouraging the national demands of the discontented elements in Yugoslavia was always balanced by an extremely doctrinaire view of the post-revolutionary system, where self-determination was only a "right," not a "duty," and in which, after national wounds had somehow miraculously been assuaged by the application of the principles of revolutionary justice, national passions would disappear forever.

The left wing, then, was actually just as centralistically inclined as the Marković faction, and a good deal more idealistic than the Comintern. When the Comintern decided to adopt the policy of the *immediate* dismemberment of Yugoslavia, in 1928, the left faction was removed from the scene, and a new type of individual appeared to carry out the Comintern line in Yugoslavia: Jovan Mališić, a Montenegrin trained in Moscow, who became Party secretary in 1928; the "Moscow student faction" made up of Serbs originally from Niš; Milan Čižinski-Gorkić, a professional Comintern agent since leaving Bosnia in 1922, who was made Party secretary in 1932; and, for that matter, Tito himself. These were a new breed, trained from an early age in Moscow for revolutionary responsibilities, with very few ties in Yugoslavia, and little or no national perspectives to start with.

It was this group that attempted to carry out the directives of the

[60] *Kommunisticheskii Internatsional,* No. 13 (1920), p. 2509.

Fourth Dresden Congress for immediate revolutionary action on the basis of a peasant uprising. Nothing came of these efforts; indeed, the local Party organizations, such as they were, simply ignored the orders of the Party, and no large-scale plans were made to launch peasant revolts. In 1932 the slogan of armed uprisings was discarded as a complete failure. At the same time, the Party continued to take an extreme position on the national question. In the spring of 1934 the Comintern was calling for the secession of Croatia, Macedonia, and Slovenia from Yugoslavia,[61] and the Yugoslav Communist Party signed a pact with the Italian and Austrian Communists to support a united (and presumably independent) Slovenia.[62] This strange agreement was paralleled by contacts with the extremist nationalist movements in Yugoslavia.[63] It is known that some form of ill-defined cooperation grew up between elements in the Party in Croatia with the United Revolutionary Youth, followers of Svetozar Pribićević, who semed to have revolutionary plans of their own against the government, of the type that Sima Marković would have described as part of the Serbian "constitutional" tradition.[64]

Following the rise of Hitler, the hostility of the Comintern toward the status quo in Europe disappeared, and efforts to weaken Yugoslavia by exploiting the national question were abandoned. Yugoslav Communist policy first reflected this change at the Fourth National Conference of the Party held in December, 1934. That portion of the conference statement which dealt with the question of national rights made no reference to immediate secession of the national regions of Yugoslavia and dropped demands for self-determination of the minorities.[65] Traces of the earlier militant policy remained, however: the conference called for revolutionary workers' and peasants' governments in Croatia and Dalmatia, Slovenia, Serbia and Montenegro, Bosnia, and Vojvodina (Macedonia was not

[61] H. Kabakchiev, "Kompartiia Bolgarii i nacionalnii vopros na Balkanakh," *Kommunisticheskii Internatsional,* No. 13 (May 1, 1934), pp. 44–50; *Proleter,* No. 4–5 (June, 1934), pp. 10–11.

[62] *Proleter,* No. 4–5 (June, 1934), pp. 10–11.

[63] Avakumović, pp. 108–9. This is also suggested by the fact that the Central Committee later found it necessary to direct the Party to reveal as fascists such persons as Mihailov and Pavelić. *Arhiv,* II, 399.

[64] *Četrdeset godina,* II, 331.

[65] *Arhiv,* II, 220.

included in the list, although the statement prepared by the conference spoke of a Macedonian nationality, the first such reference in Party literature).[66] In a decision taken by the Politburo in Moscow in August, 1935, shortly after the Seventh Comintern Congress, the CPY openly condemned the policy of secession of disaffected national regions as advantageous to the fascists, and a program of reform of the existing system was advocated as the best means of ending national oppression under the conditions that then prevailed.[67] A year later, in 1936, the Party carried the change a step further by emphasizing in positive terms the need for Yugoslav unity. The notion of self-determination as a "precondition" for the solution of the national question, rather than as a right which might or might not be exercised, was strongly condemned, and the Party adopted a position in favor of calling a constituent assembly to revise the existing constitution.[68] After January, 1937, the slogan of self-determination disappeared completely from Party pronouncements on the national question.[69]

The historic shift in policy of the international Communist movement to a position in defense of the status quo encouraged the Yugoslav Party to revive the pro-Yugoslav identification which it had abandoned in the mid-1920s. At the same time the Communists continued to present themselves as champions of the rights of the national groups opposed to Belgrade. This ruled out any return to the Marković position that the Yugoslav

[66] *Ibid.*

[67] As part of the program of realizing national rights within the existing system, the Party was to support the following reforms: (1) elimination of the banovina; (2) granting freedom for cultural groups to organize; (3) removal of Serbian colonists; (4) allowing national regions their own flags and other national symbols; (5) permitting the use of national languages; (6) ending favoritism toward industry in Serbia; (7) ending domination of the Serbs in government positions. *Arhiv,* II, 363.

[68] *Arhiv,* II, 399.

[69] The last published document available from this period which speaks of self-determination is the January, 1937, Declaration on the United Front. For parts of the declaration, see Hasanagić, ed., pp. 144–54. The statements issued by the founding congress of the Croatian Party and the First Congress of the Slovenian Party, which appeared in 1937, made no mention of self-determination. This did not mean that the CPY had "renounced" self-determination but rather that, for tactical reasons, it chose not to stress the point. One book dealing with the national question which was obviously following the Party line, Stjepan Livadić's *Politički eseji,* spoke of "self-rule" (*samoodredjenje,* not *samoopredelenje*).

peoples were all one nationality, and the Party, while shifting its position to the point where it was supporting "constitutional" solutions of the national question, never abandoned the Stalinist-inspired view that the national question could only be completely solved by revolutionary changes in Yugoslav society. It was true that demands to end the exploitation of Belgrade over the rest of the country were a standard element in Communist policy in this period, and during 1937–38 some of the nationalistic polemics of the non-Communists were echoed in the Party press. The Party in Slovenia, for example, suggested that taxes in Slovenia be reduced and that the dismantling of factories there cease.[70] The Montenegrins, in the election campaign of 1938, charged that Montenegro had given more to the community (that is, to Belgrade), than it had received.[71] But with one exception, to be mentioned shortly, these tactics were never permitted to overshadow the essentially radical nature of the Communists' approach to the national question, nor to allow chauvinism to replace revolutionary loyalties in the Party.

Ultimately, the benefits to the Communists of this approach to the national question, in which much of the revolutionary philosophy of the left wing of the Party of the mid-1920s was combined with a new patriotic spirit, were to be immense. In the short run, however, the united front period witnessed the appearance of new quarrels within the Party over national policy, and the national question continued to be a source of embarrassment and confusion to the Communists. Now, though, the Croatian Communists posed the main problem, rather than the Serbs.

In the late 1920s, following the defeat of the Marković faction,[72] Zagreb had come to replace Belgrade as the center of the Party's activities.[73] The

---

[70] Hasanagić, pp. 137–40.

[71] Batrić Jovanović, p. 284.

[72] When the temporary unity established in 1926 broke down in 1927, the Comintern called a conference of Yugoslav Communist leaders in Moscow in the spring of 1928, and afterward issued an "open letter" to CPY members criticizing factionalism in the Party. As a result of this letter, Marković was removed from his post as secretary, and an attempt was apparently made by the Central Committee, or "Bureau," of the Party to "suspend" the Belgrade Party organization. Marković responded by separating his organization from the CPY; at the Fourth Congress, he apparently reversed his position and brought his group back into the Party. *Četrdeset godina*, II, 216.

[73] The official organ of the Party, now *Srp i čekić*, started to appear in Zagreb, and in 1927, meetings of the Central Committee were held there for the first time;

Croatian section of the CPY reaffirmed its leading role at the time of the revival of the Party in the 1930s. The Croats soon found themselves out of step with the Party leadership, however, on the issue of setting up a united front. While the Zagreb Party group looked with suspicion at the effort to create a national front with the Yugoslav parties, Party secretary Milan Čižinski-Gorkić pushed vigorously for the new line, trying to reach agreement with the socialists and other parties, and as part of this strategy laying plans for the creation of an independent workers' party which could make alliances with non-Communist groups. The first real crisis arose in 1935 when the Croatian Communists resisted Gorkić's attempts to form such party; the united front plan fell through, and Gorkić, apparently in the hope of reviving a "united front from below" through exploiting the national question, persuaded the Central Committee to issue a sharp criticism of the national policy of the Belgrade government. The statement of the Central Committee was so sweeping in its attack that it seemed more anti-Serb than anti-Belgrade.[74] This in turn forced the Comintern to step in and restrain Gorkić; his erratic policies in 1935 and 1936 probably played a role in his downfall a year later.

In this muddle, the principal concern of the Croatian Communists was that the identification of the Party with the rights of the nationally exploited elements in Yugoslavia would be lost sight of in the drive for a united front. In addition, the idea of collaboration with the socialists, who had maintained the position that the Yugoslavs were all one nationality, was anathema to those elements in the Croatian Party who opposed Gorkić; instead they favored an alliance with the Croatian Peasant Party,

in 1928, the leadership of the youth movement moved to Zagreb from Belgrade after a trial of Communist youth in the latter city in February of that year. This shift was accelerated by the actions of Marković in "seceding" from the Party.

[74] The resolution attacked the Stojadinović government bitterly for its policies of national discrimination and exploitation, including Serbianization of the schools, reducing credits to scholarly institutions in Croatia and Slovenia, transferring the Maribor railway works to Kraljevo (Serbia), and so on. "The way out," the resolution stated, "lies only in broadening and deepening the national struggle against the Great Serb fascist exploitation." In the context of a call for a "united front from below," Gorkić suggested that the Party look favorably on regional demands for autonomy and support the convocation of national assemblies in Croatia and elsewhere. *Arhiv,* II, 380–95.

in the hope of gaining some foothold among the Croatian peasants. It was under the influence of these conditions that the leading Croatian playwright and Party sympathizer, Miroslav Krleža, came out in 1935 with a vigorous criticism of official Party policy on the national question, calling the appeals to self-determination and secession "platonic slogans," and urging a policy which would bring the Communists closer to the Croatian peasant, as well as extend the awareness of the Croatian peasant to the battle for the rights of the Yugoslav peasantry as a whole. This would be, as Krleža called it, a socialist movement "on an agrarian basis." [75]

This response, so heavily influenced by Croatian experience, can be considered as the Croatian national equivalent of the Marković Serbian approach of constitutional solutions to the national question. The Croatian CP at this time was not noticeably nationalistic, however; one can detect, in its statements on the national question, a more clearly articulated pro-Yugoslav position than in the stand of the Communists in neighboring Slovenia.[76] But as the pressure grew for the creation of an anti-fascist united front, so the Croatian Communists became more anxious and uncooperative. In 1938 they successfully resisted the efforts of Tito to set up an independent party along the lines Gorkić had charted three years earlier,[77] and criticized the CPY leadership for ignoring the

[75] Krleža, p. 559.

[76] The declaration on the national question issued by the First Congress of the Croatian Party in 1937 was phrased in moderate terms which carefully avoided nationalist extremes, either by focusing on the demands for self-determination, or by raising the problem of discrimination over harbors, research institutes, and the like. The proclamation of the founding congress of the Slovenian Party, prepared by Edvard Kardelj, has been referred to earlier; it demanded that taxes in Slovenia be reduced, that more be spent on Slovenian roads and railroads, and that the dismantling of factories in Slovenia cease.

[77] The preparations for the elections of 1938 had passed through several stages, complicated by the disorganization of the Party and the factional struggles going on at the time. By the fall of 1937, Tito was guiding Party policies on the united front issue; his reaction to the formation by the non-Communist parties of a united opposition in October, 1937, was quite favorable, more so, indeed, than that of the Initiating Committee of the Party of the Working People, which had only grudgingly allowed that this was a "step forward" in creating a united front. The Initiating Committee, organized in Zagreb to found a new legal party for the CPY, and having Bakarić and other Croats in its membership, seems to have represented a "Croatian" point of view at this time (or at least one side of it). For Tito's reaction to the October, 1937, formation of the united opposition, see

national struggle of the Croats for the sake of stressing Yugoslav unity at the time of the Austrian crisis.[78] Then, when the CPY adopted a defeatist line following the Nazi-Soviet pact of August, 1939, the Croatian Communists turned around and rallied to the support of the government (which now, of course, had agreed to Croatian autonomy and was made up of a coalition of Croats and Serbs). The upshot was the carrying through of a purge of the Croatian Central Committee, an action which Tito had apparently been contemplating since 1938.[79] In this shake-up,

---

Pregled istorije Saveza Komunista, p. 232; for the position of the Initiating Committee, given in the platform of the committee, see Hasanagić, pp. 157–64. As the elections grew near, an argument developed between the Initiating Committee and other elements in the Party (presumably including Tito) over the advisability of entering the 1938 elections on separate lists. Just before the elections, members of the Croatian Central Committee, joining with the Initiating Committee, blocked the Party of the Working People from participating in the elections, at least in Croatia. See reminiscences of Mladen Iveković, *Četrdeset godina*, III, 45–46. In 1940 the Croatian Party was attacked for its refusal to enter the elections of 1938 out of a fear of breaking "the unity of the Croatian national movement." *Proleter*, No. 9–10–11 (Oct.-Nov.-Dec., 1940), p. 8.

[78] The leadership of the CPY was compelled to send an "open letter" to the members of the Party in Dalmatia and Croatia attacking factions that had opposed the decisions of the Seventh Comintern Congress. These factions were accused of Trotskyism and, in addition, of "falling under the influence of national petty-bourgeois ideology." In particular, it was charged that Party members failed to follow the party line concerning the need to rally patriotic forces at the time of the German occupation of Austria. See "Materijali CK KPJ iz predratnog perioda," *Komunist*, No. 2 (Jan., 1947), pp. 74–75, and *Proleter*, No. 9–10–11 (Oct.-Nov.-Dec., 1940), p. 8.

[79] The circumstances surrounding the dismissal of the Croatian Central Committee are not entirely clear. The general impression one receives is that the Central Committee was reorganized during 1939 as a result of its mistakes during 1938. See for example, Djurdjević, p. 22, or Marjanović, *Potsetnik iz istorije Komunističke partije Jugoslavije*, pp. 56–57. Mladen Iveković, in his reminiscences, says he was in contact with Krajačić and Bukovec, members of the reorganized Central Committee, in early 1939; if Iveković is correct, the new committee was appointed even before the June, 1939, consultation. On the other hand, it is known that two very important members of the new committee, Secretary Rade Končar and Vladimir Bakarić, did not become members until 1940. The answer seems to be that the new committee came into being in 1940. *Proleter*, No. 9–10–11, (Oct.-Nov.-Dec., 1940), speaks of the fact that the leadership of the Central Committee of the Croatian Party was severely criticized at the consultation of 1939 and that when it was clear that it was sinking still deeper into mistakes—"especially" opposing the line of the Central Committee of the CPY on the question of the imperialist war in the fall of 1939—it was reorganized. The resolution of the Fifth National Conference in 1940 made the same charge. *Komunist*, No. 1 (Oct., 1946), p. 112.

Josip Kraš, secretary of the Croatian Party, was replaced by Rade Končar, a Serb from Croatia, who was to guide the Croatian Communists under Tito's orders until 1942.[80]

The emergence of a Croatian view on the national question may have been encouraged in part by the creation of national parties within the CPY in Slovenia and Croatia in 1937. The circumstances surrounding the founding of the national parties were highly involved and have never been satisfactorily explained. The proposal for taking this step was first made in 1934,[81] apparently as part of the effort to encourage autonomist tendencies in Yugoslavia; Macedonia was also mentioned in connection with Slovenia and Croatia as a region where such parties would be formed. The project was then abandoned; [82] when it was revived in 1937, the aim was not to encourage independence among the Croats and Slovenes but to help create a national image of the Party and facilitate local political alliances as part of the united front policy. This should have pleased the Croats, but there is evidence of opposition to the plan when it was first

[80] The first Central Committee of the Croatian Party, elected in August, 1937, included Josip Kraš, secretary; Andrija Žaja; Djuro Špoljarić; Pavle Gregorić; Anka Butorač; Marko Orešković-Danić; and Drago Petrović. *Osnivački kongres Komunističke partije Hrvatske*, p. 133. Of this group, two—Orešković-Danić and Petrović —seem to have been Serbs, the rest Croats. Out of this original group, only Anka Butorač remained in the new Central Committee formed sometime in 1939–40. The new committee included Butorač, Mirko Bukovec, Vladimir Bakarić, Rade Končar, Marijan Krajačić, Miha Marinko, and Martin Franekić, and perhaps others. See *Četrdeset godina*, III, 48. Rade Končar was a Serb from Croatia, Miha Marinko a Slovene. The remaining members seem to have been Croats.

[81] At the Fourth National Conference. *Arhiv*, II, 221. For another reference to the plan as it was originally conceived, see *Proleter*, No. 2–3 (1935), p. 2. In this case no reference was made to the possibility of a national party in Macedonia.

[82] The statement of the Politburo issued in Moscow in August, 1935, made no reference to the establishment of Slovenian and Croatian parties. The June, 1935, plenum of the Party has only been described indirectly, but in published reports there is no mention of its calling for the organization of national parties. The "Gorkić" plenum of the Party in April, 1936, also avoided the issue. It is understandable that Gorkić, while attempting to maneuver an alliance with the socialists, delayed the step of forming separate parties, since this would have played directly into the hands of his opponents in the Croatian Party. Later, when the united front failed, Gorkić's bitter attacks on Serbian hegemony and his stress on a "united front from below" militated against the step. With the repudiation of Gorkić's position on the national question in the summer of 1936, the call for national congresses was made one of the prominent demands in the resolution of the Central Committee in the summer of 1936.

proposed,[83] and the congresses themselves were organized hurriedly and in great secrecy,[84] perhaps out of fear that the move would be unpopular among certain groups in the Party.

It was at this time, when the Slovenian and Croatian parties were formed, that the CPY leadership underwent a reorganization which was to prove of vital significance for the future of Communism in Yugoslavia and the development of the national question as well. Following the repudiation of Gorkić by the Comintern in 1936, Josip Broz-Tito was made organizational secretary of the Party and was sent to guide Party work within the country. In August of 1937 Gorkić was removed from his post as first secretary and disappeared in the purges in Russia. In September, Tito was chosen by the Comintern to take his place.

Tito brought the Politburo and the Central Committee back to Yugoslavia and greatly strengthened discipline within the Party. Around him there appeared a group of able young men, recruited from all the major nationalities (Macedonians excepted),[85] who were without experience

[83] Vladimir Bakarić recounts how the decision to form a Croatian party was "impossible to understand" (*nerazumljiva*) for many of his comrades—one may presume first and foremost his comrades in the Communist youth movement with which he was associated at the time. The Party, on subsequent occasions, went to great lengths to justify its step; even as late as 1940, Tito carefully laid down four reasons for the creation of the Slovenian and Croatian parties: (1) to refute the argument of the enemies of the CPY in these areas that the Party was a Great Serb creation; (2) so that the masses in these areas could be more easily approached; (3) to facilitate the training of national cadres; (4) to promote initiative in these parties. For Bakarić's remarks, see *Zbornik sećanja*, II, 142–43. For Tito's arguments in 1940, see "Materijali pete konferencije KPJ održana novembra 1940 u Zagrebu," *Komunist*, No. 1 (Oct., 1946), p. 82.

[84] The First Congress of the Croatian Party met in August, 1937. A record of the meeting is contained in *Osnivački kongres Komunističke partije Hrvatske*. The First Congress of the Slovenian Party was convened on April 18, 1937; the resolution of the congress on the national question was prepared by Edvard Kardelj, who in the postwar period has become the official interpreter of national policy for the Yugoslav Communists. This was also the time at which Kardelj, under the pseudonym Sperans, published his work *Razvoj Slovenačkog nacionalnog pitanja*. A description of the congress can be found in Marinko, p. 39.

[85] Tito himself was a Croat by origin. In the Politburo which he organized, there were one Serb (Aleksandar Ranković), three Slovenes (Kardelj, Miha Marinko, and Fran Leskošek), and one Montenegrin (Milovan Djilas). The Politburo chosen in 1940, which lasted more or less intact throughout the war, included one Serb (Ranković), two Montenegrins (Djilas and Ivan Milutinović), one Slovene (Kardelj), and one Croatian Serb (Rade Končar). There were no Macedonians and no one of Croatian nationality, with the exception of Tito himself.

in the Comintern and deeply loyal to their Party secretary. Inadvertently, the purges in the Sovet Union had hastened the rise of this new leadership group by removing those of greater authority and seniority and by stemming the flow of Yugoslav Communists to the Soviet Union for training and indoctrination. For the first time since the founding of the CPY, the features of a truly Yugoslav party began to emerge.

This development had only begun, however, when the patriotic pro-Yugoslav line cultivated during the united front period was abruptly terminated by the signing of the Soviet-German pact in August, 1939. The Party, following the line set down by the Comintern, attacked the Yugoslav defense effort and urged neutrality in the struggle between the Western democracies and the Fascist powers.[86]

National policy in this period was noncommittal and cautious, reluctantly supporting the status quo. When the Sporazum (agreement) providing for Croatian autonomy was signed in September, the reaction of the Party (or at least of Tito, speaking for the Party through a Comintern publication) was reserved but favorable.[87] Only after several months had passed did the Communists begin to show some interest in the national

[86] The Party encouraged strikes in defense industries and organized demonstrations against involvement in the war; Party members in Montenegro were instructed to resist mobilization into the army (a decision which was specifically repudiated in 1940). The most detailed account of the activities of the Party in this period can be found in Lazić, *Tito et la Révolution Yougoslave,* pp. 38–47. Lazić suggests that the Party experienced hesitation and confusion over the proper course to take after August, and that a strong line against the government was only established after Tito returned from Moscow late in 1939.

[87] In an article in the Comintern journal *Die Welt,* No. 13 (Nov. 30, 1939), p. 242, Tito admitted that the agreement was one reached by the bourgeois elements in Yugoslavia, but added (without elaboration) that "it has had to a certain extent a positive meaning." Tito repeated the position that the national question could not be solved so long as the peasant question was left unresolved, but the statement seemed a hollow echo of the old Comintern position on the peasant, rather than an anticipation of the Partisan struggle to come. The Yugoslavs have published portions of a declaration issued December 1, 1939, which spoke of the need to protect Yugoslavia against fascism by "creating a brotherly harmony and agreement between the peoples of Yugoslavia." *V kongres* (1949), p. 40. This declaration, if published in full, might show the influence of the line Tito had adopted at just this same time in *Die Welt;* in fact, the declaration might have been inspired by Tito's article. On the other hand, it is clear that the Party in Yugoslavia (or parts of it) was highly suspicious of the agreement. *Proleter,* No. 7–8 (Aug.-Sept., 1940), pp. 2–3, argued that the Party expressed its suspicions of the Sporazum as a deal among the bourgeoisie from the very beginning.

issue, adopting a more critical attitude toward the Sporazum.[88] After the defeat of France in 1940 the Party dropped its policy of appeasement and adopted a more patriotic, pro-Yugoslav line; [89] by the spring of 1941 the Communists were active in the campaign against Yugoslavia's participation in the Tripartite Pact with Germany and Italy, urging alliance with the Soviet Union as an alternative. The defeat of Yugoslavia in April did not result in any major changes in the Communists' national policy, which supported, in the most general terms, the unity of the Yugoslav peoples in opposition to the occupation authorities.[90] At the same time, the Party

[88] *Proleter*, No. 1–2, 1940, voiced suspicion of the agreement and in a criticism which still showed some of the influence of the Tito line taken the previous fall declared that the agreement *"turned out* as a betrayal of the working masses and the exploited peoples" (italics added). A declaration of the Party on May 1 attacked the Sporazum but offered no alternative solutions to the national question. *Proleter*, No. 3–4 (1940), pp. 23–24. Another Party resolution adopted in May, and quoted years later by Tito at the Fifth Congress of the CPY, contained a strong attack on the Sporazum as an agreement which had taken place among the bourgeoisie at the expense of the workers and peasants. The declaration did not return to the principles of self-determination, nor proclaim that only revolution could solve the national question, but spoke in rather contradictory fashion of the desirability of Bosnia-Hercegovina and Vojvodina (Macedonia was not mentioned) deciding *their* own fate—i.e., implying that autonomy might be suitable for them as well. This line was to crystallize in the demands made at the Fifth Party Conference in the fall.

[89] See the resolution of the Fifth Party Conference, *infra*, p. 50.

[90] See the declaration of the Regional Committee of Bosnia-Hercegovina issued April 1, 1941, in *Arhiv Saveza Komunista Bosne Hercegovine*, Vol. II, Book 1, pp. 7–8; the declaration of the Central Committee of the CP of Slovenia of April, 1941, in Vojno-istoriski Institut Jugoslovenske Armije, *Zbornik dokumenata i podataka o narodno-oslobodilačkom ratu Jugoslovenskih naroda*, Vol. VI, Book 1, pp. 9–12, and the program of the National Liberation Front for Slovenia in the same volume, pp. 18–19. (This collection will subsequently be referred to as *Zbornik documenata*.) All these documents made mention of the need for unity among the Yugoslav peoples in preparing resistance to the occupier. At the same time they continued to brand the West as fascists and refused any form of cooperation with it in a struggle for national liberation. The program of the National Liberation Front of Slovenia (published June 22, 1941, the day of the German attack on Russia but clearly composed at an earlier date) stated as its first point the "right of self-determination, including the right to secession and uniting with other people!" and continued, "Whosoever does not expressly recognize this right to the Slovenes and other peoples in its entirety, that [person] is only being deceived when he claims that he fights against *imperialism* regardless of how much he preaches phrases."

continued to sabotage efforts of non-Communist democratic elements to form a resistance movement.[91]

The national policy of the Communists in this period is puzzling, and probably reflects a good deal of uncertainty within the Party and the Comintern. The Sporazum of 1939 was the epitome of the kind of "deal" between the bourgeois ruling groups which the Party had warned against even during the period of the united front. The hesitancy of the Communists to condemn the agreement was probably tied to Soviet foreign policy interests: the Yugoslav and Soviet governments were engaged at this time in negotiations which were to lead to Yugoslav recognition of the Soviet Union in the spring of 1940, and the Soviet government had reason to be grateful that the Croats had thrown in their lot with Belgrade, rather than striking a deal with the Italians. Contrary to some accounts, which have suggested that the Party returned to the national policy of the early 1930s and called for the dismemberment of Yugoslavia,[92] the Comintern and the Yugoslav Communists were primarily concerned with preserving the status quo in the Balkans. When Tito returned to Yugoslavia from a visit to Russia at the end of 1939, the Party may have decided to take the initiative and develop its own policies on such issues as the Sporazum of 1939. The fact that the Party softened its hostility to the defense effort at the same time it became critical of the 1939 agreement with the Croats was confusing, but in the

[91] Reference to the right of self-determination in the declaration of the National Liberation Front of Slovenia (see preceding note) may be interpreted not as a basic change in the national policy of the Party but as a way of creating an obstacle to cooperation between the Party (or its sympathizers) and the groups trying to form a resistance movement around the exile government, which of course could not accept the notion of self-determination for Slovenia.

[92] Stephen Clissold, in his excellent account of the Partisan campaigns, *Whirlwind*, p. 27, refers to a document prepared by the Communists calling for the dissolution of the Yugoslav state. This was supposedly drawn up after the occupation of Yugoslavia in 1941, but before the German attack on the Soviet Union. During this time, the Party fully supported the unity of Yugoslavia, however (as mentioned earlier). Indeed, there is evidence that the Party concealed certain matters from the Comintern in order to maintain its own unity (see Chapter 2). Another author who has put great emphasis on the possibility that the Party was seeking the breakup of Yugoslavia is Boris Karapandžić, *Gradjanski rat u Srbiji*. Karapandžić claims that an agreement was signed between Moša Pijade and the Ustaši that covered plans for the destruction of Yugoslavia. He also charges that the Party collaborated with the Germans in the period April-June, 1941.

last analysis not illogical. As the war approached, the Yugoslav Communists were cautiously returning to the essentials of the position of the middle 1930s on the national question. This entailed a policy not only of encouraging Yugoslav unity against foreign aggression but, just as important, of developing an independent policy on the national problem which would support the Party's contention that only the Communists were truly interested in defending national rights and reaching a genuinely just solution of the national question.

The essentials of this policy were adopted at the Fifth Conference of the CPY in November, 1940. The resolution on the national question approved by the conference was remarkably successful in anticipating much of the line to be followed during the war, taking a position in defense of the unity of the Yugoslav peoples, but dissociating the Party from the efforts of the non-Communist groups to solve the national problem.[93] To the subsequent embarrassment of the Party, the resolution did include the recommendation that Bosnia-Hercegovina should be given autonomy, presumably as a way of meeting the national demands of the Moslems. During the war, this concession to Moslem feeling was to be withdrawn.

The defeatist attitude of the Party in 1939 and 1940 is a source of embarrassment to the Communists today. The fortunes of the Party were not seriously set back by this episode, however. In 1940 and 1941 the Party gained rapidly in popularity, undoubtedly because many Yugoslavs (above all, Serbs) were looking to the Soviet Union as the last hope to stave off a German attack.[94] In the spring of 1941, prior to the fall of

[93] The resolution adopted at the Fifth Conference of the Party attacked the bourgeoisie for their suppression of national rights, while at the same time warning the Yugoslav people against the attempts of the Germans, Italians, and other revisionist powers to enslave them with promises of national liberation. The declaration spoke of self-rule (*samoodredjenje*) for the Macedonians and Montenegrins. In Bosnia it was suggested that autonomy "and similar [measures]" should be introduced; for the Serbs, Croats, and Slovenes, a "real solution of the national question"; for the minorities, freedom and equality. The resolution of the conference on the national question was published in full in *Komunist,* No. 1 (Oct., 1946), p. 117.

[94] For comments on the Serbs' and Croats' feelings on alliance with the Soviet Union, see the biting article of Anton Ciliga, "O Rusiji i Južnim Slovenima," *Nova Evropa,* XXXIII (May 26, 1940), 140–44, and the anonymous article in the same periodical, June 26, 1940, pp. 198–202, "Jugoslavija i Rusija, i rat u Evropi."

Yugoslavia to the Germans, the Party enjoyed a larger following than at any other time since the 1920s.[95] Judged in terms of leadership and popular support, it was well prepared for the events that were to follow.

There remained the problem of factionalism. Despite the authority wielded by Tito, there were elements in the Party which refused to follow the defeatist policy forced on it by the Soviet-German pact of 1939. Some Party members, both Croats and Serbs, refused to dissociate themselves from the patriotic line developed during the popular front period.[96] On the other hand, the policy of appeasement stimulated a new wave of left-revolutionary anti-Yugoslav activity on the part of Petko Miletić and his adherents in Montenegro and Kossovo-Metohija.[97] Both these factions were finally brought under control. One element could not be disciplined, however, and presented the Party with a major crisis just as it was entering the war.

This group was the Macedonians, who had been a perpetual headache for the CPY. From 1926 to 1934 the Comintern had demanded immediate self-determination for Macedonia and inclusion of the region in a Balkan federation. Then, in 1934, the organizations through which the Bulgarian Communists had worked—IMRO-United and the Balkan

[95] By April, 1941, the Party had approximately 8,000 members, according to later accounts. Moma Marković and Ivan Laća, p. 69. Tito gave the number of 12,000 in his report to the Fifth Party Congress. *V kongres,* p. 162. Of these, over 4,000 were in Croatia; from this group, many were undoubtedly Serbs living in Croatia. See *Osnivački kongres Komunističke partije Hrvatske,* Map "B."

[96] The problem of the Croats who opposed the CPY line on the Nazi-Soviet pact has been dealt with. There is less concrete evidence of opposition among the Serbs. But a "Defense Faction" is mentioned as having existed in Peć (Kossovo-Metohija). *Četrdeset godina,* III, 67.

[97] The Petko Miletić faction became the dominant group in the Montenegrin Party after Miletić was released from jail in 1939. (Miletić had strongly opposed Tito's leadership in the 1930s while in jail; the official Party histories treat him in a fashion which bears a strong resemblance to the Soviet attitude toward Trotsky.) This led to a purge of the Montenegrin Party, but factional warfare was not ended in the region until 1941. During the period between 1939 and 1941, the Montenegrin Communists cooperated with the moderate wing of the Federalist party and may also have established contacts with Sekula Drljević and his separatist wing of the Federalists. This cooperation was particularly well developed in Cetinje, the stronghold of the Federalists. Batrić Jovanović, *passim.* The Party organization in Kossovo-Metohija was also penetrated by Miletić's adherents, and in 1940, at the Fifth Party Conference, the organization was taken out of the jurisdiction of the Montenegrin Party, where it had been up until that time, and placed directly under the supervision of the Central Committee of the CPY.

Communist Federation—were dissolved, the idea of a Balkan federation was renounced, and the Comintern demanded instead the creation of a united and independent Macedonia [98] (the Fourth National Conference of the CPY in December reflected this new policy by calling for the creation of a Macedonian party and referring to the Macedonian Slavs as a distinct nationality). This brief experiment in encouraging Macedonian statehood, which paralleled similar plans for Slovenia, was quickly superseded by the policy of the united front, at which time the idea of a special solution for the Macedonian question, especially any arrangement which would involve the loss of Yugoslav territory, was quietly dropped.

During most of this period, from the late 1920s to the mid-1930s, the Party in Macedonia was weak, contacts with the CPY were poor or for long periods nonexistent, and Party membership was divided between potentially antagonistic groups: the pro-Bulgarians, the Macedonians, and the pro-Serbs. As long as Gorkić was Party secretary, little effort was made to deal with the national question in Macedonia or to establish control over the Party organizations there. Many Serbian Communists seem to have considered the region as inhabited by Serbs.

Tito tried to correct some of the failings that had marked Party activity in Macedonia under Gorkić: there is evidence that work was quietly begun, in 1937, to convince the Serbs that the Macedonians were a separate nationality.[99] At the same time efforts were made to tighten the CPY's control over the Macedonian organization. Sreten Žujović, Svetozar Vukmanović-Tempo, and Milovan Djilas were active in 1939 and 1940, working to reassert the authority of the Yugoslav Party among the Macedonians. In February, 1940, a temporary regional committee for Macedonia was formed; Metodija Šatorov Šarlo was made its secretary.

[98] Kabakchiev, p. 52. His article in the Comintern journal *Kommunisticheskii Internatsional* made it quite clear that the reason for this policy was Soviet opposition to the newly formed Balkan entente. On the future of Macedonia, Kabakchiev offered the opinion that the Macedonian Slavs did not wish to associate with any other country, but desired only one thing: "the right and possibility to determine their own nationality and to win their independence *as an independent Macedonian nation*" (italics in the original).

[99] At a conference of the regional committee of the Party in Kossovo-Metohija in the summer of 1937, its membership was informed "for the first time" that there were five separate nationalities in Yugoslavia (including Montenegrins and Macedonians), according to a participant in the meeting. *Četrdeset godina,* III, 195–96.

With the appointment of Šarlo, the pro-Bulgarian elements in the CPY found a spokesman for the first time. Šarlo began by launching a campaign against Belgrade, calling for a "national front" of all elements in Macedonia against Serbian hegemony,[100] and condemning the presence of the Serbian colonists in Macedonia.[101] These actions were apparently supported by many, if not most, of the Macedonian Party members.

On numerous occasions since the war, the CPY has condemned these acts, asserting that Šarlo was disobeying Party orders. At the time, however, the leadership of the CPY did not seem to find Šarlo's actions in the least objectionable. The account of the resolution of the Macedonian Party which called for a national front appearing in the Party organ *Proleter* did not take exception to the Macedonian position on the national question,[102] and the resolution of the Fifth Conference of the CPY in November, 1940, demanded the expulsion of Serbian colonists from Macedonia and Kossovo-Metohija just as Šarlo had wished.[103] At this conference Šarlo was made a member of the Central Committee of the CPY, the first Macedonian to hold this post.

In fact, Šarlo was well known for his Bulgarian ties and Macedonian nationalist views before being appointed Party secretary in Macedonia.[104] Tito himself had Šarlo brought to Macedonia from Paris,[105] where he had been in exile. In an effort to gain popularity in Macedonia, the CPY was apparently willing to run the risk of working with this man, and was even prepared to permit him to take a more nationalistic line than was being allowed the rest of the party.

[100] *I kongres na Komunističkata partija na Makedonija,* p. 51.

[101] Mojsov, *Bugarska Radnička Partija,* p. 89.

[102] *Proleter,* No. 9–10–11 (Oct.-Nov.-Dec., 1940), p. 21.

[103] In respect to the colonists, the resolution of the conference urged "a struggle against the colonizing methods of the Serbian bourgeoisie in those regions [Kossovo-Metohija, the Sandžak, and others] and the expulsion of all those colonizing elements with whose aid the Serbian bourgeoisie oppress the Macedonians, Albanians, and other peoples." *Komunist,* No. 1 (Oct., 1946), p. 117.

[104] According to Bulgarian accounts, Šarlo was from Prilep. Between the wars he had been a high-ranking member of the Bulgarian Communist Party and worked in IMRO-United at the time it was founded and also at the time of its demise, in 1934. In the mid-1930s he left the Balkans and went into exile in France. *Pirinsko Delo,* March 19, 1950, p. 1.

[105] According to an account given the author by one leading Macedonian Communist. The Bulgarians say that Sreten Žujović was personally responsible for arranging for Šarlo's appointment. *Pirinsko Delo,* March 19, 1950, p. 1.

It was the breakup of Yugoslavia in the spring of 1941 which put this policy in jeopardy. On the one hand, the CPY was desperately looking for ways to maintain its jurisdiction over the dismembered parts of Yugoslavia. Šarlo, on the other hand, saw this as the long-awaited opportunity for realizing Macedonian national aspirations. In a declaration issued in May, 1941, he called for a Macedonia "free and independent, one and united." [106] For this breach of the Party's line on the national question, he was summoned to a consultation of the Party in May. Instead of attending, Šarlo dissolved the Macedonian regional committee, moved his headquarters to Sofia, and attached the Macedonian Party to the Bulgarian CP.[107] The greatest threat to the Yugoslav Party in Macedonia, against which all the leaders of the CPY had fought, had come to pass: the Party had lost control over the Party organization to the Bulgarians.

The defection of Šarlo, and with him the Macedonian Party, makes it difficult to accept completely the view that Tito managed to bring unity to the CPY prior to the initiation of the Partisan campaigns. Tito had restored the authority of the Party leadership in many regions in Yugoslavia, but in the period between 1937 and 1941, disputes within the Party over the national question and other issues were almost continual, and there were many fresh wounds, apart from the Macedonian problem, which had barely begun to heal when the Party actively entered the war.

On the basis of this far from perfect record, it is difficult to understand how the Yugoslav Communists were in a position to take the initiative in finding a solution to the national question during the course of the war. That appearances were deceiving in this respect may be attributed to a number of factors, the most important of which were the confusion created by the rapid shifts of position by the Comintern and the failure of the Party to develop a satisfactory revolutionary strategy. Both these problems led to factionalism and to disillusionment within the Party during the interwar period; both these obstacles to a successful policy on the national question were largely to disappear after the Partisan struggle got under way.

[106] *Arhiv,* III, 383.

[107] Mojsov, *Bugarska Radnička Partija,* p. 89. It should be noted that in a report to the Comintern in May, 1941, Tito ascribed the absence of any delegates from Macedonia to the May consultation as due to "technical difficulties." *Komunist,* June 14, 1962, p. 9.

Despite its chronic disputes on the national question, the Party had gained important experience in dealing with the Yugoslav nationalities which was to be put to good use when the occasion arose. Above all, the Party had come to identify itself with the demands of the exploited nationalities, and in so doing, to gain a vital appreciation of the national differences that existed among the Yugoslav peoples, to which the social- ists and the early leaders of the Party had been blind. Perhaps more important for the long-term prospects of the Party, its association with the struggle for national rights slowly built up its strength in many different national regions. The Party cells thus established might have contained only a handful of members, but when the resistance struggle began they were able to organize Partisan units on a scale which the Chetniks, the Party's only rival, could not match.

At the same time, the controversy over the national problem had no apparent effect on the resolve of the Party to seek a *Yugoslav* solution to the national question. The identification of the Party with the slogans of self-determination and even secession was apt to be misleading in this respect; the Yugoslav Communists never *really* believed that these rights would have to be exercised, and Stalin's argument that the bound- aries of Yugoslavia should not be taken as the legal starting point for the solution of the national question seems to have had little influence within the Party, except in so far as it was interpreted as permission to identify the Party with the demands for Slovenian-inhabited regions in Italy and Austria.

Thus the Party had come to acquire a sensitivity to the point of view of the individual Yugoslav nationalities while at the same time being fully committed to finding a Yugoslav solution to the national question. The emergence of this attitude, and the appearance of a capable Party leader- ship to carry it out, aided the Party immensely when it was forced to deal with the national problem in the course of the resistance struggle.

Pro-Yugoslav sentiment in the Party was, it should be noted, a product of the Communist way of thinking and was different in certain important respects from the liberal tradition which saw Yugoslavia as the goal of the struggle of the South Slavs for unity.

The original affinity of the socialists for the Yugoslav state, or Balkan federation, was based on the idea that a large nation would speed the

economic development of the Balkans, and the conviction that the Yugoslavs were one nationality. In the evolution of the Party under Comintern influences, these notions were replaced, or overshadowed, by the
interests of an organization bent on seizing power and jealous of its
prerogatives to operate within certain well-established territorial limits.
A statement at the First Congress of the Croatian Party in 1937 revealed some of the reasoning which had come to play an important part
in the Yugoslav Party's thinking:

It is a generally known fact that a united and centralized organization is
far and away stronger, more solid, and has greater endurance than a divided
[party]. . . . In the struggle *against the people,* against the mass of the population, the Serb bourgeoisie has created its centralized organization—the
state—so that it could be stronger in plundering and enslaving the people.
Should we oppose that united centralized and *therefore stronger* organization of counterrevolution with a scattered, disunited, and *therefore weaker*
organization of the revolution? Or should we close together and unite our
ranks and centralize our organization and thus strengthen it in the struggle
against bourgeois counterrevolution? It is clear, the second—*for without*
this there can be no victory over the *counterrevolutionary bourgeoisie*.[108]

This tendency to duplicate, as it were, the existing power structure
was one which was ultimately to lead the Party into conflict with the
Soviet Union. At the same time, it is necessary to emphasize how important it was for the future of the nationalities question that this drive was
devoid of a specifically national (regional) bias. Among the non-
Communist parties, pro-Yugoslav sentiments had sooner or later become
entangled with Serbian interests, and this was one of the main reasons
why the once highly respected Yugoslav movement was ultimately discredited. Within the Communist Party, in its early years, the same
problem existed, but was overcome when the power of the Serbian
socialists within the Party was destroyed and the policy of seeking a
revolutionary solution to the national question made Party dogma.

For much the same reasons, the association of the Party with the rights
of the individual nationalities was not the product of regional loyalties
but was a sympathy based first and foremost on ideological principles,
rooted in the conviction that the Yugoslav peoples were exploited and
denied their rights in a fashion analogous to the exploitation of the

---

[108] *Osnivački kongres Komunističke partije Hrvatske,* p. 76.

working class. At its worst this attitude encouraged unprincipled maneuvers of the kind practiced by the Comintern aimed at exploiting national protest movements. At its best, however, the somewhat detached quality of the Party's involvement in the national question encouraged the Communists to seek just solutions of the national question which would take into consideration the competing claims of all the Yugoslav nationalities. On this concern with the total problem of national rights was built the famous slogan of the war, "brotherhood and unity."

In understanding the significance of the debates on the national question in the Party before World War II, it is essential to remember that the central problem of the time was revolutionary tactics, not the defense of local interests. The focus of the controversy, in this respect, was the insistence of the Comintern that the national question could be exploited to further the revolutionary interests of the Party, and the grave doubts of the right wing of the Party that this was possible. Here, undoubtedly, the right wing was correct. As long as well-entrenched national parties stood in the way, the policy of appealing to nationalism, especially to the peasant, was apt to meet with little success, however appropriate this strategy might have been in a semicolonial country such as China, which at this time was already developing a Communist-led peasant national movement.

In fact, the Stalinist dogma that the national question was a peasant one proved a constant source of bafflement to the Yugoslav Party, and there were few Yugoslav Communists with a natural inclination for organizing peasant rebellions in this period (one notable exception, whom it has not been able to describe in this account, was Vukašin Marković, who led a short-lived peasant revolt in Montenegro in the 1920s).[109] Ultimately, the idea of peasant nationalism was to prove to have a kernel of truth, important for the revolutionary tactics of the Party, for intentionally or unintentionally the idea focused attention on the rather elementary, raw kind of oppression experienced by one people subjugated at the hands of another. This was a Balkan phenomenon, one well known

[109] Vukašin Marković participated in the Russian Revolution and returned to Montenegro in 1921, where he tried to organize a peasant revolt. In 1922 he called the people of Montenegro to armed rebellion, was imprisoned, escaped, and in 1926, upon orders from the Party, emigrated to Austria and then to the Soviet Union. According to Anton Ciliga, he finally went to Daghistan, where he felt most at home. *The Russian Enigma*, p. 57.

to the peasant. But it was not the situation which existed in Yugoslavia in the interwar period.

Perhaps this was the ultimate reason for the failure of the Party to make a revolutionary issue out of the national question. The Yugoslavia of the period between the wars, while it was bitterly attacked from all sides, was a home-grown creation, the best possible way out of a difficult situation in which no easy alternative solutions were available. However dissatisfied the Yugoslav nationalities may have been with their condition, they were clearly not willing to pay the price demanded for the solution of the national question by the Communists, that is, revolution. The Party in fact tacitly admitted this point; however much the Communists talked about revolutionary solutions of the national question, they never dealt in specifics of the kind that might alarm the Yugoslav people. There was no public discussion of Soviet federalism, for example, as a possible way of ending the national problem. Self-determination was always urged in a vague sort of way which made it impossible to decide what the Communists really would attempt to do if they did come to power.

Despite this failure to come to grips with the immediate needs of the Yugoslav peoples, events were pushing the Party toward a role of leadership in the national question. The most decisive factor in this respect was the international situation, which, as Stalin had predicted, forced its own solution to the national problem, but one far more chaotic, and less satisfactory to the vast majority of the Yugoslav peoples, than the old system. In this crisis, the Communist Party, under Tito's leadership, seemed the only group confident that it could reunite the Yugoslav peoples, and the only movement free of the petty national grievances which had so poisoned the minds of the non-Communist parties. The unwavering confidence of the Communists proved their single most important asset during the war. Perhaps this optimism, at a time when all other groups had so obviously lost hope, was a product of the Party's fanatical faith in the victory of the Soviet Union. But one can also see in the party of the 1930s under Tito a contemporary attitude toward nationalism, unencumbered by intellectual and emotional prejudices, which was not only not afraid to face the reality of national differences but was ready to make their recognition the starting point for the building of a new Yugoslavia. Perhaps this exaggerates the progress made toward a new outlook on the national question by the

Yugoslav Communist Party. But it is beyond dispute that the Yugoslav Communists, by virtue of the very disasters that had befallen their party as a result of their own disputatious nature and the arbitrary actions of the Comintern, had made a break with the older patterns of national belief, inherited from the pre-Yugoslav era, from which the non-Communist parties could never free themselves. One might say they were the only contemporary party in Yugoslavia, perhaps the only truly Yugoslav party. This gave them the confidence needed to prevail when the Partisan movement was faced with the staggering task of creating a Yugoslav resistance after June, 1941.

2

Nationalism and the Partisan Movement

FOLLOWING the German attack on the Soviet Union in June, 1941, the Yugoslav Communist Party was freed of the restraints imposed by the need of the Soviet Union to avoid entanglement in the war in Europe. Overnight, from the role of impatient but passive spectators, the Communists became the leaders in organizing resistance forces against the occupation authorities. The patriotic slogans of the united front period were revived, and this time they struck a responsive note among many Yugoslavs. During the summer months the Party moved its organizational apparatus into the mountains of Serbia, and in August began the Partisan campaign whose success against the Germans and the remaining occupation forces was to change the course of Yugoslav history.

The national question played a crucial part in determining the outcome of this struggle. In place of its earlier failures, the Party now evolved a brilliantly successful national policy, which both admirers and detractors of the Yugoslav Communists admit was instrumental in the victory of the Partisans over the occupation authorities and rival anti-Communist groups among the Yugoslav population.

However, the national question raised many serious problems for the Party during the war, and before victory was finally achieved, nationalism threatened to be the undoing of the Communists. On occasion, too, the Party made blunders in dealing with the national question, although these mistakes never had disastrous consequences.

To understand the role of the national question in the rise of the Party's fortunes during the war, it is necessary to return to the situation in which the Communists found themselves as a result of the collapse of Yugoslavia in April, 1941. This disaster, while it did not weaken the Party internally to the extent that might have been anticipated, did create a delicate and possibly dangerous situation for the Yugoslav Communists. Duty-bound to obey the orders of Moscow, the Yugoslavs were obliged to place the interests of maintaining good relations between Germany and the USSR above their own immediate needs. But collaboration with the occupation authorities could also mean acceding to the dismemberment of Yugoslavia, and such a development would threaten the very existence of the Party.

The reaction of the Communists in this situation has been a matter of debate. Because of the apparent passivity of the Party, evident in its refusal to participate in a resistance movement with other anti-fascist groups at this time, the Communists have been accused both of collaboration with the enemy and of seeking to make the dismemberment of Yugoslavia permanent.

In actual fact, the defeat of Yugoslavia seems to have marked the first stage in the development of a truly national and independent Yugoslav Communist Party. The issue of dismemberment and self-determination for the nationalities of Yugoslavia has been analyzed in the preceding chapter, where it was suggested that the Yugoslav Communists, by the spring of 1941, were associating themselves with the policy of unity among the Yugoslav nationalities. Behind this stand were not only the directives of the Comintern, if indeed any instructions were issued by Moscow on the subject, but a determination on the part of the Yugoslav Communists to work against the settlements resulting from the April catastrophe. This was evident in May when a meeting, or consultation (*savetovanje*), was called of representatives of Party organizations from all parts of Yugoslavia. Only the Macedonian branch of the Party was not represented. The meeting went on record as opposing the breakup of Yugoslavia, asserting the right of the Yugoslav Party to jurisdiction throughout the territories of the former Yugoslav state, and even claiming the Italian portions of the Julian region for Yugoslavia.[1] It seems probable that this was also the occasion on which the Party decided that all contacts would be broken with the Hungarian Communist Party, rather than discuss the issue of Hungarian claims to Vojvodina.[2] Further evidence of the mood of the

[1] Marjanović, *Srbija u Narodnooslobodilačkoj borbi*, p. 79.

[2] The existence of this decision is revealed by a report of the Partisan organization in Vojvodina to the Central Committee of the CPY in 1942 which spoke of the

Yugoslav Communist leadership was provided by a message, sent by Tito to the Comintern at this time, describing the May consultation and the events surrounding the defeat of Yugoslavia.[3] Tito's message bristled with charges of the betrayal of Yugoslavia by elements disloyal to the country and was full of praise for the fighting qualities of the Yugoslav soldier. He omitted, however, to mention the Party's difficulties with either the Bulgarian or Hungarian Communist parties, and explained that the absence of a delegate from Macedonia was due to "technical" reasons. Already the Yugoslav Communist Party was beginning to act independently of the Soviet Union and to conceal its actions from the Comintern, if only in matters of local importance.

The events of June ended this period of uncertainty and enabled the Party to issue appeals for the organization of a wide popular front which would organize the resistance to the occupation authorities.[4] In adopting this position, the Yugoslav Communists were following a strategy laid down by Moscow for the Communist parties in occupied countries, while at the same time trying to assure themselves the leadership of the resistance movement in Yugoslavia. The revolutionary goals of the Party were no longer mentioned in Party pronouncements. National groups which had previously been the greatest rivals of the Communists were now approached with offers of cooperation in the struggle against the fascists and their collaborators. Once again, as the resistance began to gain momentum in the summer of 1941, the Yugoslav Communists found themselves involved in the delicate maneuver of forming an alliance with nationalist forces in Yugoslavia.

---

fact that it was following the line of the Party, set down in 1941, and refusing to engage in any discussion with the Hungarian Communists. *Zbornik dokumenata,* Vol. 1, Book 6, p. 151.

[3] The letter has been reprinted in *Komunist,* June 14, 1962, p. 9.

[4] For declarations and appeals to the various nationalities, see *Arhiv,* Vol. I, Book 1: *"Borba,"* 1941, and Book 2: *"Borba,"* 1942–1943, especially the proclamation of November 7, 1941, in Book 1, p. 135 and the article on the struggle against the fascist occupation in Book 1, pp. 157–67. Declarations issued by the Party in this period can also be found in *Zbornik dokumenata.* Especially useful for understanding the Party's position toward the Yugoslav nationalities upon the commencement of the Partisan campaign is the declaration of the Central Committee of July 25, 1941, which can be found in *Zbornik dokumenata,* I, 22–26. The line taken on the national question in various regions in Yugoslavia was summed up by Milovan Djilas at the Fifth Party Congress. See *V kongres,* pp. 210–11.

Events immediately indicated that this policy was not feasible. In Croatia, the Party was blocked in its efforts to organize a broad national resistance under Communist leadership by the refusal of the Croatian Peasant Party to join in the resistance. In Macedonia, the Yugoslav Communists did not even control the Party organization, which had broken off under Šarlo's leadership. In Montenegro, on the other hand, the broad coalition of national groups which participated in the uprising against the Italians in 1941 collapsed in the spring of 1942, owing to the irresponsible behavior of the local Communists, who used this opportunity to liquidate their political opponents and who took it upon themselves (contrary to the policy laid down by the Party leadership) to declare Montenegro a "Soviet republic." [5] In Serbia, the Communists and the Chetniks made a few fitful attempts at cooperation during the fall of 1941, but by the end of the year, after it had become evident that their ideological differences were irreconcilable and that neither group would permit its military units to be placed under the other's command, fighting broke out between them. Only in Slovenia did something like a popular liberation front develop [6] and here, as a result, the Communists largely dominated the resistance movement from the first moment of the fighting until the end of the war.

Developments in Serbia were particularly decisive in determining the course of the Partisan struggle. In the view of the Party, Serbia was the key to a successful resistance movement, and the first liberated territory established by the Partisans was set up in Užice, where they were able to recruit a large number of Serbs for their cause. In very short order, however, the Communists found themselves under attack from the Chetniks, and the Germans launched a powerful offensive against Užice. In the winter of 1941–42, the main Partisan forces, under Tito's command, retreated to the mountainous regions of the Sandžak and Bosnia; from that time until the end of the war Serbia, which the Communists had originally

[5] The call for a Soviet republic of Montenegro has been associated with the February, 1942, "Assembly of Montenegrin and Bokeljski Patriots" held in the monastery of Ostroga. Wolff, p. 214, and Domazetović, *Revolucija u Crnoj Gori*. The proclamation of the Ostroga assembly reprinted in Leon Geršković, ed., *Dokumenti o razvoju narodne vlasti*, pp. 53–57, contains no mention of a Soviet Montenegro, however. A general description of the mistakes committed by the Montenegrin Party during the period 1941–42 is contained in Mugoša, pp. 17–19.

[6] A useful review of the resistance in Slovenia can be found in Mikuž, *Pregled razvoja NOB u Sloveniji*.

anticipated would be their base of operations, was controlled by the Germans and Chetniks. The units under the Supreme Command (Vrhovni štab), whose core was the Serbs gathered in Serbia in the fall of 1941, fought the rest of the war in Bosnia and Hercegovina. Although they liberated large portions of Yugoslavia, the Partisans never penetrated into the main centers of the country, especially in Serbia, until the end of the war.

The Communists were now face to face with the national question in its most elementary form. Bosnia-Hercegovina was a region where Serbs, Croats, and Moslems lived side by side. By the time the Supreme Command put in its appearance, national hatreds had been inflamed by the massacres of the Serbs perpetrated by the Croatian Ustaši and Moslems, and by Serbian reprisals against the Croats and Moslems. The nationalism of the peasant, about which there had been so much academic discussion in the Party prior to the war, was no longer an abstract issue but an ugly reality which placed formidable obstacles in the path of raising a large-scale resistance movement against the occupying powers.

To try and make peasants who had fought and plundered one another one day fight side by side in the ranks of the Partisans the next was a staggering task. Nor could the Partisan units be sure of the reception they would meet in the villages through which they passed. The prevailing mood in the countryside was one of fear, coupled with a natural desire for protection against nationally-inspired atrocities. But the Partisans could only protect the villagers temporarily, and their presence always threatened to bring punitive action against the village by the local Ustaši or the occupation forces. For those in any way involved in the occupation administration, or compromised by identification with the excesses of the Ustaši, fear of retribution acted as an effective check against cooperating with the Partisans. As Vladimir Bakarić reported to the Croatian Main Command in 1941, there was a widespread belief (even within Partisan ranks) that "in case of a rapid improvement on the Eastern front, there would probably occur a massacre in the Croatian villages and that not one Croatian would be left alive." [7]

To offset the peasants' national prejudices and their suspicion of the Partisans, the Communists developed elaborate techniques for entering hostile villages and disarming the inhabitants without provoking

[7] *Zbornik dokumenata,* Vol. V, Book 2, p. 279.

resistance.[8] A policy was established that the villagers in hostile regions were not to be treated unjustly, and were even to be dealt with leniently if circumstances left no other choice; efforts were also made to arrange reconciliations among rival national groups where that was possible (one account of the resistance described a truce that the Communists arranged between the Moslems and Serbs in Bjelopolski district of the Sandžak which lasted the entire war).[9]

When the Partisans were successful the dividends could be great. A report from Bosanska Krajina early in the war described an almost textbook example of efforts to win the confidence of the Moslems of a certain district who had fled their villages upon hearing of the approach of the Partisans. The Partisan unit secured the deserted homes against plundering and placed the peasants' stock under the care of persons who had remained in the locality; the Moslems, upon hearing this, returned to their villages, and the Partisans seized the opportunity to lecture them on the aims of their struggle. "This echoed throughout all the Moslem villages," the political commissar of the unit ended his report, "and even the Serbs were pleased that the whole affair ended in this fashion politically." [10]

But these efforts, even when successful, could not completely overcome the fears and suspicions of the peasants. If it was possible, the Partisans would simply avoid entering hostile districts; Croatian villages in the regions of Lika and Kordun were never even entered by the Serbian Partisan units during the early years of the war, and contact with the Croats in these regions was almost nil. On the other hand, preaching brotherhood and unity could sometimes have tragic consequences, as in the case of the small Moslem village of Fatnica, in East Hercegovina, where the chief of police, who was a Communist, persuaded the villagers to give up their arms, only to see the population slaughtered by vengeful Serbs.[11]

[8] A number of accounts describing the manner in which Partisans occupied hostile villages can be found in *Zbornik dokumenata*. See, in particular, "Izveštaj štaba trećeg bataljona od 26 ožujka 1942," Vol. V, Book 3, pp. 376–77, and "Izveštaj Aleksandra Rankovića od 15 Avgusta 1942 god . . . drugu Titu o situaciji u Livnu . . . ," Vol. II, Book 5, pp. 307–10.

[9] Čuković, p. 237.

[10] *Zbornik dokumenata,* Vol. IV, Book 1, p. 358.

[11] Brajović, ed., p. 26.

In practice, the Partisans found they had to rely on the Serbs in the early stages of the war, and this strengthened the suspicions of the Croats and Moslems toward the Communist cause. Each region, of course, had its peculiarities. The Croats of Bosnia-Hercegovina (West Hercegovina in particular) were strongly under Ustaši influence and were totally hostile to the Partisans, while regions closer to Croatia were more under the control of the Croatian Peasant Party. Gorski Kotar, in the mountainous section of northwest Croatia, was neither fascist nor particularly disposed toward the Peasant Party, and was the first purely Croatian region to be penetrated by the Partisans. Dalmatian Croats (their territory had been annexed by Italy) had strong reasons for opposing the occupation, and sided with the Partisans in great numbers.

The problem posed by the Slav, Serbo-Croatian-speaking Moslems was particularly frustrating for the Communists, since great hopes had existed for winning this group over to the Partisan movement.[12] Some Moslem regions did support the Communists—notably the districts of Konjić and Prozor in Hercegovina—but in most areas the Moslems were to be found in the ranks of the Ustaši or in the service of the occupation garrisons. This proved to be true even in East Sandžak and Montenegro, where Moslems were exposed to Chetnik atrocities and under pressure from the Albanian occupation authorities, who wished to see the Slav Moslems adopt Albanian nationality. In one remarkable instance, on the occasion of a Partisan attack on the town of Sjenica (in the Sandžak) in December, 1941, Moslem peasants spontaneously rose up and fell on the Partisan flanks, leading to a major Communist defeat.[13]

The Communists refused to consider the demand of certain Moslem

---

[12] For appeals to the Moslems during this period, see *Zbornik dokumenata*, Vol. II, Book 3, "Poziv Muslimanima. . . ," pp. 68–70; in the same book, "Proglas Vrhovnog štaba NOP . . . od Januara 1942 god narodima Bosne i Hercegovine," pp. 229–30; and *Arhiv*, Vol. I, Book 2, p. 302, which gives an article from *Borba*, Dec. 20, 1942, on the Moslems. For a general assessment of the role of the Moslems made at the end of the war, which admits that the Moslems joined the struggle later than the other nationalities, see Sulejman Filipović, "Bosna je našla svoj put," *Nova Jugoslavija*, No. 6 (1944), pp. 24–26.

[13] Čuković, p. 209. Tito was furious with the failure of the attack, and wrote a highly critical letter to Milovan Djilas on December 28, saying that not only had the Partisans suffered a military defeat but that the events at Sjenica had led to a still greater worsening of relations with the Moslems in the Sandžak.

groups for autonomy.[14] On occasion, however, efforts were made to collaborate with local Moslem leaders in order to gain their military cooperation, even though the results were disappointing. The outstanding case of such an experiment was the cooperation developed with the Moslem Huska Miljoković from the Moslem district of Gazin in Croatia; Miljoković joined the Partisans, then deserted and formed the Moslem militia for the Ustaši in Velika Kladuša. In 1943, despite his record of collaboration, Miljoković was accepted back into the Partisan ranks.[15]

As a result of the hostility of the Croats and Moslems, the support of the Serbs in Croatia, Bosnia-Hercegovina, and the Sandžak became absolutely crucial for the success of the Partisan movement. In this situation lay one of the great and unforeseen paradoxes of the resistance struggle; driven out of Serbia by the Germans and Chetniks, the Partisans under the Supreme Command were still predominantly Serbs. This was true in a double sense: the crack units, the Proletarian Brigades, were composed principally of Serbs who had joined the Partisans in 1941, while the regular Partisan formations, operating from Kordun in the north to the Sandžak in the south, were drawn largely from the Serbs who resided in the localities in question.

In the region of the Dinaric Alps, and in other parts of Croatia where there was Partisan activity (Fruška Gora, for example), the Serbian peasant was motivated by a search for security, and much less, at least in the early stages of the war, by the patriotic motives which were behind the

[14] The promise of the Fifth Conference of November, 1944, for autonomy for Bosnia-Hercegovina was probably meant to appeal to the Moslems, although it did not mention them directly. In an article written in 1942, Veselin Masleša reviewed the problem of the Moslems in Yugoslavia and specifically rejected the notion of any form of Moslem autonomy. Veselin Masleša, *Dela,* II 148–66. The problem of autonomy was not yet dead, however. In November, 1943, the region of the Sandžak held an anti-fascist national liberation assembly. Normally, this was a privilege granted only major national groups or regions which deserved special recognition as national areas. The Sandžak had a large Moslem population, and it is possible that some of them saw the meeting as a promise that the Moslems of the Sandžak would be granted a special position after the war. When the war ended it was necessary for Moša Pijade to make a special trip to the Sandžak to persuade the Communists of the region that they should allow the area to be divided between Montenegro and Serbia. (See Chapter 3.)

[15] Miljoković was killed by the Ustaši in May, 1944. For his career, see *Zbornik dokumenata,* Vol. V, Book 19, pp. 96–97, n. 5.

uprising in Serbia proper. Chaos and terror drove the Serbian peasants into the Partisan ranks but also provided an excellent opportunity for the Italians and Chetniks. Serbian villages were particularly susceptible to the blandishments of the Italians, who offered protection against the Croatian Ustaši if the Serbs would lay down their arms. The Italians used this stratagem successfully in Dalmatia and in East Hercegovina.[16] It was not unusual for the Partisan units early in the war to negotiate with the Italians for protection, and the Partisans of Lika actually struck a bargain with the Italians, under the terms of which the Serbs of Lika were to be given "autonomy" for disbanding their guerrilla bands.[17] (Although the agreement was repudiated, the Serbian units in Lika refused to attack the Italians and it was necessary to employ Dalmatian units in the first offensive against the Italian garrison in Lika.) The Chetniks followed, collaborating with the Italians and appealing to the nationalism of the Serbian peasant as well as his desire for security. Throughout practically the entire area of the Dinaric Alps the threat arose that the situation which had developed in Serbia would repeat itself. In the shift of allegiances marked by the Chetnik appearance in the fall and spring of 1942, the Partisans lost Hercegovina, Montenegro, the Sandžak, and, for a time, eastern Bosnia. There were even cases where Partisan commanders deserted, the most well known of such persons being Bajo Stanišić, who with his followers broke with the Communists in Montenegro in early 1942 and issued a proclamation in which he claimed the support of "God and Great Russia" for the Chetniks! [18]

As a consequence of the rapid spread of Chetnik influence in their zone of operations in 1942, the Partisans were hardly in any position to place sharp restrictions on the Serbs within their own ranks. And yet, at times, the behavior of Partisan units made disciplinary action imperative. This was especially true in the best-organized and most permanent

[16] A report of the Central Committee of the Croatian Party of September 30, 1941, was strongly critical of the behavior of the Croatian Party, and gave the example of some Communists in Dalmatia and Lika who, instead of demanding that Dalmatia, Primorje, and Medjumurje be returned to Croatia, put forth the slogan "Don't provoke the Italian fascists." The Communists in the region of Brinja actually composed a proclamation which failed to make any mention of the Italian occupation but attacked the United States and Great Britain. *Zbornik dokumenata*, Vol. V. Book 1, p. 147.

[17] *Ibid.*, Vol. IV, Book 1, p. 39.

[18] *Ibid.*, Vol. III, Book 4, p. 39.

liberated areas in Croatia, where the Serbian Communists were powerfully influenced by their sense of duty to the Serbian peasants of the region, and seemed to put little stock in the Party's policy of promoting brotherhood and unity. Partisan units refused to accept Croats in their ranks, and it was reported that the practice had grown up, among the Serbian rank and file, of surreptitiously sending notes to the Croatian villages threatening them with reprisals for outrages committed against Serbs (such messages were sent in the absence of the political commissar, who was usually a Croat). Occasionally discipline would break down entirely, and a Croatian village would be burned and its inhabitants terrorized. One such setback to the Communist efforts to establish normal relations between the Serbian Partisans and Croats occurred in the district of Banija, in 1942, when the Partisans seized a mixed Serb-Croat village. The Ustaši had been active in the area and feelings were running high. "After liberation of the village," it was reported, "there began a terror over the Croatian inhabitants without any consideration of how they behaved toward the Ustaši."

One Partisan grabbed from some fellow 20,000 dinars and several days later killed this [fellow]. The village council forbade all Croats to leave their houses after seven in the evening, and took away their right to grind and to mill during the day. As a result these [villagers] were not able to mill at all. They didn't give permission to go to the neighboring village. Upon the demand of the HQ of the unit, two Croats entered into the council, but they always had to vote according to the Serbian majority, for otherwise they were threatened that they would be accompanied to the command post, whence "no one ever returns" . . . This behavior had the result of completely isolating all Croats in that village from the Serbs, without regard for the fact of whether someone in the family was Ustaši or not, and bringing the Croats closer together (which strengthened the influence of elements inclined toward the Ustaši). All without exception were frightened to death when the Partisans entered a house. The result was that the Croatian villages on the Pounj (along the narrow-gauge railway) refused to accept leaflets from the Partisans in order not to experience the fate of Gvozdanski.[19]

These developments were a source of acute embarrassment and concern to the Croatian Communists, for the Partisans of Lika and Kordun were under their command. Vladimir Bakarić, who was acting as political commissar for the Croatian Main Command, prepared several highly

[19] *Ibid.*, Vol. V, Book 3, p. 416.

critical reports, especially on developments in Kordun (it was enough, he complained, for a Croatian comrade to walk into a group discussing the Croatian problem for an embarrassing silence to ensue). But, at the same time, the Serbian units were practically the only forces the Croatian Party had at its disposal. Nor did the Supreme Command seem eager to mix in the matter, perhaps out of fear of alienating the Serbs.

Kordun, in this recrudescence of Serbian sentiment, was an extreme case, in fact a unique phenomenon in the development of the entire Partisan movement. In Kordun the Party had roots among the peasants dating back to the prewar period, and the Partisan units were strong and well organized, while the boundaries of the liberated territory were relatively stable. A sort of peasant republic was organized among the Serbs which came as close as anything could to manifesting that elusive phenomenon of peasant nationalism. The region came to be known as the "Kordun Republic," and the Partisan commanders began to abandon mobile Partisan tactics for frontal battles in defense of their little state. Croatian villagers either fled or armed themselves for defense along the republic's "frontiers." "They only carry out actions," the Main Command for Croatia complained to Tito, "in order to broaden the territory of their 'republic,' and where it is not possible to organize such actions, the units sleep." [20] The peasants of Kordun, it was reported, even composed folk songs describing the boundaries of their republic.

Serbian nationalism was a problem for the Party mainly in 1942; after this time, the local Partisan commanders, under pressure from the Croatian Main Command, took greater pains to ensure adherence to the principles of brotherhood and unity in the conduct of their units. Military developments also played a role in breaking up local cliques in the Partisan movement. In the great offensives launched by the Germans and Italians in 1943, the Partisans were forced to retreat into new regions to escape encirclement, and this severed the ties of the units to their native villages (while the Chetniks led a sedentary life perched on their neighborhood mountain top and were totally unfit for fighting outside their own locality). Kordun was an excellent case in point; the German offensive of 1943 compelled the Kordun Partisans to return to mobile tactics of warfare and awakened them to the need of working with the Croats, and this in turn

[20] *Ibid.*, Vol. V, Book 3, p. 420.

materially contributed to the spread of Partisan influences into purely Croatian areas in 1943.

There was no special quality of "rootlessness" which gave the Partisans an advantage over their opponents; the Slovenian Partisans managed—in fact insisted—on staying on their own soil, and fought extremely well under difficult conditions. Kardelj, who led the Slovenian Partisan forces, resisted efforts to be transferred to the Supreme Command, and in one letter jokingly remarked to Tito, "You know, I was always a little bit of a 'local patriot.' " [21] But the ability to engage the occupying armies whenever necessary and to maneuver freely without being tied down to one locality helped ensure the survival of the Partisans in the early and most difficult phase of the struggle. And the national antagonisms and localistic outlooks which cut deeply into the effectiveness of the Partisans' efforts to create a resistance movement hampered the Communists' opponents as well. As the war progressed, the chaotic structure of satellite states and semi-annexed provinces became the object of increasing disillusionment among those who had sided with the Axis powers. When the occupation began to show signs of weakening in 1943, the Partisans were able to move with astounding speed. The Italian capitulation in the fall permitted the Partisans to occupy Montenegro, the Sandžak, Hercegovina, and Dalmatia. The Chetniks were routed throughout all of western Yugoslavia. Although the Germans were to retake many key points seized from the Italians, the initiative had passed to the Partisans and was to remain in their hands until the end of the war.

At the same time, the problem of formulating a new approach to the national question in anticipation of the defeat of the Axis powers remained to be dealt with. In the first year and a half of the resistance, the Communists avoided committing themselves prematurely to any solution of the national problem; instead they worked to strengthen military discipline and establish Party controls over widely scattered Partisan units. By the fall of 1942 this task was by and large completed (with the important exception of Macedonia) and the stage was set for the Party to take the initiative in political matters relating to the future of Yugoslavia. In December, 1942, the Anti-Fascist Council of National Liberation of

[21] "Pismo Edvarda Kardelja od 12 Avgusta 1942 god," *ibid.,* Vol. II, Book 5, p. 279.

Yugoslavia (AVNOJ) was formed. Delegates sent by the Partisan movements of the various regions of Yugoslavia proclaimed AVNOJ the sole
representative of the resistance in Yugoslavia. During the course of 1943
anti-fascist councils were set up in Croatia, Slovenia, and Bosnia-
Hercegovina which claimed the same rights to represent the resistance
in their respective areas that AVNOJ had claimed for Yugoslavia as
a whole.[22]

The activities of the anti-fascist councils were capped by the second
meeting of AVNOJ in November, 1943, when the Communists declared
the Partisan movement, or rather AVNOJ as its political expression, the
only legal government of Yugoslavia. The resolution issued by AVNOJ
provided that Yugoslavia was to be organized according to the federal
principle; another portion of the same document indicated that this
system was to go into effect "immediately." [23] The decisions of the second
session of AVNOJ were confirmed by meetings of the anti-fascist councils
in the national regions, some held before November, 1943, some in 1944.
The last of these meetings took place in Serbia in the fall of 1944,[24] when
the German retreat from Yugoslavia permitted the Communists to return
in force to the region where the Partisan movement had originated.

The system of anti-fascist councils, despite the fact that it was obviously
not representative of the majority of the Yugoslav peoples, was an
extremely effective political instrument in the struggle of the Communist
Party to win recognition for the Partisans as a genuine national resistance
force. The structure of the councils, capped by AVNOJ, embodied the
strategy of the Communists of establishing local ties in as many of the
Yugoslav regions as possible without compromising the role of the Party
as the spokesman for Yugoslav national interests.

But to cultivate a multiplicity of national images and at the same time
organize a Yugoslav movement was a task which under ordinary circumstances would have proved difficult, if not impossible. For the Communists
to succeed in this undertaking it was necessary to maintain strict Party
discipline. This involved, furthermore, a clean break with all theories of

[22] Gršković, *Dokumenti, passim.*

[23] *Ibid.,* p. 255.

[24] Just before the second session of AVNOJ, meetings were held in Slovenia
(October 3), in Croatia (October 14), in Montenegro (November 15), in Bosnia
(November 26), and in the Sandžak (November 20). The first anti-fascist council
in Macedonia was convened in August, 1944, and in Serbia in November, 1944.

"autonomy" in Party or state relations which kept appearing in areas where the national question was particularly acute.

Discussion of the rights of the national regions was initiated in an article by Tito on the national question published in December, 1942, just after the first session of AVNOJ.[25] The most significant point in Tito's article was the revival of the principle of self-determination and secession which had been almost completely absent from Communist statements on the national question since 1937. To anyone familiar with Communist theory, this was a clear indication that the Party was not going to accept conventional constitutional solutions of the national question, but would seek to satisfy national demands through stressing the revolutionary achievements of the new system in eliminating national exploitation and ensuring national equality, while keeping the centralized controls of the Party intact. This suspicion was partially confirmed by Tito's reference to the fact that self-determination would be denied "enemies of the people." Although only the Croatian Fascists were specifically mentioned in this connection, the principle employed by Tito was obviously capable of extension to any group which might seek autonomy within a Communist Yugoslavia.

Practice confirmed the approach to the national question suggested in Tito's article. On certain occasions in the early years of the war, the Party had hinted at one form or another of autonomy for nationalities or minorities,[26] but this position was essentially alien to the Party's way of thinking. During the course of 1943, after Tito's article had paved the way, the demand for autonomy or special rights for national regions was condemned in a number of directives and communications of the Central Committee to the provincial Party committees in Macedonia and Croatia, as well as to the Albanian Communist Party.[27] That misunderstandings could arise over the nature of the relationship between the regional anti-fascist councils and AVNOJ was testified to by a curt "warning" which Tito sent to the Croats on the occasion of a declaration by the Croatian Anti-Fascist Council of National Liberation (ZAVNOH).[28] The statement, issued in September, 1943, had failed to make it clear that all the

[25] *Borba za oslobodjenje Jugoslavije*, pp. 121–30.

[26] The possibility of autonomy was raised by the CPY in connection with Macedonia and the Italian minority. Both these cases are discussed below.

[27] Each case is discussed separately below.

[28] *Zbornik dokumenata*, Vol. II, Book 10, pp. 328–29.

decisions of ZAVNOH were taken under the authority of AVNOJ, and not as the expression of the sovereign power of the Croatian people.[29] Tito attacked this omission as the adoption of a "separatist" position on the part of the Croats. (Even today there seems to be some difference of opinion in Yugoslavia concerning the sovereignty of the regional anti-fascist councils.) [30]

The fact that a federal system had been officially adopted by AVNOJ did not halt the trend toward curbing the aspirations of the national areas evident in 1943. On the contrary, administration in the Partisan areas grew more centralized after this time.[31] In addition, it was later explained [32] that the meetings of the national anti-fascist councils which confirmed the decisions of the second session of AVNOJ had also exercised, for the first and last time, the right of self-determination for the nationalities they represented; this apparently held true even for those regions (Slovenia and Croatia) which had held meetings of regional anti-fascist councils before AVNOJ had met and decided that Yugoslavia was to be organized according to the federal principle.

How smoothly the transition to the new federal system was accomplished by the local resistance movements depended on a number of factors, above all, the feelings that prevailed in the region toward the old Yugoslav state. In those areas where dissatisfaction with the prewar system was greatest, the pledges made by AVNOJ to safeguard national rights were not always sufficient by themselves to overcome local national feelings and leanings toward autonomy.

This was true above all in Macedonia, but it is also important to draw

[29] The ZAVNOH declaration did not mention AVNOJ in its signature, making it appear that the Croats were acting without reference to the Yugoslav body. The declaration is reprinted in full, *ibid.*

[30] See the discussion in Chapter 5 on the objections raised by the Croatian Party historians to the official Party history. One of the points raised by the Croatians at this time was the sovereignty of ZAVNOH.

[31] For a contrary view which claims that the system in effect during the war was really federal, see Čulinović, *Stvaranje nove Jugoslavenske države*, pp. 237–49. Although Professor Čulinović argues that a truly federal system went into effect after the second session of AVNOJ, the fact remains that centralization of the government of the liberated areas really commenced in earnest at this time, and that it was only *after* the declaration of federation that Tito felt ready to limit discussions of autonomy for Macedonia or the Albanians.

[32] At the time of the introduction of the constitution at the end of the war. See Chapter 3.

attention to the special problems posed by the national demands of the minorities, and to the behavior of the Croatian Communists, which was not entirely lacking in nationalist overtones during the war.

The minority regions may be considered first, for there the problem of reconciling the population to the idea of a new Yugoslav state was most difficult. As noted earlier, practically all the minority groups collaborated with the occupation authorities and were eager recruits for the units organized by the Germans and Italians to suppress the resistance. It was clear that, if the principle of self-determination was recognized in respect to these groups, the results could be highly detrimental to Yugoslav interests. Throughout the war the Communists therefore avoided mentioning self-determination in connection with the minorities, and no anti-fascist councils of national liberation were organized in regions where national minorities were the predominant element in the population.

A number of Partisan units were formed from minority groups, but their contribution to the Partisan cause was, with few exceptions, negligible. These formations included the Italian Pino Budučin battalion; the Albanian Zejnel Ajdini unit and the Emin Durak brigade; the Bulgarian Hristo Botev brigade; the Czech-Slovak Jan Žiška brigade; the Hungarian Petöfi Sándor unit; and the German Ernst Thälmann unit.[33] The German, Hungarian, and Rumanian units were originally formed for political purposes, not to fight; they were to make their appearance among the villages of the minorities in order to inspire confidence in the Partisans.[34] Initially, if enough persons from the minority population could not be recruited, Serbs and Croats were added to the minority units. In Kossovo-Metohija it was especially difficult to persuade Albanians to join the Partisan ranks; Vukmanović-Tempo, writing in the summer of 1943, reported that the

[33] Accounts which deal with the Yugoslav minorities during the war include Paul Shoup, "Yugoslavia's National Minorities under Communism," *Slavic Review*, XXII (March, 1963), 64–80; Ljubiša Stojković and Miloš Martić, *Nacionalne manjine u Jugoslaviji;* V. Dedijer, "Italijanske, Bugarske, Čehoslovačke i Madjarske jedinice u sastavu naše vojske," *Za otadžbinu*, No. 4 (April, 1950), p. 21; "Nacionalne manjine FR Jugoslavije," *Informativni priručnik*, II (1952), 10–12; *Komunist*, Sept. 12, 1963 (for the Czech brigade); Aug. 29, 1963 (on the German Ernst Thälmann unit); Sept. 5, 1963, (on the Slovak units); July 25, 1963 (on the Bulgarian unit). An excellent eyewitness account of the operation of the Italian Pino Budučin battalion in Istria is contained in "Izveštaj operativnog štaba za Istru od 23 Aprila 1944 . . . ," *Zbornik dokumenata*, Vol. V, Book 26, pp. 500–18.

[34] The formation of these groups in Vojvodina is recorded in *Zbornik dokumenata*, Vol. V, Books 18, 19, and 20, *passim*.

Albanians were "truly chauvinistically inclined toward the Serbs," and instead of armed struggle, recommended that the Communists pursue a policy of organizing mass demonstrations for bread, as well as other nonmilitary actions which would serve to unite the Serbs and the Albanians.[35] Plans were also set afoot for the transfer of Albanian Partisan units from Albania to western Macedonia and Kossovo-Metohija.[36] Mixed Albanian-Yugoslav brigades finally began to operate in western Macedonia in October, 1943, and in Kossovo-Metohija in the spring of 1944.

In the closing years of the war, the ranks of the minority units were filled by conscription and by volunteers hoping to rehabilitate themselves. This was not always an entirely satisfactory answer to the problem of mobilizing the minorities; for example, a report to the Regional Committee of the Party in Vojvodina spoke of how, in the closing phase of the war, of 800 Hungarians who volunteered from Bačka Topola, 200 later deserted; of 180 who volunteered from Sente, 50 later deserted; and so on for other towns. Rumanian conscripts deserted the Partisans en masse and fled to Rumania, and as a countermeasure, camps were set up in which the families of the soldiers were interned. (At the end of the war, these deserters were pardoned, and most returned to their homes.) [37]

At the same time that the Partisans were trying to form units among the minority population, the Party had to contend with strong pressures from the Communist parties of neighboring states, all of whom had a natural interest in the minority question in Yugoslavia. The problem of the Hungarian minority was especially delicate, for the region in which the Hungarians were located was annexed by Hungary, and the Hungarian Communists supported this decision (so say the Yugoslavs). In order to avoid being drawn into discussions over the matter, the Yugoslav Communists decided in the spring of 1941 to break off all contacts with the Hungarian Party. This position was maintained for several years thereafter.[38]

[35] *Arhiv*, III, 238–39.

[36] *Ibid.*, p. 228, and Glavna politička uprava Jugoslovenske armije, *Stvaranje i razvoj Jugoslovenske armije*, II, 359–60.

[37] From unpublished reports examined by the author.

[38] A report from the Partisan organization in the Vojvodina to the Central Committee of the CPY in 1942 spoke of the fact that it was following the line of the Party, established in 1941, and refusing to enter into any discussion with the Hungarian Communists. *Zbornik dokumenata*, Vol. I, Book 6, p. 151.

Meanwhile, the Partisan movement met such stiff resistance from the Albanians that Miladin Popović, who was attached to the Albanian Communist Party as a representative of the CPY, proposed an arrangement under which the Party in Metohija would be placed under the jurisdiction of the Albanian CP.[39] Despite the fact that the Albanian Communists were carefully guided by their Yugoslav advisers during the war, the Albanian CP supported the claims of Albania to Kossovo-Metohija at the Mukaj Conference of the Albanian resistance movements held in 1943.[40] The Yugoslav Communist Party would not consider any special concessions to Albanian national sentiment in Kossovo-Metohija, however, and both the suggestions of Miladin Popović and the claims of the Albanian CP were rebuffed in the course of 1943 by the Central Committee of the CPY.[41]

In the case of the Italian Communist Party the tables were turned, for the prewar boundaries left many Slovenes and Croats in Italy, and the Yugoslav Communists were determined to get them back. In this instance the Yugoslavs were not reticent to discuss the minority question, and as early as 1941 the Yugoslav Party was pressing the Italian CP to recognize Yugoslav territorial claims in Istria and the Julian region.[42] The Italian Communists finally gave way in 1944 [43] (much to the disgust of

[39] Popović proposed that separate Serbian and Albanian units, with the latter operating primarily in Metohija, be formed under their own commands which would in turn be under the direction of the Albanian Partisan movement, and that the Party in Metohija be put under the jurisdiction of the Communist Party of Albania. *Zbornik dokumenata*, Vol. II, Book 10, p. 148.

[40] Skendi, ed., p. 21. For the charge that the agreement made claims on Kossovo-Metohija, see Dedijer, *Jugoslovensko-Albanski odnosi*, p. 93.

[41] For Tito's negative reaction to the proposals of Miladin Popović, see Tito's letter to Vukmanović-Tempo, *Zbornik dokumenata*, Vol. II, Book 11, p. 42. The Albanian Party was informed by the Central Committee of the CPY that any consideration of the Albanian claims would be "grist to the reactionaries' mill," and the Albanians had to be content with the assurance that Yugoslavia had no intention of mistreating her Albanian minority after the war. Dedijer, *Jugoslovensko-Albanski odnosi*, p. 133.

[42] The May, 1941, consultation of the CPY had claimed the Julian region for Yugoslavia, provoking a dispute with the Italian Communist Party, whose representative in Yugoslavia (Umberto Masola) only agreed, with the greatest reluctance, to permit Party organizations of the Slovene minority in Italy to attach themselves informally to the Slovenian Communist Party. See the report of Edvard Kardelj, *Zbornik dokumenata*, Vol. II, Book 2, p. 34.

[43] At the Milan agreements of 1944 by which cooperation was established

the non-Communist Italian resistance).[44] At the same time, the Croatian and Slovenian parties both offered the Italian minority "autonomy" in Yugoslavia after the war.[45] This was, of course, contrary to Party policy, and Tito reprimanded the Croatian Party (although not the Slovenian CP) for its promise to the Italian minority to-be.[46]

Finally, a brief and emotional encounter took place with the Bulgarians over the Bosilgrad and Caribrod districts when the Fatherland Front government sought permission to continue administering these two districts after the capitulation of Bulgaria in the fall of 1944. The Partisan headquarters for Serbia reacted sharply to this request and demanded that the two areas be given up to the Yugoslavs at once, since they were "already now an integral part of the sovereign territory of free democratic federal Yugoslavia." [47]

In Croatia the Communists were not as handicapped by the national question as in minority areas. On the other hand, the Croatian Communist Party experienced great difficulties in preparing for the resistance struggle in the spring of 1941. Some Communists simply deserted the Party in a panic, while others hastily organized guerrilla actions which failed disastrously.[48] In an incident which has never been fully explained, the City

---

between the Italian resistance and the Partisans operating in mixed areas. By December, 1944, the Slovenians had set up a city committee for Trieste, thus claiming control of the city for the Yugoslavs. Only in March, 1945, did the Italian CP finally give in and accept completely the Yugoslav claims and the Yugoslav position toward the Italian minority.

[44] For an Italian anti-Communist view, see G. F., "Sacrifice of Free Men," *Trieste,* No. 2 (July-Aug., 1954), p. 20. The Yugoslav position can be found in Mikuž, and Plenča, pp. 364–66.

[45] A declaration of the National Liberation Front of Slovenia issued in September, 1943, contained a promise of autonomy for the Italians of the Julian region and called for immediate discussion of this suggestion by "authorized representatives" of the Italians and Yugoslavs. Gersković, *Dokumenti,* p. 189. ZAVNOH, at its meeting in September, 1943 (critized by Tito for failing to refer to AVNOJ), repudiated all prior international agreements in respect to the Julian region, claiming it for Yugoslavia. At the same time the Croatian Communists promised the Italian minority-to-be autonomy. *Zbornik dokumenata,* Vol. II, Book 10, p. 328.

[46] *Zbornik dokumenata,* Vol. II, Book 10, p. 328.

[47] Plenča, p. 349.

[48] The disorganization in the Croatian Party is described in "Izveštaj operativnog vojnog rukovodstva pri CK KPH od avgusta 1941 god glavnom štabu NOP . . . ," *Zbornik dokumenata,* Vol. II, Book 2, pp. 43–45. Kardelj reported in

Committee of Zagreb defied the rest of the Croatian Party and the CPY leadership by attempting to usurp the powers of the Croatian Central Committee.[49] In September the Central Committee of the Croatian Party found it necessary to circulate a lengthy and strongly worded criticism of the actions of Party members in Croatia, attacking the "great weaknesses, mistakes, and shortcomings of individual organizations and of the CPC [Communist Party of Croatia] as a whole." [50] Tito was also critical of the Croatian Party and, in a letter sent to the Croatian Main Command in 1941, alluded pointedly to the contribution being made by the other nationalities of Yugoslavia to the national liberation struggle.[51]

August that the Croatian Party was hesitant to begin Partisan warfare, giving as its reason the fact that conditions for such tactics were not yet ripe. *Zbornik dokumenata,* Vol. II, Book 2, p. 28.

[49] According to the accounts given by Party historians, the City (Mesni) Committee of the Party, under the influence of one "N. N.," became impatient with the fact that the Croatian Communists were not taking swifter action in the resistance struggle and convinced the Communists of Zagreb, at least for a brief moment, that *it* should take over control of the resistance from the Croatian Central Committee. The incident is discussed by Jovan Marjanović, "Još o jednom pitanju Jugoslovenstva u ustanku 1941," *Jugoslovenski Istorijski Časopis,* No. 1 (1963), pp. 47–54. The matter is a sensitive one for the Croatian Communists, since there is the implication that some of the Croats were plotting against Tito. Marjanović hints at this, and Kardelj, in describing the incident in a report during the war, says that "N. N.'s" actions were directed "unconsciously at the leadership" and that he played the role of an "objective provocateur." *Zbornik dokumenata,* Vol. II, Book 2, pp. 28–29. On the other hand, "N. N." could hardly be criticized for wishing to begin a resistance movement; for this reason, he has further been charged with simple incompetence in organizing a prison break for Communists at the time, and in certain other matters. To confuse the matter even further, the chief of the Soviet Intelligence Service in the Balkans at the time, Ivan Antonov, has been accused of involvement and of egging on "N. N." Indeed, one letter from the Central Committee of the CPY to the Central Committee of the Croatian Party dated September 4, 1941, indirectly criticizes Antonov for attacking the CPY leadership! *Zbornik dokumenata,* Vol. II, Book 2, p. 57. The case is discussed by Vladimir Bakarić in his report to the Second Congress of the Communist Party of Croatia. *Drugi kongres Komunističke partije Hrvatske,* p. 60. Ranković also mentioned the case at the Fifth Congress of the CPY. *V kongres,* p. 149. For a Croatian reply to Marjanović's article, see Ivan Ceranić, "Dogadjaji i činjenice," *Vjesnik* (Zagreb), Dec. 12, 1962.

[50] "Okružnica br. 3 Centralnog komiteta KPH od 30 rujna 1941 godine," *Zbornik dokumenata,* Vol. II, Book 2, pp. 143–53.

[51] *Zbornik dokumenata,* Vol. V, Book 2, pp. 21–23.

There were quarrels between the Croatian Provincial Committee and the Zagreb Committee of the CPC, and in August, 1942, Ivo Lola Ribar told of how he (in his capacity as the Party leader responsible for nonliberated territories) was compelled to take over command in the Zagreb area in a complicated organizational tangle which had resulted in the separation of the Croatian Main Command from the temporary Central Committee, and which led to the creation of two headquarters for the Second Operative Zone around Zagreb.[52] There were other incidents involving the Croatian Communists later in the war, chief among them Tito's anger over the failure of the Croatian Main Command to send a proletarian brigade to join the main Partisan forces, and the poor showing of the 8th Corps in the winter of 1943, which had made it necessary to turn command of the unit over to Sreten Žujović, a representative of the Supreme Command, for a short time.[53]

Although these incidents did not raise the national question in a direct form, the Croatian Party was placed in an embarrassing position which invited unfavorable comparisons between the Croats and the remaining nationalities (such as was hinted at in Tito's letter to the Croatian Main Command in 1941). The situation was made all the more difficult for the Croatian Communists when the national liberation struggle in Croatia became an almost entirely Serbian affair during the course of 1942.

By the end of 1942 the Partisan movement was active in many parts of Croatia, including the city of Zagreb itself.[54] For the Yugoslav Communist Party, the addition of the Croats in great numbers to the ranks of the Partisans was a significant step toward creating a broad Yugoslav movement. For the Croatian Communists this was the moment when their own national pride could assert itself more boldly. That this did happen in the course of 1943 is suggested in part by the disagreement over ZAVNOH, to which reference has already been made. More serious was the charge, made after the war, that the Party secretary in Croatia between January, 1943, and September, 1944, Andrija Hebrang, was guilty of

[52] *Ibid.*, Vol. II, Book 5, pp. 189–207.

[53] *Ibid.*, Vol. II, Book 11, p. 20 and pp. 242–49.

[54] For a fairly sober assessment of the spread of the Partisan movement among the Croats, see Bakarić's speech, made in the closing phase of the war, in *Narodna vlada Hrvatske formirana u gradu Splitu dana 14 travnja 1945*, p. 28, and his article "Nešto o nacionalnoj vitalnosti Hrvata u ovom ratu," *Nova Jugoslavija*, No. 2 (March 15, 1944), pp. 17–19.

chauvinistic behavior in his attitude toward the Serbian minority in the liberated portions of Croatia.[55]

The accusation cannot be accepted at face value because it was brought after Hebrang had sided with the Soviet Union in the dispute with Yugoslavia in 1948. When he was still in favor, Hebrang was praised for the "tremendous contribution" [56] he had made to the cause of unity between the Serbs and Croats in Croatia, and his removal in September, 1944, while it may have been associated with the national question, came too late to have been prompted by his behavior toward the Serbs. It is more likely that Hebrang's frequent clashes with the Party leadership over the proper policy to pursue toward the Croatian Peasant Party,[57] or his involvement in the border dispute which arose between Croatia and Serbia at the end of the war,[58] led to the decision to replace Hebrang as Croatian Party secretary. Of these two possibilities, the latter seems more probable, but conclusive evidence concerning the reasons for Hebrang's removal is lacking.

[55] Owing to Hebrang's influence, it was said, the use of Cyrillic in Serbian-liberated areas of Croatia was discouraged, and cultural and historical monuments of the Serbs were removed. These actions were said to have led to intervention on the part of the Central Committee of the CPY on several occasions. *Drugi kongres Komunističke partije Hrvatske*, p. 72, and Milatović, p. 14. For useful biographical data on Hebrang, see *Zbornik dokumenata*, Vol. II, Book 2, p. 85, footnote.

[56] From an election pamphlet issued in Croatia at the end of the war.

[57] Tito gave his views on how to handle the Croatian Peasant Party in a directive of August, 1943, when he told the Croatian Central Committee that he was against forming a separate Croatian Peasant Party and favored seeking agreement on the basis of the platform for the struggle against fascism laid down by ZAVNOH, while at the same time criticizing the behavior of Maček. *Zbornik dokumenata*, Vol. II, Book 5, p. 205. Kardelj took the same position a short time later. Apparently Tito had been meeting with strong resistance from Hebrang and others, for it was Tito's plan to send a high-powered delegation including Lola Ribar, Dedijer, and others to Croatia to discuss the problem. *Ibid.* What became of the delegation is not revealed. Hebrang was accused of "attacking Maček from all sides." *Drugi kongres Komunističke partije Hrvatske*, p. 71. He may have also favored setting up a separate Croatian Peasant Party in opposition to Maček. Such a party *was* formed in the fall of 1944, the Croatian Republican Peasant Party, with Franjo Gazi as president of its Executive Committee. Although this corresponded to Hebrang's general approach to the problem of the Croatian peasants, it was at just this time that Hebrang lost his post as Party secretary.

[58] The dispute over whether Serbia or Croatia was to get the area of the Srem after the war has been identified as the cause of Hebrang's removal in Jareb, p. 123. This dispute is described in the following chapter.

The fact remains that Hebrang and the Croatian Party were at least during one period at odds with the CPY, and it seems very likely that the Croatian Party began to assert some of its old national outlook at the time it freed itself from dependence on the Serbs and began to strike roots among its own people. Thus, in their own way, the Croatians in 1943 were repeating the experience of the Serbs, among whom the creation of a mass base within the peasantry in 1942 in Kordun had led to the recrudescence of nationalism in the Partisan ranks.

The phenomenon of rising national feeling and local self-assertiveness in connection with the establishment of a mass base for the Partisan movement was also evident in Macedonia, but in this case national feelings were already strongly aroused by years of agitation for Macedonian national rights before the war. Šarlo, by breaking off relations with the CPY in 1941, had brought the problem to a head even before the Partisan resistance movement could be organized in Macedonia. The result was a tangled struggle between the CPY and the Macedonian Communists in which nationalism rooted in resentment of Yugoslavia was ruthlessly stamped out, only to be replaced by feelings of local pride and national self-assertiveness among former national leaders and Partisan commanders who pledged their loyalty to Tito and the CPY.

The defection of Šarlo to the Bulgarians in 1941 had posed a major dilemma for the Yugoslavs. A brief but sharp conflict followed between the Yugoslav Communists and the Bulgarian Communist Party; a high point of confusion was reached in the fall when Šarlo was expelled from the CPY by the Yugoslavs; the agents sent by the Yugoslavs to Macedonia (Lazar Koliševski and Dragan Pavlović-Šilja) were expelled from the Communists' ranks by the Bulgarian Party, and the entire regional Committee for Macedonia was expelled by the Yugoslav Central Committee for siding with Šarlo.[59]

The quarrel was patched up in the fall of 1941 by the decision of the Comintern that, for "practical" reasons, jurisdiction in Macedonia should fall to the CPY.[60] Beneath the surface, however, intense factional war-

[59] For various accounts of the confusing events in Macedonia in the fall of 1941, not all of which are in agreement on the details, see *Plenča*, pp. 64–65; Mojsov, *Bugarska Radnička Partija*, pp. 108–9; *Arhiv*, VII, 43–44 and 48. The most detailed account is to be found in *Zbornik dokumenata*, Vol. IX, Book 2, pp. 155–57.

[60] *Arhiv*, VII, 388–89.

fare continued between the Bulgarians and the Yugoslavs,[61] and it was evident that the sympathy of the majority of the Party members in Macedonia lay with Šarlo's policy of supporting the creation of an independent Macedonia, within some form of Balkan Communist federation, while at the same time there existed a good deal of reluctance—encouraged by Bulgarian advisers who had stayed on in Macedonia—to engage in Partisan warfare against the Bulgarian army. The CPY sent several instructors to Macedonia in 1941 and 1942 to straighten out the affairs of the Party, but all of them took a pessimistic view of the situation, urging the Supreme Command to make concessions to Macedonian national feeling.[62] At the same time, a number of attempts to organize Partisan units were broken up by the occupation authorities.

Conditions in Macedonia finally improved for the Yugoslav Communists in the spring of 1943, when Svetozar Vukmanović-Tempo, one of the most able Partisan leaders, arrived to take charge. Tempo succeeded in forming Partisan units in western Macedonia (the portion occupied by the Italians). The success of these units generated a wave of enthusiasm in other parts of Macedonia. By the fall, the area on the right bank of the Vardar stretching from Veles to Gevgelija, which had once been a stronghold of Bulgarian and IMRO influences, was supporting the Partisans.[63]

[61] After the Comintern decision the Yugoslavs reorganized the Party, but factional warfare persisted. Šarlo left Macedonia and worked for the Bulgarian Party for the remainder of the war. He was killed in the resistance struggle shortly before Bulgaria capitulated. Bane Andrejev was made temporary secretary of the Macedonian organization (Koliševski had been arrested by the occupation authorities). Instead of following the Yugoslav line, Andrejev began acting according to the instructions of the Bulgarian Party adviser on the scene. Only after a prolonged controversy did the pro-Yugoslav elements manage to secure the removal of Andrejev in June, 1942. For the Yugoslav account of these events, see *Zbornik dockumenata,* Vol. IX, Book 2, pp. 155–57.

[62] The first to make such reports was Dragan Pavlović, who in August, 1941, in a report to the Central Committee of the CPY, showed a good bit of sympathy for Šarlo's view and suggested that the question of which party was to be in command in Macedonia should not be considered the crucial issue. *Arhiv,* VII, 43–44. Dobrivoja Radosavljević, in 1942, followed a line which stressed "free Macedonia" and played down the connections of the region with Yugoslavia, for which he was criticized at the time. *Ibid.,* p. 177.

[63] Tempo reported in August that the fighting spirit of the Macedonians was especially strong in the Italian-occupied regions, the Kavardorsko, Gevgelija, and Veleški regions, and also in the Prilep-Bitolj districts. *Zbornik dokumenata,* Vol.

Following the Italian capitulation, the Partisans occupied all of western Macedonia (although they were forced to give up many key points to the Germans and Albanians temporarily during hard fighting in 1944). By the fall of 1944 Partisans were appearing in Pirin Macedonia, that is, in Bulgaria proper. Furthermore, the units that participated in these actions were Macedonian, not Serbian.[64] By the end of the war, the Macedonians could boast that they had provided more recruits for the Partisans than neighboring Serbia.

The rapid growth of the Partisan movement ended Bulgarian influence in the Macedonian Party, but in its place it encouraged the open expression of Macedonian nationalism, with which the Yugoslavs had to contend until the end of the war. To understand the complex development of the Macedonian question in 1943 and 1944, however, it is necessary to return to certain decisions taken by the Yugoslav Party leadership in the fall of 1942.

In September of that year, Tito made a seemingly minor concession to the Macedonians by informing the provincial committee that, because the CPY was not then in a position to render adequate assistance to the Macedonian Communists, he was not opposed to the suggestion of the Bulgarians that the Macedonian committee exercise some autonomy in its activities and develop closer ties with Sofia.[65] The reasons Tito made

---

II, Book 10, p. 148. For a revealing report on the switch of allegiance of persons in Kavadarci, Veles, and Prilep to the Partisans see, "Izveštaj člana CK KP Makedonije od 4 Jula 1943 . . . ," *ibid.,* Vol. VII, Book 1, pp. 272–302.

[64] The Serbian element in Macedonia is most pronounced around Kumanovo in the north and the Skopska Crna Gora just north of Skoplje. In November, 1943, the Skopsko-Kumanovski Partisan unit numbered 75 Macedonians, 3 Serbs, and 1 Montenegrin. In Kumanovo, it was reported, the Serbs were afraid of the Chetniks who held many of the surrounding mountains, while the Partisan units got most of their recruits from persons mobilized into the Bulgarian army. *Zbornik dokumenata,* Vol. VII, Book 2, pp. 198–207. There was also a unit operating in the Šar mountains that had some Serbs or Montenegrins. According to one report, it was made up of 25 Macedonians and 25 comrades from Kossovo-Metohija (Serbs or Montenegrins and perhaps a few Albanians). *Ibid.,* p. 167.

[65] For the directive, see "Uputstvo sekretara CK KPJ druga Tita od 22 septembra 1942 god . . . ," *Zbornik dokumenata,* Vol. II, Book 6, pp. 148–52. Tito's words were: "From grandfather [the Comintern] we received certain suggestions from the side of the CC of the Bulgarian CP that we should give the Macedonian CP certain autonomy (*izvjesnu autonomiju*) at the same time that [it] remains in connection with (u sklopu) the CPY and under our leadership, and in so far as our

this suggestion, apart from those set down in his letter, are obscure, all the more so since Tito had once already turned down a request from the Comintern along similar lines.[66] Later developments strongly suggest, nevertheless, that Tito was thinking in terms of a new Communist coalition in the Balkans, in which a semi-autonomous Macedonian party would be part of a Communist Balkan federation under Yugoslav leadership. Alternatively, Tito may have considered this concession to the Macedonians a temporary stratagem to appease the Comintern and the Bulgarian CP, while gaining some support among the Macedonians for the first session of AVNOJ, which was then pending, unaware of the tenuous hold of his representatives over the Macedonian Party.

The reaction to Tito's suggestion revealed that autonomy was clearly popular with the Macedonian Party, and that the proposal had been interpreted in a much more sweeping fashion than was originally intended.[67] When Vukmanović-Tempo left for Macedonia in the fall of 1942, he took with him further instructions to set up a national party along the lines of those that existed in Croatia and Slovenia, for one of his first acts upon arrival in Macedonia was to create a Macedonian Communist Party and Central Committee.[68] In addition Tempo—again, it must be assumed, with Tito's authority—began at once to enter into negotiations with the Albanian, Greek, and Bulgarian Communists over

---

connections are made more difficult, to get more help from the CC of the Bulgarian CP. Naturally we agreed with this entirely and had nothing against such a solution. You have had full free self-initiative until now."

[66] The Comintern telegram had spoken of the desirability of organizing an "independent" (*samostalna*) Macedonian party. *Arhiv*, VII, 59. Tito replied briefly and evasively, saying that he did not understand the meaning of the term "independent." *Ibid.*, p. 60.

[67] See the report of Radosavljević to Tito in October, 1942, to the effect that the Central Committee letter (presumably Tito's "Instruction" of September, or a decision of the Central Committee of the CPY embodying Tito's position) had a very positive effect on the Party in Macedonia and met with the approval of the Bulgarian Central Committee. *Zbornik dokumenata*, Vol. IX, Book 2, pp. 155–60.

[68] In his report to the Central Committee of August 8, 1943, Tempo described how he had set up the Central Committee of the Macedonian CP, and that the mass of the workers openly welcomed "the decision of the CC of the CPY on giving autonomy to the CPM." Tempo added: "Naturally I directed the whole movement in the direction of union with the remaining Yugoslav peoples." *Zbornik dokumenata*, Vol. II, Book 10, p. 148.

the creation of a joint command to coordinate the resistance forces in the Balkans. Political considerations loomed large in these discussions, and Tempo pressed the other parties to accept the principle of the union of all Macedonia (its Yugoslav, Greek, and Bulgarian portions),[69] presumably prior to the entry of Macedonia into a Balkan federation, or even within the framework of the Yugoslav federal system.[70]

These developments, beginning with Tito's original reference to autonomy and ending with the plan for a united Macedonia, served to create the impression among the Macedonian Communists that the CPY was in favor of some special solution to the Macedonian problem which would satisfy Macedonian nationalist sentiment, especially its aversion to any settlement which would be accompanied by the return of Macedonia to Yugoslavia. The attitude of the Macedonian Communists was revealed in June, 1943, when the Central Committee of the Macedonian Party, in the absence of Vukmanović-Tempo, issued a declaration calling for an independent and united Macedonia. No reference whatsoever was made to Yugoslavia in the statement.[71] Emotions ran high over the

[69] Tempo described his negotiations to form a joint command, and the reluctance of the other parties to accept the idea of a united Macedonia, in his report to the Central Committee of the CPY, "Izveštaj Svetozara Vukmanovića Tempa od 8 Avgusta," *Zbornik dokumenata,* Vol. II, Book 10, pp. 143–62. The Greek Communists balked at the idea of union, and promised Tempo only that the Macedonians would receive full minority rights after the war. They did agree that, when a Balkan command was formed, the Greek Party would issue a declaration recognizing the right of all Balkan peoples to self-determination. Later, the Greek Party drew back from the idea of a Balkan command but made some concessions to the notion of Macedonian unity, agreeing that the Macedonians would gain "full national freedom and equality with other Balkan peoples" after the war. *Zbornik dokumenata,* Vol. II, Book 10, p. 232. Relations between the Greek Communists and the Yugoslav Partisans are discussed in greater detail in Chapter 6.

[70] Vukmanović-Tempo did not speak of any plan for Balkan federation in his correspondence with the Central Committee of the CPY in August of 1943, but kept stressing the desire of the Macedonian nationality for unity. Balkan federation was not mentioned until the Manifesto of the Main Command for Macedonia in October. Still, the idea must have been part of the discussions from the very outset.

[71] The declaration spoke of the "ideal" of the Macedonian people through the ages: "*national freedom, equality, and brotherly* cooperation with all Balkan peoples." The aim of the liberation struggle, the declaration continued, was not only to free Macedonia of the occupiers but to attain "*complete national freedom and equality, the right to decide our own fate and create a genuine people's democratic authority in Macedonia*" (italics in the original). *Arhiv,* VII, 222 and 224. Curiously, the inspiration for this document came not from the Macedonian members of the

justification of the Macedonian Central Committee's action; Tempo, upon his return, sharply criticized the committee for acting in a way which would divide the Macedonians from the rest of the Yugoslavs; the Macedonians, according to Tempo's own testimony, argued the point vigorously and admitted their error only with the greatest reluctance.[72]

Meanwhile Tito had second thoughts on the issue of autonomy. In January, 1943, he reversed his earlier stand on the issue in a directive addressed to the provincial committee (*not* the Central Committee) of the Macedonian Party in which he strongly criticized the idea of autonomy for the Macedonians or the notion of any "possible specific Macedonian conditions," and made it absolutely clear that the Macedonian resistance was to be treated as an integral part of the Yugoslav national liberation movement.[73] Now confusion ensued, for Vukmanović-Tempo, it can be assumed, had been sent to Macedonia with different instructions. To complicate matters, six months elapsed before Tito's message arrived in Macedonia (this in itself is a suspicious fact, never adequately explained). Vukmanović-Tempo was clearly embarrassed upon receiving Tito's directive, and engaged in what was for him a rare act of self-criticism, expressing doubts over whether he had acted correctly in setting up the Macedonian Central Committee.[74] This made it appear as

Central Committee (although they obviously approved of it) but from their Yugoslav adviser, Radosavljević, who continued to follow the line he had taken in 1942, prior to the arrival of Vukmanović-Tempo, of emphasizing Macedonian interests at the expense of unity with the remainder of the Yugoslavs.

[72] Tempo describes the scene that took place upon his return in his report to the Central Committee of the CPY of August 8. *Zbornik dokumenata,* Vol II, Book 10, pp. 151–52.

[73] Said Tito: "Raising the question of 'autonomy' or 'possible specific Macedonian conditions' does not fall into the range of our position and line, and those who pursue (*potržu*) this question in essence are in the last analysis identified with those who, because of the name Yugoslavia, isolate the Macedonian people from the common struggle of all the peoples of Yugoslavia." *Arhiv,* VII, 190.

[74] Tempo, in a letter to the Central Committee of the Macedonian Party, admitted that he had failed to fight against autonomist tendencies energetically enough, and added, in respect to the formation of the Macedonian Party, "I am afraid, comrades, that we were hasty with the creation of our CC of the CPM. It is true that for these several months we have succeeded *in strengthening and solidifying our Party organization in Macedonia, cleansing it of all unhealthy and opportunistic elements.* . . . But we are still behind in the work of getting the Party to stand on its own two feet (*osamostaljivanju*)." *Zbornik dokumenata,* Vol. II, Book 10, p. 179. Italics in the original.

though the Central Committee had been formed on Tempo's own initiative; in this unlikely instance the Macedonian national party had been formed by accident! More likely, Tempo had acted under orders from the beginning, but Tito had reopened the question of the status of the Macedonian Party's Central Committee (at least in Tempo's mind) by his sharp attack on autonomy.

Tito's directive placed the Communist Party in Macedonia in a quandary, for the Party was on record (in the June statement of the Central Committee) as favoring quite a different aproach to the Macedonian problem from that now being insisted upon. The Party procrastinated and delayed in issuing a public statement incorporating Tito's new views on autonomy.[75] The situation was made more difficult when Tito, probably reacting to Soviet pressure, abruptly broke off negotiations in the fall for a combined Balkan command.[76] At the same time, Macedonian Partisans were demanding a statement from the Party concerning the national aims of the Partisan struggle; urgent appeals were directed to the Central Committee from the Bulgarian-occupied areas in the fall, pointing out the harmful effects on the resistance movement of the lack of any clear-cut statement on the future of Macedonia.[77] Finally, in October, on the eve of the second meeting of AVNOJ, the Main Command for Macedonia issued a "Manifesto" which, while employing evasive language, made it clear that Macedonia was to remain an integral part of Yugoslavia after the war. At the same time, the Main Command

[75] A declaration of the Committee of the People's Liberation Front of Macedonia, issued in September, 1943, made a ringing appeal to the Macedonian people to join in the resistance struggle along with the other peoples of the Balkans. The question of autonomy or independence for Macedonia was avoided. The declaration did speak of the struggle against the fascists side by side "with the remaining peoples of Yugoslavia," which was presumably meant to hint delicately at the status of Macedonia within Yugoslavia. *Zbornik dokumenata,* Vol. VII, Book 2, p. 69.

[76] In a letter written October 9 to Vukmanović-Tempo, Tito spoke of the "so-called Balkan command" and displayed bemusement over the origins of the idea. *Zbornik dokumenata,* Vol. II, Book 10, p. 361.

[77] In October, 1943, Kuzman Kosifovski reported that the Macedonians in Bulgarian-occupied areas were awaiting some word on their future, and that there was great uncertainty over the policy of the Party. He urged the issuance of a proclamation from liberated territories on Macedonia's future for those who were asking "kuda idemo, Makedonci" (Where are we going, Macedonians?). *Zbornik dokumenata,* Vol. VII, Book II, pp. 151–54.

strongly supported the union of all Macedonia and the eventual creation of a Balkan federation.[78]

The declaration of the Main Command, which appeared without the endorsement of any political body representing the resistance movement, received a mixed reaction. Tito, in November, expressed dissatisfaction with the idea of Balkan federation and the strongly worded statement over Macedonian union [79] (Vukmanović-Tempo was later to claim that the reference to Balkan federation was inserted in the declaration upon the insistence of the Greek Communist Party).[80] To a number of Macedonians, on the other hand, the document did not go far enough in meeting national demands. The declaration was strongly criticized by a group in Skoplje who were members of the Action Committee formed to organize an anti-fascist national liberation council for Macedonia. Instead of the union of Macedonia with Yugoslavia, the group proposed a joint command with other Partisan movements, the union of all Macedonia, and eventually Balkan federation,[81] more or less the program Vukmanović-Tempo had been trying to put into effect the previous summer.

[78] The portion of the declaration relating to Balkan union read: "Today all Balkan peoples are united in the struggle for the creation of a *brotherly federative union of the Balkan peoples* on the basis of full national equality and recognition of the right to self-determination of peoples. Never before, Macedonian people, have we had such a good opportunity and so many allies for the creation of this great ideal—*the union of Macedonia*" (italics in the original). *Arhiv,* VII, 260.

[79] In a "warning" to Tempo dated November 9, 1943, Tito stated that it was incorrect to raise the question of the union of Macedonia, and that "federation of the Balkan peoples is for us now [only] an agitational slogan." *Zbornik dokumenata,* Vol. II, Book 11, pp. 196–97. In a letter to Tempo dated December 6, Tito came out strongly against the idea of a Balkan federation and a Balkan command. On the former point, Tempo was warned that any plan for federation at the moment would play into the hands of the Western powers. On the question of the union of all Macedonia, Tito said nothing directly, but warned the Macedonians against becoming overly concerned with the principle of self-determination. Self-determination was their right, said Tito, but it was being exercised by the participation of the Macedonian people in the resistance struggle. *Ibid.*

[80] *Ibid.,* Vol. II, Book 11, pp. 34–35.

[81] Mojsov, *Bugarska Radnička Partija,* p. 64. There were also some reports of favorable reactions to the declaration. A letter written to the Central Committee of the Macedonian CP by Kuzman Josifovski, Dec. 20, 1943, spoke of the "overwhelmingly favorable" reaction among the Macedonians. See *Dokumenti od sozdavanjeto i razvitokot na N.R. Makedonija,* pp. 265–68.

In August, 1944, after a delay of over a year occasioned by the opposition of the Action Committee and the pressure of the Germans on Partisan positions in Macedonia, the first session of the Macedonian Anti-Fascist Council of National Liberation (ASNOM) was convened. The assembly recognized the existence of the Macedonian nationality and declared Macedonian the official language of the region, and at the same time supported the idea of a united Macedonia.[82] The decisions of the second session of AVNOJ were approved, thus terminating the right of the Macedonians to exercise self-determination. All hopes that Macedonia might receive a special status in Yugoslavia, or that it would be permitted to enter into some new combination of Balkan powers after the war, were thus ended.

What had taken place in Macedonia was not unlike the evolution of the resistance movement in other parts of the country, in so far as the initial stages of the struggle were marked by confused efforts to reach accommodation with the occupation authorities, followed by the growth of a new kind of national pride, impatient and sometimes self-assertive, but fundamentally loyal to the leadership of the Yugoslav Communist Party.

The peculiarities of the Macedonian problem lay in the depth of national resentment against Yugoslavia and—closely connected with this fact—the way in which the Yugoslav Communists so long misled the Macedonians concerning their future status in a Yugoslav state. A further complicating factor was the elusive character of Macedonian nationalism, at one moment pro-Bulgarian in orientation, at another, supporting the idea of a separate Macedonian nationality.

The idea of a Macedonian nationality had a complex history, about which more will be said in a subsequent chapter. It is enough to point out here that there was no one moment, prior to ASNOM at the end of the war, when the principle was clearly set forth that the Partisans were struggling for the rights of the Macedonian nationality as distinct from the people of Macedonia, designating those living in the region. The fact seems more or less to have been assumed, and was not the subject of debate between the CPY and Šarlo, or between the Yugoslav and Bul-

---

[82] Gerškovtić, *Dokumenti,* pp. 343–54. A short time later, the Central Committee of the Macedonian CP issued a statement emphasizing that the goal of the struggle of the Macedonian people was the unification of all the Macedonians. *Dokumenti od sozdavanjeto i razvitokot na N.R. Makedonija,* p. 7.

garian Communists. Because the idea of the existence of a distinct Macedonian Slav nationality was not widely propagated before the war, even in the ranks of IMRO, the influence of the Partisan movement on the development of nationalism was potentially broader and deeper than in other parts of Yugoslavia, where the sense of belonging to a distinct nationality was already well established. How widespread and intense a national consciousness was developed by the Macedonians during the war is difficult to judge, but there is no doubt that a change did take place, spurred by Communist propaganda, and encouraged by the disillusionment of the Macedonians with the occupation regime.[83] The benefits the Yugoslav Communists could gain by being present at the beginning of the process were demonstrated by the decision of ASNOM to recognize the Macedonian language, a landmark in the development of the idea of a Macedonian nationality.

Because the Yugoslav Communists, acting through the Macedonian Party, were instrumental in encouraging the Macedonians to think along national lines, and at the same time (inadvertently it appears) participated in a deception in respect to Macedonia's future which lasted until the time of the Manifesto of the Main Command for Macedonia in October, 1943, there was bound to be resentment toward the outcome of the resistance struggle by those who had thrown in their lot with the Partisans. How great a reaction took place remains a matter of speculation on which there is very little concrete evidence.[84] In the last analysis, what was of crucial importance was the fact that the new Party members, recruited from the peasantry and trained in the Partisan ranks, were loyal to Tito and the CPY, and with their support the Party leadership managed to isolate and contain the intellectuals and former members of IMRO who were working for the complete independence of Macedonia.

This same process of creating a new leadership for the country was taking place all over Yugoslavia, although in less dramatic form than in Macedonia. The Partisan movement reared a whole new generation of local and regional cadres whose first loyalty was to the Yugoslav Party, persons with strong local roots but ready to follow the Party in its

[83] According to Yugoslav sources, Traicho Kostov, the prominent Bulgarian Communist, wrote in May, 1941, that, according to reliable information from those on the scene, not less than 80 percent of the Macedonian Slavs felt themselves "Macedonian" rather than Bulgarian. *Arhiv*, VII, 22.

[84] Some additional remarks pertaining to this problem appear in Chapter 4.

essentially unitary approach to the national question. In this lay the real secret of the ability of the Communists to overcome the deep contradiction between regional ties and loyalty to Yugoslavia which had been at the root of so many of the problems of the prewar system.

By 1944 the Communists had made such progress in identifying themselves with the national aspirations of the Yugoslav peoples that the national issue, instead of being a liability, served the Party as a powerful instrument in advancing its claims to power. In the agreement reached between Tito and Ivan Šubašić in June, 1944, which settled on the postwar form of government, Šubašić was compelled to recognize the federal system proclaimed by AVNOJ.[85] The London government reluctantly agreed to the principle of a federation several months later.[86] Although it could hardly be expected to believe in the sincerity of the Communists, the London government had little choice in its decision, for to have rejected the Communists' proposals would have made it appear that the non-Communist parties were not sincere in seeking a solution to the national question.

There were nevertheless some who decided not to accept the solution imposed by the Communists. One group within the Croatian Peasant Party tried to evade the Tito-Šubašić agreements and deal directly with the Croatian Communist Party, to no avail.[87] The Chetniks also re-

[85] The agreement for a federal form of government was spelled out in more detail in November, 1944, at the second meeting of Tito and Šubašić. This agreement of November stated: "The sovereignty of [each] nation's individuality will be honored in the spirit of full equality and guarded as it was decided upon at the second session of the Anti-Fascist Council of National Liberation of Yugoslavia. The predominance of any one nation over another will be excluded." "Sporazum nacionalnog komiteta oslobodjenja Jugoslavije i kraljevske Jugoslovenske vlade od 1 novembra 1944 godine," *Službeni List DFJ,* No. 11, 1945, p. 121. The agreement also stipulated that the first postwar government would include ministers without portfolio for each of the six republics. This provision was honored in the government formed March 9, 1945. All the ministers representing the republics, with the exception of the Croatian and Slovenian ministers, were Communists, and those from Croatia and Slovenia were fellow travelers. The posts were of no great significance, and were abolished with the reorganization of the government in 1946.

[86] For the statement of the London government of August 8, 1944, see *V kongres,* p. 100–1.

[87] A delegation led by Košutić conferred with the Croatian Communists in Otačac, Sept. 8, 1944. Košutić proposed to the Central Committee of the Communist Party of Croatia a "Supreme Assembly of the Republic of Croatia" which would have representatives of the Croatian Peasant Party and ZAVNOH

pudiated the compact between Šubasić and Tito, but were forced to come up with their own proposal for a federal Yugoslavia in the last days of the war, in a desperate effort to broaden their national appeal.[88]

Following the capitulation of the London government and the collapse of the anti-Communist national movements, the Party's policy in respect to the national question seemed secure. Party propaganda in the closing year of the war took advantage of the unchallenged position of the Communists to claim that the national question in Yugoslavia was a thing of the past, a line that was to be carried over into the postwar period.[89]

The Party's claim was, of course, exaggerated. Rather than resolving the national question, it would be more accurate to say that the Party had proved that it was the only group capable of ruling in the face of the national problem. To describe the Communists' success in this fashion in no way diminishes the significance of their achievement, but suggests that national contradictions could be neutralized by a determined authoritarian regime which was able, as the Communists were, to develop strong national roots while remaining essentially Yugoslav in its outlook.

In respect to public opinion, if it is possible to use such a phrase under the conditions that prevailed during the war, it is safe to say that most Yugoslavs were not ready to accept the Communists as authentic national spokesmen. But this was not necessary. For many people, the Party had established its right to attempt a solution to the national question, and this was sufficient to assure the Communists that their national policy would not be actively resisted by the majority of the Yugoslavs.

The ability of the Party to gain *any* national following remains something of a mystery, however, in the light of the failures of the Communists to exploit the national question before the war. While it is generally agreed that the Party did attract national support away from the established

---

combined into one body, while the home guard of Croatia, the *domobrani,* was to be combined with the Partisans. The Central Committee of the Croatian Party and the Main Command for Croatia turned down Košutić's demands and broke off further negotiations. The Communist version of the Košutić mission can be found in Plenča, pp. 306–7.

[88] At the Congress of St. Sava, which organized a Yugoslav Democratic Union, in favor of a federal Yugoslavia with a hereditary monarchy. Karapandžić, *Gradjanski rat u Srbiji,* pp. 291–92.

[89] Contained in the Djilas article, "O rješenju nacionalnog pitanja u Jugoslaviji," *Članci, 1941–1946,* pp. 254–70.

parties, the reasons for this have never been fully clarified. Many theories on the relationship between the Partisan movement and national feeling have appeared, but still the source of the appeal of the Partisan movement remains a subject of debate.

The single most important event which contributed to the Communists' victory was the military and political collapse of the nationalist forces which had blocked the road to the seizure of power in the past. The reasons for the failure of these groups to exercise their traditional leadership role will always be a matter of controversy. But it is clear that the anti-Communist national forces never grasped the long-range implications of deserting Yugoslavia in her hour of need, and made a serious mistake in underestimating the national appeal of the resistance struggle to the Slav nationalities. By allowing the Communists to seize the initiative in the fight for liberation, the nationalist forces placed themselves in a position which grew more and more difficult as time passed, and from which it eventually became impossible for them to extricate themselves.

The Party saw in the collapse of the anti-Communist opposition vindication of its assertion that the bourgeoisie would eventually be forced to betray the national interests of its own people. Whether collaboration was really betrayal of national interests is a delicate point, not only because many persons considered themselves persecuted by the old regime, but because national choices made during the war were inescapably linked with political predispositions and loyalties to foreign powers. It was the tragedy of Yugoslavia, and many other European countries at the time, that nationalism was so influenced in its expression by nonnational interests and ideologies. To the fascist, collaboration with Hitler could no more be considered a betrayal of national interests than the waging of a struggle to drive out the Germans and seize power by the Partisans under the orders of the Communist International. In all of this, authentic, or natural, national positions were often hard to discern or justify. Practically speaking, however, the willingness of the Chetniks to collaborate with the hated Germans, or the acquiescence of the Croatian fascists in the decision of Italy to annex portions of Croatia, worked to support the Communists' contention, and cut the ground out from under the nationalist elements.

A second factor which contributed to the Communists' success was the strong support which certain groups gave to the Partisans, above all, the Serbs outside Serbia, the Montenegrins and Dalmatians, the Slovenes, and, in the closing years of the war, the Macedonians.[90] It is obvious that without these groups—especially the Serbs—the Communists could not have organized an effective resistance movement. It is less clear what other conclusions can legitimately be drawn from this pattern of national participation in the Partisan movement. It does not seem justified, for example, to rely solely on ethnic or racial factors and attribute the success of the Partisans to the fighting qualities of the Dinaric stock which inhabit the mountains of western Yugoslavia. It is enough to remember that Jovan Cvijić, the eminent Yugoslav ethnologist, considered the Slav Macedonians (or Šopski type) to be temperamentally averse to suffering and warfare, and to compare the performance of the Macedonian Partisans to their Chetnik counterparts in neighboring Serbia, to see how misleading such racially oriented thinking can be when applied to concrete historical situations.

It would also be a mistake to conclude that those who sided with the Partisans were motivated by pro-Yugoslav sentiments. This *was* true in some cases—most notably the Dalmatians—and probably had a strong influence on individuals in Montenegro and Slovenia and on some Serbs. But among the Serbs, the Croats, and especially the Macedonians, the resistance struggle was largely inspired by more narrow regional loyalties. How this attitude was in turn modified by Communist influences is a subject about which more shall be said shortly.

This account has also touched on other possible reasons for persons wishing to join the Partisans: not nationalism, for example, but the desire to escape the atrocities committed by the occupation troops and the local fascists. The role of fear in driving the peasant into the ranks of the Partisans has been noted on many occasions, and has encouraged the

[90] There are very few meaningful figures on the national composition of the Partisans. Tito, *Borba za oslobodjenje Jugoslavije,* p. 180, gave the following figures in the spring of 1944: 44 percent Serbs, 30 percent Croats, 10 percent Slovenes, 4 percent Montenegrins, 2½ percent Moslems, and 6 percent others. By this time, the Partisans were conscripting heavily, and the percentage of Serbs must have been considerably less than in early years of the resistance. One of the most ambitious attempts to provide data on the national make-up of the Partisans can be found in Burks, pp. 124–26. His general conclusions correspond with what has been said here. See also D. A. Tomasić, "The New Class and Nationalism," *Journal of Croatian Studies,* I (1960), 53–74, and by the same author, "Nationality Problems and Partisan Yugoslavia," *Journal of Central European Affairs,* VI (July, 1946), 111–25.

belief that the key to the Partisans' success lay in the workings of a process by which national persecution created a homeless and terrorized peasant mass which became the recruiting grounds for the Partisan armies. This suggests that, Communist propaganda for brotherhood and unity notwithstanding, the Party benefited from the national strife of the occupation period. From such a premise, it is a short step to the conclusion that the Communists climbed to power on the backs of the demoralized and divided Yugoslav peoples—and, to take the argument further still, that the Communist revolution was the final, all-encompassing disaster which the national question inflicted on Yugoslavia.

If one simply asks whether the Partisan movement would have been possible if national persecution had not occurred, the answer would have to be in the affirmative. The uprisings in Serbia in 1941, or in Dalmatia, were proof of that. Broadly speaking, the results of employing terror against the peasant were unpredictable. Whole regions (one thinks of Serbia and Vojvodina) were cowed into submission as a result of the unrestrained savagery of the occupation authorities, while in other areas, persecution released a flood of manpower into the Partisan ranks (the Ustaši in particular were forced to give up their persecution of the Serbs because of the stimulus this gave the Partisans in Croatia). The Partisans considered that the tactic of visiting retribution on the peasants for aiding the Partisans worked to their advantage,[91] but only a few cases are on record of staged incidents, organized by the Communists to provoke the occupation authorities. When such methods were used—as in certain

---

[91] Early in the war, Kardelj wrote to the Central Committee of the CPY: "There exists a difference in the fighting spirit of the Croatian and Serbian villages. If we followed the line of least resistance, we would lead these two villages into conflict. *Willy-nilly we must raise up into battle the Croatian villages, or the Serbian population will be completely annihilated.* And that most definitely can be done. Some comrades fear reprisals (not those in the leadership) from the destruction of villages and people and so on. Just this fear is most responsible for preventing decisive action in the mobilization of Croatian villages. But I take the position that just these reprisals will swing the Croatian villages to the side of the Serbian villages. In war we need not fear the destruction of whole villages. Terror will inevitably lead to armed action." Later in the same report, Kardelj went even further, suggesting that in respect to Maček's forces, *"We must provoke their action. Terror against Maček's [forces] will raise all of Croatia in resistance."* Partisan practice did not follow this latter path, however, and doubtless Kardelj felt, later in the war, that this was putting the matter too strongly. *Zbornik dokumenata*, Vol. II, Book 2, pp. 31–32. Italics in the original.

instances in Croatia—the results were usually disappointing to the Partisans.[92]

The role of nationalism in the Partisan movement has been posed in a different fashion by the theory, now quite widespread, that the Partisan struggle illustrated the success of the Communists in awakening nationalism in the peasant by mobilizing him for guerrilla warfare in a national-liberation type of struggle. With the discussion of this point in respect to wars of national liberation in Asia and elsewhere in recent years, the national question has come full circle and is again being posed as a "peasant question" just as Stalin did in the 1920s.

The discussion of the theory of the mobilization and national awakening of the peasant has not, unfortunately, been accompanied by a careful analysis of the process so that its elements might be identified and closely analyzed in terms of actual experience. Chalmers Johnson has made the greatest contribution to clarifying the dynamics of the peasants' reaction to participation in a resistance movement. Writing with Yugoslavia and China in mind, he has suggested that the "political meaning of this destructive challenge, and subsequent resistance, was the replacement of territorial, ethnic provincialism by allegiance to nationalistic goals." [93] Going a step further, he has suggested that, in Yugoslavia, Marxism was the official rationale for what was essentially a national (that is, Yugoslav) movement; in this he has the support of another student of the phenomenon of Communist nationalism, R. V. Burks.[94]

A careful examination of the Yugoslav resistance suggests the need to introduce some refinements into this theory. For example, the proposal that the crucial transformation in the peasant is from a provincial outlook to a broader and more sophisticated type of nationalism can be misleading; the behavior of the Yugoslav peasant during the war shows that his nationalism was far from devoid of localistic tendencies. The "peasant republic," despite its amusing side, was a genuine expression of the

[92] Early in the war, for example, the Croatian Communists (perhaps following Kardelj's advice) tried to mobilize the peasants of the Hrvatsko Zagorje by provoking clashes betwen the peasants and the Ustaši. To do this, Partisan units were sent into the region to carry out attacks against the occupation authorities. The maneuver failed, according to later reports. *Zbornik dokumenata*, Vol. II, Book 2, p. 85.

[93] Johnson, pp. 172–73.

[94] In his work *The Dynamics of Communism in Eastern Europe*.

peasants' reaction to the war. In a very real sense (although this too is not the whole story), the emotional feelings sparked by the resistance encouraged regressive, atavistic behavior,[95] notwithstanding the noble goals which were placed before the participants in the movement and the constant effort to broaden the horizons of the Partisan soldier through lectures on political subjects or current events.

The peasant, once he was persuaded to move, or perforce had to march from his own locale, acquired new perspectives and developed new loyalties. But his own national consciousness remained regional in outlook and ethnocentric in quality. Party propaganda never really attempted to persuade the Partisan that he was a Yugoslav rather than a Serb, Croat, or Macedonian, but sought rather to get him to tolerate persons of other national origins. Further, while the peasant may have been motivated by national pride, the Partisan experience was not a national awakening (with the exception of the Macedonians), since the national traditions of the Yugoslav peasant were already well developed.

The direct link between the peasant and the Partisans was not some quality of nationalism in the abstract but the desire of the peasant to escape foreign rule. The Communists responded to this desire by demonstrating, through their brilliant tactics, that Partisan warfare could prevail against superior force. When the feeling of subjugation was there, and the terrain for guerrilla tactics was suitable, the Partisans gained supporters from Thrace to Istria, even among peasants who had no highly developed tradition of resistance such as existed among the Serbs and Montenegrins.

The importance of this aspect of nationalism may itself be overestimated. By itself, it was unable to develop broad enough horizons to be effective, as numerous examples from the Partisan campaigns (and the experience of the Chetniks) demonstrated. But it is incontrovertible that the driving force behind the peasants' nationalism was an attitude which had played an important role in the history of the Balkan peoples for centuries: deep-rooted hostility toward rule by ethnically alien elements. It was a sentiment with a glorious tradition. It was also primitive,

[95] A social anthropologist who was with the Partisans during the war has commented to the author on the appearance of certain terms among the Partisans which had their origins in the struggle against the Turks or even earlier, such as *zbeg* (hideout), but which had practically disappeared from popular speech before the war.

ethnocentric, and provincial. The Partisans capitalized on this sentiment but they did not essentially alter its perspectives.

Yugoslav nationalism, on the other hand, was not natural to most of the participants in the resistance struggle, and had to be acquired through the example of the relatively small circle of Communists who directed the Partisan campaigns. In this respect, one cannot help but be struck by the difficulties which the Party faced, despite its superb leadership and rigid discipline, in inculcating in the new cadre an appreciation of the interests of the Party in a *Yugoslav* approach to the resistance. Not only the new recruits, but the older Party members often lost sight of this principle under the pressure to adapt to local or regional national outlooks.

By the same token, the astute and farsighted approach of the Party leadership to the complex problems of the war was remarkable. From the very first, Tito and those around him seem to have understood the vital importance of aligning themselves with Yugoslav interests, and this course was pursued unwaveringly during the entire war.

The presence of this relatively sophisticated attitude toward national interest among the leadership of the Yugoslav Party may come as a surprise in light of the tradition of obedience of the Party to the commands of the Communist International. It is often said that the Party gained the habit of independent thinking only after it was forced to fend for itself during the war. But from what is known of the communications Tito sent the Comintern in the spring of 1941, it would seem that the CPY was well attuned to the interests of Yugoslavia before the Partisan struggle ever began. It must be remembered, in respect to Tito in particular, that service for the Comintern was unsurpassed as an introduction to the art of power politics and was an excellent school for developing an understanding of the importance of national interests—even if these interests were those of the Soviet Union.

The development of the national question after the war was to be profoundly influenced by the relationship between the two extreme types in the Party: the local Party member, still largely provincial in his habits and his approach to the national question, although loyal to the leadership and to the larger aims of the movement, and the small group of Party leaders, with broad horizons and a more sophisticated understanding of national interest. Of course this is something of an exaggeration. There were Party members who fell between these two opposite poles. Nor should it be thought that there existed some kind of cultural gap between the two groups which prevented the penetration of the outlook of the leadership down into the rank and file of the Party.

Still the difference was there. The Party leaders were by temperament accustomed to thinking in Yugoslav terms, while the Party members in the lower ranks were deeply provincial at heart. Party loyalty and revolutionary ambitions made these two groups work as one, and through their cooperation the seemingly impossible task of mastering the national question was accomplished. Only in later years was it to become apparent that, as long as this difference in attitude existed, the national question could not be considered as finally solved.

3

The National Problem
After World War II

THE END of World War II witnessed great changes in the character of
the national question. As the Communist regime consolidated its power,
discussion of national relations was more and more limited to official
propaganda issued by the regime. In most parts of Yugoslavia, the
passions of the interwar period and the occupation gave way to a passive
attitude over the issues which had incited national antagonisms in the past.
National feelings remained strong, but the Party could with justification
claim that the advent of Communist rule was marked by a sharp decrease
in national tensions.

There were a number of reasons for this change. Although national
passions could easily be aroused in postwar Yugoslavia (some examples
of this will be cited shortly), many Yugoslavs welcomed the opportunity
to escape from the nationalistic mood of the preceding years. The
Communist take-over encouraged a withdrawal from involvement in the
national question by posing new challenges and hardships for all classes
in society. Most important of all, the old national parties and their spokesmen were scattered or suppressed, leaving most nationalistic forces without leadership or links with the people.

At the same time, the national question was very much alive in the
postwar period, and continued to pose numerous difficulties for the Party.

The most immediate problem which the Communists faced at the close
of the war involved the nationalist elements (both Slav and minority) who
remained unreconciled to the Communist victory. The extreme fringe of
this nationalist resistance was made up of terrorist bands [1] which operated

---

[1] Chetnik bands were known as the White Eagles (Beli orlovi), the Movement
of National Rebirth of Yugoslavia (Pokret nacionalnog preporoda Jugoslavije), and
the United Movement for National Resistance (Ujedinjeni nacionalni pokret

for many years following the official cessation of hostilities in the same mountains that had sheltered the Partisans. If one can rely on Communist accounts of these groups, their main activity was assassination (or attempted assassination) of Communist officials. The best-known victim of such an attack was Miladin Popović, Party secretary in Kossovo-Metohija after the war, who was killed by Albanian terrorists in the spring of 1945.[2] The last of these groups was reported to have been apprehended only in 1955,[3] and official figures give the impressively high total of 3,000 secret police who lost their lives in stamping out the terrorist-nationalist bands.[4] It is probable that the secret police exaggerated the difficulties of their task somewhat (and inflated their casualty figures as well by including losses suffered in the war). In any case, the bands which operated in Serbia, Croatia, and Bosnia-Hercegovina do not seem to have been a great problem for the Communists, despite the stubbornness with which they resisted capture.

Among the minorities, who had amply demonstrated their hostility to the Communists during the war, the problem of stamping out strong nationalistic anti-Communist sentiment was far more difficult than among the Slav population. The Czechs and the Slovaks, as Slavs who had been in the ranks of the Partisans, did not oppose the Communists on national grounds, although the Slovaks, thanks to their great internal cohesiveness, maintained democratic institutions within their community longer than any group in Yugoslavia. The German minority, on the other hand, was never given the opportunity to prove its loyalty to the new regime. In 1944 the Yugoslav government deprived all Germans of their rights as Yugoslav citizens.[5] Those Germans that remained in Yugoslavia at the end

---

otpora). Perhaps the most well known, and the strongest of these groups, were the Ustaši bands known as Crusaders (Križari), whose activity was particularly pronounced after the crises provoked by the split between Yugoslavia and the Soviet Union in 1948. Followers of IMRO in Macedonia were also accused of terrorist activities. For terrorist and subversive activities by IMRO elements in Macedonia, see Chapter 4.

[2] A notice of the commemoration services held a year after his death can be found in *Jedinstvo* [Priština], March 18, 1946, p. 1.

[3] *Zakon o organima unutrašnjih poslova,* p. 18.

[4] New York *Times,* May 17, 1964, p. 4

[5] Two decrees took away the German's rights. Decision No. 1 of AVNOJ, November 21, 1944, never published, and decision No. 2, of the same date, "Odluka o prelazu neprijateljske imovine u državno vlastništvo," *Službeni List DFJ,* No. 2 (1945), p. 13.

of the war were placed in concentration camps or deported to the Soviet Union.[6] The remaining minorities were absolved of any collective responsibility for collaboration and were promised recognition as national minorities with the right to receive education in national schools and organize national cultural organizations.[7]

The behavior of the minorities during the war could not simply be forgotten, however, and behind the promises made by the Communists there lurked a deep distrust of the entire minority population. The appearance of the Partisans in minority regions at the close of the war was marked by widespread arrests among elements considered dangerous to the new regime.[8] The effect of these punitive acts was to deepen the

[6] The most reliable estimate of the number of Germans deported to the Soviet Union can be found in Markert, ed., p. 36. He calculates that some 320,000 could be accounted for in Germany, that some 50,000 were known to be deported, and that 180,000 were unaccounted for. For other estimates of the size of the German exodus from Yugoslavia, see J. B. Schechtman, "The Elimination of German Minorities in Southeastern Europe," *Journal of Central European Affairs,* VI (July, 1946), 160–62, and Dolfe Vogelnik, "Demografski gubici Jugoslavije u Drugom svetskom ratu," *Statistička Revija,* II (May, 1952), 29.

[7] The basic rights of the minorities were provided for in a general way by Article 13 of the constitution of 1946, which stated that "the national minorities in the Federal People's Republic of Yugoslavia enjoy the right and protection of their cultural development and the free use of their language." The right to use one's native tongue before the courts was guaranteed in various laws dealing with criminal procedure and other subjects. Minority schools were set up in the immediate postwar years according to a directive issued August 9, 1945, which provided that a minority school, with courses conducted in the language of the minority, would be set up if there were twenty students requesting it. This was finally superseded by the General Law on Schools of 1958, which dealt with the minority schools, and by republic laws. For the cultural and educational societies of the minorities prior to 1950, see the statement by Aleksandar Ranković in *Borba,* Dec. 28, 1949, which lists the number of cultural, hunting, and physical education groups for each of the minorities. The total of all groups mentioned by Ranković was 174, the vast majority of which were located in Vojvodina for the Hungarians, Czechs, Slovaks, and Rumanians. Only three organizations were given for the Albanians in Kossovo-Metohija.

[8] Hungarian exiles in the United States claim that thousands were killed at the hands of the Partisans, but no evidence is available to prove or disprove these charges. An exchange of populations was discussed between the Yugoslav and Hungarian representatives at the Paris Peace Conference as a method of ending the minority problem which existed for both countries, but in the end no action was taken to carry out this plan. In Carinthia, hundreds of persons were summarily executed. For a description of this incident, see Thomas M. Barker, *The Slovenes of Carinthia,* p. 240. For another account, see Karapandžić, *Kočevje, Titov najkrvaviji zločin.*

hostility which was felt on both sides and to reenforce the old nationalist sympathies of the minority population. Although the Communists took a wide variety of measures to ensure impartial treatment of the minorities after the first wave of hostility had been spent, the intransigence of nationalist elements in the minority population remained a thorn in the side of the Party for years after the war was over.

The Albanians were the most hostile element among the minorities, and in dealings with them the Communists were guilty of extreme measures which at times differed little from those employed by the occupation authorities during the war. One incident was described by Aleksandar Ranković, who was then head of the secret police, as follows:

On the occasion of transporting one group of Albanians to strengthen the IV Army one incident occurred which was such that it could not be localized [and] the results of which could not be contained. . . . One Albanian provoked by some guard took down his rifle and killed him. That is, he killed one of our fighters. But our comrades obviously didn't recover their wits and instead of settling the whole thing in such a way as to prevent any further clash, wished to punish them, wished to carry out reprisals, wished to execute 40 Albanians for one dead fighter. This stupid intention and completely foreign method for us was taken advantage of by enemy elements in that group of Albanians and [they] succeeded in provoking an uprising (*pobuna*). . . . On this occasion about 200 Albanians were killed.[9]

The behavior of the Partisans toward the Albanians was criticized at the first Congress of the Serbian Communist Party in the spring of 1945.[10] But by this time the Communists were already reaping the bitter harvest of the atrocities committed in Kossovo-Metohija, for open revolt had developed among the Albanians against the new regime.

The Albanian uprising, although it took place just after the war had ended, was notable as the only instance of an armed rebellion against the Communist government in Yugoslavia. The Communists claim that the revolt was organized by the Germans; there may be some truth to this, but the action of the Albanians was mainly inspired by national feelings, in protest against Communist terror. Although little is known of the political aims of the uprising, the intellectual leader of the rebellion, Imer Berisa, was apparently an advocate of the idea of a "Greater Albania,"

[9] Ranković, *Izabrani govori i članci, 1941–1945*, p. 46.
[10] *Ibid.*

that is, the inclusion of Kossovo-Metohija in Albania.[11] The revolt broke out in Urošec in December, 1944, and spread to Gnjilane, Drenica, and Trepča. In Drenica Yugoslav accounts (probably exaggerated) say 30,000 Albanians were engaged in the battle for the town.[12] The rebellion was finally pacified in the summer of 1945, and on the surface everything became calm in Kossovo-Metohija. In the constitutional elections held in the fall, more registered voters went to the polls in Kossovo-Metohija than in any other region in Yugoslavia. But the position of the Communists in the region was never completely secure; the population remained alienated from the new regime while the resistance went underground, and the Communists were never able to stamp it out completely.[13]

The Party had not wished to incite the national feelings of the Albanians, and considerable efforts were made after the war, through the establishment of Albanian schools and the introduction of Albanian as one of the official languages of Kossovo-Metohija, to undo some of the injustices visited upon the peoples of that region in the past. In recognition of the mixed national character of the region, Kossovo-Metohija was declared an autonomous *oblast* (later it was promoted to the rank of an autonomous province); [14] although this did not mean that the Albanians had been granted autonomy, the establishment of the *oblast* did give the minority population in Kossovo-Metohija access to local administrative posts and Party positions which would otherwise not have been open to them.

The interest of the Party in reaching some kind of a settlement with the minorities, despite the hostility which existed on both sides, contrasted strongly with the political calculations which dominated the Communists'

11 For an account of the revolt, see *Jedinstvo,* June 8, 1964, p. 4.

12 *Ibid.,* Jan. 21, 1946. For other accounts see *ibid.,* July 9, 1946; Aug. 4, 1946; May 11, 1964; June 1, 1964; June 8, 1964; and June 15, 1964.

13 At the Seventh Conference of the Kossovo-Metohija regional Party organization in 1956, Fadilj Hodža, regional Party secretary, mentioned the great Albanian chauvinism still being spread by "various committees of the National Democratic [Movement]." *Sedma konferencija Saveza Komunista Srbije za Kosovo i Metohiju,* p. 135. Hodža's speech at the 1956 conference is a useful summary of the successes and the difficulties the Communists had encountered in Kossovo-Metohija in the preceding years. For further information on unrest in Kossovo-Metohija in this period, see Chapter 5 on the Ranković case.

14 The system of autonomous regions is discussed in more detail later in this chapter and in Chapter 5.

campaign against the last remaining stronghold of the traditional national forces in Yugoslavia, namely, organized religion. The churches were closely associated with the nationalist foes of the Party, and the struggle between the Party and the churches very quickly assumed national overtones, especially in the case of the Catholic Church.

For a very brief period, in the spring of 1945, the Communists spared the Catholic Church direct attack. In Zagreb, in May, Tito proposed the terms of a truce between the Communists and the Church: the Yugoslav Catholics were to form a "national" church, cutting their ties with the Papacy.[15] The Catholics of course refused, and a bitter struggle between the Church and the Party ensued, which reached its most dramatic moment during the trial of Archbishop Stepinac in the fall of 1946.[16] During the trial, the Communists used questionable evidence in an attempt to prove that Stepinac had collaborated with the Germans during the war, and tried to create the impression that the Catholic Church was antinational for having given support to the enemies of the resistance movement. Stepinac defended the view that he had acted only with the interests of the Croatian people at heart. Without going further into the tangled history of the case, it is clear that the Communists were interested not only in discrediting the Catholic Church but in trying to drive a wedge between the Croats and the Church as a national institution. The attempt failed; the Church in Croatia remained a symbol of non-Communist nationalism, and the prelates themselves continued to hold (in private, of course) strongly nationalist views similar to those expressed publicly just before the Communists seized power.[17] The trial of Stepinac did

[15] Tito first made his proposal to a gathering of Church dignitaries in Zagreb on June 2. Several days later he repeated his plan publicly: "For my part, I would say that our church should be national, to belong more to the nation. Perhaps it is a little strange to you that I defend nationalism so strongly. But . . . I would like to see the Catholic clergy in Croatia more deeply tied to the people. . . . I would like to see the Catholic Church in Croatia now, when all the conditions for it exist, to have more independence. That is what I wish, and all other questions are secondary." *Borba*, June 5, 1946, p. 1.

[16] Pattee gives an account of the trial from the point of view of one sympathetic to the Archbishop. For the Yugoslav Communist view, see Novak, *Magnem krimen*.

[17] In a pastoral letter of March, 1945, it was stated: "The church has imbued the priests and peoples of Croatia with the will to render to God what is God's, and to its own country its due. History testifies that the Croatian people for nearly a thousand years have never renounced their right to nationhood." Pattee, p. 417.

make a deep impression on the Serbs, however, who accepted the evidence presented by the Communists as further proof that Yugoslavia was betrayed by the Croats in 1941.

The Serbian Orthodox Church, despite the reputation of its Patriarch as an archfoe of the Communists, reached an accommodation with the new regime,[18] and the Communists never undertook a campaign against the Orthodox prelates and clergy of the kind that was directed against the Catholic Church. The Communists chose to ignore the fact that the Serbian Orthodox Church had favored the Chetniks during the war, and were content to allow the Orthodox religion to survive as a symbol (without any great influence) of Serbian national traditions.

The Communists always had a lever to enforce obedience from the Serbian Orthodox Church, for there existed strong pressure from Macedonia, resisted by the Patriarch in Belgrade, to form a national Macedonian Church. In 1958 this change in the organization of the Serbian Orthodox Church was finally pushed through by the Macedonians and an autonomous church for Macedonia was formed with the reluctant approval of the helpless Serbian Patriarch.[19]

The Slav Moslems posed a special problem for the Communists. Although the majority of Moslems had sided with the occupation authorities, the Party at first tried to avoid a head-on clash with the Moslem Religious Community, or IVZ. Moslem charitable organizations, influential in the IVZ before the war, were dissolved or reorganized,[20] but the leaders of

[18] The return of the Patriarch, Gavrilo, was arranged through the intercession of the Czechs. Shortly after his arrival in Belgrade, Gavrilo visited Tito; the result seems to have been some kind of understanding between the regime and the Serbian Orthodox Church. For mention of the meeting, see New York *Times,* Dec. 9, 1946, p. 5.

[19] The creation of the Macedonian church and the appointment of the Metropolitan were carried out by a "Church National Assembly" (Crkveno-narodni sabor) made up of Macedonian clergy and lay personages from Macedonia. The meeting re-created the archbishopric of Ohrid, which had existed in medieval Serbia; a former official of the Patriarch in Belgrade was chosen as Archbishop of the new archbishopric and Metropolitan of the Macedonian Orthodox Church, which was to remain in canonical union with the Serbian Orthodox Church. For the creation of the Macedonian church, see *Borba,* Oct. 7, 1958, p. 5.

[20] In 1945, from the two prewar organizations Gajreta and Narodna uzdanica, the Communists in Sarajevo formed a new organization, Preporod. In August, 1946, the one remaining charitable group, Merhameta, was brought into Preporod. *Nova Doba* [Sarajevo], Oct. 6, 1945, p. 5, and August 28, 1946, p. 3.

the Community were spared public criticism for their contacts with the occupation authorities during the war. The Communist tactics of appeasing the Moslems were not successful, however. In the fall of 1945 elections for official posts in the Community were won by anti-Communists, and the following year saw a rapid growth of anti-Communist feeling throughout the Moslem Community.[21]

For a brief moment, it seemed as though the Moslem faith was going to emerge as an anti-Communist force of some importance, parallel to the Catholic Church. In 1947, however, the Communists moved against the IVZ,[22] cutting off state support and making it impossible for the Moslems to gather their own funds on a voluntary basis for the medresa (confessional schools) and other activities of the Community.[23] In dire financial straits, the IVZ capitulated. On August 5, 1947, a statement of the deliberative body of the Community for Bosnia-Hercegovina, the Vakufski sabor, appeared, in which all those who had opposed the regime were criticized, and the support of the sabor was pledged to the government.[24] Several weeks later a Supreme Vakufski sabor representing the Moslems of all Yugoslavia met and approved a new constitution for

[21] The opposition within the IVZ was strongly attacked by a Communist-sponsored meeting of Moslems held in Sarajevo in August, 1946. *Nova Doba,* Aug. 28, 1946, p. 5. Other mention of the opposition appeared in *Nova Doba,* Sept. 6, p. 1; Oct. 2, pp. 2–3. For an admission by the Communists that elements hostile to the regime were elected, see *Referat druga Hasana Brkića održan na trećem sastanku plenuma Glavnog odbora muslimana 9–IX–1946.*

[22] In January, 1947, a group of six Croatians and Moslems were tried in Sarajevo for organizing Ustaši and Chetnik (*sic*) activities in Bosnia-Hercegovina. One of the defendants was Mehmed-Meho Sahinagić, who had been the subject of public attacks several months earlier as one of the chief trouble makers in the IVZ. Sahinagić received a prison term of eight years. *Oslobodjenje* [Sarajevo], Jan. 14, 1947, p. 4. In the fall of 1947, twelve Moslems were also sentenced to terms in prison for anti-state activities. The leader of the group, Kasim Dobrača, had been active in the prewar organization of Moslem priests, El Hidaje. The sentences given these men were short enough to suggest that they were being jailed for political reasons and not for terrorist activities. *Ibid.,* Sept. 26, 1947, p. 4.

[23] When government support was cut off, the IVZ turned to voluntary contributions. A fund was established into which each Moslem was to pay two dinars a month. The plan showed promise in early trials but was forbidden by the government, which ruled that collections could only be taken within the mosques. See the report of the committee of the Vakufski sabor reproduced in *Glasnik Vrhovnog Islamskog Starještinstva,* No. 1–3 (Jan.-March, 1951), p. 81.

[24] *Oslobodjenje,* Aug. 5, 1947.

the IVZ.[25] Under its provisions, the IVZ was to be an autonomous organization representing all the Moslems of Yugoslavia. The Supreme Vakufski sabor was to be made up of representatives of the Vakufski sabori of the four Moslem regions: Bosnia-Hercegovina, Serbia, Macedonia, and Montenegro. Local administrators were to be democratically elected, but steps were taken to prevent any repetition of the November, 1945, elections: the regional Vakufski sabor was to be elected by direct and secret vote of the Moslem population, but the local committees were to be chosen by open voting, while the district committees, where anti-Communist elements had shown great strength, were to be appointed by the Vakufski sabor. In return for these concessions the government renewed its financial support of the church; of 31½ million dinars spent by the Community between 1945 and 1951, 23 million came from the state treasury.

The Moslems remained strongly conscious of the cultural and religious differences which separated them from the remaining Slavs of Yugoslavia, but with the support of the Community assured, the Communists were able to carry out many changes in the traditional Moslem way of life. Sheriat courts were dissolved in 1946, and with the active support of the IVZ, wearing of the veil was prohibited in the period 1950–51.

The IVZ never ventured an opinion on any political aspect of the national question; the idea that the Slav Moslems should receive some form of autonomy was never publicly broached by Moslem spokesmen when the federal system was under discussion in 1945. The official policy of the Communists was to treat the Slav Moslems as a religious group, not as a separate national or cultural community. Moslems could declare themselves as Serbs, Croats, or (as most frequently was the case in the first census of 1948), "Yugoslavs." Only later, in the Titoist period, was this general attitude toward the national status of the Moslems to be challenged and the suggestion put forth that the Moslems should be considered a separate nationality.[26]

Publicly, it appeared after the war that the Communists had routed their nationalist opponents. Furthermore, through control of the press

[25] The constitution can be found in *Glasnik Vrhovnog Islamskog Starještinstva*, No. 1–3 (Jan.-March, 1951), pp. 59–67. For election procedures, see decrees published in the same issue, pp. 93, 96, and 97.

[26] See Chapter 5.

and ceaseless agitational activities, the Party gave the impression that prewar national attitudes had few supporters among the Yugoslav population. A more accurate picture of the situation would have to take into account the fact that, while the prewar national groups were largely paralyzed, traditional national attitudes remained largely unchanged. How deeply entrenched these sentiments were was to become apparent in later years, not through the appearance of anti-Communist organizations, but in the adoption of local national outlooks by the Communists themselves.

National prejudices were also strong as a result of the bitter memories of the occupation. The feeling of brotherhood and unity encouraged by the Party was not a myth, and among those who accepted the Party line, one would normally expect to find a tolerant attitude toward other nationalities. But it cannot be said that these persons represented more than a small percentage of the population.

The Party was conscious of the existence of these national prejudices and the fact that it would take time for the wounds created by the war to heal. Notwithstanding the official claim that the national question was a thing of the past, the Communists were quick to pass a law at the end of the war which severely punished as a criminal offense any act which incited national, racial, or religious antagonisms.[27] Granting privileges on the basis of race, nationality, or religion was also prohibited.

The law was vigorously enforced [28] and made an important contribution

[27] "Zakon o zabrani izazivanja nacionalne rasne i vjerske mržnje i razdora," *Službeni List DFJ,* No. 36, 1945, p. 198. The law is no longer considered in effect, for its provisions have been restated in the Criminal Law of 1951, articles 148 and 119. See "Krivični zakonik," *Službeni List FNRJ,* No. 13, 1951, p. 185. Article 148 makes it an offense punishable by up to five years' imprisonment to limit the rights granted citizens in the constitution or to grant favors and advantages on the basis of nationality, race, or religion. Article 119 makes punishable by up to fifteen years' imprisonment exciting or inflaming national, racial, or religious hatred.

[28] Statistics on the enforcement of the provisions of the law for the period 1947 to 1959, which cannot be published here in full, can be found in Paul Shoup, "Communism and the National Question in Yugoslavia" (Unpublished doctoral dissertation, Columbia University, 1961), p. 111. A semiofficial account of the Yugoslav minorities stated that "especially during the period immediately following the war, when chauvinistic hatred and national and religious intolerance fanned by the forces of the occupation and quislings were still smoldering, there were cases in which the national feelings of the members of various nationalities and national minorities were violated. Punishment was very severe in such cases." Stojković and Martić, p. 85.

to limiting nationalistic outbursts, especially in areas of mixed nationality. The minorities above all had reason to be grateful for the protection they received in this fashion from the anger of the Slav population.

In at least one case, however, the Communists were unable to prevent an open clash between national groups. The violence occurred in Macedonia, in the spring of 1945, between Macedonian peasants and the Serbs returning to claim the land they had owned before the war.

Antagonism between the Serbs and Macedonians had come to the surface as a result of the problem of disposing of land tilled by the colonists before the war but abandoned during the occupation and seized by local peasants. The Communists had attempted to settle the issue, temporarily, by a law which returned all land to its earlier owners, pending final legislation on the whole agrarian question.[29] It was in part as a reaction to this law that the Macedonians sought to take revenge on the Serbian peasants who had returned to claim their plots.[30] As a result the Communists found themselves caught in a difficult situation, unwilling to make a decision which would anger either the Serbs or the Macedonians. After several months of indecision,[31] a law was adopted which distinguished between colonists who could keep the land they had held before the war and those to whom it would not be returned, either because

[29] In March, 1945, a decree was passed forbidding all colonists to return to their homes. "Odluka nacionalnog komiteta oslobodjenja Jugoslavije br. 153 . . . ," *Službeni List DFJ,* No. 13, p. 137. A week later those from Vojvodina were allowed to return. "Rešenje o dozvoli preseljenja kolonista za Vojvodinu," *ibid.,* No. 15, p. 145. Then in May the law was passed returning the land to its former owners. See "Zakon o postupanju sa imovinom koju su vlasnici morali napustiti u toku okupacije i imovinom koja im je oduzeta po okupatoru i njegovim pomagačima," *ibid.,* No. 36, 1945. Under the provisions of this law, all land which the owners had to leave during the occupation, as well as all land taken out of racist, religious, national, or political reasons, was returned immediately. There were no qualifications which might limit this right to a certain class or exclude any group from its provisions.

[30] *Borba,* June 5, 1945, p. 2, and June 17, p. 2.

[31] During this period, the problem was discussed in the legal committee of the Presidium of AVNOJ. Sreten Vukosavljević, a venerable Serbian patriot who had cooperated with the Communists, and Emanuel Čučkov, minister for Macedonia, crossed swords in the committee. Vukosavljević defended the colonists, while Čučkov criticized Vukosavljević for stating that the Macedonians acted "crudely" toward the colonists. Moša Pijade, chairman of the committee, remarked that the unnecessary delay in bringing the law had done much to exacerbate the situation. Privremena narodna skupština DFJ, *Rad zakonodavnih odbora,* pp. 546–51.

they had been officials of the old regime or had not worked the land themselves before the war.[32]

The Serbs in Croatia, who had suffered so terribly at the hands of the Ustaši while contributing so much to the Partisan cause, also posed a serious problem for the Communists. As the war drew to a close, the Party took a number of steps to mollify the Serbian population in Croatia, and it appeared that the Serbs might be granted special rights, similar to those enjoyed by the minorities, within Croatia.[33] The high point in this policy was reached in the fall of 1945, when a congress of Serbs was organized in Zagreb.[34] Following this display of Serbian sentiment, the privileges which had been introduced during the war were gradually

[32] "Zakon o reviziji dodeljivanja zemlje kolinistima i agrarnim interesantima u Makedoniji i u Kosovo-Metohijskoj oblasti," *Službeni List DFJ*, No. 56, p. 511. The law provided that all those who had been awarded land as the result of agrarian reforms carried out before 1941 would lose ownership if the land had been the private property of another agricultural worker, and if any one of the following conditions obtained: (1) the land had been worked by a sharecropper (the Macedonian *čivčija*); (2) the colonists did not directly work, but only rented, the land; (3) the land had been, prior to settlement, the property of a "political emigrant"; (4) the colonist was a former police official or other agent of the old regime or had been given the land in return for services rendered the regime before the war. All cases were to be decided by September 1, 1945. (Later this was extended to December, 1946). In Kossovo-Metohija, most of the colonists in these four categories were entitled to other land in the region itself. In Macedonia, those who lost their land were to be "supplied with land in other places." According to official figures, out of 11,283 colonist households in Macedonia and Kossovo-Metohija, 1,791 had their holdings entirely confiscated and 9,492 partially confiscated under the provisions of the law. Brashich, p. 48. Prewar figures had given the number of colonist households at over 30,000 in 1936; the discrepancy between these two sets of figures may be explained by the fact that the Yugoslavs have listed 12,732 holdings as "abandoned" throughout Yugoslavia by the colonists.

[33] In the fall of 1944 a Serbian cultural and educational society, "Prosveta," was formed, and a Serbian choir, "Obilić," organized. The Serbian newspaper in Croatia, *Srpska Riječ* had appeared throughout the war. In the fall of 1944, Moša Pijade promised the Serbs in Croatia that "the Serbian and Croatian nations have and will have in Federal Yugoslavia all the possibilities and all the means necessary to organize their national life as complete national entities. The borders of the federal units will not and cannot be any kind of obstacle to this." Pijade, *Izabrani govori i članci, 1941–1947*, p. 270. This suggested that the Communists foresaw some form of cultural autonomy for the Serbs of Croatia, or even direct ties in cultural matters with Serbia. While it did not come to this, the Serbs did gain special representation on the "Main Committee" of the Communist front organization in the spring of 1945.

[34] *Srpska Riječ*, Oct. 5, 1945, gives a description of the congress.

withdrawn,[35] and no more mention was made of the special status of the Serbs in Croatia. In contrast to Macedonia, the Serbs who returned to Croatia after the war to claim their land were apparently resettled without difficulty.[36]

The policies adopted toward the Serbs in Croatia and Macedonia were a good example of the reluctance with which the Party granted special concessions to any one national group, out of a fear that this would lead to a reaction among the remaining nationalities. The Communists were not averse to providing a safe outlet for national feelings, but were keenly aware of the limits of such a policy under the conditions that prevailed at the time. The same type of consideration governed the cautious introduction of the federal system, whose primary purpose was to serve as a lightning rod for national emotions, without limiting the power of the Party or the jurisdiction of the centralized administration built up during the war.

The groundwork for a federal system was laid by the decision of AVNOJ in 1943 to adopt the federal principle in Yugoslavia and, on the political front, by the successful struggle against autonomist currents within the Party. Although the federation was theoretically in existence during the war, the actual introduction of federal institutions had to await the adoption of a new constitution after the conflict had ended.

This step was taken after elections to a constituent assembly were carried out in the fall of 1945. The Communists were in such firm control of the entire proceedings, from the elections to the meetings of the

[35] The Main Committee of the Croatian front organization ceased to function soon after the congress of Serbs in Zagreb. The congress itself was the last demonstration organized for the Croatian Serbs. The Serbian choir "Obilić" was joined, later, with the Croatian group "Lisinski" into a choral society called "Bratstvo i Jedinstvo" (Brotherhood and Unity). Certain organizations were retained by the Serbs. Prosveta was allowed to continue its cultural work, and a Serbian museum was founded in Zagreb to which Serbian schoolchildren would come to be told of the struggle of the Croatian Serbs during the resistance.

[36] Those Serbs who had fled Croatia and planned to return to their homes were processed through the Ministry of Transportation in Belgrade; to each family was explained the necessity of suppressing any hostile feelings toward the Croats. The writer has been told that all questions outstanding between the Croats and the returning Serbs were left in the hands of the parties concerned, to settle as their sense of justice and fair play dictated. The matter could hardly have been so simple. In all probability the local officials, very likely the Party committee, used their discretion, employing whatever rough standards of justice they deemed appropriate.

constituent assembly itself, that the new constitution was adopted without a dissenting vote at any stage of the ratification process. Shortly thereafter, the same procedure was repeated in each of the newly formed republics, where constituent assemblies were held and republic constitutions adopted.[37]

The federal system was patterned very closely after the Soviet model. Six republics were designated (Serbia, Croatia, Slovenia, Bosnia-Hercegovina, Montenegro, and Macedonia), and two autonomous regions, Vojvodina and Kossovo-Metohija. The major departure from the Soviet constitution of 1936, as amended, was the absence of any reference to the right of the republics to maintain armies or foreign offices, and the power of the federal legislature to adopt "general," or "basic," laws, which would be completed by the republics. Otherwise, most of the provisions of the constitution followed Soviet practice closely. This was especially evident in the organization of the legislature, in which one house, the Chamber of Nationalities, represented the republics, and in the organization of the administrative apparatus, which was built around All-Union, Union-Republic, and Republic ministries in which the federal and republic governments shared powers.[38]

Five nationalities were recognized in the constitution of 1946: Serbs, Croats, Slovenes, Macedonians, and Montenegrins. The members of a nation were not restricted to the republic in which the nationality predominated, but included all those of like ethnic (or national) background,

---

[37] The proceedings of the constituent assembly can be found in Narodna skupština FNRJ, *Ustavotvorni odbori Savezne skupštine i skupštine naroda*. For the texts of the federal and republic constitutions, see *Ustav FNRJ i ustavi narodnih republika*.

[38] See articles 86 and 87 of the federal constitution. The constitution provided for six All-Union and nine Union-Republic ministries. The All-Union ministries were given the right to carry out directly all tasks that fell to them. They could place representatives in the republic governments. While the republic constitutions promulgated on December 31, 1946—Bosnia-Hercegovina, Macedonia, and Montenegro—did not say that this representative need be chosen with the approval of the republic government, the republic constitutions promulgated after the third week in January, 1947—Serbia, Croatia, and Slovenia—contained this stipulation. The very fact that the republic constitutions were promulgated in two groups, and that the three major republics held off for several weeks in adopting their constitutions, suggests that some issues had come up for discussion between the federal government and the governments of the republics.

whatever part of Yugoslavia they inhabited (Serbs in Croatia for example, were referred to as part of the Serbian nation). At the same time, each republic was considered a nation-state in the sense that it served as a rough equivalent of the homeland of the dominant nationality within its boundaries. The minorities had a special status, and it was clear that the right of self-determination was not intended to apply, even in theory, in their case. Autonomous regions were not considered areas where minorities could enjoy a homeland analogous to that available to the Slav nationalities, but were thought of rather as regions of mixed nationality, which required special status in the light of the difficult problem of adjusting relations among groups with different national origins.[39]

The most striking aspect of this federal system was the sweeping grant of rights to the republics as national units. The six republics were sovereign, and they were considered "states," although self-determination was limited by the federal constitution, which was phrased in such a way as to make it appear that the right had already been exercised.[40] Although the federal government was granted the power to pass laws on most subjects, the right to legislate in areas not specified in the constitution lay

[39] The only peculiarities in the organization of the autonomous areas which set them apart from other inferior administrative units in the republics were their statutes, their representation in the Chamber of Nationalities, and, in Vojvodina, the existence of a Supreme Court equal in rank to those of the republics. It was implied that there was a difference in rank between the two autonomous areas (Vojvodina was termed a province, or *pokrajina,* while Kossovo-Metohija was identified as a region, or *oblast*), but the practical difference between the two was never clear, and later they were equalized in status. The rights and duties of the autonomous areas were fixed in the Serbian constitution and in the statutes of the respective areas. For the 1948 statute of the Autonomous Province of Vojvodina, see *Statut Autonomne Pokrajine Vojvodine u Narodnoj Republici Srbiji,* for Kossovo-Metohija, *Službeni list Autonomne Kosovske Metohijske Oblasti,* No. 10, 1948, p. 74.

[40] While the declaration made at the AVNOJ meeting of November, 1943, had contained the phrase that "on the basis of the right of every nation to self-determination, including the right of secession or uniting with other nations . . . AVNOJ brings the following decisions . . . ," Article 1 of the constitution read: "The Federal People's Republic of Yugoslavia is a federal people's state, republican in form, a community of peoples equal in rights who, on the basis of the right to self-determination including the right of secession, have expressed their will to live together in a federative state." One constitutional lawyer called this an "indirect right" of self-determination. Stefanović, *Ustavno pravo FNR Jugoslavije,* p. 397.

with the republics, which were also supposed to exercise responsibility over their own administrative organs.

The intent of these provisions was clearly not to supply the republics with powers that could be used contrary to the wishes of the federal government.[41] The very fact that these rights were *not* used, although granted the republics, was part of the image that the federal system was designed to present of a voluntary union of equal independent states firmly united by a common revolutionary outlook under the leadership of the Communist Party. However much this may have concealed the true nature of national relations, the very willingness to adopt such principles was evidence of a widespread consensus among the Communists themselves that the rights of the republics, while they should reflect the importance of the multinational character of Yugoslavia, should not be interpreted in such a way as to impinge on the powers of the Party.

At the same time it was obvious that the character of the federal system was strongly influenced by the long-standing conviction of the Communists that centralism was a supreme virtue. In this respect, the Party had not changed fundamentally since it first advocated a strong unitary system of rule for Yugoslavia in 1919. There was also much that was specious, or confusing, in the theory of Yugoslav federalism as it was set out in the constitution of 1946, as Yugoslav constitutional lawyers were later to admit. How could the republics be "sovereign" when the federal government held real power and was responsible for foreign affairs and military matters? Some aspects of the theory of nationality were unclear. Was not a Serb in Croatia part of the Croatian

41 Tito expressed this idea very clearly in a statement which, perhaps because of its frankness, has not been cited in Yugoslav works on federalism. On the occasion of his first visit to Zagreb in May, 1945, he made the following remarks on the federal system: "Many people do not understand what federal Yugoslavia means, federal Croatia, federal Serbia, and so forth. That does not mean emphasizing the borders between this and that federal unit, that you there do what you know how [to do] and can, and I will do what I know. No! These borders, if I may present them in this fashion, should be something similar to those white lines on a marble column [*sic*]. The borders of the federal states in federal Yugoslavia are not borders which divide, but borders which unite. What is the meaning of federal units in today's Yugoslavia? We don't consider them a group of small nations; rather they have a more administrative character, the freedom to govern oneself. That is the character of independence of each federal unit, full independence in the sense of free cultural and economic development." *Borba*, May 22, 1945, p. 1.

nation? If not, was Croatia "multinational," in fact a multinational state within a multinational state? Apparently this problem did provoke some thought in Serbia, for the Serbian constitution was corrected before its promulgation to make clear that, despite the presence of other nationalities in the republic, Serbia was a state of the Serbian nation.[42]

In practice, these doctrinal points were not to be discussed until the period of the Titoist reforms, when a more critical attitude was adopted toward the federal system. In the immediate postwar years, the main elements of the federal structure, including the Chamber of Nationalities, the republic national assemblies, and the autonomous areas, worked together as one well-oiled machine. Perhaps the most difficult moment in organizing the federal system was passed in 1945, when the borders of the republics were fixed and the location of the autonomous areas decided upon. Momentarily, national feelings came to the surface within the Party, especially between the Serbs and the Croats over the location of the autonomous area of Vojvodina and the Srem. Before the war, the Croatian Communists had tended to favor autonomy for Vojvodina, treating it as a separate national region (such as Bosnia-Hercegovina). The Croats had an even greater interest in the Srem, for it had traditionally been part of Croatia-Slavonia, and the Croatian Main Command had exercised jurisdiction over most of the area during the war. The Serbs, for their part, tended to view Vojvodina as part of Serbia and the Srem as part of Vojvodina, because of the large number of Serbs in both regions. The arguments over these areas reached a peak in the spring of 1945.[43] After some hesitation, Vojvodina and the Srem

---

[42] Jovan Djordjević, *Ustavno pravo,* pp. 33–35.

[43] In November of 1944, a delegation from Vojvodina, attending the Great Anti-Fascist National Liberation Assembly of Serbia as observers, announced that the peoples of Vojvodina "at various assemblies and conferences" had come out in favor of autonomy for the area, but did not state which republic they wished to join. Stefanović, *Ustavno pravo FNR Jugoslavije,* p. 215. As an apparent result of the indecision over the future of the area, Vojvodina remained under military rule into 1945, well after the area had been cleared of the Germans. Ranković, *Izabrani govori i clanci, 1941–1945,* p. 34. In April, 1945, the representative for Vojvodina at the first meeting of the Anti-Fascist Assembly of National Liberation for Serbia (ASNOS) announced that, at a meeting of the Main National Liberation Council for Vojvodina, "the question of the position of Vojvodina was discussed and it was decided unanimously that it should be clearly announced in which federal unit the autonomous region of Vojvodina should enter." *Slobodna*

were made one autonomous province within the republic of Serbia.[44]

There were also misunderstandings over the autonomous status of the Sandžak. The convening of an Anti-Fascist Assembly for the Sandžak in November, 1943, gave the impression that the area was being prepared for autonomous status after the war. When it was decided to divide the area between Serbia and Montenegro, a special commission, headed by Moša Pijade, was formed to go to the spot and explain the move to the local Communists.[45] In March, 1946, the Sandžak assembly gave its approval to the division of the region.

Several other territorial disputes arose but were dealt with inside the inner circle of the Party without reference to the constituent assembly,[46] which by law was supposed to approve all the republic boundaries before they could be incorporated into the federal and republic constitutions.

The centralism which characterized the organization of the govern-

---

Vojvodina (Novi Sad), April 8, 1945, p. 1. The Council then voted unanimously for inclusion in Serbia.

[44] ASNOS approved the inclusion of Vojvodina in Serbia in April; in July, 1945, elections were held for an assembly which ratified the decision of the Vojvodina delegates to ASNOS; in August, AVNOJ approved the decision of ASNOS; in September, 1945, Serbia brought forth a law governing the administrative organization of Vojvodina; the formal statute for the region was promulgated in 1948.

[45] Prezidium Narodne skupštine FNRJ, *Zakonodavni rad pretsedništva Antifašističkog veća narodnog oslobodjenja Jugoslavije*, pp. 53–56.

[46] Moša Pijade, speaking to a committee of the national constituent assembly, spoke of minor disputes over boundaries between Slovenia and Croatia, and Croatia and Bosnia-Hercegovina in the region of Lika. Voices from the floor interjected that boundaries were at issue between Serbia and Croatia and Serbia and Macedonia as well. Narodna skupština FNRJ, *Ustavotvorni odbori Savezne skupštine i skupštine naroda*, p. 119. The area in dispute between Croatia and Slovenia was the Hrvatsko Zagorje. The specific issues which divided Serbia and Macedonia are not known. Pijade promised that a special commission would be formed to examine the situation and that the National Assembly would determine the final borders. Instead, the borders appeared in the republic constitution in 1947 without prior assembly approval.

Since the delimitation of the republic boundaries sometime in 1946, the following adjustments have been made in accordance with the provisions of the constitution that republic approval will be obtained: (1) in 1949, two villages were transferred from Montenegro to Bosnia-Hercegovina; (2) in 1953, some villages in the districts of Bihać and Bosansko-Grahovski were transferred from Bosnia-Hercegovina to Croatia; (3) in 1956, in the commune of Buja, the district of Pula, half a dozen villages were switched from Croatia to Slovenia; (4) in 1956, the village of Bušević in the Bihać district was transferred from Bosnia-Hercegovina to Croatia.

ment was even more evident in the structure of the Party. The Party leadership, making its decisions in the Politburo, was served by a large bureaucracy, whose main sections reached down to the republic and local levels. In deference to national feelings, republic parties were created in Serbia in 1945, and in Montenegro and Bosnia-Hercegovina in the period 1948–49. The republic parties did not of course exercise any real powers, although each had its own Politburo and Central Committee. In those rare instances when the republic party made a decision contrary to the wishes of the CPY leadership, or perhaps simply failed in the execution of its duties, it was the practice to hold joint sessions of the Yugoslav Central Committee and the Central Committee of the republic to straighten the matter out.[47] With Party controls almost 100 percent effective throughout the country, any tendency to adopt a nationalist position, in the government or elsewhere, could be quickly brought under control.

Because Yugoslavia was clearly a unitary state which concentrated all real power at the center, it was difficult to assess the contribution of the federal system to the betterment of national relations. The lack of complaints about the system could not be taken to mean that it met with universal approval, since all opposition to the regime was silenced. On the other hand, the federal structure could not be dismissed as window dressing, for it helped satisfy important psychological needs of the Yugoslav peoples for recognition of their national individuality, and perhaps more important, it gave each nationality the assurance, for the first time, of enjoying a truly equal status with the other national groups. Concretely, the Macedonians won recognition as a nationality enjoying equal rights with other Yugoslav nationalities, and the perpetual insult to Croatian pride provoked by the dominant position of the Serbs before the war was removed.

Despite the monolithic character of the totalitarian form of rule set up after the war, a real effort was made to establish the importance of

[47] Two such meetings are mentioned by Aleksandar Ranković in his report to the Fifth Congress of the CPY: one with the Macedonian Party in 1946, and one with the Slovenian Party in 1947. *V kongres,* p. 166. The meeting with the Macedonians took place because of a failure to "coordinate organizational-political" and economic activity in Macedonia; the meeting with the Slovenes was held in order to correct weaknesses in the organization of the Slovenian Party which were not specified.

the nationalities in Yugoslav life. This was in harmony with the goals of the Party's national policy, which hoped to incorporate the emotional attachments of nationalism into the revolutionary ideology of Communism by identifying Communism with the abolition of all forms of national exploitation. While many national rights which are considered important in the West were withheld by the Communists, the principles of national equality, respect for national differences, and an end to the exploitation of one nationality by another were treated as basic rights which the Yugoslav Party sought with a good deal of success to introduce into postwar life.

It is therefore essential, when speaking about national relations after the war, to go beyond the narrow limits of the federal system. Other policies were equally, if not more, important in determining the status of the nationalities and confirming the multinational character of the Yugoslav state.

One of the most important steps taken by the Party was to continue the practice, developed during the war, of employing national cadres in the republics. In the immediate postwar years, when the Communists were still consolidating their power, this took several forms: deploying politically reliable and nationally acceptable personnel among the minorities to overcome hostility to the Communists; or using national cadres to spread Yugoslav influence into neighboring states, as in the case of the Pirin district in Bulgaria. The most important application of this principle, meanwhile, was the practice of staffing government and political posts with indigenous personnel *representative of the national composition of the region in question.*

Exact proportionality was not, however, observed at all levels or in all regions of the country. The most painstaking efforts were made to apply this principle in the elective bodies which had the least real power; on the other hand, at the apex of the system, in the Politburo, proportionality of national representation did not play a great role.[48] Secondly, while one could be sure of finding nationally indigenous personnel in positions of power in republics with a relatively pure national population (Slovenia and Montenegro), there was almost always some distortion in the local picture in regions of mixed nationality, reflecting

[48] See Appendix C for data on this problem, and the remarks to follow on national cadres.

local prejudices, the strong resistance of certain groups to participating in the system, or both together. Minorities, for one, were a constantly underrepresented group, and no great efforts were made in this period to improve the representation of the non-Slav elements in the Party, or in government posts.[49] A potentially more serious imbalance among the Slav nationalities became apparent after the war in Bosnia-Hercegovina, where the Serbs had far more influence than the Croats,[50] undoubtedly because of the close association of many Croats in Hercegovina with the Ustaši during the war.[51] In West Hercegovina the situation was particularly serious because of the influence of Ustaši elements. In the Čitlučka district there were no militiamen of Croatian nationality, while almost 90 percent of the teachers, although Croats, were brought in from other districts.[52] In Croatia, the Serbs were overrepresented in government and Party positions, using the scale of proportionality in the population, but this did not seriously endanger the position of the Croats, since the

[49] In 1950 the Party organizational journal, *Partiska Izgradnja,* charged the Party with taking a sectarian attitude toward accepting minorities into the Party, and admitted that the minorities themselves were not eager to join. Vida Tomšić, "Ličnom sastavu KPJ," *Partiska Izgradnja,* No. 6 (June-July, 1950), p. 8. For figures giving minority representation in the republic parties, see Appendix B. The first Albanian was made a member of the Central Committee of the CPY in 1953. In the Titoist period, great efforts were made to draw more of the minorities into the Party. See Chapter 5.

[50] Although the Serbs did not constitute a majority of the population according to census figures (44 percent Serbs in 1953), they did enjoy predominant influence in Party and government posts in Bosnia-Hercegovina, as Appendix 3 suggests.

[51] Mention of the problem of getting Croats and Moslems into the Party in Bosnia-Hercegovina is rare. No figures on the national composition of the Party in the republic have been published, and this in itself is a cause for suspicion. At the First Congress of the Party for Bosnia-Hercegovina in 1949, the difficulties of recruiting outside the Serbian population was admitted, however. The congress spoke of the fact that "the growth of the Party was particularly slow in those areas which were liberated later, although there as well there were many people who by their attitude toward the Party, in their honesty and personal lives and so forth, could have been accepted into the Party. Such sectarianism appeared everywhere and especially in Croatian and some Moslem districts (e.g., Derventa, Tuzlanski, and Samački districts, some districts of West Hercegovina)." *Osnivački kongres Komunističke partije Bosne i Hercegovina,* p. 72. Reference to this problem was also made later, in 1952, at the Fifth Plenum of the Central Committee of the republic Party, which complained about the "Maček and pro-Ustaši forces" in Bosnia-Hercegovina who "stress the lack of equality of the Croats and the suppression of the church." *Oslobodjenje.* April 16, 1952, p. 1.

[52] *Vjesnik u Srijedu,* Oct. 12, 1966, p. 5.

Serbs were a definite minority in the republic to begin with.[53] The stories of "Serbian domination" of Croatia after the war seem to have little foundation.[54]

Considering the Party as a whole, the Serbs were clearly the single most important nationality, constituting something over half of the members of the Party,[55] but still not distributed in such a way as to represent a controlling element outside the two republics of Serbia and Bosnia-Hercegovina. To talk of Serbian hegemony in Yugoslavia, or to draw other parallels to the situation that existed before World War II, would be quite misleading.

The utilization of national cadres, therefore, was a contribution of substance to the elimination of grievances over the national question which had sprung from the domination of the Serbs prior to the war. The Party also made a considerable concession to national feeling in the cultural field, allowing the republics, within the limits established by Communist ideology, to develop their own cultural, artistic, and scientific institutions, to publish their own textbooks for the schools, and to cultivate a feeling of national loyalty to the republic and its leaders.

These concessions amounted to a policy of cultural autonomy for the nationalities, although the Party, for doctrinal reasons, avoided describing the principles guiding its approach to the national question in these terms. The autonomy of national cultures was not, however, strictly comparable to that which the minorities had enjoyed in Yugoslavia before the war or that which, for example, had been discussed for the Austro-Hungarian Empire by the socialists prior to World War I.

[53] The Serbs enjoyed an especially prominent position in the Croatian Central Committee and the Politburo prior to 1949 (see Appendix C), but were less strongly represented in government positions. After 1949, with the defection of some of the Serbs to the Cominform, the role of the Serbs in the top Party bodies declined somewhat. With only about one quarter of the Party membership, the Serbs of Croatia were in no position to control the Party in Croatia.

[54] See the views of Anton Ciliga, "Nacionalizam i komunizam u hrvatsko-srpskom sporu," *Hrvatska Revija*, IV (Dec., 1951), 365–96.

[55] No figures were published in these years giving the national composition of the CPY as a whole. One could calculate, however, that in 1953, when Serbs made up 48.5 percent of the total population of the three republics of Serbia, Croatia, and Macedonia, 57.2 percent of the aggregate of Party members of these regions were Serbs. In 1958, Serbs accounted for 56.7 percent of the aggregate membership in the three republics. If Bosnia-Hercegovina were added, the disproportion would undoubtedly be more marked.

On the one hand, cultural freedom was circumscribed by ideological considerations which sharply limited the extent to which national figures (especially those of the recent past) could be held up for praise and emulation. On the other hand, cultural autonomy took on special importance under the Communists because of the absence, in the postwar period, of national (Yugoslav) cultural and scientific institutions. There simply was *no* Yugoslav theater, Yugoslav ballet, or Yugoslav Academy of Sciences. In the field of history, the Partisan campaigns were the only subject in the curriculum of the schools which dealt with the common problems and shared experiences of the Yugoslav peoples, and even in this case the tendency was to present the resistance movement as a struggle for the liberation of the nationality of the republic in question, rather than as an all-Yugoslav affair.

To have placed more emphasis on Yugoslav themes in the fields of culture and education would have run the risk of associating the Party with the practice of cultural and national assimilation, and this the Communists were determined to avoid at all costs. And yet the anomalous result was that the rigid uniformity imposed on Yugoslav society by the Stalinist system after World War II did not extinguish the *feeling* of national differences. If anything, these sentiments were sharpened by the lack of any contact among the republics (the bureaucratic structure worked through vertical connections between the local government and the capital at the expense of horizontal ties between regions), by the absence of the idea of a Yugoslav nationality, and by the insistence on determining nationality by place of birth, regardless of one's background or personal preferences. If these tendencies did not appear contradictory to the Party, it was largely because of the conviction prevailing that with the destruction of the conservative nationalist forces, and the constant exposure of the population to the Communist line on the national question, the national pride of the Yugoslav peoples could be channeled into cooperative, nonantagonistic relationships, completely the reverse of the kind that had existed prior to the revolution.

This expectation, in turn, could not be understood apart from developments in the country as a whole. In the immediate postwar years the Yugoslav Communists were experiencing the exhilarating effects of their successful climb to power. As a result, unbounded optimism characterized the attitude of the Party toward Yugoslavia and her future development. Foreign relations were conducted with aggressive self-assurance. In diplomacy, in which national feelings were strongly expressed, claims on Yugoslavia's neighbors—for Trieste, the Slovenian-inhabited portions of Carinthia, and Pirin Macedonia—played a large part. Whatever defects might have existed in the federal system or the conduct of relations among the nationalities, the national problem itself no longer represented a threat to the stability of the regime. So great, indeed, was the confidence of the Yugoslav Communists in their ability to cope with the national question that plans were already afoot before the war had ended to expand the Yugoslav federation by adding new members. This, if successful, would have led to the transformation of the Yugoslav state into a new type of Balkan or South Slav federation of Communist nations under the leadership of the Yugoslav Communist Party.

It was through the involvement of the Yugoslav Communists in plans for a Balkan federation that the Yugoslav national question became intertwined with developments in the Balkans generally in the immediate postwar period. The fate of the idea of Balkan federation in the past had not been such as to inspire confidence in the Yugoslavs' plan. The Comintern had utilized the scheme as part of its attack on the status quo in southeastern Europe in the 1920s and summarily dropped the idea after the theme of Balkan cooperation was endorsed by the governments of Yugoslavia, Greece, Rumania, and Turkey in 1934. Although the plan was revived from time to time (in isolated statements issued by the Croatian Communist Party, and in the declarations of Šarlo), the idea of Balkan federation remained discredited in Communist circles until the Yugoslavs began to lay plans in 1943 for a joint command in the Balkans. But this project, as has been explained in the preceding chapter, was given up by the Yugoslavs as a result of Soviet objections.

Despite the necessity to abandon plans for a Balkan command in 1943, the Yugoslav Communists were determined to press forward and establish their leadership of the Communist forces in the Balkans. Tito, while dissociating himself from the idea of a Balkan command in his letter of October, 1943, to Vukmanović-Tempo, left no doubt on this point, emphasizing to Tempo that the primacy of the Yugoslavs in the Balkans was recognized by the Soviet Union. As Tito put it, "Yugoslavia in any case occupies a leading role in the Balkans, both from the point of view of the military power of the People's Liberation Army and from the point of view of her experience in creating people's rule through national liberation committees and anti-fascist assemblies. Therefore, in our opinion, and also in the opinion of grandfather [the Comintern], we should be the center for the Balkan nations, both in a military and in a political sense." [56]

Thus it was only a matter of time before negotiations were reopened with other Communist parties in the Balkans with the aim of consolidating the revolutionary movement under Yugoslav leadership. This opportunity arose in the fall of 1944, following the events which led to the entry of Bulgaria in the war on the side of the Allied powers and the accession to power in Sofia of the Fatherland Front, under Communist domination. Negotiations were quickly opened between the Yugoslav and Bulgarian Communists on the creation of a Balkan federation, or, as the Yugoslavs preferred to call it, South Slav federation, in which Yugoslavia and Bulgaria would be joined in some type of confederative or federal relationship. Part of this plan, as the Yugoslavs envisaged it, was the inclusion of the Bulgarian portions of Macedonia (the Pirin district) into the Macedonian People's Republic of Yugoslavia. At the same time, in a parallel move, the Yugoslav Communists were pressing the Albanian Communist Party for the establishment of intimate relations between Yugoslavia and Albania.

Accounts of the conversations which took place between the Yugoslavs and the Bulgarians in 1944 have been contradictory in many details but are in essential agreement on the main issues that arose in the course of the negotiations. The tone of the exchange between the two parties was established in September when a Yugoslav delegation attended a meeting of the Bulgarian Central Committee and practically compelled the Bulgarians to make sweeping concessions to the Yugoslav point of view on Macedonia.[57] Shortly thereafter negotiations began, in the greatest secrecy, for the formation of a South Slav federation. In conversations in Sofia in December, Kardelj tried to reach agreement with Traicho Kostov and other Bulgarians over the details of the federation. According to Yugoslav accounts, the Bulgarians had prepared a plan for union based on messages received from the Bulgarian Communist leader, Di-

[56] *Zbornik dokumenata*, Vol. II, Book 10, p. 361.

[57] More details on the September meeting will be found in Chapter 4 on the Macedonian question.

mitrov, who was still in the Soviet Union at the time. The Bulgarian proposal foresaw a defense pact between Yugoslavia and Bulgaria which would at the same time involve the creation of a commission, in which Yugoslavs and Bulgarians would be equally represented, whose task would be to draw up plans for a federal union between the two states.[58] Kardelj found the defense pact inadequate, however, and argued that immediate steps should be taken for the union of the two countries.[59]

Agreement was reached between the Yugoslavs and Bulgarians that a proclamation of the new federation should be issued on New Year's Day, 1945. But the negotiations held in December had revealed that the two parties were basically at odds over the character of the new state. Kardelj insisted that the commission which was to draw up the details of the federation include representatives from all the Yugoslav republics.[60] Although the Bulgarians did not, at this time, insist on a federation between Yugoslavia and Bulgaria as equals, rather than the entry of Bulgaria into Yugoslavia as a seventh republic, the arguments over the make-up of the commission reflected fundamental differences on this issue. Dimitrov, for his part, would not consider the annexation of the Pirin district by the Macedonian People's Republic prior to the creation of the federation,[61] thus injecting an issue into the negotiations which was to be a source of discord in the years to follow.

In these negotiations for the creation of a South Slav, or Balkan, federation, the Bulgarians were at a great disadvantage. They were clearly not eager to enter into a federation in which Bulgaria would lose her independence and fall completely under the control of the Yugoslav Communist Party. On the other hand, the Yugoslav Communists were at the height of their power and prestige, and could argue convincingly that the Bulgarians themselves had been the strongest proponents of a Balkan Communist federation before the war. Caught in a dilemma, the Bulgarians chose to draw out the negotiations. On one pretext or another, they evaded demands made by the Yugoslavs that a delegation be dispatched to Belgrade to sign the declaration of union between the two countries.[62]

[58] Glavna politička uprava Jugoslovenske armije, *O Sofiskom procesu,* pp. 15–16. Hereafter referred to as *O Sofiskom procesu.*

[59] *Ibid.*

[60] *Ibid.,* p. 8.

[61] *Ibid.,* pp. 18–19.

[62] *Ibid.,* pp. 20–21.

The Bulgarian proposal for a federation, finally prepared and sent to the Yugoslavs in January, 1945, called for the establishment of a Federation of South Slavs (FJUS) with common ministries and a common national assembly. The heart of the proposal was the provision for the creation of a governing body, to be called the Temporary Council of South Slav Union, whose seat would be in Belgrade, and which would be composed of an equal number of Bulgarians and Yugoslavs.[63] It also seems likely, from remarks made in Moscow by Dimitrov not long after, that the Bulgarians envisaged equal representation in a Council of Nationalities (to be established in the legislative branch) between Yugoslavs and Bulgarians.[64]

This Bulgarian plan was rebuffed by the Yugoslavs, who insisted that Bulgaria must unite with Yugoslavia as a seventh republic, equal in stature with the existing republics of the Yugoslav federal system. In place of the Bulgarian scheme, the Yugoslavs suggested the creation of a "Commission of Yugoslav Unity," representing all seven republics of the new federation, whose task would be to prepare a constitution in which a federal government would have responsibilities over matters of common concern (including foreign affairs, defense, as well as other matters), while remaining powers would fall to the republics.[65]

Thus it happened that the Yugoslavs and Bulgarians were actually drawing farther apart in their views of the new federation when the Great Powers, alarmed by rumors of the impending union, began to bring pressure on the two governments. The British, late in January of 1945, informed the Bulgarians that any agreement with the Yugoslavs would meet with Western opposition.[66] The Soviet Union also began to show concern over the project, and even before British objections became known, it summoned the Yugoslavs and Bulgarians to Moscow for talks on the impending union.[67]

If we are to believe Yugoslav accounts, the attitude of the Soviet Union toward the creation of a federation was favorable, and Stalin was ready,

[63] *Ibid.*, pp. 24–25.
[64] *Ibid.*, p. 23.
[65] *Ibid.*, pp. 25–26.
[66] *Ibid.*, p. 23.
[67] This aspect of developments is dealt with in Moša Pijade's account of the negotiations which appeared in *Borba*, Dec. 29, 1949, p. 3, as well as in *O Sofiskom procesu*.

in principle, to accept the merger of the two countries on the terms proposed by the Yugoslavs.[68] But both parties to the negotiations were
warned in Moscow that the time was not yet ripe to consummate the
union. Instead, apparently with Soviet approval, the Yugoslav and Bulgarian delegations to the Moscow conversations drew up an agreement
on economic, military, and political cooperation between the two countries.[69] Plans were also laid for a secret exchange of letters between Tito
and Kimon Georgiev, which would interpret the agreements as the first
step toward federation of Bulgaria and Yugoslavia.[70] (Whether this step
was taken with the knowledge and approval of the Soviet Union is not
entirely clear from existing accounts of the Moscow meeting.)

Why the Bulgarians agreed to this substitute for federation when they
had just been freed of the obligation to join in a South Slav state with
Yugoslavia is not entirely clear, nor is it known for certain if the Moscow
agreements were ever ratified by the Bulgarian and Yugoslav governments. By the spring of 1945, in any case, the Yugoslav Communists
had been forced to alter their tactics. Instead of presenting the West
with a *fait accompli,* the Yugoslavs found it necessary to wait until 1947
before once more taking up the campaign for a South Slav federation.

In the spring of that year negotiations between the Yugoslavs and the
Bulgarians began in earnest once again. In July, Tito and Dimitrov met
at Bled and signed a series of agreements which provided for close economic cooperation between the two countries, the eventual abolition of
customs barriers, and mutual assistance in such cases as the "provoca-
tions" of the Greek "monarcho-fascists." [71]

The announcement of the Bled agreements was not accompanied by
any reference to Balkan federation, and because the treaties themselves
were not made public, it was impossible to know the actual terms of the
agreements worked out between the Yugoslavs and the Bulgarians. Dimitrov, several weeks after the conference, denied categorically that
the subject of South Slav union or Balkan federation had been dis-

[68] *Borba,* Dec. 29, 1949, p. 3.

[69] *O Sofiskom procesu,* p. 22.

[70] *Ibid.,* p. 23.

[71] The most complete account of the protocol announced at the time of the Bled
agreements can be found in Royal Institute of International Affairs, *Documents
on International Affairs, 1947–1948,* pp. 290–92. Hereafter referred to as *Documents on International Affairs.*

cussed.[72] After the Cominform dispute broke out, however, the Bulgarians gave an entirely different version. The resolution adopted by the Sixteenth Plenum of the Bulgarian Central Committee in July, 1948, repudiated the idea of federation with Yugoslavia as long as that country opposed the Cominform, and suggested strongly that such a project had been discussed, presumably by Tito and Dimitrov at Bled.[73] Later, Dimitrov himself was to insist that the Bled agreements had laid the groundwork for a Balkan federation.[74] The Yugoslavs, who after 1948 revealed so much of what took place in the negotiations over federation, kept silent about the content of the Bled agreements, revealing only that concessions were made in the Pirin district by the Bulgarians, permitting the Yugoslavs to send cultural workers into the region to encourage Macedonian nationalism, but that, contrary to the wishes of the Yugoslavs, the Bulgarians refused to consider the annexation of this Bulgarian district by the Macedonian People's Republic of Yugoslavia until a federation between Yugoslavia and Bulgaria had been achieved.[75]

The Bulgarian testimony, and the Yugoslav description of the agreement over the Pirin district, gave the impression that some plan for federation was approved at Bled. But by the fall of 1947, if not earlier, it had become apparent that federation was not about to take place. Tito, when he visited Sofia in the fall, hinted at this when he remarked that "we are creating such all-sided forms of cooperation that the question of federation represents only a formality," [76] a fairly clear indication that the Yugoslavs were settling for something less than actual union. Tito, in his visit to Bulgaria, agreed to sign a pact of friendship with the Bulgarian government, although the Yugoslavs had turned down a similar proposal in 1945 on the grounds that it would not be necessary if the federation were created. Shortly thereafter Dimitrov made the reluctance of the Bulgarians to enter into union with Yugoslavia clear by proposing a broad Danubian customs union in place of a Balkan federation.[77] In 1948 the whole scheme became entangled in the growing differences between the

[72] *Ibid.,* p. 292.

[73] *Ibid.,* pp. 293–94.

[74] Dimitrov, p. 65.

[75] According to Tito's account of the Bled negotiations given in his speech in Skoplje, printed in *Borba,* Aug. 3, 1949, p. 1.

[76] *Borba,* Nov. 25, 1947, p. 1.

[77] *Documents on International Affairs,* p. 297.

Soviet Union and Yugoslavia. The Soviet government, reacting after a short delay, expressed dissatisfaction with the plan of Dimitrov,[78] and then shortly thereafter agreed to support the Yugoslav project of federation with Bulgaria.[79] The Yugoslavs, alarmed at possible trickery behind the Soviet suggestion, began to argue that the time for federation was not yet at hand, and dissociated themselves entirely from the plan for forming a Balkan federation, informing the Bulgarians of this decision in March.[80]

The whole episode, beginning with the Bled agreements and ending with the Soviet maneuver to draw Yugoslavia into a union with Bulgaria, had an odd, even bizarre, quality about it. The Yugoslavs later claimed that they were not disappointed by the outcome of the negotiations,[81] despite the obvious eagerness with which they had pursued the goal of South Slav federation. The Bulgarian Communists, at one point in the series of shifts which marked their policy on federation after 1948, actually asserted that they had never at any time entertained the idea of setting up a Balkan federation.[82] Meanwhile, what really occurred in the negotiations for federation during 1947 and 1948 remained as much a mystery as ever.

Despite frequent suggestions to the contrary, it does not seem that the Bled agreements dealt with the actual mechanics of unification or the creation of a federation between Bulgaria and Yugoslavia. Most descriptions of what took place at Bled suggest that the two parties agreed to "create the conditions" for union.[83] What is puzzling is just what these conditions were. Permitting Macedonian nationalists to operate in the Pirin district of Bulgaria was obviously one of them; the decision to form a customs union and create close economic ties was another. It is also quite possible that territorial concessions were considered by both parties. The Bulgarians almost certainly demanded that the Bulgarian districts in Serbia be returned to Bulgaria, and it is possible, although not likely,

[78] *Ibid.*

[79] Dedijer, *Tito,* p. 317.

[80] Dimitrov, p. 65.

[81] Milovan Djilas, "Lenjin o odnosima medju socijalističkim državama," *Komunist,* III (Sept., 1949), 14.

[82] See Chapter 4.

[83] Thus Blagoje Nešković, speaking at the First Congress of the Macedonian Communist Party, in 1949, said that Bled foresaw a series of steps which would "create the conditions" for the formation of a South Slav federation. *Borba,* Dec. 20, 1948, p. 1.

that both the Bulgarians and the Yugoslavs hoped to acquire territories in Greece if the revolt in that country were successful.[84] In their essentials the Bled agreements seem to have been a revival of the Moscow plan of 1945, brought up to date and broadened to cover the question of Pirin Macedonia and possibly other territories. Balkan federation was still the ultimate objective, although the method of joining the two countries was probably left undecided and was still a matter of controversy when the Cominform dispute broke out in the spring of 1948.

Why the Bulgarians were willing to agree even to the principle of federation remains something of a mystery. It might have occurred to them that as the largest single nationality in the projected South Slav state they could dominate the remainder, but second thoughts would have revealed the impracticality of such ambitions in the light of the strength and unity of the Yugoslav Communist Party at this time. Union on practically any terms held great dangers for the Bulgarians, and very few for the CPY.

Negotiations over Balkan federation held at least one great advantage for the Bulgarian Communists, nevertheless. For the creation of a broad union of Communist states in the Balkans could be made the precondition for granting the Yugoslavs some of their more immediate demands, above all, the unification of Macedonia. By agreeing to the principle of federation, the Bulgarians obviously gained time in their negotiations with the Yugoslavs over the future of Pirin Macedonia. In pursuing this strategy, the Bulgarians would have been following the precedent established by the Greek Communists in 1943 when they insisted, in connection with the demand for the unification of all Macedonia in the Manifesto of the Main Command of the Macedonian Partisan movement, in having a reference to Balkan federation included as one of the goals of the Partisan movement in the Balkans.[85]

[84] Philip Mosely, *The Kremlin and World Politics,* p. 231, suggested in 1950 that the Bled agreements foresaw an exchange of territory according to which Yugoslavia would obtain all Bulgarian and Greek portions of Macedonia, and Bulgaria would be compensated with western Thrace. Such a deal would of course have been possible only if the Greek Communists were successful in taking over Greece. This suggestion fits in with the guarded references to the "series of measures" agreed upon at Bled. But by the summer of 1947 the Yugoslavs had made extensive concessions to the Greek Communists and were willing to concede that the Macedonians in Greece should be treated as a Greek minority. See Chapter 4.

[85] See the preceding chapter.

In addition, the Bulgarian attitude was undoubtedly influenced by emotional and personal considerations. Not only was the tradition of South Slav union attractive to the Bulgarian Communists (or at least to some of them), but there was also a desire to emulate the Yugoslavs and accept Tito's leadership in the Balkans. On this issue, a tangled rivalry apparently grew up within the Bulgarian Party among those favorable to accepting Yugoslav leadership and those who wished to maintain the independence of the Bulgarian Party, or who bore the Yugoslav Communists some special grudge. Subsequent purge trials, the desire to play on the reputation of eminent Party figures such as Dimitrov, and even personal animosities have so obscured the record on the question that it is impossible to state with certainty what role the individual Bulgarian leaders played in this situation. Traicho Kostov, denounced by the Bulgarians at his trial in 1949 for selling out to the Yugoslavs,[86] and bitterly attacked by the Yugoslavs for aiding Šarlo in his defection from the CPY in 1941 as well as for blocking plans for federation after the war,[87] seems to have been one of the genuine Bulgarian nationalists who was also willing to look to Yugoslavia for leadership. Contrary to the Yugoslav account, he seems to have given his support to federation.[88] Dimitrov, whom the Yugoslavs have identified as the greatest champion of the idea of a South Slav federation, apparently remained uncommitted in the struggle over whether to accept Yugoslav leadership in the Balkans, hoping to maintain friendly relations with Belgrade by carrying on negotiations for union, but at the same time carefully guarding Bulgarian interests, especially in respect to Macedonia.[89]

Soviet policy on the question of a South Slav union was extremely

[86] *The Trial of Traïcho Kostov and His Group, passim.*

[87] *O Sofiskom Procesu,* p. 58.

[88] Kostov was the leading figure in the original negotiations for federation in 1944, and both Yugoslav and Bulgarian accounts of these negotiations suggest that Kostov was ready to make concessions to the Yugoslavs. He is accused of sabotaging the Bled agreements, but has been quoted at the time of the pact between Yugoslavia and Bulgaria in November, 1947, to the effect that "our people are impatiently awaiting the unfolding of the new pages [in our history] which by the iron logic of historical necessity will soon lead to complete unification of the South Slavs, to the creation of one common Yugoslav motherland." Radulović, p. 228.

[89] Dimitrov's attitude toward the federation after the outbreak of the Cominform dispute is examined in more detail in the chapter to follow.

devious, and shifted several times without any apparent reason. It is natural to assume that the Soviet Union supported the union of Yugoslavia and Bulgaria in 1948 as a way of curbing the Yugoslavs, but it is also apparent that, if such a union were in fact carried out, the pro-Tito faction in Bulgaria would have been greatly strengthened and a powerful new rival to Moscow created in the Balkans. Better knowledge of the Soviet position on Balkan federation prior to 1948 would help clarify this matter, but Yugoslav accounts of the discussion among Soviet, Bulgarian, and Yugoslav representatives in Moscow in February, 1948, during which the history of the question of Balkan federation was discussed, are vague and evasive. In particular they confuse the Dimitrov proposals of December, 1947, with the Bled agreements of the previous summer in connection with the sharp exchanges that took place among the Bulgarians, the Yugoslavs, and Stalin over the fate of Balkan federation.[90] In the light of this ambiquity, it must still be considered a possibility that Stalin, far from seeking to bring about a Balkan federation, was aware of the rift that had grown up between the Yugoslavs and the Bulgarians over the methods by which federation was to be achieved and meant to aggravate this division by pressing the Yugoslavs into a reckless move. At the same time, it appears likely that Stalin was not completely convinced he had received the true story of the Bled agreements, and suspected the Yugoslavs and Bulgarians of attempting to make a deal behind his back.

The objective of Yugoslavia in supporting South Slav union was not difficult to discern, for the creation of such a state would have given the Yugoslav Communist Party control of a large section of the Balkans. Bulgaria was only one of the objects of Yugoslav ambition. Much more vulnerable to Yugoslav pressure than Bulgaria was the new Communist regime in Albania.

The Yugoslavs had helped found the Albanian Communist Party and had guided the Albanian Communists closely during the war. There was no doubt that the Yugoslavs felt they had the right to play a leading role in Albanian affairs by virtue of their endeavors. After the war, a purge of elements opposed to Yugoslav influence was carried out in the Albanian Party. In 1946 the Yugoslavs intervened directly in the domestic affairs of Albania by forcing the Albanian government to expropriate the property of large landowners. Joint stock companies were formed after

---

[90] Dedijer, *Tito*, pp. 498–99.

the model of those being established by the Soviet Union in Eastern Europe; Albanian military units were standardized along Yugoslav lines; and currency reforms were carried through, over the objections of the Albanian Communists, in order to prepare for the merger of the currencies of the two countries.[91]

The Yugoslavs have been sensitive to the charge that they acted in an arbitrary fashion toward the Albanians. Vladimir Dedijer, Tito's official biographer, devoted an entire book to the defense of Yugoslav policy, attempting to demonstrate that the Yugoslavs were generous with economic aid and always acted with the best interests of the Albanians at heart.[92] Milovan Djilas, after he broke with the CPY, admitted the inconsistencies in the Yugoslav attitude toward Albania, but claimed that the Party, although misled, was at all times sincere.[93]

But no matter how sincere or generous in giving economic assistance, the Yugoslavs treated Albania as a Yugoslav satellite. The irony in this situation became evident in the spring of 1948, for just as the Yugoslavs were preparing to defy Stalin, the Albanian Nakon Spiro organized a nationalist faction in the Albanian Party against the Yugoslavs. Spiro opposed the decision to accept credits from Yugoslavia and authored a three-year economic development plan which the Yugoslavs condemned as "unrealistic." Spiro lost his struggle, but before he could be expelled from the Party he committed suicide.[94] At the time, it apparently did not occur to the Yugoslav Communists to compare Spiro's position to their own resistance against Soviet domination.

In the light of the aggressive attitude of the Yugoslavs toward neighboring Communist states, the decision of Stalin to take action against the Yugoslavs was not entirely without justification. The circumstances surrounding the dispute between Yugoslavia and the Soviet Union have been discussed by many authors,[95] and no further mention of the events leading up to the break between Yugoslavia and the Soviet Union will be made in this account of the national question. What role nationalism played in the behavior of the Yugoslav Communists does deserve com-

[91] Dedijer, *Jugoslovensko-Albanski odnosi*, pp. 173–75.
[92] *Jugoslovensko-Albanski odnosi*.
[93] Djilas, *Conversations with Stalin*, pp. 144–45.
[94] *Ibid.*, p. 134.
[95] See especially Adam Ulam, *Titoism and the Cominform*.

ment, nevertheless, because of the importance of the relationship between the national feelings of the Yugoslavs in the dispute with Moscow and the development of the national question in Yugoslavia.

The identification of the CPY with the interests of Yugoslavia can be traced to the period following the defeat of Yugoslavia in April, 1941, and even earlier if one takes into account the interest of the Party organization in the interwar period in maintaining a Yugoslav state as the stage for its revolutionary activities. During the war, this identification with the Yugoslav state became an emotional force stimulated both by patriotism and by pride in the achievements of the Partisan movement. In the period after the war, revolutionary zeal, patriotic feeling, and a highly developed sense of national interest laid the foundation for a new type of Yugoslav Communist nationalism, ready to adapt itself to the needs of the Communist movement as a whole when necessary, but supremely confident in the correctness of its own behavior and the right of Yugoslavia to play a leading role among the Communist states of Eastern Europe generally and the Balkans in particular.

For several reasons, Yugoslav behavior did not appear to be inspired by traditional nationalism. The radical character of Yugoslav Communism after the war seemed antithetical to national feeling and more apt to emphasize proletarian internationalism and solidarity with the Soviet Union than to stress national interests. The Soviet Union helped to encourage this picture of Yugoslav Communism by suggesting, in its correspondence with the Yugoslav Central Committee preceding the open break between the two countries (and later published by the Yugoslavs), that in conversations with the Russians Edvard Kardelj had spoken favorably of the eventual annexation of Yugoslavia by the Soviet Union.[96]

The Soviet assertion—although sometimes accepted at its face value— must be treated with a good deal of skepticism, and only after making allowance for the fact that the remark was clearly taken out of context. The Yugoslav leadership, whatever its devotion to international Communism, was far too cautious in its dealings with the Soviet Union to make impulsive gestures of this kind.

In the last analysis, the revolutionary mood of the Yugoslav Communists was not incompatible with nationalism. In the Balkans, revolu-

[96] Royal Institute of International Affairs, *The Soviet-Yugoslav Dispute*, p. 38.

tionary movements often combined strong local attachments with pas-
sionate internationalism. Perhaps more important in the Yugoslav case,
the revolutionary spirit of the Communists bred a desire to emulate the
Soviet Union. While this might normally have brought the two countries
closer together, the fact that the Yugoslavs believed (largely as a result
of their understanding of Soviet experience) that this goal could be
achieved only through a national effort, without dictation from without,
meant that the desire to copy the Soviet Union made the two countries
rivals, rather than creating harmonious relations between them.

These considerations did not directly touch on the question of relations
among the Yugoslav nationalities in the immediate postwar years but were
to become important in a later period, when nationalism in the republics
began to create difficulties. At the same time, the national problem became an issue in the dispute with the Soviet Union, for the members of the
Cominform organization, through which the Soviet Union exercised her
control over Eastern Europe, attempted to probe the national question
for issues which would divide the Yugoslav Party in its support for Tito.

On the whole, this effort failed. There were naturally defections to the
Cominform, and in a few cases it can be determined that the national
issue played a role in motivating an individual to break with the Yugoslav
Party. In 1950 a group of highly placed Serbs in the Croatian Party from
Lika—Rade Žigić, Duško Brkić, and Stanko Opačić—declared for the
Cominform, and in the short time before they were apprehended they
attempted to rally support by spreading stories among the Serbs in Croatia
about the ill treatment they were receiving at the hands of the Croats.[97]
In Macedonia, where there were a small number of defections, national
feelings also played a role.[98]

The greatest opportunity for playing on national discontents to the
advantage of the Soviet bloc lay among the minority population, and the
Hungarian and Albanian governments, in particular, outdid themselves
in the output of propaganda attacking the treatment of the minorities by
the Yugoslav Communist regime.[99] Agents were also sent across the

[97] *Borba,* Sept. 11, 1950, p. 1.

[98] See Chapter 4.

[99] Typical of the propaganda issued by the Albanians is the following passage,
which appeared in the Cominform journal, *For a Lasting Peace, For a People's
Democracy,* Nov. 23, 1951, p. 4: "Before me are two documents. One, consisting
of hundreds of pages, shows how the Tito-Ranković clique is exterminating the

Yugoslav border into minority regions. The Yugoslavs responded to these actions by setting up their own organizations among the minorities. An "Albanian League" was formed in Prizren in 1949, and in 1951 a congress of the organization was held and a "Supreme Albanian Council" organized whose task, it was stated at the time, was to liberate Albania from the regime of Enver Hoxha.[100] The Bulgarians who fled to Yugoslavia were organized through a League of Bulgarian Emigrants, and Macedonian escapees from Bulgaria were also brought together in organizations meant to counter Cominform propaganda and activities in Macedonia.[101] The mood within these organizations can be judged in part by a resolution adopted by the second conference of the Committee of the League of Bulgarian Emigrants held in Niš in July, 1952; the resolution called for a continuing struggle against "the traitorous and anti-people's government of Vladko Chervenkov," and pledged to fight for the final removal of the Soviets from Bulgaria.[102]

What effect the plotting and intrigues of the Cominform agents and their Yugoslav opponents had among the minorities is difficult to judge. Some Hungarians were influenced by Cominform propaganda; a report to the regional Party Committee of the CPY for Vojvodina admitted that Hungarian propaganda was having harmful effects on all classes among the Hungarian population. A curious plot which led to the arrest of a group of Albanians at the time of the outbreak of the Cominform dispute suggests that there were elements in Kossovo-Metohija which tried to take advantage of the break with the Soviet Union.[103] In Dimitrovgrad,

---

800,000 Albanian people in Yugoslavia. On the basis of facts confirmed by witnesses, this document describes how the Titoists machine-gunned thousands of Albanians in Kossovo and Macedonia; how thousands of Albanians were killed by means of poison gas and by spreading typhus; how the fascist degenerates bury people alive and subject others to brutal torture before death." See also *ibid.*, May 18, 1951, p. 4, "Titoist Clique—Rabid Enemy of the Albanian People"; Jan. 27, 1950, p. 4, "Vojvodina under the Yoke of the Tito Clique." See *Pravda*, Feb. 24, 1950, p. 6, and Sept. 12, 1952, p. 4, for articles on the mistreatment of the Albanian minority.

[100] *Christian Science Monitor*, April 4, 1953, p. 3. For material on the Union of Albanian Emigrants, headed by Apostol Tenesi, see *Nova Makedonija*, Feb. 28, 1953, p. 1.

[101] See Chapter 4.

[102] *Politika*, July 23, 1952, p. 3.

[103] An account in *Jedinstvo*, June 15, 1964, p. 4, tells of the activities of the secret police in Kossovo-Metohija and relates a curious episode in which a plot

center of the Bulgarian minority, the head of the Teachers Institute and a group of his followers were arrested, although the Yugoslavs denied that they had encountered wholesale opposition from the Bulgarian minority.[104]

None of these incidents add up to a major show of resistance to the Yugoslavs, however. The only record of any widespread arrests among any ethnic group at the time of the Cominform dispute occurred when many Russian émigrés were detained on suspicion of being Soviet spies.[105] The action provoked a bitter protest from the Soviet government and caused considerable publicity at the time.

If there was a national group in Yugoslavia markedly susceptible to the appeals of the Cominform, the Montenegrins would have to be singled out even before the national minorities. The Montenegrin Party reported a higher rate of expulsions for Cominform sympathies than any other republic party.[106] While the data are incomplete (the Serbian and Slovenian parties never issued figures on expulsions), and while the Montenegrin figure may reflect merely an excess of zeal among local cadres to weed out supposedly unreliable elements, the fact that the Montenegrin Party hesitated to report on conditions in Montenegro to the central Party organs when the dispute with the Soviet Union broke out into the open [107] suggests that some degree of difficulty was encountered in persuading the rank and file of Party members in Montenegro that the break with the Soviet Union was the right course for the Party to take. In addition, a high rate of defection in the Sandžak—reportedly the highest

---

was supposedly prepared by Enver Hoxha just at the time of the outbreak of the dispute, to trick the Yugoslav secret police into arresting and killing a group of innocent Albanians in order to turn Albanian sentiment against the Yugoslavs. The plot, according to this account, was discovered in time. This may, however, be an intentionally misleading version of an anti-Yugoslav incident that took place when the dispute began, perhaps among anti-Communist Albanians who were not supporters of the Albanian regime.

104 *Glas na B'ulgarite v Jugoslaviia,* June 27, 1949, p. 2.

105 The Yugoslav version of this incident is contained in *Ministry of Foreign Affairs, White Book,* p. 40.

106 In Montenegro the ratio of Party members to expulsions was six to one, while in Bosnia-Hercegovina it was twenty-three to one; in Croatia, twenty to one; and in Macedonia, thirty-one to one.

107 See the remarks of Aleksandar Ranković, *Partiska Izgradnja,* No. 8 (Oct., 1949), p. 4.

in the country—would have contributed to the problem of containing Cominform sympathies in the Montenegrin Party (as well as in Serbia).

There have also been claims, which cannot be substantiated, that the rate of defection to the Cominform was high among the postwar colonists in Vojvodina [108] and that widespread purges took place in Bosnia-Hercegovina.[109] In a later chapter the arrest for Cominform sympathies of the leadership of the trade union apparatus in Macedonia will be described. None of these incidents added up to a major crisis within the CPY, however, even in the case of the Montenegrins. It seems reasonably certain, even making allowances for incidents which the Yugoslav Party has concealed, that the Slav nationalities, and even many of the members of the minority population, stood behind the Yugoslav Communist leadership in the crisis brought about by the conflict with the Soviet Union and her satellite partners. This display of unity was a great political victory for the Party and an indication that the Yugoslav Communists maintained firm control over national feelings, at least as far as any threat from the Cominform was concerned.

The Party's success was in part the result of the dislike felt by most Yugoslavs, regardless of nationality, for the policies advocated by the Cominform. There is no doubt, however, that the Yugoslav Communists had managed, in a remarkably short time, to eliminate many sources of the national antagonisms which had plagued Yugoslavia before the war.

The major constructive change resulting from the policies of the Communist regime probably lay in greatly reducing the feelings of inequality and humiliation which had embittered prewar national relations. The victory of the Communists ended Serbian domination of Yugoslavia and also marked the elimination of discriminatory policies against the Macedonians and most of the minority population. One feels sure that if these practices, or their equivalent, had persisted, the reaction of many Yugoslavs during the Cominform dispute would have been different from what it was.

Further, it was beyond dispute that the Yugoslav Communist Party exercised both firmness and impartiality in settling questions which it would have been impossible to resolve before the war. Establishing the boundaries of the republics, solving the problem of the Serbian colonists,

[108] Antun Novak, *I Served Tito.*
[109] *La Yougoslavie sous la terreur de la Clique Tito.*

and encouraging the use of national cadres were good examples of this skill. Finally, although the state apparatus was highly centralized, the Party radically altered the character of the Yugoslav unitary system by the introduction of federal forms, thanks to which the importance of national differences was recognized in many areas of Yugoslav life.

The shortcomings of Communist national policy were nevertheless real and were to have unfortunate consequences in later years. It was characteristic of the Yugoslav Communists that they showed practically no appreciation of the need to take steps to overcome the isolation of the nationalities. Concealed behind the optimistic statements of the Party on the national question was a large element of wishful thinking, often resulting in a tendency to put off measures until they were absolutely unavoidable. For example, republic parties were not established in Montenegro or Bosnia-Hercegovina until the outbreak of the dispute with the Cominform; certain steps designed to protect the rights of the minorities were taken only as a result of the Cominform threat.[110] Local Communist officials were not always bound by the principles observed by the Yugoslav Party. Thus the 1945 law prohibiting nationalistic manifestations made it a punishable offense to grant privileges to national groups or to curtail national rights, but in the period 1952–59 only two persons were convicted for the crime of limiting citizens' rights or granting favors on the basis of nationality (Article 148 of the 1951 Criminal Code),[111] and the record was probably no different for earlier years. (That many abuses were in fact taking place at the local level was revealed many years later. This was especially true in the behavior of officials toward the Albanians in Kossovo-Metohija and in the treatment accorded the Croats in West Hercegovina.) [112] On occasion, one suspects that the Party was not so much interested in solving the national question as in simply putting it out of sight. This impression is strongly reenforced by the behavior of the Yugoslav Communists toward Albania and Bulgaria: to have thought that these two countries could also be incorporated into a federation reveals a mentality which could only think in bold strokes and total

110 For example, certain aspects of a dual-language administration in Rijeka (Italian and Serbo-Croatian) were introduced in August, 1948; the statutes for the two autonomous areas were promulgated only in 1948.

111 Shoup, "Communism and the National Question in Yugoslavia," p. 111.

112 *Vjesnik u Srijedu,* Oct. 12, 1966, p. 5.

solutions, and which was unwilling to face the possibility that a long and tedious struggle was still ahead before the Yugoslav peoples could be truly united in one nation-state.

What was best in the Yugoslav approach, it may be suggested, was Yugoslav in origin; what was less commendable could by and large be attributed to the Stalinist influences which pervaded the early years of the Yugoslav revolution. But what was the Stalinist approach to the national problem? The question requires consideration, since it looms so large in understanding national relations under Communist rule.

Stalinist national policy had its special set of slogans and constitutional forms, most of which were accepted uncritically by the Yugoslavs in 1945. The policy behind these forms was often less attractive, tending above all to glorify the achievements of the leading nationality in the Soviet Union, the Great Russians. This aspect of Soviet policy was antithetical to Yugoslav feelings and experience in dealing with the national question, and was not considered as adaptable to Yugoslav conditions.

Stalinist national policy also relied upon centralized methods of administration, notwithstanding the provisions for a federal system contained in the 1936 Soviet constitution. In this respect, the Yugoslavs adhered closely to Soviet practice in the immediate postwar years. When Stalinism was finally repudiated, both bureaucracy and a high degree of centralism were criticized by the Yugoslavs, and their own mistakes in following the Soviets down this path were used as an explanation for the failure to get at the roots of the national problem during the Stalinist period in Yugoslavia.

The Stalinist approach to the national question was also characterized by a revolutionary, or quasi-revolutionary, content. This fact was never adequately explained in Yugoslav writings on the national question, and yet it was in many ways the key to understanding how, in the expectations of the Party, a final solution to the national question was to be realized.

The revolutionary implications of the national question were first insisted upon by Stalin and the Comintern in the interwar period, with consequences for the Yugoslav Communists that have been examined in detail in an earlier chapter. When the Party came to power, it was a logical extension of earlier views to assume that the Communization of Yugoslavia would lead to a total solution of the national question by curtailing the power of the bourgeois elements who were responsible for perpetuating national exploitation during the interwar period.

By tying the final solution of the national question to the deepening of the revolution and the victory of Communism over the remnants of the bourgeois society, the Yugoslav Communists were compelled to place a high priority on totalitarian methods of dealing with the nationalities: for example, reliance on ideological explanations of the origins of nationalism; the suppression of all nationalistic tendencies in the population; and the widespread use of propaganda methods in place of more fundamental methods of reeducation aimed at breaking down barriers among the nationalities. In the short run, these policies were successful in smothering the national question. But by assuming that Communists were immune to nationalistic feelings, and that political indoctrination of the population could eradicate deeply rooted attitudes on the national question, the Party was shutting its eyes to many problems which were to cause great difficulty after the rigid controls of the Stalin period were relaxed.

In addition, the constant effort of the Party to inject an ideological and revolutionary content into the national question reduced the whole problem of nationalism to something very primitive and emotional, quite contrary to the scientific spirit in which Marxist socialism originally approached the question. This became evident in 1948 and 1949, when the Yugoslavs had broken with the Cominform but were still attempting to behave like orthodox Stalinists. During this period, the revolutionary and ideological approach to the national question received great emphasis, and textbooks and other materials on national history were rewritten to increase their "Marxist" content. Instead of diminishing the importance of nationalism, however, this politicizing of the national question had exactly the reverse effect; the emotional content, if not the logic, of the policy they were pursuing led the Yugoslav Communists to adopt the position that the revolution had actually led to a strengthening and deepening of national traditions (at least, those that were considered worthy of the revolution). In a remarkable statement, which showed to what extent the revolution had tried to appropriate national sentiment for its own uses, one commentator in this period offered the opinion that "the working class of each country is the legal (*zakoniti*) inheritor of all that is great and significant for the development of the nation and all the humanism (*čovečanstvo*) which was created in the history of that country." [113] At the same time, the conviction of the Party in its ability to build socialism in a national, *Yugoslav* context, and the statist and authoritarian currents of the period, led to an unexpected stress on the virtues of the Yugoslav state; one meets references, at this time, to the idea of Yugoslavia as a "socialist fatherland" of the Yugoslav peoples, and even a hint that the Yugoslav state was a higher synthesis of the individual nations or the republics which made up the federation.

This way of thinking, so contrary to the Yugoslav's own experience with the national question, did not last long, perhaps a year at the most. Nor should too great stress be laid on doctrines which were obviously patterned after Soviet practice (as well as Soviet theory), in the hope of making Yugoslavia appear as the champion of orthodoxy in the Communist world. Still, the convergence of several elements of the Stalinist pattern was clear enough to see, and the direction of that convergence led not to a solution of the national question but to the reappearance of some form of Yugoslav integralism. This, it can be surmised, was the path laid out for Yugoslavia if the break with the Cominform had not intervened and completely changed the course of Yugoslav development, as well as the evolution of the national question itself.

[113] Ziherl, *Komunizam i otadžbina*, p. 34.

4

The Macedonian Question

FOLLOWING World War II, the national question was raised in its most acute form in Macedonia. In certain respects, it is true, the problems that arose in Macedonia were quite similar to those encountered by the Communists in other parts of Yugoslavia. The minority problem, the struggle of the Communists against the nationalist anti-Communist organizations, and the difficulties that accompanied the resettlement of the Serbian colonists, for example, were not restricted to any one republic.

Nevertheless, the situation in Macedonia was unique in a number of ways. One problem that the region faced might be called that of nation-building. Macedonian national institutions did not exist when the Macedonian People's Republic (or MPR as it shall be referred to here) came into existence as the result of the decisions taken at ASNOM in 1945. This posed formidable practical problems, for example, in the development of the Macedonian literary language, and was partly responsible for the fact that nationalism was more volatile and unpredictable in Macedonia in the immediate postwar years than in the other, more mature, Yugoslav republics.

A second and more well-known aspect of the Macedonian national question after World War II concerned the relationship between Yugoslav policy in the Balkans and the desire of the Macedonians to create a united Macedonia by annexing portions of Bulgaria and Greece to the MPR. In the period under consideration here Macedonian and Yugoslav national ambitions, which had so often clashed in the past, were at least temporarily reconciled by an identity of interests. For the Yugoslavs, the appeal of Macedonian nationalism was a weapon to be exploited in spreading Communist influence and assuring the CPY of a leading role among the Communist states of the Balkans. For the Macedonians, the long-sought-for goal of unification was brought within reach by the support of the powerful Yugoslav Party.

In the day-to-day development of the national question in Macedonia, problems of nation-building and the ambitions of the Yugoslavs and the Macedonians in the Balkans were intertwined and interdependent. For practical purposes, however, it is convenient to treat the two problems separately, turning first to the fate of the plans for Macedonian unification and the crisis which ensued as a result of the outbreak of the dispute between the Cominform and Yugoslavia, and then considering the main problems which were encountered during the process of nation-building within Macedonia after the war.

The origins of the Yugoslav plan for the unification of Macedonia can be traced back to 1942, when it appeared that Tito was contemplating such a step as part of his design for gaining control of the Balkans after the war. Vukmanović-Tempo argued strenuously with the Greek Communists over the issue of unification in 1943, without winning anything but token acceptance of the Yugoslav position from that quarter. Soviet opposition was the decisive factor leading to the abandonment of the Yugoslav campaign, but it did not alter the determination of the Yugoslav Party to press for unification at a more opportune moment. Thus, when the war drew to a close, the Yugoslavs renewed their demands. This time they were in an excellent position to apply pressure on the Communist parties in Greece and Bulgaria, and at the same time to work through Macedonian Partisan units and political organizations loyal to the Yugoslavs. If the Great Powers had not finally intervened, the Yugoslavs would probably have succeeded in enlarging Yugoslav Macedonia at the expense of Bulgaria and Greece.

The campaign to separate the Pirin district from Bulgaria began immediately after the capitulation of Bulgaria in September, 1944. In their first confrontation with the Bulgarian Communists in Sofia, the Yugoslavs put intense pressure on the Bulgarians to admit publicly all past errors over the Macedonian question and to recognize the claims of the MPR to the Pirin district.[1] It was finally agreed that, "for the time being," political and military bodies in the district were to remain under Bulgarian control.[2] But the Bulgarians gave way to the Yugoslav demands that

[1] See Vukmanović-Tempo's speech reproduced in *Borba*, Dec. 22, 1948, p. 2. In his report to the Central Committee of the Macedonian Party, Tempo related with obvious satisfaction how "we really tied them up" (*dobro smo ih pritegli*). *Arhiv*, VII, 357.

[2] *Arhiv*, VII, 359.

all-Macedonian military units and Macedonian national committees be set up in the Pirin district.[3] The Yugoslavs, for their part, made it clear that the establishment of these bodies was the first step toward annexation, "the preparation of the Macedonian people for union with the Macedonian democratic federal state in new Tito's Yugoslavia," in the words of Lazar Koliševski.[4] Vukmanović-Tempo (so the Bulgarians later charged) [5] actively urged the officials of the Pirin district to press for autonomy in their relations with Sofia. And the Macedonian Partisan unit in the district flouted the Sofia agreement, acting independently of the Bulgarians. At one point they even seized military supplies from a local army camp,[6] although Bulgaria was by this time fighting on the Allied side against the Germans.

To the surprise of the Yugoslavs, the Bulgarians did not capitulate under these pressures. Although forced to accept Yugoslav advice on Macedonia, the Bulgarian Party successfully avoided implementing the most distasteful of the Yugoslav demands. The confession of errors on Macedonia was never published. Ignoring the criticisms of the Yugoslav advisers sent to the Pirin district, the Bulgarian Communists kept firm

[3] According to Tempo's September, 1944, letter to the Central Committee of the Bulgarian Party. The details of what was agreed upon at the September meeting differ somewhat here from the account Tempo gave in 1948 (see preceding footnote). The letter to the Bulgarian Central Committee mentioned an agreement to permit the Macedonians in Bulgaria to exercise self-determination, including secession and voluntary union with other peoples; this demand is not mentioned in Tempo's account of 1948, and it is possible that the 1944 letter enlarged upon the matters actually agreed upon as a new form of pressure on the Bulgarians. On the other hand, Tempo's 1948 account claims that the Bulgarians promised to give the Pirin Macedonians "administrative autonomy," and this is not mentioned in the 1944 letter. Nor does that letter mention the self-criticism which the Bulgarians were supposed to prepare for their past mistakes over Macedonia. A second letter, reproduced in *Arhiv*, VII, 360–61, was sent to the Bulgarian Central Committee by Lazar Koliševski in September, and repeats the demands made by Tempo. According to a Bulgarian account, Tempo demanded the secession of the Pirin district in the near future, to be followed by its annexation by Yugoslavia. See the report of Georgi Madolev to the Fifth Congress of the Bulgarian CP, published in *Rabotnichesko Delo* (Sofia), Dec. 23, 1948, p. 1.

[4] *Arhiv*, VII, 361.

[5] K'osev, *Borbite na Makedonskiia narod za osvobozhdenie*, pp. 157–58.

[6] *Rabotnichesko Delo*, Dec. 23, 1948, p. 1. Vukmanović-Tempo admitted in his letter to the Bulgarian Central Committee that Yugoslavs in the Pirin district had demanded that the military units be placed under their control. This decision was "premature," in Tempo's words, and the action was condemned by him. *Arhiv*, VII, 359.

control over their own party and government bodies in the region. In a letter from the Bulgarian Central Committee to Tito sent in November, 1944, the Bulgarian Communists praised the formation of the Macedonian republic, but informed the Yugoslavs that an *oblast* Party committee was being formed in the Pirin district under the supervision of the Bulgarian Party which would be "Communist in content, national [Macedonian] in its form of work." [7] Yugoslav hopes for a quick and painless separation of Pirin Macedonia from Bulgaria then evaporated in the complicated negotiations over Balkan federation which took place in the spring of 1945. Although the Yugoslav Communists subsequently made considerable inroads into the Pirin district, they never came as close to winning control over the region as in late 1944.

In Greece, the question of Macedonian union was tied up with the activities of the resistance movement which developed among the Slav population, known as Slavo-Macedonians by the Greeks. This group, although not a majority of the inhabitants in the regions bordering on Yugoslavia, was to play a key role in the war and postwar struggles for control of northern Greece, or as the region was called by the Macedonian nationalists, Aegean Macedonia.

At first, the anti-fascist resistance had been weak among the Slavo-Macedonians, many of whom sided with the Bulgarians or IMRO-ists. In 1943 the success of the Partisans in Macedonia encouraged the formation of Macedonian Partisan units in Greece, and in November, 1943, the Macedonian Communists formed their own front organization, the Slavo-Macedonian National Liberation Front, or as it was known by its Macedonian initials, SNOF.[8] SNOF began to agitate for Macedonian union,[9] putting pressure on the Greek Communists not long after Vukmanović-Tempo had pressed for a commitment by the Greek Party to self-determination for the Macedonians in Greece during the discussions over a combined Balkan command. In the spring of 1944 the question of SNOF

[7] *Arhiv*, VII, 368.

[8] A Yugoslav account of the founding of SNOF can be found in *Nova Makedonija*, April 26, 1950, pp. 2–3.

[9] In January or February of 1944, SNOF sent a letter to the regional committee of the Greek Communist Party supporting the stand on unification taken by the Manifesto of the Main Command for Macedonia issued in September, 1943. The Greek Communists answered that the letter was an unfriendly document which took an IMRO-ist position on the Macedonian question. Pejov, p. 31.

came to a head when the Greek Party dissolved the Macedonians' organization in accord with agreements reached with the Greek government-in-exile. The Greek Communists apparently used this moment to settle some old scores with SNOF; its leaders were arrested, according to Yugoslav accounts, and Macedonian Partisan units were ordered to disband. Some units, in the face of this demand, retreated into Yugoslav Macedonia, while others continued to operate in Greece and on several occasions were engaged in skirmishes with ELAS, the Greek Partisan movement.[10] To halt this alarming deterioration of relations, the Greek Party and the Yugoslavs were forced to come to terms. In an agreement reached at Kajmakčalan [11] in the summer of 1944, the Greeks agreed to permit Slavo-Macedonians to fight within the ranks of ELAS, and a formula over

[10] Accounts of these clashes are given in Pejov, p. 37; Vukmanović-Tempo, "Komunistička Partija Grčke i narodnooslobodilačka borba," *Komunist*, No. 6, (Nov., 1949), p. 47; *Arhiv*, VII, 330–31; and Kofos, *Nationalism and Communism*, pp 123–28. *Arhiv* reproduces a radiogram written by Tempo and Radosavljević in August, 1944. This account does not speak of the dissolution of SNOF, but says that the trouble began when the Greek Partisans attempted to conscript the Macedonians, triggering an exodus of Macedonians into Yugoslavia, where they were organized by the Mihailov IMRO groups into units to fight the Greeks. At this point, says Tempo, the Partisans also began to organize the Macedonians, and permitted the belief to grow up that Macedonians from Greece were welcome in the Yugoslav Partisan movement. This led to a massive flow of Macedonians across the border into the Partisans, and one unit of Macedonian-Greek Partisans even returned across the border to fight in Greece. The Greeks, Tempo went on, then engaged in reprisals against the Macedonians, arresting those in the Greek Partisans and forbidding any Macedonians to cross the border and join with the Yugoslavs. In the negotiations that followed between the Greek and Yugoslav Partisans, the Yugoslavs took the position that the Greeks should not form any units in the Macedonian regions, but that if they insisted in doing so, the Yugoslavs would do likewise. Pejov's account stresses the agitation for self-determination that was going on among the Macedonians in the winter and spring of 1944, leading to the dissolution of SNOF in April. Following this, says Pejov, the Macedonians formed their own unit, in Kastoria. This led to attacks on the Macedonians by the Greek Partisans of ELAS in the spring and summer. The Kofos account does not mention the dissolution of SNOF, and gives the time of the confrontation between the Macedonian Gotsev battalion and ELAS as October.

[11] Elisabeth Barker, in her account of the Macedonian question, mentions a "Mount Kaimaxiller" agreement which was supposed to have made between the Greek Communists and the Bulgarian authorities over Aegean Macedonia. The rumors of the existence of such an agreement may have originated from some garbled account of the Kajmakčalan agreement. Elisabeth Barker, p. 115; Kofos, *Nationalism and Communism*, p. 128.

the question of Macedonian unity was worked out which left the door open for the affirmation of Macedonian national claims but did not formally commit the Greek Communists to self-determination of the Macedonians in Greece, that is, to the unification of Aegean Macedonia with Yugoslav Macedonia.[12]

The events of the summer of 1944 showed how deeply the national feelings of the Greek Communists were aroused by the Macedonian issue. The Greek Party, although it had made some vague promises to the Yugoslavs, first to Vukmanović-Tempo in connection with the question of a combined staff, then in the Kajmakčalan agreement, stoutly resisted demands for the separation of Aegean Macedonia from Greece. The official position of the Greek Party, established during the period of the United Front in the 1930s, remained that the Macedonians were a minority within Greece who enjoyed full equality with the Greek people but could not claim the right to separate in any way from the Greek state.[13]

The policy of the Greek Party was challenged a second time when the German occupation of Greece ended in the fall of 1944. The Macedonian Communists pressed the Greeks, unsuccessfully, for the right to organize independently along the lines of the old SNOF, with freedom to inculcate Macedonian nationalism in the Slav population of the Aegean region and to agitate publicly for the unification of all Macedonia.[14] Although the circumstances have never been entirely clarified, the Greek Party apparently reacted to the Macedonian demands with new reprisals against the Macedonian population, and forced the retreat of at least one Macedonian Partisan brigade into Yugoslavia in October.[15] The arrival of the British in Greece, at just this time, increased tensions between the Greek

12 Pejov, p. 37.

13 Yugoslav accounts stress the fact that the Greek Communists, in the early years of the resistance, would not even recognize the existence of a Macedonian minority, and treated the Slavo-Macedonians as Greeks. In the winter of 1943–44, after SNOF was formed, the use of Macedonian was recognized, and schools were even permitted to be organized for the Slavo-Macedonians. But the Greeks stood fast on the issue of self-determination, leading to the dispute with SNOF and the dissolution of that organization. Vukmanović-Tempo, *Komunist*, No. 6, pp. 46–47.

14 The existence of a memo giving the demands of SNOF has been described in Kofos, "The Making of Yugoslavia's Peoples Republic of Macedonia," *Balkan Studies,* III (1962), 383.

15 Vukmanović-Tempo, *Komunist*, No. 6, p. 80; Kofos, *Nationalism and Communism,* pp. 125–28.

and Yugoslav Communists. The Yugoslavs strongly disagreed with the policy of the Greek Party to seek an agreement with the British, and it is possible that some Partisan commanders favored sending Yugoslav troops to Salonica to occupy the port before the arrival of the British, over the objections of the Greek Communists.[16]

The outbreak of the civil war in Greece in December put an end to the Yugoslav hopes that Aegean Macedonia could be separated from Greece and annexed to the MPR through the actions of the local resistance movement. In February, 1945, the Greek Communists were forced to come to terms with the British and resistance to the Greek government ended. Yugoslav propaganda against the "monarcho-fascists" in Greece was bitter, but unavailing. Although the Yugoslavs did not forsake their claims, the opposition of the Greek Communist Party, and then the intervention of the British, had combined to thwart the drive for the incorporation of Aegean Macedonia into the MPR.

When the Greek and Bulgarian Communist parties refused to permit the Yugoslavs to carry out their plans, and the opportunity for the quick separation of the Macedonian portions of Bulgaria and Greece was lost, the CPY drew back and temporarily dropped the campaign for Macedonian unification. Pressure was renewed in 1946, both on Bulgaria and on Greece. This time, although the possibility of taking control of the Pirin district and Aegean Macedonia was less than in 1944, the Yugoslavs were more persistent and more vocal in pressing their claims. It appears likely that the Yugoslavs at one point contemplated making territorial claims on Greece at the Paris Peace Conference which was in session during the spring and summer of 1946, although such a demand was in fact never officially placed before the conference; nor was it brought up with the Great Powers, in whose hands the decision in these matters rested.

The Yugoslav task of advancing Macedonian claims was made easier by the fact that the Bulgarian Communists, although having blocked the separation of the Pirin district from Bulgaria in 1944, cooperated closely with the Yugoslavs in efforts to build up the MPR as the new national homeland of the Macedonian people. Shortly after the capitulation of Bulgaria in September, 1944, the Fatherland Front officially recognized

[16] After the outbreak of the Cominform dispute, Zahariades charged that Tempo, in October, 1944, informed the Greeks that he had asked for two divisions to occupy Salonica. *For a Lasting Peace, For a People's Democracy*, Aug. 1, 1949.

the existence of the Macedonian nation and the right of the Macedonians to self-determination.[17] (The Bulgarian Communists were later to make much of this statement to counter the Yugoslav charge that in 1943 the Fatherland Front had opposed the creation of a Macedonian national republic.) In October the remains of the nationalist Goce Delčev were transported from Sofia to the Macedonian Republic. At the same time, the Institute for the Scientific Study of Macedonia, which had been disseminating Bulgarian propaganda on Macedonia since the 1920s, was dissolved and its materials transferred to Skoplje,[18] where they were later incorporated into the library of the Institute for the Study of National History, set up to combat Bulgarian influences in Macedonia after the dispute with the Cominform broke out.

The Bulgarians did not consider that the policy of amicable relations with the MPR entailed concessions over the Pirin district. No stand was taken on the sensitive issue of the future of Pirin Macedonia until 1946, when the Bulgarian Communist Party adopted a secret resolution on the problem at its Tenth Plenum in August.[19] Later, the resolution was to be the subject of conflicting interpretations. The Yugoslavs claimed that the resolution approved the immediate unification of Macedonia, while the Bulgarians took the position that the statement foresaw unification only after the formation of a federation with Yugoslavia. Judging from a portion of the document published by the Bulgarians themselves, the Yugoslavs were closer to the truth. Despite obvious misgivings the Bulgarian Communists agreed in principle at the plenum that the Pirin district should be joined to Macedonia as one of a number of steps which would precede the creation of a Balkan federation.[20]

[17] *Otochestven Front* (Sofia), Sept. 18, 1944, p. 1.

[18] In December, 1946, Kiril Nikolov delivered the swan song of the institute in a lecture taking the position that the Macedonian language and Macedonian nationality did exist. His essay was later reprinted in Yugoslavia under the title *Za Makedonskata nacija.*

[19] The public version of the resolution of the Tenth Plenum is given in *Bulgarskata Komunisticheska Partiia v rezoliutsii i resheniia,* Vol. IV: *1944–1955,* pp. 60–69. The Yugoslavs published their version of the portions of the resolution dealing with Macedonia in Mojsov, *Bugarska Radnička Partija,* pp. 263–64. The Bulgarians have admitted to the existence of this portion of the resolution, and parts of it have been reproduced in K'osev, *Borbite na Makedonskiia,* p. 165.

[20] The resolution, in the version given by K'osev, stated that "it is in the interest of the Macedonian people, both those in Bulgaria and those in Yugoslavia, to unite

The position of the Bulgarian Party at this juncture was a difficult one, for the Yugoslav Communists were able to argue that Macedonian unification had long been accepted as the goal of the Bulgarian Communists when they had been advocating Balkan Communist federation in the 1920s. The Yugoslavs could also offer the Bulgarians support for Bulgarian claims to Western Thrace, and the resolution of the Tenth Plenum of the Bulgarian Party may have been based on an understanding with the Yugoslav Communists concerning territorial realignments in the Balkans which were then under consideration at the Paris Peace Conference.

On the other hand, there were certainly many persons inside and outside the Bulgarian Party strongly opposed to concessions over Macedonia.[21] The fact that the Bulgarian government was now controlled by the Communists did not completely solve the problem of public opinion, for the opposition press still existed in Bulgaria and was bitterly critical of developments in Macedonia. This was true even as late as the fall of 1946, when representatives of the immigrants from Macedonia, traditionally a powerful group in Bulgarian politics, attacked the Communists' policies on Macedonia, charging that the idea of a Macedonian nationality was "born in a retort of the political alchemy of the Communist Party," and called for a united, free, and independent Macedonia as part of a federation of Balkan peoples in which there would be complete freedom to chose one's own nationality without any form of coercion.[22]

The course of action chosen by the Bulgarian Communists in this situation was similar to that followed in 1944. A great show was made of complying with Yugoslav demands, especially in recognizing the Macedonian character of the Pirin district. Criticism of the Yugoslavs within the Bulgarian Party seems to have been held to a minimum, and the rank and file, at least in the Pirin district, apparently believed that the Bulgarian

---

the Pirin region to the Macedonian People's Republic in such a way that there exist no customs on the borders between Macedonia and Bulgaria, just as no such [customs exist] between PR Macedonia and the remaining units in the FPRY. The union of the Pirin region to the PR of Macedonia should not only not worsen economic and cultural ties between the united part and Bulgaria, but, on the contrary, will increase even more the common ties between Macedonia (Yugoslavia) [sic] and Bulgaria."

[21] Slijepčević, pp. 228–29.

[22] *Svoboden Narod* (Sofia), Oct. 24, 1946.

policy was identical to that of the Yugoslav Communists. At the same time, the Bulgarians never let control of the Party and the government slip out of their hands. The pledge contained in the resolution adopted by the Tenth Plenum, that the Pirin district would be transferred to the MPR as a step toward federation, was ignored and was later repudiated completely.

Steps to speed the Macedonianization of the Pirin district, in response to Yugoslav pressures, began at the end of 1946. The Bulgarian census of December was administered in such a fashion that the people of the district had little alternative but to declare themselves Macedonians.[23] On the basis of the results of this census, the regional committee of the Fatherland Front for the Pirin district issued a resolution in January, 1947, which stated that the inhabitants of the region were "part of the Macedonian people," and granted them "recognition of their national life." [24]

During the spring and summer of 1947, the Bulgarians stepped up their pro-Macedonian campaign in the district. The Fatherland Front even went to the extent of distributing propaganda within its ranks which supported the union of Pirin Macedonia with the MPR, although this met with an adverse response from many Bulgarians in the organization who wished the area to remain part of Bulgaria, or who felt that the MPR should not be part of Yugoslavia but associated with Bulgaria.[25]

The Bled agreements of July came at a moment when the campaign to encourage a Macedonian national outlook among the inhabitants of the Pirin district had gained such momentum that union with the MPR appeared imminent. It is known, nevertheless, that at Bled the Bulgarians refused to consider the idea of unification of Macedonia prior to the formation of a Balkan federation.[26] At the same time the Bulgarians

[23] The local press in the Pirin district promised that the registration of nationality was a voluntary affair, but went on to add: "The Oblast Committee of the Fatherland Front . . . considers that the registration of the Macedonians of our region as Macedonians [*sic*] is the most correct, which answers to our Macedonian origin, to our battle for liberation and union of Macedonia, as well as to the resolution of the Balkan question." *Pirinsko Delo*, Dec. 30, 1946, p. 1. The results of the 1946 census have never been completely published, and to the best of this author's knowledge, the figures on the nationality of the inhabitants of the Pirin region were never made known publicly.

[24] *Pirinsko Delo*, Jan. 13, 1947, p. 1.

[25] *Ibid.*, March 24, 1947, pp. 1 and 4.

[26] See Chapter 3.

agreed to permit Macedonians from the MPR to conduct cultural and educational programs in the district. As a consequence, the period following the Bled agreements witnessed a noticeable increase in pro-Macedonian propaganda there. After Bled, the region was referred to as "Pirin Macedonia," and articles in the Macedonian language in the local press became more frequent. The height of the campaign was reached in October with a rousing celebration of the national holiday of the MPR.[27] Shortly thereafter, the cultural workers, as the Macedonian teachers and propagandists called themselves, began to make their appearance in the district. A Macedonian theater was set up in Gorna Džumaja in November.[28] In January, 1948, the Bulgarian government introduced the study of Macedonian history and language into district schools; [29] close to a hundred teachers were brought in from Yugoslavia in the early part of the year to conduct these courses.[30]

Week by week, the agitation for unification of the Pirin district with the MPR gained momentum. About the time of the arrival of the Yugoslav Macedonians in November, however, a change in the attitude of the Bulgarian officials of the district was discernible. On the occasion of Tito's visit to Bulgaria in November, Madolev, secretary of the Fatherland Front and leading proponent of unification in the Pirin district, took the position that Pirin Macedonia was a "nation" on equal terms with the other nations in Yugoslavia.[31] On the occasion of the announcement that Macedonian would be taught in the schools, the responsible Bulgarian official could only say that "between the peoples of Yugoslavia and Bulgaria there do not exist any questions which cannot be solved in a fraternal [fashion]." [32]

It is not clear whether the change in the attitude of the Bulgarians in the Pirin district was prompted by the arrival of the Yugoslavs or reflected a decision on the Macedonian question reached by the Bulgarian Communist leadership in Sofia. In any case, the self-styled cultural

[27] *Pirinsko Delo,* Oct. 6, 1947.

[28] *Ibid.,* Nov. 3 and Nov. 10, 1947.

[29] *Ibid.,* Jan. 1, 1948, p. 1.

[30] *Pirinsko Delo* set the number at 93. See the issue of Aug. 23, 1948, p. 1. Koliševski said there were 135. *Nova Makedonija,* May 24, 1948, p. 1.

[31] *Pirinsko Delo,* Nov. 24, 1947, p. 1.

[32] *Ibid.,* Jan. 1, 1948.

workers immediately fell to quarreling with the Bulgarian Communists and government officials of the district. According to accounts given by the Bulgarians at a later date, the conduct of the Macedonians was arrogant and offensive.[33] It was claimed that everyone was compelled, regardless of his wishes, to study Macedonian and to read Macedonian newspapers. It was also the practice of the teachers, the Bulgarians said, to send telegrams to Skoplje, in the name of a Pirin town or village, in which the locality would announce its enthusiastic approval for the unification of the district with the MPR. The Yugoslavs, for their part, admitted that cooperation between the teachers and the local population was not always satisfactory, but blamed the Bulgarian officials for hampering the Macedonians' work.[34]

What the consequences of these antagonisms in the Pirin district would have been if the dispute between Yugoslavia and the Soviet Union had not broken out can only be guessed at. Although Bulgaria and Yugoslavia were ostensibly in agreement over the desirability of encouraging the Macedonian language and culture in the district, the struggle for influence going on in the region was strikingly reminiscent of the old rivalry between the Bulgarian and Serbian priests and national workers in Macedonia during the era of the Bulgarian Exarchate, and it is difficult to believe that the Bulgarians could have tolerated the presence of the Yugoslavs in the Pirin district for any great length of time.

Developments in the spring of 1948 conclusively demonstrated the impossibility of carrying out the plan for the Macedonianization of the area as it had been envisaged at Bled. In March the Yugoslavs informed the Bulgarians of their decision, taken after the February conference with Soviet leaders in Moscow, to oppose the establishment of a Balkan federation.[35] This did not materially alter the prospects for South Slav union, which had already grown dim in the previous fall because of Bulgarian opposition to federation. But the categorical nature of the Yugoslav move made it imperative to reach some decision on the future of the Pirin district. The Yugoslavs, perhaps afraid that they could not maintain their position in the region, stepped up their pressure on the Bulgarians,

[33] *Ibid.*, Aug. 23, 1948.
[34] Mitrev, pp. 107–9; Mojsov, *Bugarska Radnička Partija*, p. 274.
[35] Dimitrov, p. 65.

criticizing the Bulgarian Communists for chauvinistic behavior in the district and demanding the immediate incorporation of the region into the MPR.[36]

The Bulgarians, influenced greatly by the course of the Yugoslav-Soviet dispute, decided to resist Yugoslav pressure and halt the spread of Macedonian influences in the area. Sometime in May or June (most probably after the meeting of the Cominform at which the Yugoslavs were expelled from the organization), a letter was distributed among the Communists of the Pirin district clarifying the Bulgarian Party line on the Macedonian question.[37] The contents of the letter indicate that the Bulgarians had not yet broken fully with the Yugoslavs over Macedonia, for Party members were admonished for giving in to chauvinistic Bulgarian feelings. At the same time, the Communists of the Pirin district were informed that there could be no consideration given to the demand for the incorporation of the district into the MPR unless a Balkan federation had first been established. The letter also made known the decision of the Party to revive Bulgarian influences in the region, especially the Bulgarian language. Party members were informed that the use of Bulgarian was not a "serious barrier" to developing Macedonian national consciousness, nor even to realizing the goal of unification of the Pirin district with the MPR.[38]

This new position on the Macedonian question was incorporated into the resolution of the Sixteenth Plenum of the Bulgarian Workers' (Communist) Party, which convened in July. In the resolution, the Bulgarians pledged to continue developing cultural autonomy for the Macedonians of the Pirin district.[39] Party members on the spot were told, on the other hand, that the Bulgarian Communists had rejected "Koliševski's Macedonian national consciousness" for Macedonian consciousness which would "cultivate brotherhood with the Bulgarian people." [40] Macedonian

[36] *Nova Makedonija,* May 24, 1948, p. 1.

[37] K'osev, *Borbite na Makedonskiia,* pp. 165–66.

[38] *Ibid.*

[39] Royal Institute of International Affairs, *Documents on International Affairs,* p. 293.

[40] The meeting of the Party leadership in the Pirin district at which the decisions of the Sixteenth Plenum were discussed is given in *Pirinsko Delo,* July 26, 1948, p. 1. At the meeting, Vladimir Poptomov used the words just cited in explaining the new Bulgarian position toward the national question. Poptomov stressed the

teachers and other cultural workers were summarily expelled from the Pirin district, and all contacts with the MPR were severed. From erstwhile allies and collaborators in the project for unifying the Macedonian peoples, the Bulgarians and Yugoslavs had become open rivals for Macedonian national sympathies.

Yugoslav designs on Aegean Macedonia were also frustrated, despite the strong support which the Yugoslav Communists gave to the demands of the Macedonian nationalists in Greece for self-determination (that is, for the separation of Macedonian areas from Greece and their inclusion in the MPR). In this case the Yugoslavs were forced to abandon their plans by 1947, after the Greek Communists failed to gain a decisive victory in the Greek civil war.

The first round of fighting between the Greek Communists and the British had ended in a truce in 1945. The Yugoslav Communists, true to their reputation for militancy, opposed the decision; to rally support for prolonging the struggle while serving their own interests in Greek Macedonia, the Yugoslavs encouraged the formation of a new organization in April along the lines of the old SNOF, with the initials NOF (National Liberation Front).[41] NOF immediately issued a declaration calling for a renewal of the civil war,[42] perhaps with the expectation that the Macedonians would lead and eventually dominate the struggle.

The hopes of NOF were not fulfilled until the summer of 1946, when guerrilla activity against the Greek government assumed the character of a full-scale civil war. In the interim, the Greek Communist Party had established close ties with the Yugoslavs, whose support was indispensable for the success of any new uprising. What price, if any, the Greeks had to pay for Yugoslav aid has been the subject of considerable speculation, but conclusive evidence on the subject is lacking. If the Greek Party reached a secret agreement with the Yugoslavs over Macedonia, this would almost certainly have been revealed later by the Yugoslavs. More important still, the resolution issued by the Second Plenum of the Greek Communist

---

fact that the Bulgarian Party still supported Macedonian national rights. *"Not the BWP(k)* [Bulgarian Workers' Party—Communist] *nor any progressive force in our country wishes to make a Bulgarian out of a Macedonian, nor has the slightest intention of joining Macedonia to Bulgaria."* Italics in the original.

[41] *Nova Makedonija,* April 26, 1950, pp. 2–3.

[42] *Ibid.*

Party in 1946 took an uncompromising stand on the question of Macedonia, refusing to make any concessions to the Yugoslav point of view.[43] NOF, however, managed to maintain its autonomy in this period, perhaps as a result of Yugoslav pressure on the Greek Party.

When the fighting broke out in Greece in the summer of 1946, the Yugoslav press took up the theme of self-determination for the Aegean Macedonians with unprecedented bluntness. The peak of excitement was reached in August when *Borba* printed a claim which had originated in the Macedonian press that there were 250,000 Macedonians residing in Greece. The article warned that "our country cannot remain indifferent toward the annihilation of our inhabitants in Greece nor toward their demands for self-determination and union (*priključenje*) with their brothers in Yugoslavia." [44]

The Yugoslav press campaign over Aegean Macedonia put the Greek Communists in an awkward position, and it is difficult to understand why the Yugoslav Communists chose this particular moment to renew their demands for Greek Macedonia. The Yugoslav Party leadership may have felt that the Macedonian units in Greece would do most of the fighting and should be encouraged even at the price of Greek support; more likely, the Yugoslav Communists expected a quick victory and were trying to put pressure on the Greek Communists to permit the Macedonians, acting through NOF, to declare themselves part of the MPR.

As hopes for an easy victory in Greece vanished, the excitement over Macedonian unification subsided. It must have become evident to the Yugoslavs that they would have to support Greek national aims if the revolution was to succeed. Concessions to the Greeks followed: at the end of 1946, an agreement was worked out by which NOF was to be put under the control of the Central Committee of the Greek Communist Party, and its military units under the General Staff of the DSE (Democratic Army of Greece), while it was to be awarded representation in the Central Committee, military commands, and Communist organs of local

43 Vukmanović-Tempo, *Komunist,* No. 6, p. 46.

44 *Borba,* Aug. 26, 1946, p. 1. See also *Nova Makedonija,* Aug. 31, 1946, p. 1, which reprinted a map of Macedonia giving the national composition of the Aegean region, and claiming that in the whole area, which included Salonica and all of western Thrace, there were 251,000 Macedonians and 250,000 Greeks. Another blunt demand for the region was made by Dimitar Vlahov in a speech in September in Bitolj. *Nova Makedonija,* Sept. 22, 1946, p. 1.

government in the Aegean region.[45] Although the Yugoslavs did not officially reverse their position on the right of the Macedonians in Greece to exercise self-determination, an interview with Markos Vafiades, the Greek Party secretary, published in *Borba* in March, 1947, indicated that Belgrade had decided to make concessions to the Greek point of view.[46] Markos was quoted as saying that the Macedonians in Greece were fighting for the exercise of the national rights they had enjoyed in the Communist-occupied regions of Greece at the close of the war. In effect, this meant that the Macedonians were to be considered as a minority in Greece; this impression was confirmed by the fact that Markos did not mention the right of self-determination for the peoples of the Aegean region in his interview.

The failures in Greece and Bulgaria marked the end of Yugoslav efforts to unify Macedonia. The Yugoslav Communists had been able to arouse strong emotions among the Macedonians in Yugoslavia, Greece, and Bulgaria by appealing to the right of self-determination and the aspirations of the Macedonians for unification. But the actions of the Yugoslav government were always marked by a considerable degree of caution, based on a desire to avoid arousing the Western powers, and stemming also from the need to give some consideration to the interests of the Greek and Bulgarian Communist parties. Belgrade never engaged openly in the kind of strident nationalistic polemics over Macedonia which marked the dispute over Trieste or the arguments over the fate of the Slovenes in Austrian Carinthia. Needless to say, this failure to back the Macedonians to the limit was a potential source of friction between the Macedonian Communists and Belgrade, and played a role in at least one defection from Communist ranks in 1946, as shall be seen.

Following the outbreak of the dispute with the Soviet Union, the Yugoslav Communist leaders felt they would be running too great a risk in continuing the campaign for Macedonian unification. Overnight Belgrade became the staunch defender of the status quo in the Balkans, while the Soviet-led Communist parties began to exploit the Macedonian issue for their own ends by associating themselves with the aspirations of the Macedonians for union.

This reversal of positions on the Macedonian question did not develop

[45] *Nova Makedonija,* April 26, 1950, pp. 2–3.
[46] *Borba,* March 25, 1947, p. 1.

at once. The appearance of the Cominform resolution of June, 1948, released the Bulgarian and Greek Communists from their distasteful role as accomplices in the Yugoslav designs for the unification of Macedonia, and there was an obvious desire on the part of both parties to avoid further involvement in the Macedonian issue. As long as Markos remained Party secretary in Greece, the Greek Party kept silent. The Bulgarians, for their part, could not decide whether to take the offensive against the Yugoslavs in the name of Macedonian nationalism, or give in to popular feeling in Bulgaria and treat the Macedonians as Bulgarians. Rather lame references were made by the Bulgarian Communists to "self-determination" for the Macedonians, but it was far from clear what this was supposed to entail. At the same time the resolution of the Sixteenth Plenum of the Bulgarian Party accused the Yugoslavs of curbing *Bulgarian* national traditions in the MPR, and, using a new approach, attacked the Yugoslavs for refusing to admit the existence of a Bulgarian minority in the Macedonian republic.

The Cominform offensive against the MPR began to gain momentum in December, 1948, when articles appeared in the Bulgarian press advocating a free and united Macedonia as part of a Balkan federation.[47] Dimitrov endorsed this plan at the Fifth Congress of the Bulgarian Party in the same month.[48] In Greece, the way was paved for the adoption of the new Cominform line by the defeat of the pro-Tito faction in the Greek Communist Party and the replacement of Markos by Nikos Zahariades, who supported the Soviet Union. NOF split; some of its members took refuge in Macedonia, but others sided with the Cominform. This group of Macedonian nationalists now became a tool in Cominform plans for subverting the MPR; in February, a meeting of its Central Council convened and issued a declaration for an independent united Macedonia as part of a "democratic" (i.e., Cominform-controlled) Balkan federation.[49] In March, a congress of the organization was held, and the decision was reached to form a Communist party for Aegean Macedonia (KOEM) which would exercise "political, party, and organizational autonomy"

[47] *Pirinsko Delo,* Dec. 6, 1948.

[48] Dimitrov, p. 65.

[49] Elisabeth Barker, p. 120; Royal Institute of International Affairs, *Chronology of International Events and Documents,* Vol. V, No. 6, p. 174; and Kousoulas, *The Price of Freedom,* p. 78.

within the Greek CP.[50] It was foreseen that a general conference of Macedonians would be convened sometime in the near future, presumably
with representatives from Yugoslav and Bulgarian Macedonia, to give
support for the creation of a new Macedonian state.[51]

The Communists of NOF were undoubtedly in earnest in calling for a
new approach to the question of Balkan federation and Macedonian unity.
On the other hand, the cynicism which led the Cominform to support
such an operation was only too clear. The 1949 campaign for Balkan
federation marked the final and complete debasement of the once lofty
ideal of Balkan unity which had inspired Balkan socialists in the past.
In so far as can be determined, the move had little effect within the MPR,
where the Yugoslavs countered by organizing their own propaganda
campaign against NOF. In the summer a rally of refugees from Aegean
Macedonia was organized in Skoplje to protest the actions of the
Cominform-led forces in Greece. Koliševski, in addressing the group,
spoke of the MPR as the "Piedmont" of Macedonia,[52] but the resolution
of the refugee organization stayed carefully within the established Yugoslav policy of avoiding any challenges to the status quo, and pledged
support for the Greek Macedonians in Greece without reviving any
demands, directly or indirectly, for Greek territory.[53]

In Greece, the actions of NOF were met with alarm. The Greek Communist Party, under its new secretary, Zahariades, had at first accepted
the claims of NOF as the only way in which to gain support for the
guerrilla movement from the Slavo-Macedonians.[54] But following the
announcement of the plan to set up an independent Macedonia, the non-
Communists in Greece quickly accused the Communists of betraying
Greek national interests, and the Greek Party was compelled to offer a
series of explanations modifying the position taken by NOF.[55] After
several months, Moscow came to the assistance of the Greek Communists
by modifying its own position. In June, *Pravda* reprinted an interview
between the Greek Partisan leaders and a French journalist, in which the

[50] *Rabotnichesko Delo,* May 19, 1949, p. 6.
[51] *Ibid.*
[52] *Nova Makedonija,* Aug. 3, 1949, p. 1.
[53] *Ibid.,* July 29, 1949, p. 1.
[54] Kousoulas, *Revolution and Defeat,* p. 263.
[55] Elisabeth Barker, p. 122; Kofos, *Nationalism and Communism in Macedonia,*
p. 182.

territorial integrity of Greece was made one of a number of preconditions for settlement of the Macedonian question.[56] At the Sixth Plenum of the Greek Communist Party in October, 1949, the policy of independence for Macedonia was officially abandoned by the Greek Communists.[57]

With the end of the ill-fated Cominform plan, the Macedonian question entered a new phase, for once Soviet backing was withdrawn there was no one left to support the plan of unification. Reports originating in Greece in the spring of 1949 persisted in attributing the whole scheme for setting up a new Macedonian state to the Bulgarians. It was suggested that a number of the Partisans captured on Greek soil at this time were in fact Bulgarians of Greek origin.[58] One document which the Greek government claimed to have captured from the rebel leaders spoke of the creation of an autonomous Macedonia within a "People's Democratic Bulgaria." [59] While such evidence may in fact have pointed to Bulgarian involvement in the Greek guerrilla movement in the spring of 1949, it does not seem that the Bulgarians were the real force behind the reorganized NOF, or KOEM. The Bulgarians could not have viewed with equanimity the development of a new nationalist Macedonia movement so soon after having escaped from the humiliation of being dictated to by the Macedonian Communists in Skoplje. When news of the NOF declaration of February became known, Vasil Kolarov, the Bulgarian foreign minister, declared the Bulgarian government had not the slightest interest in Balkan federation, nor indeed had ever supported such a plan.[60] This announcement drew ridicule from the Yugoslavs; [61] perhaps, indeed, it was no more than a hasty and poorly conceived attempt to disguise the responsibility of Sofia for the demands of NOF. On the other hand, the Bulgarian attitude toward the formation of KOEM was noticeably reserved; [62] the founding of the organization was reported cautiously and noncommittally, without drawing any connection between this act and the idea of Balkan federation or Macedonian unification. This statement, and the reaction

[56] *Pravda,* June 13, 1949, p. 4.

[57] Kousoulas, *Revolution and Defeat,* p. 271.

[58] Burks, pp. 100–1.

[59] New York *Times,* June 6, 1949, p. 6. For more on alleged Bulgarian designs on Greece, see Kousoulas, *The Price of Freedom,* p. 178.

[60] Elisabeth Barker, p. 122.

[61] See Koliševski's speech to the Second Congress of the Macedonian union organization, *Nova Makedonija,* May 11, 1949.

[62] *Rabotnichesko Delo,* May 19, 1949, p. 6.

of the Bulgarian government to the NOF announcement, seemed to add up to something far short of enthusiasm for the new scheme of a Cominform-backed Macedonian state within a Balkan federation.

By the summer of 1949 the Bulgarians were taking a somewhat different line; the polemics issued at the time on the Macedonian question praised the struggle of the Macedonians for Balkan federation and associated the Bulgarians with past efforts to unite the South Slav peoples.[63] This new emphasis on Balkan federation was paralleled by, and was perhaps even the result of, the removal of Kolarov as Bulgarian foreign minister. In his place was appointed Vladimir Poptomov,[64] a Macedonian nationalist who had played a leading role in the national liberation movement in Macedonia during the war (he had attended the second session of AVNOJ as a delegate from Macedonia), but who had subsequently emigrated from the MPR and sided with the Bulgarians.

This last in a long series of shifts in Bulgarian policy toward the Macedonian question was not, however, accompanied by any demands for the creation of an independent unified Macedonia along the lines that had been proposed by NOF. On the contrary, Bulgarian policy was very closely attuned to the Cominform position on Greece and the undesirability of raising sensitive territorial issues. Balkan federation was therefore presented as something which had been desirable in the past but was not appropriate to present conditions, while the solution of the Macedonian question was linked to the success of the Cominform bloc in its struggle with Yugoslavia. In the words used by one of the Bulgarian polemics of the period, "The guarantee of national independence and the solution of unresolved national questions generally, which earlier were thought of as soluble through federation of the Balkan peoples, today can be solved only through one mighty world democratic front in fraternal and close association with the Soviet Union." [65]

As the dispute between Yugoslavia and the Cominform deepened, the controversy over Macedonia took on harsher forms. The Yugoslavs accused the Bulgarians of seeking to annex Vardar Macedonia, while the Cominform countries, in their purge trials of Titoist elements in the

[63] A good example of this is the work of the indefatigable K'osev who in August, 1949, published a résumé of the Bulgarian position, *Makedonskiiat vupros i Titovata klika.* See also his *Borbite na Makedonskiia narod za osvobozhdenie.*

[64] New York *Times,* Aug. 7, 1949, p. 1.

[65] K'osev, *Makedonskiiat vupros,* p. 35.

summer and fall of 1949, charged Yugoslavia with plotting in collaboration with the Western powers to set up an anti-Communist federation in the Balkans. Both camps engaged in vociferous propaganda over the question of the Macedonian nationality (some of the points at issue will be examined shortly). Provocateurs were sent across the Macedonian border, and both sides organized groups of émigré Macedonians who engaged in activities meant to demonstrate that they were the only authentic representatives of the Macedonian people in Vardar Macedonia, the Pirin district, or Greece, as the case might be.[66]

For the MPR this crisis was an unexpected and severe test of its stability and of the unity of the Macedonians of Yugoslavia in the face of divisive national appeals from abroad—appeals of a kind which in the past had never failed to have some effect. The ability of the MPR to weather the crisis can best be judged by returning, briefly, to the conditions that prevailed in Macedonia after the war, and the feelings of the Macedonian people concerning their status as a nationality within a Macedonian republic which was part of a Yugoslav state.

The popularity of the Macedonian Communist regime in Skoplje had been enhanced after the war as a result of the support given Macedonian unification by the Yugoslav Communist Party, and also by other steps designed to appeal to Macedonian national feelings in the field of domestic policy. The border with Serbia was drawn in such a way that it closely followed the proposals made by IMRO before the war, rather than following a line further to the south which would correspond to the Serbian view of the limits of Macedonia.[67] The spread of the Macedonian language was encouraged at the expense of Serbo-Croatian and, of course,

---

[66] When Tito withdrew his support from the Greek Communists in 1949 and the revolution there collapsed, the members of the KOEM were forced to flee to Eastern Europe; from the Slav refugees there was formed, in 1951, an organization meant to represent the Macedonian national movement, "Ilinden." In Skoplje an organization existed under the title Club of Aegean Refugees; there was also a Main Committee of Macedonians from Aegean Macedonia, which published a newspaper, *Glas na Egejcite*. In addition, there was an organization founded in 1951 which went under the title Union of Pirin Macedonians. For a vivid description of conditions on the border, see Dragomir Stojik, "Den na graničarite," *Nova Makedonija*, March 1, 1953, p. 1.

[67] The version of the northern boundary prepared before the war by the Institute for the Scientific Study of Macedonia, which was supported by the Bulgarians, generally adopted the present line, with deviations in Macedonia's favor in the mountains east of the South Morava River (the Kokura, Patarica, and Dukat

Bulgarian. Also, the Macedonians were left free to interpret their past in a far more nationalist, and less Marxist, fashion than Communists in the other republics.[68]

These measures had a great impact in Macedonia and aided the Macedonian Party in consolidating its rule and pushing forward with the revolutionary policies which were in the last analysis the main concern of the new regime. But the MPR still faced many difficulties in connection with the national question. The new republic had only the rudiments of a written language, an uncertain and much disputed history, and no cultural traditions which it could really call its own. Lurking in the background was the memory of past injustices suffered at the hands of the Serbs, and uncertainty over the intentions of Belgrade toward Macedonian unification in the future. Koliševski, the leader of the Macedonian Party, although native-born, was closely connected with the Serbian Party from before the war and was therefore vulnerable to attack as an agent of Belgrade.[69]

Several incidents did in fact raise the question of the loyalty of the Macedonians to Yugoslavia at the close of the war. The circumstances under which they took place tended to limit their significance, however. Prior to ASNOM, opposition to the policies of the CPY had originated in closely knit groups within the Party or sympathetic to it. After ASNOM many of these persons made their peace with the Yugoslav Party, while a number who could not reconcile themselves to the new situation simply left Macedonia altogether and later reappeared in Bulgaria, playing the

---

mountains). Other prewar sources usually drew the boundary of Macedonian influence further to the south (for example, the area said to be inhabited by Macedonian-Slavs by the Serbian ethnographer Cvijić). H. R. Wilkinson has prepared an excellent illustration of the boundary lines proposed for the northern extent of Macedonia to illustrate the fact that the Macedonian Slavs were generally considered to be south of the present boundary. See his "Yugoslav Macedonia in Transition," *Geographical Journal,* CXVIII (Dec., 1952), 402. Wilkinson, in his book *Maps and Politics,* states that the boundary between Serbia and Macedonia was adjusted slightly in favor of the former between 1946 and 1947. The author has been unable to discover proof of this change. Minor adjustments may have been made. But if so, they have not been recorded in the official gazette.

[68] A good example of such national writings is the collection of articles and speeches of Dimitar Vlahov, *Kroz historiju Makedonskog naroda: Zbirka Članaka.*

[69] Koliševski was born in Sveti Nikola but was raised in Kragujevac, Serbia, and in 1935 joined the Communist Party in Serbia. He participated in the Fifth Conference of the CPY in 1940 as a delegate from Kragujevac, and was sent to Macedonia after the war broke out.

role of Bulgarian nationalists opposed to the MPR.[70] The incidents which were reported as taking place after ASNOM originated largely in a new element, the young cadres whom the Communists had placed in positions of responsibility in the Partisan units and Party organizations, often without adequate indoctrination in the Party line.

These persons, loyal in the overwhelming majority to Tito, were not always reliable. On several occasions in the fall of 1944, discipline broke down within Partisan units because of inadequate indoctrination, or as a result of outbursts of national emotions among the Macedonians. The Goce Delčev unit, which had been recruited from Macedonians in Bulgaria, was disbanded by the Yugoslavs in the fall of 1944 for deserting en masse when sent into battle against the Germans; the incident led to lengthy arguments between the Bulgarians and the Yugoslavs over the organization and leadership of the unit, but the questionable bravery of the Bulgarian Macedonians does not seem to have been motivated by specifically national grievances.[71] The influence of the national question was more evident when several Partisan units rebelled in the Skoplje area at about the same time. Although information on the incident is scanty, it appears that a number of officers of nationalist persuasion refused to obey orders to send their troops to fight on the Srem front in Serbia, and demanded instead to be sent to fight for Salonica.[72]

How much importance should be attached to such isolated incidents, and to rather vague references to "foreign bourgeoisie and non-Party understanding" of the national question in the Macedonian Party after the war,[73] is difficult to say. National feeling in Macedonia, as in other parts of Yugoslavia, was a potential danger rather than a manifest prob-

[70] For example, Vladimir Poptomov, referred to earlier, and Peco Traikov, a Partisan commander placed in charge of the Yugoslav garrison in Skoplje after the war who decided to leave Macedonia and later engaged in polemical writings against the MPR.

[71] For the Yugoslav view on this incident, see Apostolski *et al., Završnite operacii na N.O.B. za osloboduvanjeto na Makedonija*, pp. 245–48. For the Bulgarian view concerning the founding of the Delčev brigade, see Traikov, *Natsionalizmut na skopskite rukovoditelie.*

[72] The incident is described in Uzunovski, "UDB-moken organ na našeta narodna revolucija," *Socialistička Zora*, I, No. 2 (March-April, 1949), 1–17, and Popovski, *Špiuni vo odbrana na linijata na informbiroto.* The slogan of the units in rebellion was "Ne sakame na sremskot front, sakama na Solun," roughly, "We don't want to go to the Srem, on to Salonica."

[73] At the First Congress of the Macedonian Party in 1949, it was reported:

lem, and the Party was extremely cautious to avoid any actions which would give the Macedonians an opportunity to vent their past resentments against Yugoslavia. The most serious challenge from within the ranks of the Party arose in 1946 when Antunov Čento, who had once been associated with IMRO and was president of ASNOM during the war, broke with the Party over the national question. At the moment he chose to take this step, Čento was occupying a minor ministerial post in the Macedonian government. Apparently disillusioned with the failure of the Yugoslavs to unite Macedonia,[74] and impatient with the controls which Belgrade had imposed on the Macedonian Communists, he delivered an attack against the policies of the Yugoslav Party in the Macedonian national assembly and then, according to Yugoslav accounts, was arrested while attempting to flee abroad and deliver a petition to the Paris Peace Conference in favor of an independent Macedonia under some form of Western Condominium.[75] Čento was not a key figure in the Party, and his outburst in the national assembly does not seem to have had wide repercussions.[76] But Čento's prominent role in the national movement during the war made the incident extremely embarrassing to the Party, which did not acknowledge his defection until news of the incident leaked out during the Cominform dispute.[77]

"As a result of the low ideological work and political level of young Party members on the one hand, and because of insufficient and unsatisfactory alertness and insufficiently sharp criteria for accepting new members [on the other], there appeared in some places foreign bourgeois and non-Party understanding of the national question [and also] of a series of other questions." *I kongres na Komunis-tičkata partija na Makedonija,* pp. 170–71.

[74] According to the Macedonian Political Organization in the United States, Čento was also motivated by anti-Yugoslav feelings, and had become disillusioned by the uprooting of the Bulgarian language and Skoplje's dependence on Serbian administrative experts. U.S. Department of State, "Macedonian Nationalism," p. 103.

[75] The most complete account of the incident in a Yugoslav source is given in Popovski, pp. 51–52.

[76] Appraising the effect of such an incident is difficult. There was no visible reaction, at least as far as the outside world could tell. The Yugoslavs minimize the affair. According to émigré accounts, on the other hand, Čento called for self-determination in the assembly and then made a rousing speech in the Prilep town square attacking Belgrade, following which 37 were killed in demonstrations in Resen.

[77] The first Yugoslav reference to the incident of which the author is aware is in *Nova Makedonija,* March 5, 1949, p. 3.

Part of the caution displayed by the Communists in dealing with Čento was undoubtedly the product of the exaggerated fears which the Party entertained of a resurgence of IMRO. During the war, IMRO had failed conspicuously to rally popular support, and thus had opened the way to Communist domination of the national struggle. The Party, nevertheless, considered the followers of IMRO a great potential danger, or at least feared the influence of certain prominent non-Communist nationally minded Macedonians who had chosen to collaborate with the Germans rather than the Bulgarians during the war. Kitinčev, mayor of Skoplje during the occupation and advocate of the right of Macedonia to autonomy, was imprisoned and then executed after the war. Jordan Čkatrov, another prominent figure during the occupation, was arrested but not brought to trial until 1949, when the Communists, probably as a gesture to demonstrate that Yugoslavia was not pampering class enemies as the Cominform charged, brought Čkatrov before a court for playing the role of a collaborator during the occupation.[78]

According to the information supplied by the Yugoslav Communists, anti-Communist IMRO organizations were indeed widespread after the war. It was claimed, in a report published in 1949, that 134 terrorist groups were uncovered between 1945 and 1948 in the MPR, and 600 members of terrorist bands were arrested.[79] Like the figures supplied by the secret police from other parts of Yugoslavia, this report probably exaggerated the size of the opposition. The two most important IMRO organizations uncovered were headed by Konstantin Terziev and Metodija Kolarov. Both, along with their accomplices, were tried in the spring of 1947 for carrying out terrorist activities and trying to create an independent Macedonia with Western aid.[80] Perhaps the most significant thing revealed by these arrests was the fact that the opposition looked to the

[78] For reference to the trial, see *Pirinsko Delo,* July 3, 1949, p. 1, giving excerpts from Peco Traikov's book, *Natsionalizmut na skopskite rukovoditelie.* Similar actions took place in other parts of Yugoslavia, especially in the trial of Božidar Kavran and Ljuba Miloš, leaders of the largest group of anti-Communist agents uncovered after the war, and identified with the Croatian Crusaders. Although apprehended in 1947, they were not tried until 1948.

[79] Uzunovski, pp. 1–17.

[80] Reports on the trials were carried in *Nova Makedonija,* March 25 through March 30, and April 26, 1947.

creation of an independent Macedonia under Western protection. At just the time Čento was making his bid for aid from the West, Terziev was also preparing a plea to the meeting of foreign ministers in Paris, calling for a reexamination of the Macedonian issue by the Great Powers.[81]

These activities, which reached their height in 1946, made the Communist leadership in the MPR visibly uneasy, and their concern was reflected in the lengthy attacks on Mihailov's IMRO launched by Koliševski and others in the summer of 1946.[82] IMRO, however, was no longer in a position to exercise influence in Macedonia; despite Communist fears to the contrary, it did not receive support from abroad. National feeling within the ranks of the Party was a far greater danger to the MPR than the national movements of the anti-Communist forces. But following the stir caused by the Čento incident, this threat also seems to have subsided.

Upon the outbreak of the dispute with the Cominform new pressures on the national loyalties of the Macedonians suddenly were generated. It became necessary for the Party leadership to restrain those who were loath to abandon the goal of Macedonian unification as a result of the dispute. Those elements in the population with sentimental ties or family connections in Bulgaria posed another problem. The large Albanian minority, and the smaller Turkish element in Macedonia, were also open to influence by the nationalist appeals and anti-Yugoslav propaganda which issued from Cominform sources.

There was, therefore, no overt opposition to the Communists when the dispute with the Cominform began, but potential sources of disaffection were present in Macedonia. While the policy of the Cominform was to play on the issue of Macedonian unification (and also to stir up minority discontent), it was the tactic of the Bulgarian Communist regime to stress the ties of the Macedonians and their national movement with Bulgaria, and to try to reawaken old fears among the Macedonians that they were the object of exploitation by the Yugoslav government in Belgrade. These emotional issues proved the real focus of debate between the Macedonian Communists and their chief Cominform protagonists, the Bulgarians, following the Cominform resolution of June, 1948.

[81] *Ibid.*, March 28, 1947, p. 3.
[82] See Koliševski's speech to the First Congress of the Macedonian front organization. *Ibid.*, Aug. 4, 1946, p. 1.

In the polemics which developed between Skoplje and Sofia, the Macedonians were the first to take the offensive, attacking the Bulgarian Communist Party for failing to recognize the existence of a Macedonian nationality prior to the war.[83] This calculated effort to destroy the reputation of the Bulgarian CP as the prewar champion of Macedonian national rights met with a strong rejoinder,[84] and the two parties quickly found themselves embroiled in a dispute over which Communist party had first asserted that the Macedonians were a distinct nationality. The Yugoslavs, in their desire to get the better of the argument, were led to make the dubious assertion that the CPY had recognized the existence of a Macedonian nationality in the 1920s [85] (a claim which was later admitted to be exaggerated). The Bulgarians claimed that IMRO-United had advocated the creation of an independent Macedonian nation in 1934,[86] neglecting to explain that this was a step taken on the deathbed of that ill-fated organization, and never fully accepted by the Bulgarian Party.

The arguments between the Bulgarians and the Yugoslavs over the origins of the Macedonian nationality quickly spread to many other issues, including the attitude of the socialist movement toward Macedonian nationalism,[87] the influence of Bulgarian on the Macedonian language,[88] the

[83] Mitro H. Vasilev, *Majska Manifest i deklaracijata na VMRO (obedinena)*, *passim*.

[84] *Pirinsko Delo,* June 6, 1949.

[85] The assertion has been difficult to retract since it was made by Tito himself at the Fifth Party Congress. In his speech on the prewar history of the Party, he claimed that the Macedonians were recognized as a distinct nationality at the Third Party Conference of December, 1923. *V kongres,* p. 28. No documents on the conference support this position, however.

[86] *Pirinsko Delo,* June 6, 1949. The Yugoslavs claimed that the Bulgarians first recognized the existence of the Macedonian nationality shortly before World War II. Mojsov, *Bugarska Radnička Partija,* p. 50.

[87] See the elaborate critique of Bulgarian socialists given by Lazar Mojsov. For the Bulgarian view, see *Otochestven Front,* Aug. 1, 1948, and *Rabotnichesko Delo,* Aug. 3, 1948. Mojsov is able to talk about the view of the Bulgarian Narrows toward Macedonia without mentioning either Glavinov or the views of the Bulgarians given at the meetings of the Balkan socialist parties before the Balkan Wars.

[88] For various polemics on the question of the Macedonian language, see K. Mirchev, *Za Makedonskiia literaturan ezik; Rabotnichesko Delo,* Oct. 9, 1948, and May 7, 1949; and the work by Traikov. Some of these attacks were summarized and rebutted in the Macedonian volume by Blaže Koneski, *Po povod najnoviot napad na našiot jazik.*

contribution of Bulgaria to the Macedonian national movement,[89] and the national loyalties of the leadership of the Macedonian Communist Party.[90]

The immediate objective of both sides in these polemics was to sew the seeds of doubt in the minds of the Macedonians over the sincerity of the opposing camp in supporting the Macedonian national movement. The real hope of the Bulgarians, meanwhile, was to awaken the Macedonians to their Bulgarian ties and to prove that the Macedonian national movement was an offshoot of the Bulgarian struggle for independence. The leadership of the MPR was intent on demonstrating that Macedonian nationalism had developed *parallel* to the national awakening of the other Balkan peoples, but had been stifled by the pretensions of the stronger Balkan nationalities, including the Bulgarians, to Macedonia.

Both the Macedonians and the Bulgarians were guilty of distorting the facts to serve their own purposes. But the Macedonians made a much greater effort to prove their case through the device of issuing scholarly works on Macedonian history. This left the Macedonians vulnerable, if only because they tried to defend their claims in detail. The attempt to discredit Bulgarian socialists was especially questionable, not only because it did not give a balanced picture of the Bulgarian socialist position, but because by implication the attack cast doubt on the motives of *all* socialists in Macedonia—Serbs, Bulgarians, and Macedonians alike. None had shown any lasting enthusiasm for the idea of a Macedonian nationality; among all there had been the tendency to think of the Macedonian question in terms of the larger problem of ending conflict among the Balkan powers. At the same time that they were directly or indirectly denigrating the socialists, the Macedonian Communists were placing nationalists such as Goce Delčev on a pedestal as national heroes. By implication this elevated the bourgeois nationalists of the nineteenth-century IMRO movement to a higher and more exalted position in Macedonia's past than the socialists, an anomalous view for a Communist, but the logical outcome of placing nationalism above ideological considerations, as had evidently taken place in the debate over Macedonia.

[89] For a good statement of the Bulgarian position, see K'osev, *Makedonskiiat vupros*, p. 35.

[90] For an attack on Koliševski as a police spy of the Serbs, see *Rabotnichesko Delo*, March 24, 1950, p. 4. The main attack on the Macedonian leadership came in the polemic by Peco Traikov, *Natsionalizmut na skopskite rukovoditelie.*

The real victim of the polemics between the Bulgarians and the Macedonians of the MPR was the Macedonian national movement itself. The Macedonian nation was still young and in a formative stage. In the process of gaining self-awareness as a nationality, the Macedonians had drawn on many cultural traditions from the Balkans, and were hastened down the path of national development by events over which they had very little control. But in the controversy with the Bulgarians, the Macedonian Communists insisted on dating the birth of Macedonian consciousness as a nationality from the nineteenth century, representing the phenomenon as a completely indigenous development taking place against the opposition of the surrounding Balkan states. In particular, all references to Bulgarian influence on Macedonia's national development were made the object of criticism.

Very quickly, the dispute with the Bulgarians and the remaining members of the Cominform led to a campaign to rewrite Macedonian history. The first move in establishing a new line for the Macedonian historians was taken in 1949, and was aimed at placing more emphasis on the role of the Yugoslav Party in Macedonian national development.[91] This policy might actually have encouraged the Macedonians to recognize the importance of contemporary developments in the emergence of a Macedonian national consciousness, but the effect of the change was overshadowed by a decision to launch a frontal attack against all Bulgarian influences in Macedonian historiography. The tone of this campaign was set by a harsh polemic first appearing in 1949 [92] attacking the work of Macedonian historians since the war for exaggerating the role of the Bulgarians in the Macedonian national movement. The author complained as follows:

Some of our people cannot understand correctly the activity of Kuzman Šapkarev in publishing textbooks, his struggle for the Macedonian language, and are suspicious of the national character of our entire national liberation (*prerodbeničko*) movement simply because Šapkarov or someone else in the movement was not clearly, definitely, and to the last degree nationally "in-

[91] The line was first laid down by Koliševski at the First Congress of the Communist Party of Macedonia. *I kongres na Komunističkata partija na Makedonija*, pp. 13–90. On the basis of his report there appeared an article in the journal *Komunist* on Macedonian national history by Video Smilevski, "Osvrt na razvoj Makedonskog nacionalnog pitanja," No. 1 (Jan., 1950), pp. 81–116.

[92] Kiro Miljovski, *Za nekon prašanje od rabota nad našata nacionalna istorija*.

clined," because some of them felt "now a Macedonian, now a Bulgarian." In the same fashion, some people fall into helplessness, suspicious of the Macedonian character of the national liberation movement in Goce's time simply because Goce Delčev wrote in Bulgarian, because he didn't say definitely that Macedonia is one nation and Bulgaria another.[93]

The article ended with an unprecedented order to the Macedonian historians on their style of writing, proscribing the use of certain language when dealing with the national history of Macedonia. Thus it was deemed impermissible to speak about "independent Macedonia in a Balkan federation," which was labeled as "nonsense" and "a confusion of contradictory terms of independence and federation." The phrase "spiritual slavery" was ruled out as a Bulgarian term used to describe the pre-Exarch period; reference to "Macedonian Supremists" (Macedonian members of the Supreme Committee) was forbidden, since only Bulgarians belonged to the committee, and so forth.

The effort to put Macedonian history in a strait jacket must have provoked hostile feelings among intellectual circles in the MPR. It was not easy to desert the Macedonian Party leadership for the Bulgarians, however, and out of loyalty and perhaps sometimes fear, the Macedonian nationalists kept their unity in the face of the Cominform attack and the efforts of the Bulgarians to appeal to old ties.

Some idea of the impact of the Cominform campaign against Macedonia can be gained from data published on the number of persons purged from the CPY for Cominform sympathies. In Macedonia, the ratio of those expelled from the Party to the total Party membership of the region was less than in any republic that published figures.[94] There were no defections from the top echelons of the Party, and the only government-controlled organization penetrated by the Cominform was the trade unions, whose leadership in Macedonia sided in a block with the Cominform. (Here, national considerations may have been important, for the leader of the group was a Turk, and the Turkish minority was in a difficult position in Macedonia at this time.) [95] The only person of political importance in

[93] *Ibid.,* p. 8.

[94] The ratio of expulsions to total Party membership in Macedonia was thirty-one to one. *Vtori kongres na Sojuzot na Komunistita na Makedonija,* p. 3. For expulsions from the other republics, see Chapter 3.

[95] Remzi Ismail was the leader of this group. The position of the Turks is described below. Turkish national feelings were only part of the explanation for the

Macedonia who was associated with the Cominform was Bane Andrejev, who had been Party secretary in Macedonia for a brief period during the war and had shown some partiality for the Bulgarian approach to the national question. Despite the fact that he supported the Yugoslav position on the Macedonian question after the dispute with the Cominform broke out, Andrejev was arrested in 1950. At the time he was occupying only a minor post in the Macedonian government.[96]

Figures on Cominform sympathizers in the Party do not necessarily tell the whole story. It is possible that the lower level of expulsions for Cominform sympathies in Macedonia was the result of a deliberate policy of being lenient on wavering elements in the Party in Macedonia, or the consequence of a careful weeding out of all suspect elements long before the Cominform attack. Other imponderables arise in assessing the effect of the Cominform campaign on Macedonia, the greatest of these being the reaction of the mass of the Macedonian people in this situation. The absence of any overt protests against the regime in Skoplje is not in itself convincing proof that the Macedonians were behind their government. An indication of this was provided by the Yugoslav elections of 1953, when experimentation with a more liberal voting system led to a show of un-expected opposition to the regime in Macedonia. In several Macedonian districts two candidates succeeded in being nominated for the same office

defection from the ranks of the unions, however, for many involved were Macedonians. For reference to the Ismail case, see *Rabotnichesko Delo,* March 24, 1950; *Pirinsko Delo,* March 27, 1949; and the speech of Dimitar Aleksievski, the successor to Ismail as head of the unions, at the Second Congress of the Mace-donian Unions, *Nova Makedonia,* May 10, 1949. Aleksievski implicated, in addition to Ismail, Sotir Tačevski, Metodie Avramovski, Vladimir Salabov, Blagoja Arizankov, Angelo Petrovski, Strahil Trajkovski, and Koce Zlatev, all of whom seem to have been associates of Ismail. In addition, Bulgarian sources reported the following as arrested: Lazo Sokolov, who had been a member of the Action Committee and a signer of the Objection to the Manifesto of the Main Command; Pavel Šatev, an old Macedonian revolutionary who was for a short time minister of justice after the war, and who was released after a short period of detention; Mire Anastasov, who had been arrested before the war for Com-munist activities and served in the foreign service and the Macedonian Ministry of Labor, and others. *Pirinsko Delo,* Aug. 21, 1949. The Macedonian poet, Venko Markovski, was reportedly incarcerated at about this time for views hostile to the regime.

[96] According to information supplied the author by the Institute for National History in Skoplje.

(Macedonia was the only part of Yugoslavia where such a thing occurred). In the campaign that followed, the contestants began to appeal, among other things, to national feelings, necessitating the removal of the nonofficial candidates from the ballot.[97]

Still there is reason to believe that, as the dispute between Yugoslavia and the Cominform dragged on, the Macedonians were less and less attracted to the propaganda hostile to Yugoslavia. There were two moments when the Cominform was moderately effective in penetrating into the ranks of the Macedonian nationalists: immediately after the dispute broke out in 1948, and late in 1949 and early 1950, when the idea gained acceptance that an all-out attack from the East was imminent, and something like panic seized certain groups and individuals in the Yugoslav Party (Bane Andrejev was the victim of this momentary hysteria). But the over-all effect of the struggle with the Cominform was undoubtedly to encourage many Macedonians to take a more favorable view of the Yugoslav federation than they had held earlier. For the threat of Soviet domination acted to draw the Macedonians closer to the rest of the Yugoslavs; then, as the danger receded, the Macedonians found themselves bound to Yugoslavia by new political sympathies originating in the widespread preference for the new Titoist reforms over the harsh forms of Communism still practiced in Bulgaria and other Communist nations.

If this interpretation of Macedonian sentiment is correct, the dispute with the Cominform accomplished what the most strenuous efforts of the Communists and the prewar Yugoslav regime, each in its own way, had failed to achieve: giving the bulk of the Macedonians a reason for wishing to preserve the Yugoslav state. Although this did not eliminate the problem of relations between Macedonia and the rest of Yugoslavia, it did at least take the sharp edge off the Macedonian question, relieving the Yugoslav federation of the burden of controlling a completely disaffected element in its midst.

This milestone in the development of relations between Macedonia and the rest of Yugoslavia was realized at the same time that the Yugoslav

[97] For an account of the 1953 elections, see Thomas T. Hammond, "Yugoslav Elections: Democracy in Small Doses," *Political Science Quarterly*, LXX (March, 1955), 57–74. Kofos, *Nationalism and Communism in Macedonia*, p. 193, takes the position that the situation in Macedonia was grave and that the Yugoslav Communists were hard-pressed by the Cominform attack.

government was working toward a solution of many of the problems which had made Macedonia the focus of international disputes in the Balkans. The conflict with Greece was finally resolved in 1952 when the Yugoslavs agreed to accept the position that the Aegean Slavs should be content with minority status. In the mid-1950s relations with Bulgaria were normalized and polemics over the Macedonian question officially ceased, although sniping between Skoplje and Sofia continued over the nature of the Macedonian language and other issues relating to the role of the Bulgarians in Macedonia.[98] The Pirin district was administered as an integral part of Bulgaria; occasionally the Bulgarian government would pay lip-service to the Macedonian character of the region, but in the 1960s even this pretense was discarded.[99]

These steps contributed to stability in the Balkans but were not entirely welcome to the Communists in the MPR. Rapprochement with the Greeks and permanent renunciation of Macedonian unification were especially difficult to accept, and reports in Macedonian newspapers concerning the defense pact signed between Yugoslavia and Greece in 1953 differed in certain minor respects from the official accounts issued in Belgrade.[100] By this time, however, the danger among the Macedonian Communists of defection from the Yugoslav Party was remote. The Macedonians' distrust of the Greeks and dislike of the settlement of the problem of the Slav minority in Greece remained a source of friction in relations between Greece and Yugoslavia in the years that followed, for the Greek government was loath to take the step of recognizing the existence of a Macedonian minority on Greek soil, while the Macedonians from time to time

[98] For example, see the brief furor raised in 1958 over the remarks of Professor Emil Georgijev at the Congress of Slavists in Moscow, which the Macedonians intepreted as an assertion that the Macedonian language did not exist. See *Borba,* Sept. 12, 1958. As part of this flare-up, the Yugoslavs began to suggest that Bulgaria, in contrast to her propaganda at the time of the Cominform campaign, was taking the position that the Macedonians were Bulgarian. For this view, see *Politika,* Sept. 21, 1958, and *Borba,* Sept. 24, 1958. For a more recent complaint by the Yugoslavs over the anti-Macedonian bias of Bulgarian scholars, this time over the role of the Bulgarians in liberating Skoplje, see the New York *Times,* April 3, 1964.

[99] Official Bulgarian statistics published since the war give no figure for the number of Macedonians recorded by the 1946 census. The 1956 census recorded 187,789 Macedonians, while the 1965 census indicated that only 8,750 persons had given their nationality as Macedonian. *Nova Makedonija,* Feb. 6, 1967, p. 3.

[100] *Nova Makedonija,* March 24, 1953, p. 2.

engaged in propaganda activities among Greek nationals crossing the border into Yugoslavia. On at least two occasions (1963 and 1967) free transit of local inhabitants across the Yugoslav-Greek border was suspended: in the first instance, owing to friction over Macedonian nationalist propaganda; in the second case, because of the hostility toward the Yugoslav government of the Greek military leadership that seized power in May of 1967.[101]

Within Macedonia, the immediate postwar period was a time of nation-building which saw the CPY engaged in the task of creating national institutions, seeking to maintain harmony among the peoples of Macedonia, and pressing forward with economic development. Problems in each of these areas were as important for the development of the national question as the dramatic events taking place in the realm of foreign policy.

There is little question that, with Communist encouragement, nationalism in Macedonia grew rapidly in the postwar period. The success of the Macedonians in affirming a distinct national personality and developing authentic national institutions is more difficult to assess. While the Yugoslav Communists went to great lengths to encourage Macedonian national sentiment, they also had strong ideas concerning the direction in which nationalism in Macedonia was to develop. Moreover, Macedonia was too poor and too dependent on Belgrade to permit real freedom of action in the task of nation-building. The growth of the Macedonian nation was not therefore a spontaneous process, in which local Macedonian sentiment was the decisive factor, but was instead a mixture of genuinely popular reforms with politically motivated decisions reflecting the interests, both ideological and national, of the Yugoslav Communist Party.

That this could result in anomalies in the development of nationalism in Macedonia was illustrated by the tactics used to combat Bulgarian influences in the MPR. This campaign fitted into the need of the Macedonian national movement to assert its equality with the other Slavic nationalities of the Balkans, but at the same time it was clear that Belgrade viewed the move as an indispensable step toward securing the region against outside influences. The policy in respect to Bulgaria's past role in Macedonia was maintained with very little change after the dispute with the Cominform had subsided. Only in 1959 did Lazar Koliševski call for

[101] New York *Times,* May 16, 1967.

a less dogmatic view toward Macedonian history,[102] but even after this time (to continue the story up to the mid-1960s) Macedonia did not make much progress in coming to terms with its Bulgarian heritage.

The introduction of a literary Macedonian language was more successful in winning the allegiance of the Macedonians to the MPR than the experiments in rewriting history, although implementing the reform was not a simple matter. The Macedonians did not speak either Serbian or Bulgarian, but neither did they have one manner of speech of their own which could be called Macedonian.[103] It was necessary for the new regime in Macedonia to pick one of several alternative dialects; that of southwest Macedonia was finally chosen, presumably because it bore least resemblance to either Serbo-Croatian or Bulgarian.[104] There were very few examples of written Macedonian on which to base the new language, and even after the language was developed [105] the formidable task remained of teaching it to the Macedonians, all of whom were of course accustomed to writing in either Serbo-Croatian or Bulgarian. Notwithstanding these difficulties, use of the language spread rapidly. By the mid-1950s, one trained observer was of the opinion that Macedonian had acquired widespread acceptance among the people of the MPR.[106] How quickly the

[102] In *Istorija, stvarnost, aspiracii*, also published in English under the title *Macedonian National Question*. Koliševski criticized those who wished to "overemphasize our particular characteristics, to ignore any common qualities only because the other side was making use of such common qualities." His whole thesis remained centered around the earlier claim that the Macedonian language and nationality were developing rapidly in the nineteenth century.

[103] For a concise summary of the similarities of the Macedonian dialects to Serbo-Croatian and Bulgarian, see Horace G. Lunt, "A Survey of Macedonian Literature," *Harvard Slavic Studies*, I (1963), 365.

[104] For a Yugoslav account of how the dialect for the Macedonian literary language was chosen, see Drum Tošev, "Die mazedonische Schriftsprache," *Südost Forschungen*, XV (1956), 491–503. Elisabeth Barker, p. 106, suggests that the dialect of the northern part of Macedonia around Skoplje and Tetovo was originally chosen by the Yugoslavs because of its resemblance to Serbo-Croatian but later dropped because of resistance by the Macedonians. The same story also appeared in Mihailov [Macedonius], p. 34. The author has been unable to find evidence to support this contention.

[105] By the spring of 1945 the basic problems of the grammar had been solved and incorporated into law. A grammar was published in 1950 and a book on orthography in 1951. The first volume of a two-volume dictionary appeared in 1961.

[106] Horace Lunt remarked on the "almost incredible fact that, by the time the *Macedonian Orthography* had appeared in March, 1951, the language had achieved

language was mastered by the population, and how rapidly its use spread from public documents and the press to private correspondence, are more difficult to judge. By the 1960s, however, it was possible to encounter functionaries in the lower echelons of the administration in Macedonia who either could not, or would not, speak Serbo-Croatian.

Political considerations were not entirely lacking in the development of the Macedonian language. In expanding the meager vocabulary on which the written language was based, words were borrowed from Serbo-Croatian, from Russian, and from other languages, but seldom from Bulgarian. Thus the language served as an instrument for reducing Bulgarian cultural influences in Macedonia and, to some degree at least, as a means for familiarizing the Macedonians with the technical and professional vocabulary employed in the rest of Yugoslavia.

Despite concessions made to Macedonian national feeling at the end of the war over the boundary question and certain other matters, the MPR also labored under political and economic handicaps in asserting itself within the Yugoslav federal system. At first, Macedonia did not enjoy a completely equal position with the remaining republics. Until 1952, the Macedonians were not represented in the Politburo of the CPY, and their participation in other Party bodies, and in the government, was somewhat less than one would expect, using as a measure Macedonia's share of the total Yugoslav population.[107] Contrary to the widely held view that Macedonia was developing industry at a rapid pace, economic growth in the Macedonian republic was not as impressive after the war as in the rest of Yugoslavia. Between 1947 and 1956, Macedonia experienced the lowest rate of economic growth of the three underdeveloped republics (Macedonia, Bosnia-Hercegovina, and Montenegro).[108] In

---

a remarkable uniformity and almost universal acceptance." Lunt, *Harvard Slavic Studies*, p. 372. For Lunt's views on the language, see also his *Grammar of the Macedonian Literary Language*.

[107] See Appendix C, which suggests that the Macedonians were slightly under-represented in the governments from 1945 to 1949. This is not true of governments after that time; nor could one say that Macedonians had less than their fair share in the Central Committee of the CPY at any time.

[108] For reference to the data on which these conclusions, and those immediately following, are based, see the discussion of the development of underdeveloped regions in Chapter 6. A useful summary of the economic development of Macedonia during the First Five-Year Plan, which gives a balanced view of the difficulties as well as the successes of the MPR, is *Industrijata vo NR Makedonija*.

this same period she received less investment per capita than any other republic with the exception of Serbia, although her stock of capital goods per capita remained the lowest in the country.

This did not necessarily mean that Macedonia was the object of conscious discrimination by the federal government. Many factors, among them the exposed strategic position of Macedonia during the dispute with the Cominform bloc and the absence of opportunities for profitable investments, contributed to the region's lack of rapid economic progress. On the other hand, Macedonia simply was not able to lay claim to federal funds with the success of other republics. This is clear, for example, when the inflated grants-in-aid which Montenegro received for raising her social standard are compared with the financial assistance which Macedonia received for the same purpose.[109]

During the Second Five-Year Plan, Macedonia received a greater share of the economic aid distributed to the republics, and improved her representation in Party and government organs in Belgrade. Most of the anomalies in the national development of the MPR were eliminated or reduced, and Macedonia became a full-fledged participant in the affairs of the Yugoslav federation. Certainly, by the end of the 1950s, it was not possible to point to any obvious problem, or issue, which singled out Macedonia as an area of special concern for the Yugoslav Party in the conduct of national relations.

Meanwhile, the Macedonian Communists faced considerable difficulties in the immediate postwar years in maintaining harmonious relations among the national groups situated within the boundaries of the republic. This problem, in turn, involved two distinct issues: developing a consensus among the Slav Macedonians over the question of nationality; and overcoming the hostility and suspicion of the minority population toward Yugoslavia generally, and the Communists in particular.

As far as the Slavs were concerned, the recognition of a Macedonian nationality raised the possibility of a new form of discrimination against those persons who preferred to retain their old national ties. Perhaps the Bulgarian element in Macedonia was content to be known as Macedonians, but the fact remained that there was no real choice in the matter. Serbian schools existed for the families of Serbian officials or others whose work brought them to Macedonia, as well as in villages

[109] See Chapter 6.

where Serbian colonists resided, but they were not available for those indigenous to the area who might feel themselves more Serbian than Macedonian.

Macedonian nationalism could not in all fairness be viewed as an alien imposition on the Slavs of the Macedonian People's Republic, regardless of the sentimental or political ties of individuals with either Bulgaria or Serbia. The minorities, on the other hand, were clearly unhappy with their lot, despite the fact that large-scale efforts were made to meet their educational and cultural needs. The origins of this problem lay in the age-old hostility which existed between the Slavs and the Albanian-Turkish element in Yugoslavia, but was also the responsibility of the Communists themselves. In Macedonia, as elsewhere in Yugoslavia, questions of race and politics unavoidably became mixed during and after the war, and the strong anti-Communist feelings of the minorities, as well as their alleged loyalty to foreign powers, made them subject to greater political persecution than the Slavs.

For several years after the war it was the Turkish minority which was under a cloud of suspicion, because of the friendship between Turkey and the West. In January, 1948, seventeen Turks were tried as members of a group identified as "Judzel." The trial was accompanied by a great deal of publicity of the kind that could be counted on to intimidate the Turkish minority, spread by protest meetings organized in the Turkish villages.[110] The effects of this situation could be documented in the first postwar census of 1948, in which many Turks gave their nationality as Albanian. After 1953, when Yugoslavia and Turkey became allies in the Balkan pact, the Turks were granted permission to emigrate; there was an immediate exodus of Turks from Macedonia, to the embarrassment of the Macedonian officials, who attacked what they considered to be the hasty and ill-considered desire of the Turkish minority to leave Yugoslavia "while the getting was good." [111]

When the dispute with the Cominform broke out in 1948, the onus of being the suspect group in Macedonia fell upon the Albanians. In a revealing statement made by one high Party official in 1953, it was admitted

[110] Zemski odbor na Narodniot front na Makedonija, *Procesot protiv špionsko-teroristićkata organizacija "Judžel,"* and *Nova Makedonija,* Jan. 20, 21, 22, 23, 24, and 25, 1948.

[111] *Borba,* March 28, 1954, p. 2.

that many Macedonian Communists felt that the Albanians could only be dealt with "by force." [112] In the census of 1953, many Albanians gave their nationality as Turkish. As a consequence of this change of fortune for the Turks and Albanians before and after the outbreak of the dispute with the Cominform, the number of "Turks" in Macedonia grew from 95,940 in 1948 to 203,938 in 1953; [113] of the Turks in Macedonia in 1953, 32,392 gave Macedonian as their native tongue, 27,086, Albanian. (In Kossovo-Metohija at the same time, 6,041 Turks gave their native tongue as Serbo-Croatian, 7,343 as Albanian.)

A realistic assessment of Macedonian national development must recognize the many difficulties that the MPR encountered in the postwar period and the fact that, while *de jure* equality was established with the other peoples of Yugoslavia after the war, *de facto* equality—in political representation in Belgrade, or in economic assistance—was slower in coming. Undoubtedly there was just a trace of the old suspicion of the Macedonians in Belgrade, enough to slow up the process of development, in the initial stages, in comparison with the other republics in Yugoslavia. Using the conditions that prevailed in prewar Macedonia as a standard, on the other hand, one can see that the progress made by Macedonia was impressive—a credit to the Communists' desire to overcome the inequalities which prevailed among the nationalities in prewar Yugoslavia.

On the whole, it has been difficult for outsiders to assess the strength of Macedonian nationalism and predict its future development. In the late 1940s the strident nationalism of Macedonian Communism left a deep impression on Western observers. As a result it was easy to overlook the dependency of the MPR on Belgrade and the extent to which Macedonian nationalism was being shaped by Yugoslav national interests. At the same time it was often not appreciated that the Macedonian Communists after 1945 were less apt, on the whole, to disobey the Yugoslav Party's commands than, say, the leadership of the Croatian or Slovenian Party. This fact certainly could not be attributed to a lack of national feeling among the Macedonian Party members. On the contrary, one can sense in the Macedonian attitude (just as in the attitude of the local spokesmen on the minority question in Yugoslavia) a reluc-

[112] Crvenkovski, p. 653.
[113] See Appendix A.

tance to pursue certain lines of thought too far, for fear that they might open a veritable Pandora's box, or bring a swift and harsh reaction from Belgrade. Thus, to cite an example which will figure in the discussion later, it was possible for Slovenian Communists to speak of "secession" for Slovenia without apparently provoking severe disciplinary action from the Yugoslav Party. One is justified in wondering if this lenient attitude would prevail if the Macedonian Communists were to make a similar claim.

Also, some consideration must be given to the Bulgarian ties of many Macedonians, especially those in the eastern half of the MPR. Clearly the MPR had difficulty in coming to grips with this problem. In the 1950s and early 1960s progress was made in normalizing relations between Bulgaria and the MPR, but by and large it remained true that Bulgarian influences on Macedonia's national development were considered in a consistently negative light. Perhaps this anti-Bulgarian attitude served a useful purpose in the early stages of nation-building in Macedonia, but with the Macedonian national personality firmly established such a policy might well have appeared to many Macedonians as a concession to Belgrade, rather than in the best interests of the Macedonians themselves.

Finally, Macedonian national ambitions in the Balkans worked to keep the national question alive. As long as the Balkan powers supported the status quo, Macedonian aspirations for unity were not likely to become a political or diplomatic problem. But from the point of view of the Macedonians the issue was still very much alive, and could be used to incite national feeling in the MPR against Belgrade if national relations in Yugoslavia experienced a general deterioration.

5

Titoism and the National Question

WHEN the Yugoslav Communist Party broke with the Soviet Union in 1948, Stalinist totalitarianism was the only recognized model of a Communist state. Since seizing power during the war, the Yugoslav Communists had been moving steadily toward the introduction of this system of rule, a process which was actually speeded up by the events of 1948. There is little doubt that the Yugoslav Communists did not initially anticipate any reform of the Stalinist system as a result of their quarrel with the Soviet Union, but rather expected, in the course of time, to be recognized by the bloc as an orthodox, ultrarevolutionary regime whose institutions would be above reproach even in Soviet eyes.

In practice the Yugoslav Communists were able to sustain the Stalinist system about a year after the dispute began. As a result of the intensification of bureaucratic controls, the introduction of collectivization, and other Stalinist measures, the country was brought to the verge of economic collapse. The fear of military intervention after 1949 forced the Yugoslav Communists to recognize that, as a result of Stalinist practices, the morale of the people had been seriously weakened and defense efforts placed in jeopardy. For these reasons, and in order to speed a rapprochement with the West, the Yugoslav Communists began to discard the harsh form of rule which they had adopted in imitation of the Soviet Union, decentralizing the economy, limiting the power of the secret police, and opening up Yugoslavia to the West. In place of Stalinism there emerged a unique Yugoslav form of socialism, more authoritarian than totalitarian, which soon became known in the West as Titoism.

The national question was greatly influenced by these changes. The Titoist system, unlike Stalinism, encouraged a frank examination of the state of national relations in Yugoslavia, and this brought in its wake a more critical attitude toward the accomplishments of the revolution in solving the national problem. At the same time, decentralization of the economy thrust new and unexpected responsibilities on regional and local organs of authority. These developments encouraged the reappearance of national feelings on many levels, especially within the Party itself. The result was the emergence of a new national question, unique because it was a combination of old national feelings and a new nationalism created through the workings of the Titoist system.

The first effects of the Titoist reforms on the national question were felt in the field of administration. As the result of a campaign to decentralize powers amassed by the federal government, the republic ministries acquired new duties, especially in the economic sphere.[1] This situation was only temporary, however. The republics soon gave up part of their economic responsibilities to the enterprises, and part to the organs of local government. As the reforms went forward, the role of all levels of government in the management of the economy was reduced, and centralized planning was replaced in part by the market-oriented decisions of the enterprises themselves.

Decentralization, in the early stages of Titoism, was not linked with the concept of increased freedom for the republics or greater rights for the nationalities. On the contrary, the theory of the reforms foresaw quite a different end: the reduction of state interference at all levels in the economy and the society. In this spirit, national relations were reexamined, and it was decided to make their further development more dependent upon the influence of the new social forces, rather than upon the actions of the state.

Thus it was that the first step away from the statist system in Yugoslavia was also marked by a change in national policy, one whose central feature was deemphasis of the federal system in effect up to that time. There was undoubtedly a feeling, in taking this step, that the time was ripe for a move toward emphasizing the unity of the Yugoslav peoples. But even more important were the great hopes held out for the new reforms in the social and economic sphere, and the expectation that the Titoist system would be more effective in harmonizing

---

[1] A series of decrees in 1950 and early 1951 took the administration of the economy out of the hands of the federal government and gave it to the republics. The new law on the social plan for 1952 took administration of the enterprises away from the state completely and gave it to the workers' councils.

national relations than the federal system by creating, in the course of time, an enlightened and responsible society unencumbered by the nationalistic prejudices of the past.

In theoretical writings which first made their appearance in 1952, the Yugoslavs began to develop this new approach by suggesting that socialist relations would soon come to have more influence in society than national ones; this in turn was linked to the effect of self-management by workers on the attitudes of individuals. Edvard Kardelj explained the process in theoretical terms in 1953 as one in which "all society's means for production are general people's property, that is, in a practical sense [the property] of *all toilers* of our country. Their maximum exploitation and advancement represents the common interest of every single toiler, for whom that collective property, in a certain sense, is at the same time his personal property. This is the new factor which creates a socialist community of a new type in which language and national culture become a secondary factor." [2]

This highly abstract formulation of national relations of course had its practical side. In down-to-earth terms, the Yugoslavs hoped to create the conditions under which social change and economic progress would lead to a mixing of the nationalities and a lessening of their parochial national outlooks (something along the lines of the American experience), rather than continuing to rely indefinitely on the revolutionary formulas and techniques of political indoctrination employed as a means of transforming national attitudes in the immediate postwar years.

The influence of this new approach toward the national question was evident in the constitutional law of 1953, which amended the Stalinist constitution of 1946 so completely as to be in effect a new constitution. The role of the federal system was deemphasized, chiefly by eliminating the sweeping promises of the 1946 constitution in respect to the rights of the republics.[3] The right of self-determination was no longer mentioned in the new constitutional law, while sovereignty was ascribed to the republics only in an indirect fashion. The Chamber of Nationalities, which during its lifetime had failed to exer-

[2] Kardelj, *O osnovama društvenog i političkog uredjenja FNRJ*, pp. 51–52.

[3] *Novi ustav; Ustavni zakon od 13–1–1953 i ustav od 31–1–1946 (delovi koji nisu ukinuti).*

cise any initiative on behalf of the republics, was merged with the National Assembly, where it could still, under certain conditions, constitute itself as an independent body with the right to debate certain types of acts touching on matters of direct concern to the republics.[4] In place of the Chamber of Nationalities, a new second house was formed, the Council of Producers, intended as a place for the representation of the working people of Yugoslavia.

These changes did not markedly affect the operation of the federal system, and certainly did not deprive the republics of any important rights. On the contrary, it was characteristic of the new period that, as some of the more dogmatic aspects of the Stalinist federal theory were abandoned, the substantive rights of the republics tended to grow, often through informal practices not recognized in the constitution. The same could be said in respect to the rights enjoyed by the minorities. Thus, for example, there grew up the practice of providing for the representation of the republics in the cabinet, or Federal Executive Committee, and in the subcommittees of the FEC.[5] Attempts (admittedly not very successful) were made to revive the legislative activity of the republics and

[4] The republic assemblies, under the new system, chose deputies to the National Assembly (ten deputies per republic). This "national" representation was obliged to convene as a separate house—the Chamber of Nationalities—when a change of the constitution or the social plan had been brought before the National Assembly. They would also meet to discuss general laws proposed for adoption by the legislature; if their approval was not forthcoming the law could not come up for ratification in the National Assembly. The Chamber of Nationalities could also meet separately to discuss laws dealing with the relations between the Union and the republics if six of its deputies from one republic so requested. The rights of the Council of Nationalities were somewhat altered in 1954. The Council would still meet separately in the instances cited above, but doing so was no longer made obligatory. The procedure by which the Council might meet when considering a law which touched on the relations between the Union and the republics was considerably simplified. See "Zakon o izmeni člana 45, 46, 47, 48 i 51 ustavnog zakona o osnovama društvenog i političkog uredjenja FNRJ i saveznim organima vlasti," *Službeni List FNRJ,* No. 13, 1954, p. 257.

[5] Besides having a minimum of one member plus the republic president as an ex-officio member of the Federal Executive Committee under the provisions of the constitutional law of 1953, the presidents of the republic Executive Committees were members of the Committee for the Prospective Social Plan, while the Committee for Education and Culture and the Committee for Welfare and Health had representatives of the republic Executive Committees responsible for these particular fields.

halt the practice of the federal assembly of adopting "general" and "basic" laws in such detail that the republics could not bring their own supplementary legislation, a practice that had been foreseen in the 1946 constitution.[6] Efforts were also made to increase representation of the minorities in the party,[7] and there was a franker discussion of the national feelings of the minorities, a discussion which did not hide the fact that animosities continued to exist between the Yugoslavs and the minority population in many regions.[8]

The changes in national policy which accompanied the introduction of the Titoist system in Yugoslavia were not therefore in practice harmful to the interests of the individual nationalities. In place of sweeping grants of certain abstract rights such as self-determination, the republics received small, but tangible, benefits which assured them some voice in making policy and greater attention to their local needs. Although the Party leadership was clearly impatient with the national sensitivities of the Yugoslavs, what was abandoned or modified was in a large part the most negative or dogmatic elements of the national policy of the Stalinist period, above all the sacrosanct nature of the federal system embodied in the theory of republic sovereignty.

This franker attitude toward the national question seemed well timed, following a period of steady improvement in national relations in Yugoslavia capped by the united resistance of the Yugoslav peoples against the Cominform attack. In directing their attention to the effects of social change on national attitudes, the Yugoslav Communists were coming face to face with a crucial but previously neglected aspect of the national question in Communist nations which was of great concern to all multinational states undergoing the process of modernization. In fact, the Yugoslavs now became conscious that what they sought to accomplish in the field of national relations could serve as a model

[6] In the years 1955–57, the republics passed a number of laws in the fields of education, culture, health, and welfare. Soon thereafter, however, the federal government passed basic and general laws in these areas which tended to supersede the republic legislation.

[7] See articles cited below on the complaints that the minorities were underrepresented in the Party.

[8] For example, Krste Crvenkovski, "Treba se upornije i sistematskije boriti za sprovodjenje pisma CK SKJ u delo," *Komunist*, No. 9 (Sept., 1953), pp. 653–59.

for the newly developing nations of Africa and Asia with problems similar to their own.

But these auspicious circumstances went for nought. Not only did the national question stubbornly persist, but with the introduction of the Titoist reforms, national relations unexpectedly took a turn for the worse.

The fact that a relaxation of totalitarian controls could lead to an increase in national feeling was evident in the Party when, in the spring of 1953, it became necessary to criticize Communists for falling victim to nationalistic emotions.[9] Manifestations of nationalism within Party ranks continued to plague the Communist leadership in the years to follow; the problem will be examined later in the chapter. At the same time, nationalistic behavior, or unacceptable national attitudes, became obvious in other groups as well.

This was especially true among artists and intellectuals. The relaxation of tight ideological controls made it possible for the intellectuals to express their national attitudes more forcefully, while the demise of Marxist and Communist subjects in the theater and other cultural fields revived national themes in the arts. The problem received wide attention in 1953, when a broad attack was launched against the appearance of romantic national works on the stage, while cultural associations, especially among the minorities, were criticized for their exclusive concern with narrow national themes.[10] The campaign was later extended to the field of education; Kardelj, speaking to the Sixth Plenum of the Party which convened in 1956 to study the problem of the youth in Yugoslavia, complained that the textbooks used in the republics dealt with history "in the spirit of national romanticism, foreign to Marxism and socialist internationalism," and charged that the existing texts in the country's schools were a "nourishment for nationalism." [11]

[9] "Svim organizacijama Saveza komunista Jugoslavije," *Komunist*, No. 7 (July, 1953), pp. 430–31.

[10] For a criticism of the theater in Serbia, see Mirko Tepevac, "Povodom reportoara pozorišta u Srbiji," *Komunist*, No. 10 (Oct., 1953), pp. 726–33. For the "national romantic" character of the activities of the Cultural Artistic Societies in Vojvodina, see "Jedan aspekt problematike kulturne delatnosti u Vojvodini," *Naša stvarnost*, No. 7–8 (July-Aug., 1956), p. 96.

[11] *Komunist*, No. 3–4 (1956), pp. 260–61.

Most in evidence was the growth of nationalistic attitudes among persons working in the creative arts, disturbingly enough among the youth. The problem of intemperate nationalism among the younger artists in Belgrade burst into print on several occasions: in an incident in 1953 when certain remarks of the Croatian playwright Miroslav Krleža, mildly critical of Belgrade, provoked a bitter tirade by a young Serbian poet who was enraged by what he felt to be a smugness and Germanic disdain displayed by Krleža toward the crudities of life in Serbia; [12] then a number of years later, when the young painter Milić Stanković caused a sensation by displaying a nationalist "manifesto" in defense of the Cyrillic alphabet at an exhibition of his paintings in a Belgrade gallery.[13] Tito, in a speech at Split in 1962, may well have had this latter incident in mind when he voiced concern over the attitude of the youth, remarking on how "it is simply revolting when one sees how chauvinism is beginning to spread among our youth." [14]

To the credit of the Party leadership, no attempt was made to resort to the harsh controls of the Stalinist period to stem the rising tide of nationalism that accompanied the introduction of Titoism. Instead, the Yugoslav Communists began to take a more active concern in the improvement of national relations at every level of Yugoslav society. As a result, a search began in the mid-1950s for a new concensus on the national question, arrived at through an honest, if not perhaps entirely free, discussion of national relations. Steps were also taken to bring the nationalities in closer contact with each other, especially in their cultural activities, and a campaign was organized (for the first time) to elevate the Yugoslav idea to a level of respectability which would make it an effective contender for the national loyalties of the Yugoslav peoples.

[12] For Krleža's article, see "Na grobu Petra Dobrivoica," *Svedočanstvo,* No. 1 (March 22, 1952), pp. 1–2. For the criticism of Krleža, see Marko Ristić, "Da mržnje više ne bude," *ibid.,* No. 1 (April 19, 1952), p. 5, and Oskar Davičo, "Levantinstvo: recidiv zla," *ibid.,* No. 1 (May 6, 1952), p. 8. A mimeographed protest was also circulated clandestinely around Belgrade against the offending piece. In his article, Oskar Davičo ended the debate with a vicious attack on the young man. Perhaps there was no connection, but *Svedočanstvo* ceased publication soon after this affair.

[13] For accounts of this incident, see *Beogradska Nedelja,* Feb. 25, 1962, and *Danas,* Feb. 28, 1962, pp. 3 and 9.

[14] Supplement to *Komunist,* May 10, 1962.

The course of action adopted in the 1950s gave every indication of being a landmark in the evolution of national policy after World War II. In the many attempts that had been made to solve the national question since 1918, very little headway had been made in inculcating Yugoslav feeling in the various national groups. The original ideals of the Yugoslav Committee, which had been shared by the socialists, had become a vehicle for Serbian interests in the interwar period, while the Stalinist epoch had manifested its Yugoslav nationalism largely in foreign affairs. With due consideration for the differences of time and in the temperaments of those involved, the experiment in developing Yugoslav nationalism in the mid-1950s could be compared, in its idealism and its stress on the common characteristics of the Yugoslav peoples, with the Yugoslav movement of the period before and during World War I.

However, the task of gaining support for this new approach to the national question proved more difficult than could have been anticipated. Eventually the leadership of the Party was forced to retreat, and, in the face of increasing resistance by the republics to *any* steps which would detract from the importance of the nationalities in Yugoslav life, to adopt a position toward the national question which left very little of the Yugoslav idea intact. This unexpected reversal of policy, although accompanied by many statements concerning the party's dedication to the goal of creating a new Yugoslav national spirit, was a major setback for the Party leadership. The change, further, was a personal defeat for Tito, perhaps the most serious the Yugoslav leader experienced in the field of national policy.

The obstacles which stood in the way of any frank discussion of the national question first became evident in connection with the modification of the federal system brought about by the constitutional law of 1953. To the Western mind, the mystique of the revolutionary solidarity of the sovereign nationalities enshrined in the principles of the self-determination and sovereignty of the republics was not always easy to appreciate. But in the Yugoslav case, these ideas concerning the rights of the republics filled a psychological need for recognition of national individuality, and eliminating them was not always easy. On the occasion of the discussion of the draft constitutional law, it became obvious that widespread differences existed among the constitutional lawyers in Yugoslavia over the intention of the act to eliminate references to the "sovereignty" of the republics. The debate quickly developed into a broad discussion of the federal system, in which those persons with more centralistic inclinations pushed for realism in assessing the true character of Yugoslav federalism, while those writers from the republics with a greater stake in federalism (Macedonia and Croatia) tried to defend many of the old principles concerning the sovereign status of the republics.[15] The debate ended on an inconclusive note; no one was able to apply realistic criteria to the Yugoslav system and still call it a federation,[16] while very few, out of consideration for national sensibilities, were willing to call Yugoslavia a unitary state. The vagueness of the principles finally adopted in the constitutional law, and the inability of the constitutional lawyers to agree on the essential character of Yugoslav federalism, were among the first indications of how difficult it was going to be to find new principles to replace the beliefs of an earlier period.

[15] For the debate over the federal system, see Maks Šnuderlj, "O državnosti Narodne Republike Jugoslavije," *Anali Pravnog Fakulteta u Beogradu,* I, No. 3–4 (1953), 277–86; Jovan Stefanović, "Primjena federativnog načela u saveznom ustavnom zakonu," *ibid.,* I (1953), 257–70; Evgeni Dimitrov, "Karakter federativnih odnosa u našoj zemlji," *ibid.,* pp. 277–86; Ferdo Čulinović, "Problem o višedržavnosti jugoslovenske federacije," *Zbornik Pravnog Fakulteta u Zagrebu,* V, No. 3–4 (1955), 119–33; Jovan Stefanović, *Ustavno pravo FNR Jugoslavije i komparativno* (2d ed.), I, 413–15; Radomir Lukić, "O nekim pitanjima iz oblasti teorije države i prava," *Anali Pravnog Fakulteta u Beogradu,* III (1955), 57–60; Dan Gjanković, "O federativnom karakteru naše države," *Zbornik Pravnog Fakulteta u Zagrebu,* IV (1954), 230–41.

[16] Two of the frankest discussions of the system were presented by Professor Lukić and Dan Gjanković. Gjanković was particularly blunt. He saw the republics as having little or no powers. They did not have the right to self-organization, for "the Union constitutional law describes the most minute relations between these republic organs." The division of powers carried out in the constitutional law gave the Union government the power to act on almost all questions of importance to a government, it was asserted. Gjanković strongly criticized the use of "general" and "basic" laws, pointing to the fact that the Union government had drawn up these laws in such detail that there was no need for republic legislation. Gjanković suggested that the emasculated Chamber of Nationalities still served to protect the rights of the republics, but added that since 1946 the Chamber never felt it necessary to oppose any decision of the Union Assembly, and "there is no doubt that in the future she also will not have to make use of this right." Such a critical view of the federal system did not lead Gjanković to deny the existence of federalism in Yugoslavia but rather, like Professor Lukić, to redefine federalism as a high degree of decentralization in administration.

The battle on the cultural front began with the organization of a campaign against the cultural isolation of the republics. Artists, writers, and performers were urged to exchange delegations or participate in guest performances in other republics. Newspapers were criticized for not devoting space to events taking place in other republics, and a great effort was made to point out the waste involved in the duplication of effort that was taking place in such fields as scientific research and publishing.[17] A favorite object of attack was the practice of publishing school textbooks separately, and at great expense, in each of the six republics.[18]

Against this background of criticism directed at the republics, the possibility was cautiously raised in the late 1950s that the cultures of Yugoslavia would eventually be merged into a single Yugoslav culture.[19] At the same time, steps were taken to encourage exchanges and end duplication, partly through establishing coordinating bodies in various educational, scientific, and cultural fields. In 1954 an Assembly of the Cultural Educational League of Yugoslavia (Veće kulturno-prosvetnih saveza Jugoslavije) was formed as a coordinating body among the autonomous cultural societies of the republics. In December of 1954

[17] For example, Zagorka Stoilović, "Problemi izdavačke delatnosti," *Komunist,* No. 2–3 (March-May, 1950), pp. 258–61, or Puniša Perović, "Neki problemi naše kniževnosti," *Naša Stvarnost,* No. 4 (April, 1954), p. 12.

[18] A good example of these complaints, appearing more recently, is "Školska knjiga i 'tezga,' " *Komunist,* March 16, 1963, p. 9.

[19] This idea was inherent in the arguments against the isolation of the republics and the creation of new socialist relations. It gained widespread notice with Kardelj's theoretical work on the national question which, while emphasizing the importance of republic cultures, introduced the idea of a new form of loyalty, *Jugoslovenstvo.* With this encouragement, one group of cultural workers and writers became advocates of a Yugoslav culture. Tito, in a cautious way, showed support for this view, expressing the belief that "our cultural life should develop in a Yugoslav framework," and arguing that, while each republic should have its own culture, there could not be separate socialist cultures for each republic. Milan Ranković, "Zapažanja o integraciji Jugoslovenske kulture," *Socijalizm,* No. 6 (1962), p. 126, and *Komunist,* Jan. 14, 1963, p. 3. No one advocated the simple elimination of the republic cultures by the Yugoslav culture; always in an effort to avoid offending local sensibilities, the argument was put in a much more roundabout fashion. The opposition to this view is described below. For a strong statement of the view that there should be one Yugoslav culture, see Radomir Lukić, "O jedinstvu Jugoslovenske kulture," *Književne Novine,* XIV (Nov. 2, 1962), 1.

representatives of the national cultural societies and leading literary figures from Croatia and Serbia met in Novi Sad and issued a declaration affirming that Serbian, Croatian, and Montenegrin were one language, and at the same time forming a commission to prepare a dictionary of Serbo-Croatian, which finally appeared in 1960.[20] Other joint projects were organized among the republics, and some limited forms of cooperation among scientific institutions were developed.

These actions did not impinge greatly on the cultural life of the republics. It was a much more serious matter when the Party decided to attack the problem of the isolation of national minorities from the remainder of the Yugoslavs. The cultural societies of the minorities were merged with parallel groups in the Slav population;[21] the use of Serbo-Croatian was encouraged in the minority schools;[22] and in areas of mixed population the minority schools were merged with the schools for the Slavs,[23] leaving only sections or classes within the school in which the child would be taught in his native tongue.

How successful these steps were in reducing the cultural isolation of the nationalities was debatable. For one thing, the efforts at cultural

[20] *Pravopis hrvatsko-srpskog književnog jezika.* For the Novi Sad agreement, see pp. 5–10 of this volume.

[21] The process of reorganization actually began when the Union of Cultural-Educational Societies of Vojvodina was replaced by the Cultural-Educational Community of Vojvodina (Kulturno-Prosvetna Zajednica Vojvodina), which administered the cultural activities of the autonomous province along strictly functional (not national) lines. Provincial cultural committees continued to exist for each of the minorities, but only on paper, and were finally abolished in 1957. Figures for the dissolution of the cultural societies at the local level, given above, can be found in Hadžić, ed., p. 332. The only organization in Yugoslavia today actively responsible for the over-all cultural program of a minority is the Union of Italians of Istria (Unione degli Italiani dell' Istria), located in Rijeka.

[22] Teaching of the official language now begins in the third year of primary school.

[23] Yugoslav statistics do not give the number of consolidated and separate schools. In 1951–52 there were only seven consolidated schools in Yugoslavia for Albanians. Stojković and Martić, English edition, pp. 200–1. The author was told in 1958 by a member of the Commission for Education and Culture of Kossovo-Metohija that there were 344 separate and 202 consolidated primary and secondary schools for Albanians in the *oblast*. However, see Koča Jončić, *Nacionalne manjine u Jugoslaviji,* who gives figures for minority schools in 1958–59, showing 852 primary schools for Albanians in all of Yugoslavia, considerably above the previously stated figure. The Jončić volume provides a useful review of the status of the minorities in the Titoist period.

cooperation and exchange among the republics were carried out with a good deal of caution in order to avoid offending local sensibilities. The Serbian author Dobrica Ćosić, in an article appearing in 1961, wrote with a touch of sarcasm that cooperation in the literary field was often reduced to organizing literary dinners—"one of the lowest forms of literary activity," [24] as Ćosić put it. Even the inoffensive activity of encouraging cultural exchanges could backfire, for not infrequently the appearance of guest stars from other republics would cause jealousy among local performers.[25] Some projects, such as the Yugoslav Drama Theater in Belgrade, simply did not maintain their all-Yugoslav character. In 1963, the secretary of the Macedonian Council for Culture complained that in Macedonia, partly because of the expense, cultural exchanges had dropped off, and the cultural isolation of the republic remained as great a problem as before.[26] The argument over standardizing textbooks carried on into the 1960s, with the only apparent change coming in Montenegro, which agreed to cooperate with Serbia in the publication of educational materials.[27]

The most severe setback to cultural cooperation came in the spring of 1967 when all of the important cultural organizations of Croatia signed a resolution repudiating the 1954 Novi Sad agreement on the Serbo-Croatian language and asking that a constitutional amendment be adopted to recognize Serbian and Croatian as two distinct tongues, both with the status of official languages.[28] This widely publicized incident met with a sharp rebuke from the Party and served to deepen existing differences between Serbian and Croatian intellectuals; more will be said about it later in this chapter.

The difficulties which were experienced in developing cultural cooperation were perhaps to be expected, and pointed to the need for a long-range program to overcome the opposition of the republics. In any

[24] *Borba,* Dec. 6, 1961, p. 6. For several critical discussions of cultural exchange in the literary field, see *Književne Novine,* No. 163 (Nov. 2, 1962).

[25] See the article by Draža Marković on the progress of cultural exchange in *Komunist,* March 29, 1962, p. 8.

[26] *Borba,* March 5, 1963, p. 7.

[27] The agreement between Serbia and Montenegro is discussed in more detail in Chapter 6.

[28] *Borba,* March 21, 1967, p. 1. The declaration was originally published in *Telegram* (Zagreb), March 17, 1967.

case, the idea of cooperation was not discarded but was extended to new areas when possible.[29] In one instance, a program of joint cultural activities was initiated across republic boundaries among several adjoining districts located in the region where Bosnia, Serbia, and Montenegro come together.[30]

In the case of the minorities, the effort to merge schools was strenuously resisted in certain areas. In Sombor the attempt to dissolve the cultural societies of the Hungarians met with such opposition that it had to be temporarily abandoned.[31] When the proposal was made to merge the Hungarian and Serbian schools in Zrenjanin, the Commission for Education and Culture of the local People's Committee rejected the plan on the grounds of a shortage of teachers and lack of space.[32] The merger was nevertheless approved two weeks later by the committee.[33] Complaints were also published in the local press in Subotica concerning misunderstandings that had arisen over the merger of the schools.[34] Merger plans nevertheless went ahead throughout the country, and the change was carried to completion among the schools of all the minority groups with the exception of the Italians, whose minority rights were governed by treaty between Italy and Yugoslavia.

When the attempt was made to popularize the idea of a gradual blending of the cultures of the Slav nationalities, on the other hand, the opposition viewpoint prevailed. It was the intent of the new approach

[29] Thus, in the publishing field, in addition to the Association of Publishing Enterprises formed in 1954 to coordinate the publishing efforts of the republics, cooperation has been developed between individual publishing houses, such as Prosveta, Zora, and Omladinska Knjiga from Belgrade, Zagreb, and Ljubljana, respectively. Guest performances of the republic symphony orchestras was begun in 1963. Republic cooperation in fields outside of culture has developed to a limited degree, such as between Croatia and Slovenia in developing tourism. Cooperation in the cultural field across international boundaries has been initiated to aid the minorities. Thus, agreements exist between publishing houses in Yugoslavia and Hungary for the publication of materials in Hungarian, and similar arrangements have been worked out for the Italian minority with publishing houses in Italy.

[30] These are districts along the river Lim, which have a common cultural center to which outside performers and groups are invited.

[31] *Somborske Novine,* May 25, 1956, p. 3.

[32] *Zrenjanin,* Aug. 13, 1955.

[33] *Ibid.,* Aug. 27, 1955.

[34] *Hrvatska Riječ,* March 30, 1956, p. 6.

to encourage the development of a Yugoslav culture side by side with the cultures of the republics, not to fuse the local traditions or replace them entirely. The reaction in the republics, which was strongest in the early 1960s, nevertheless revealed that many persons in the cultural field had the gravest doubts over the new policy, fearing that it would lead to Serbian cultural domination or the compulsory adoption of a new integral Yugoslav culture.

The exchange between Ćosić and the Slovenian Dušan Pirjevac in 1961 brought these feelings out into the open. Ćosić, in an interview with a Croatian reporter, was quoted as remarking that interrepublic cooperation would remain passive as long as republics existed and as long as the problem of cooperation was the subject of discussion. The manner in which these seemingly innocuous remarks were interpreted by Pirjevac offered an enlightening glimpse of the state of mind that had come to prevail in Yugoslav cultural circles:

But look: first there was put here the question about interrepublic relations being too passive. Then there is also in question Ćosić's conviction that this question will be an actual one as long as the republics exist, which could mean that we shall be too passive in interrepublic relations as long as we have republics. From this the conclusion follows logically that the existence of the republics above all is responsible for the passivity in interrepublic relations. And from this it certainly is not far to the sinful thought that this whole thing will be settled and the passivity of the republics will disappear only when there are no more republics.[35]

Pirjevac, convinced on the basis of his reasoning that the real issue raised by Ćosić was the merger of the republics, attacked Ćosić roundly for giving moral support to the cause of the "two-headed ghosts," "the unitarian integralist ghosts . . . the bearded and shaved centralists who do not know what republics are and what people are." [36]

Ćosić, in his reply, defended the need for developing a socialist type of unity among the Yugoslav peoples and denied the relevance of the problem of Serbian hegemony to his position.[37] Nevertheless the Party was forced to reiterate at every step the principle that any merging of

[35] *Borba*, Dec. 6, 1961, p. 6.
[36] *Ibid.*
[37] *Ibid.*, pp. 6–7. A rebuttal to Ćosić by Pirjevac was published in *Borba*, Dec. 14, 1961, pp. 6–7; Dec. 15, pp. 6–7; Dec. 16, pp. 6–7.

cultures would only take place as the result of the fullest development of republic, or national, traditions.[38] Even this, however, was not sufficient to quiet those who feared the appearance of integralist views toward cultural development. Eventually, as shall be recounted shortly, the party leadership was forced to reverse itself and a new position was adopted in which the forces behind Pirjevac were victorious over the Yugoslav philosophy for which Ćosić had become something of a symbol.

The field of historiography was also a testing ground for the development of a new national outlook. In 1950, at a time when the threat of an armed attack on Yugoslavia by the Cominform bloc seemed very real, the official Yugoslav Party journal had called for a reassessment of the history of Yugoslavia in order to demonstrate that the Yugoslav state was no "accident," but a long-standing aspiration of the Yugoslav peoples.[39] Several years later, when Party controls in the field of history were relaxed, this theme was picked up by historians, and works began to appear by Čulinović and others in Croatia on the events surrounding the formation of Yugoslavia in 1918,[40] while materials connected with the lives of Fran Supilo and Svetozar Pribićević were republished.[41]

Although the Party had initiated the movement for developing a Yugoslav view of history, the works that appeared in the early 1950s were not well received by Party historians. From the Communist point of view, these works were deficient because they lacked ideological content and because certain historical events, such as the union of 1918, were treated in a way that was obviously contrary to Party policy. On the other hand, the historical material which did not deal with Yugoslav

[38] In 1958, for example, the Cultural Educational Assembly devoted a session to the question of cooperation among cultural workers of the republics. The president of the assembly used this occasion to state the official view that "although in the process which is developing in Yugoslavia the structure of the nations is changed in the direction of ever-greater inter-relatedness, the independent cultural development of each nation was, and remains, the condition for cooperation and the further drawing together of our peoples." *Politika,* Jan. 21, 1958, p. 4.

[39] Rodoljub Čolaković, "Rešenje nacionalnog pitanja u Jugoslaviji," *Komunist,* No. 4–5 (July-Sept., 1950), pp. 48–87.

[40] Ferdo Čulinović, *Razvitak jugoslovenskog federalizma* and *Nacionalno pitanje u jugoslovenskim zemljama.*

[41] Fran Supilo, *Politika u Hrvatskoj;* Svetozar Pribićević, *Diktatura Kralja Aleksandra.*

themes was too nationalistic for the Party's tastes. Much of the new literature ignored revolutionary themes, such as the class struggle, to the annoyance of the Communists.

In 1956 steps were taken to correct this situation. A Party commission reviewed the activities of the historians and reached the conclusion that future works on Yugoslav history should continue to deal with the theme of Yugoslav unity, but that the manner in which this goal was pursued should be explained by a purely *Marxist* form of analysis.[42]

This new directive of the Party placed the historians in a difficult position, for it was not easy to adopt a negative attitude toward the bourgeois statesmen who had taken part in the creation of Yugoslavia, while approving the goals for which the advocates of the Yugoslav idea had labored. One effort was made to meet the Party's requirements by the Croatian historian Vaso Bogdanov. Bogdanov suggested that Yugoslavia was in the process of formation in the first half of the nineteenth century thanks to the efforts of the rising bourgeois class among the South Slavs, which was struggling to free itself from the exploitation of the provincial feudal classes. Following the reaction of 1848 within the Austro-Hungarian Empire, however, and the coming of the bourgeoisie to power, the attitude of this group became "opportunistic, conservative, and even reactionary," and the "natural, progressive current of our entire national development was halted and replaced with an opposite, reactionary, abnormal separatist direction." [43]

Bogdanov's questionable ideas received a mixed reception, however, and no firm line could be established on what was desirable, or even permissible, in analyzing the birth of the Yugoslav state and the character of national relations among the Yugoslav peoples in the interwar period.[44]

To add to the difficulties facing the Party in the field of historiography, nationally oriented scholars began to reopen controversial issues

[42] See *Komunist*, No. 3–4 (1956), p. 265.

[43] Bogdanov, *Historijska uloga društvenih klasa u rešavanju južno-slovenskog nacionalnog pitanja,* p. 66.

[44] One attempt was made by Franjo Tudjman, director of the Institute for the Study of the Workers' Movement, in Zagreb, in his work *Stvaranje socijalističke Jugoslavije.* The approach was not strictly Marxist and was favorable toward the union of 1918 and the Sporazum of 1939, thus running contrary to official policies.

from the past. While there was nothing surprising in this, the debates that quickly developed showed how easily emotions could be aroused among historians over the national issue. This was especially evident in exchanges between Serbian and Croatian historians over the responsibility of Croatia for the collapse of Yugoslavia in 1941,[45] and in a debate over the errors made by the Croatian Communist Party during the resistance.[46] In 1964, the republic institutes for research on the history of the Party created a stir when they strongly attacked a new official Party history; the Institute for the Study of the Workers' Movement in Zagreb issued a particularly blunt criticism of the history, which defied the Party line by approving the Sporazum of 1939.[47] For this

[45] The argument over the role of Croatia in the collapse of 1941 was provoked by a volume that appeared in 1960, Velimir Terzić, *Jugoslavija u aprilskom ratu 1941.* Croats interpreted Terzić's work as placing the blame on Croatia for the collapse of Yugoslav resistance to the Germans, and for suggesting that the Croatian politicians favored the separation of Croatia. See *Vjesnik* (Zagreb), July 26, 1964, pp. 6–7, and Vaso Bogdanov, *Porijeklo i ciljevi šovinističkih teza o držanju Hrvata 1941.*

[46] One article which prompted such a discussion was Jovan Marjanović, "Prilog uzučavanju jugoslovenstva u ustanku 1941," pp. 33–45. Marjanović alluded to the incident in 1941 in which the City Committee of Zagreb tried to take over from the republic leadership. For an attack on Marjanović, see the article of Ivan Ceranić in *Vjesnik* (Zagreb), Dec. 12, 1962. For other criticisms of Marjanović, see Franjo Tudjman, "Uvod u historiju socijalističke Jugoslavije," *Forum* (Zagreb), No. 2, (1963), pp. 292–352, and France Klopčić, "O nacionalnoj politici KP Jugoslavjie," *Naši Razgledi*, Jan. 27, 1962, p. 26. The debate was not restricted to the war, and a polemic also developed over the correctness of the Party's nationalities policy in the 1920s, with Marjanović taking the position that it was not correct until the 1930s, when the Party came out for union of the Yugoslav peoples.

[47] The criticism issued by the Institute also attacked the Party history for an entirely negative attitude toward the Croatian Peasant Party and for being less harsh toward the London government; for giving the impression that the national liberation struggle was not well developed in Croatia; for not granting ZAVNOH a larger role, which it was claimed by the Institute was one of a "carrier of sovereignty of Croatia in the creation of a new Yugoslav federation." A further point the Zagreb institute made which later caused the Party leadership considerable irritation was that the national liberation movements of the prewar period (here referring, apparently, to the Croatian Peasant Party and other national groups) had a progressive role to play because national exploitation harmed all classes, and because the unsolved national question represented a great obstacle to the economic, cultural, and social development of the exploited nationalities. (This of course was reminiscent of the position of Sima Marković.)

outspoken attitude, the Institute received a public reprimand from the Party.[48]

On many occasions in the late 1950s and early 1960s, the Party was impelled to criticize manifestations of nationalism among historians.[49] But the situation was confused, because the Yugoslav historians (especially in Croatia) all energetically supported the Yugoslav idea. They displayed their nationalism not by revealing doubts over the wisdom of forming a Yugoslav state but in defending what they considered slurs on the reputation of their republics, especially in regard to the role the republic had played in the defense of Yugoslav unity. To complicate matters the Party, as a result of antipathy toward everything associated with the old regime, often found it necessary to criticize the historians for "nationalism" because they expressed favorable opinions about actions taken before the war which strengthened the Yugoslav state— for example, the act of union of 1918, or the attempt to solve the Serb-Croat problem by granting autonomy to Croatia in 1939. In 1962 a historian close to the Party revived the idea that the union of 1918 was the "lesser of two evils" for the working classes of the South Slav peoples,[50] but the apparent change in attitude on this one issue did not mark any retreat by the Party from its hostility toward the prewar regime. Like the constitutional lawyers and the intellectuals engaged in cultural activities, the historians found it extremely difficult to contribute much to Yugoslav unity, either because of dissension within their own ranks, or as a result of the opposition of the Party to certain lines of research.

It was natural that Marxist theory should be drawn into the discussion over national relations at some point. As remarked earlier, the theoretical justification of Titoist national policy was first couched in terms of the proposition that socialist relations of a new type would become more important than, and perhaps eventually replace, older methods of accommodating and reconciling national differences. But Marxist-Leninist doctrine, in the narrow sense, only entered the picture in 1958 when Kardelj reissued his prewar work, *The Development of*

---

[48] *Komunist,* March 26, 1964, p. 4.

[49] See especially Tito's remarks at the Eighth Party Congress. *Osmi kongres Saveza komunista Jugoslavije,* pp. 31–33.

[50] Marjanović, "Prilog uzučavanju jugoslovenstva u ustanku 1941."

the Slovenian National Question,[51] revised and with a lengthy theoretical introduction which dealt with the position of Marxist theory toward nationalism and the national question.

The reasons which prompted Kardelj to discuss the doctrinal aspects of the national question were related to foreign policy considerations as much as to problems of domestic national policy. Titoism, despite its importance as the first national revolt against Soviet domination of the international Communist movement, had never developed a clear-cut doctrine of "national communism." The phrase, in fact, was a Western one, and one not commonly employed by the Yugoslavs. Each nation, the Yugoslav Communists argued, enjoyed equality with other socialist nations and had the right to develop in accord with local conditions. But this defense of the rights of the countries of the Communist bloc had not been accompanied by an attempt to justify in *theoretical* terms the equality which was being demanded in practice.

The Yugoslav Communists therefore had been hesitant to formulate a comprehensive ideological justification for their national communism, but instead followed a pragmatic approach which emphasized the inherent rights of all nations to independence and equality. In the mid-1950s, meanwhile, not only had the question of nationalism become important within Yugoslavia, but pressure had arisen from the Soviet Union for Yugoslavia to reverse her policy of independence and recognize Soviet leadership over the Communist bloc as the price for the *détente* which had just been achieved between the two countries. In addition, Yugoslavia was engaged in an effort to extend its influence among the highly nationally conscious nations of Africa and Asia. Thus a number of considerations, international and domestic, prompted Kardelj to engage in the ambitious undertaking of revising Marxist-Leninist theory on the national question, a task which no Yugoslav Communist had attempted since Sima Marković.

Kardelj's theoretical opponent was Stalin, whose works on the national question still reigned supreme in Marxist-Leninist theory. To establish his own Marxist point of reference, Kardelj did not dispense with Stalin's writings entirely (an approach subsequently employed by

[51] Sperans (Edvard Kardelj), *Razvoj Slovenačkog nacionalnog pitanja* (2d ed.; 1958). Hereafter referred to as *Razvoj*.

the Soviet Union) but chose to use the classical work *Marxism and the National Question* as a starting point for constructing a broader and more contemporary theory of nationalism. In addition to the factors which Stalin had considered essential to the formation of a nation, Kardelj added his own: the "social division of labor in the epoch of capitalism." The description of a nation which Kardelj proposed thus read as follows:

A specific community of peoples arising on the basis of the social division of labor in the epoch of capitalism, in a compact territory and within the framework of a common language and close ethnic and cultural similarity in general.[52]

The definition was not really self explanatory, and a good deal of confusion came to prevail over its implications. The significance of Kardelj's position on the character of the nation could be deduced from the context in which the new ideas were presented, however. The reference to the "social division of labor in the epoch of capitalism" was not an effort to emasculate the concept of the nation by resorting to some form of economic determinism; instead it represented an attempt to view the development of the nation as a necessary response to the needs of organizing production under the conditions created by capitalism. Kardelj's apparently very orthodox definition of the nation was in fact a revision of Marxism-Leninism, for it not only pointed to the importance of economics in the development of nations (Stalin himself had made this point) but emphasized the importance of the nation in the development of economic relations.[53]

Perhaps Kardelj's description of the nation would not have represented such a striking departure from the tenets of orthodox Marxist thought if Kardelj had not suggested that the positive role attributed

[52] *Ibid.,* p. 104.

[53] See Kardelj's remark that "the struggle for the affirmation of the nation in the epoch of capitalism was not only the struggle for the democratic and cultural rights of man, for the right to his own language and independent cultural affirmation, [or] even for improved economic conditions, but for the social and cultural progress of humanity in general. *And that struggle will not cease as long as nations do not objectively complete that socioeconomic function for which they appeared in history, that is, not until the progress of productive forces and socialist relations outgrows this function.*" *Razvoj,* p. 60. Italics added.

to the nation, which originated in capitalist societies, continued to exist regardless of the political form assumed by the state.[54] The opposite, erroneous view was attributed to Stalin:

Stalin saw a bourgeois creation in the nation, and not the creation of the *societal-economic relations* of the epoch of capitalism, that is, the degree of development of the productive forces which was characteristic for this epoch. For this reason he contrasted the so-called "bourgeoisie" nation with the "socialist nation" which was simply the result of the change in government and property. . . . That such a theory cannot contribute to the direct practice of leading socialist forces in treating the national question in the transitional period from capitalism to socialism is also quite clear.[55]

This criticism of Stalin did raise problems, for it would not seem unreasonable to argue that, with the collapse of capitalism, the "societal-economic relations" which had led to the formation of the nation would expire as well. But regardless of the lack of precision in Kardelj's argument, the effect of his position was clearly to reduce the impact of revolutionary upheavals on national relations and the solution of nationality conflicts, thus opening to question fundamental dogmas which had been accepted by the Party since the 1920s. If the nation was a vital institution to both capitalist and socialist stages of development— and Kardelj made it clear that he felt this to be the case—there had to exist a continuity in national development which defied revolutionary upheavals and the subsequent changes in class relations.

Kardelj's theoretical analysis was well adapted to the task of defending each country's right to national development within the Communist bloc. But there remained the question of relations among the Yugoslav nationalities. Since the role of the nation had been equated with progressive social forces, and since the republics were commonly accepted as nations in their own right, the new respectability acquired by nation-states in Kardelj's theory would seem to accrue to the republics as well. But the problem was not so simple. First one had to determine whether in Yugoslavia the conditions required for the creation of a nation existed in the republics, or in the country as a whole.

---

[54] "It [the national question] is organically tied with the social relations of the epoch of capitalism and with the transitional period from capitalism to socialism." *Razvoj*, p. 62.

[55] *Ibid.*, p. 63.

On this crucial point Kardelj was vague. He seemed to take the position that each republic was a nation while Yugoslavia, as a state, was a manifestation of a new higher form of supranational relationship which would eventually replace the nation-state system throughout the world.[56] The national feelings of the republics were identified as "democratic national consciousness." Such feelings were not condemned, but they were obviously of a more primitive type than Yugoslav nationalism, which was given the designation of "Yugoslav socialist consciousness." For the first time, this Yugoslav feeling was referred to as "Yugoslavianism" (*Jugoslovenstvo*), implying that the bond of Yugoslavs to their country went deeper than simple Yugoslav patriotism or loyalty to the Yugoslav Communist Party.

Alluding to "Yugoslavianism" was sure to raise the hackles of the advocates of republic rights, especially because it suggested a new attempt to hasten the cultural assimilation of the Yugoslav peoples. Kardelj went to great lengths to explain that his interpretation of the national question was in no way aimed at curbing the rights of the nationalities in the cultural field. The right of each national culture to develop separately, and free of pressures for assimilation in any form, was made a central tenet of a correct Marxist view toward the national question.

Nevertheless, in his treatment of the nationalities question in Yugoslavia, Kardelj adopted a position which saw little that was progressive in regional national outlooks. In discussing the growth of national feeling during the Titoist period, Kardelj unleashed a criticism of nationalism unprecedented in Yugoslavia for its frankness and lack of respect for local sentiment:

In nationalistic manifestations there is expressed everything that is reactionary, ideologically backward, or momentarily disorienting in our social life. . . . Nationalism in our conditions is one of those reactionary ideological factors which draws people backwards, shuts out socialist perspectives, hinders the formation of socialist consciousness, and cripples that practical socialist creative activity which does not act all at a moment but [only] ensures lasting results [in the course of] an entire determined historical period. As

56 "Yugoslav socialist consciousness is by no manner of means in contradiction to democratic national consciousness, rather [it is] its necessary international supplement in conditions of a socialist community of peoples." *Ibid.*, p. 53.

such, nationalism is a reactionary force which undermines many of the results of the National Liberation War and revolution, deforms equal relations
among the peoples of Yugoslavia, and would significantly cripple the socialist enthusiasm which initiated the revolution if socialist forces did not
actively fight against its manifestations and sources.[57]

This attack reflected adversely on the role of the republics and sharpened the dilemma, apparent in Kardelj's theoretical innovations, concerning the role of the Yugoslav republics as "nations." Perhaps, out
of consideration for national sensibilities, Kardelj's ambiguous statements on this point were left unchallenged, or unexplained, by Yugoslav
commentators and experts on the national question. But a careful examination of the new theory of the development of the nation left little
doubt over what Kardelj felt the status of the republics should be.

For it was clear from Kardelj's new definition of a nation that the
only true nation could be Yugoslavia. The republics performed no
progressive economic function (according to opinion prevalent at that
time). They had "democratic" consciousness—that is, they were organs
of local government, just like the communes. They had "national"
cultures, but this did not, in itself, make the republics nations according to Kardelj's definition of that latter term. By adding an economic
criterion of the kind described earlier to Stalin's definition of a nation,
Kardelj had in fact attacked the Yugoslav republics at what was their
weakest point: their role in the economic system of Yugoslavia, which,
as shall appear shortly, had always been depreciated, if not openly
denied. Examined in this light, Stalin's long-accepted definition of a
nation was far more suited to the purpose of justifying the national
stature of the Yugoslav republics than was Kardelj's.

This issue has been examined at some length because Kardelj's work
is frequently and mistakenly interpreted by the Yugoslavs themselves as
a defense of the right of the republics. This was to come later. But as
originally conceived, the result of modifying Stalin's definition of a nation worked through several lines of reasoning to the same end: to make
Yugoslavia the only authentic "nation," free to resist the pressures for
proletarian internationalism emanating from Moscow, and at the same
time, to assert its authority over the republics. Kardelj's reasoning was

[57] *Ibid.,* p. 39.

not always precise, but his effort to introduce a new ideological justification for the role of the nation in Marxist thought *and* at the same time to diminish the status of the republics in Yugoslavia was a remarkable tour de force, not fully appreciated at the time it appeared.

In 1958, at the Seventh Congress of the League of Communists (as the Party was known after the Sixth Congress of 1952), the Party adopted a new program which carefully balanced the traditional elements of Yugoslav national policy with the ideas produced in the Titoist period.[58] "The basic principle," the program stated, "has been to recognize the individuality, equality, and the right of self-determination of all the Yugoslav peoples—Serbs, Croats, Slovenes, Macedonians, and Montenegrins—as well as their unity on the basis of a federal state structure." [59] Nevertheless, the future of national relations lay in the development of socialist relations, "the common interest [which] has already appeared and is appearing still more in the general social and cultural consciousness of the working masses." [60] On this basis, the program predicted, there was developing a "socialist, Yugoslav consciousness, in the conditions of a socialist community of peoples." [61] Although the statement was careful not to offend national sensibilities, and specifically stated that there was no intention of creating a Yugoslav "nation" to replace the republics, it was clear at this time that the Party was intent on transforming national relations through emphasizing their socialist content, at the expense of local nationalism and the rights of the republics.

The Party program of 1958 marked the high point of the campaign to create a climate favorable for the growth of Yugoslav nationalism. Although certain issues such as the encouragement of cultural cooperation were to be debated in the years that followed, the policy of supporting "Yugoslavianism" was abandoned, and in the 1960s a completely different approach to the national question was adopted. The circumstances under which this change took place form one of the most curious episodes in the complex history of Communist Yugoslav national policy. They were important not only because they signified a basic change in national policy but even more so because they marked the first signs of

[58] *VII kongres Saveza komunista Jugoslavije: Stenografske beleške,* pp. 1055–58.
[59] *Ibid.,* p. 1055.
[60] *Ibid.,* p. 1058.
[61] *Ibid.*

strain in the top Yugoslav Communist Party leadership, a group which had displayed remarkable unity over the national question since Tito took command of the Party in the 1930s.

The growing complications encountered in the campaign to infuse the spirit of socialist Yugoslavianism into the culture and history of the country were contributing, but not decisive, factors in the shift of policy that took place in respect to the national question. Two developments in the Titoist period, it slowly became clear, were most responsible for bringing this change about: the growth of economic nationalism, and splits within the Party over the policy of liberalization of the Titoist system. These problems, in turn, were closely linked to the appearance of nationalistic attitudes in Party organizations, and even among the top Party leadership. So important was the economic issue for the national question in the Titoist period that a separate chapter will be devoted to this problem.

Complaints over the behavior of Party members, as noted earlier, began in 1953, when the Party was passing through a severe crisis as a result of uncertainty over its future role in the Titoist system (this was the period when Djilas began to develop his revisionist theories). In February of 1958 the Party leadership was again compelled to issue a sharp reprimand to Party members, and among the malpractices which were the subject of criticism were what was described as "powerful particularistic tendencies appearing above all in the economy [which] frequently assume a nationalistic and even chauvinistic form." [62] The campaign to reform the Party in 1958 had a sequel in 1962, when Tito, in a speech delivered in Split, publicly rebuked Communist Party members for seeking privileges and for thinking only of their own interests.[63] Once again, the nationalism of many Party members was the subject of strong criticism. At the same time, the Executive Committee of the Party distributed a letter to Party members condemning a wide range of practices, including nationalism and particularism.[64] This letter, published in June, 1962, was particularly significant, for it admitted something which earlier had been hinted at indirectly: that opposition of the republic parties to federal policies which were contrary to local interests had gone so far that

[62] *Komunist,* Feb. 28, 1958, pp. 1–2.
[63] *Ibid.,* May 10, 1962, supplement.
[64] *Ibid.,* June 14, 1962, p. 3.

the Central Committee was no longer assured that its directives would be obeyed.[65]

The reappearance of nationalism within the Party was a severe setback for those who had anticipated that the Titoist system and a socialist economy would eliminate the last vestiges of national rivalry in Yugoslavia. Far too rapidly for their own interests, the Yugoslav Communists had tried to devolve responsibility, break up the Party bureaucracy, and decentralize the administration and the economy while at the same time leaving the individual Party member free to maintain and even increase his power and privilege within the locality or enterprise. These tendencies were only partly offset by the quasi-democratic institutions of workers' self-management in the enterprises and the encouragement of communal self-governing organs in the localities and districts. Rather than encouraging socialist morality, the new emphasis on the pursuit of self-interest by the enterprise and the individual undermined the élan of the Party and encouraged the development of regional interests over those of the country as a whole.

The complex institutional structure of the Titoist system was therefore working to encourage particularism within the Party. This was no less true at the regional and republic levels than in the localities, as events were to prove. Economic competition became fierce; in addition, opposition to the Titoist reforms began to crystallize along regional lines, finally coming to focus among the followers of Aleksandar Ranković in the Serbian Party. Ranković, who had been head of the secret police, was Organizational Secretary of the League of Communists in control of cadres and *de facto* leader of the Serbian Party. For a number of years he had been considered a successor to Tito, and was indisputably the most powerful figure in the Party leadership after Tito himself. His resist-

[65] According to the Executive Committee, there had grown up a double standard, according to which the decisions of the plenums, congresses, and the like were considered to apply only to the ordinary Party member, not the important figures in the Party. The letter also strongly attacked the fashion in which Communists protected one another, leading to the Yugoslav equivalent of the Soviet "family circles," making it impossible for the Party organs to check up on actions taken at lower levels. Tito had already revealed that the Party was not acting in a united fashion several years earlier, at the Second Plenum of 1959, when he complained that the Central Committee was making decisions by a majority, not unanimously. *Drugi plenum Centralnog komiteta Saveza komunista Jugoslavije*, pp. 12–13.

ance to the line of the CPY began in the late 1950s. At a stormy meeting of the Central Committee in March, 1962, Ranković's opposition to
the policy of further reform of the economy was overcome.[66] The meeting, which had strong nationalist overtones, nevertheless formalized the
split within the Party, and Ranković commenced a policy of sabotaging
the liberalization of the economy, both through his control over the
secret police and through his power within the Serbian Communist Party.

The fashion in which this split in the CPY leadership reenforced the
trend toward manifestations of economic nationalism within the Party
will be examined in more detail in the following chapters. Its effects
on national policy, meanwhile, were already evident in the late 1950s.
In the course of the struggle against Ranković, concessions were
made to those who wished to see a greater role for the republics in
Yugoslav life and who sought to reverse the policy of developing a new
form of Yugoslav nationalism. Although conclusive evidence on the origins of these pressures is lacking, it seems clear that Croatian and Slovenian Communists were advocating changes in national policy. On the
other hand, the Serbian Communist Party was not united in opposition
to this pro-republic stand; spokesmen for greater republic autonomy
could be found among the Serbs in the discussions that took place over
the federal-republic relations in the early 1960s.[67]

The fact that a change in national policy had indeed taken place was
suggested by the new ideas that began to appear concerning the economic
contribution of the republics to the Yugoslav federation. Prior to the
1960s no one had suggested that the republics had a special role reserved
for them in the organization of the economy or the execution of the economic plan, although it was often emphasized that economic development
was important for the republics, especially those that were underdeveloped. In the early 1960s suggestions were made that republics performed significant economic functions. Miloš Minić, an important figure
in the Serbian Party, was quoted as being critical of the disharmony
which existed between "the actual general political role of the people's
republic as one of the most important factors in our political and social
system and the special influence of her organs in determining and carry-

[66] More on this meeting will be found in Chapter 6.
[67] See the remarks of Miloš Minić on this page.

ing out economic policy for the entire country on the one hand, and on the other, her really narrow formal-legal and actual potentialities for influencing in a more significant fashion the economic means and methods of . . . the economic policy of the country." [68] This new approach was approved by Kardelj, in 1964, at the Eighth Congress of the League of Communists,[69] and a subcommittee of the Central Committee which convened to discuss nationalities policy at the congress, while criticizing unrestrained economic rivalry among the republics, spoke for the first time of an opposite danger, of the "unitarian ignoring of the economic functions of the republics and autonomous regions." [70]

Debate over the prospects for integration of the national cultures of Yugoslavia also revealed that the Party had reversed its direction in nationalities policy not long after adopting the Party program in 1958. The idea of "Yugoslavianism" simply dropped from view, although the desirability of the eventual merger of national cultures continued to receive support in some quarters. The preparation of a new constitution provided the opportunity to reverse sharply the practice of encouraging persons to identify themselves as Yugoslavs when registering their nationality. The draft constitution debated in 1961 contained the provision that a person could give his nationality either in terms of national origin or as "nationally undetermined," and it was made clear, in authoritative discussions of the draft, that "Yugoslav" would not be acceptable as a designation of nationality.[71] This extreme position was modified somewhat in the final constitution (promulgated in 1963), which granted a person complete freedom to choose his nationality, including that of Yugoslav, or to refuse to give any national designation if he so wished.[72]

[68] *Borba,* Oct. 14, 1961, p. 1. See also "O nekim pitanjima nacionalnih odnosa u prednacrtu ustava," *Komunist,* Nov. 8, 1962, p. 4.

[69] Said Kardelj: "Every nationality has the right and the realistic possibility to live and to develop in harmony with the results of its work and with the development of productive forces, and no force outside of it—that is, outside mutual relations of the working people and nationalities confirmed by the constitution—can dispense the fruits of its labor." *Osmi kongres,* p. 84.

[70] *Komunist,* Oct. 22, 1964, p. 3.

[71] *Ibid.,* November 8, 1962, p. 4.

[72] See Article 41 of the constitution in *Ustav Socijalističke Federativne Republike Jugoslavije sa ustavima socialijstičkih republika i statutima autonomnih pokrajina,* and the comments of Kardelj in *Komunist,* March 7, 1963.

The constitution of 1963 also showed the influence of the new trend toward recognizing republic rights by making certain changes in the constitutional law of 1953 favorable to the republics. In addition to the provisions dealing with the choice of nationality just discussed, a broad statement of the rights of the republics to self-determination and secession was reintroduced into the statement of general principles which prefaced the constitution. The practice of preceding years, that republic representation would be considered in determining the composition of the Federal Executive Committee, was now written into the constitution.[73] The distinction between "complete," "basic," and "general" laws, which had been part of the Yugoslav federal system since its inception, was retained, and the rights of the republics to legislate under this system somewhat strengthened.[74] There was also a new provision which dealt with the possibility of voluntary cooperation among the republics.[75] Finally, the Yugoslav constitution was put under the protection of a constitutional court, and theoretically at least this body could test the constitutionality of federal laws which infringed on republic rights, as well as republic laws which violated the federal constitution.[76]

The new importance of the republics was also evident in the statute adopted by the League of Communists at its Eighth Congress in 1964. It had never been the practice to allow republic parties any real power within the highly centralized and tightly disciplined ranks of the Party; at the Sixth Party Congress in 1952, a slight concession was made in the wording of the statute which suggested that the republic Party congresses might enjoy some policy-making functions,[77] but this clause was elimi-

[73] Article 226.

[74] Thus the extent of "complete" legislation was reduced in Article 119; it was provided (in the same article) that the republic could even legislate in areas of federal competency (e.g., complete legislation) if the federal government had not done so; general laws, until they were completed by the republic legislatures, were to be considered as principles, not enforceable legislation (Article 120).

[75] The relevant section of Article 110 read: "For the purpose of realizing certain specific goals of common interest, the republics by agreement form common organizations, undertake common actions, and develop exchange of experience and other forms of economic cooperation."

[76] Article 241 of the constitution.

[77] The statute adopted at the Sixth Congress recognized the right of the republic Party congress to "determine, within the framework of the political line of the League of Communists of Yugoslavia, the political line of the League of Communists of the People's Republics." Section VII, paragraph 26.

nated at the Seventh Party Congress in 1958 as being out of harmony with the principle that the Party was a "united organization." [78] In the statute adopted in 1964, however, it was provided that the republic congresses should convene immediately *before* the congress of the entire Party, and the republic congress was given the right to "determine the policies, positions, and tasks of the League of Communists of the socialist republic in harmony with the policy of the League of Communists of Yugoslavia." [79] These changes were potentially more significant than anything contained in the new constitution. That a new role for the republic parties was envisaged seemed to be confirmed by the explanation that the new statute sought

to express more precisely the independence (*samostalnost*) of the League of Communists in the socialist republics on the basis of the national character of the economic development of the republics. [It] emphasizes that independence will make it possible for Communists in the republics to discover (*iznalaze*) creatively, freely, and with full responsibility the most adequate paths for realizing the general line of the League in specific circumstances.[80]

The federal system of Yugoslavia was still highly unitary by Western standards, and not all the changes in the constitution of 1963 were to the advantage of the republics. The constitution held to the position that the peoples of the republics were "sovereign," and did not grant the republics themselves this right,[81] while the Chamber of Nationalities maintained the form it had acquired in 1954.[82]

[78] See the remarks of Moma Marković at the Seventh Congress. *VII kongres Saveza komunista Jugoslavije*, p. 446.

[79] *Osmi kongres*, pp. 224–25; Articles 27 and 28 of the statute.

[80] Koliševski's speech on the new statute. *Osmi kongres*, p. 184.

[81] The federal constitution, in Part I of the preamble, referred to the "sovereign rights" of the working people and the nationalities (*narodi*) of Yugoslavia which were exercised through the federation *and* by the socialist republics. The formula of divided exercise of sovereignty which ultimately resides in the people was repeated in the republic constitutions of Bosnia-Hercegovina, Montenegro, and Croatia, and in the resolution of the Slovenian National Assembly preceding adoption of the Slovenian constitution. The Serbian constitution contained no reference to sovereignty, either of the federation or of the republics. For the Macedonian approach to sovereignty, see *infra*, p. 223.

[82] The republic assemblies would choose ten representatives each, who would enter into the National Assembly and constitute themselves as a Chamber of Nationalities on matters involving the equality of the republics or republic rights

The direction of thinking on the national question was nevertheless unmistakable, and the trend toward recognizing the role of the republics was given further impetus in 1966 after Ranković was dismissed from his Party and government posts.[83] In the purges following Ranković's ouster, plans were initiated to reorganize the Party's central organs and give greater power to the republic Party organizations. In place of the all-powerful Executive Committee, it was foreseen that a purely administrative body would be created, shorn of power to make policy, while a new organ, a Party Presidium, would stand between the Executive Committee and the Central Committee, and take over the responsibilities for policy formulation.[84] The plan was clearly aimed at preventing any small clique from blocking the decisions of the Central Committee, as the Ranković faction had attempted to do. Republic Party organizations would be reorganized along similar lines; at the same time it was evident that the net effect would be to give more power to republic parties. Vladimir Bakarić, secretary of the Croatian League of Communists, spoke of the change as leading to a "free hand" for the republic committees,[85] although to gain such a position they too would have to accept a weakening of their commanding organs.

By the mid-1960s, the national question had come to occupy a place in the domestic concerns of the Yugoslav Communists second only to the issue of economic reform. The scope of the problem can be briefly summarized in terms of three interrelated factors: manifestations of nationalism; the trend toward "polycentrism" in federal-republic relations; and the absence of a clear-cut policy to deal with the problem of national relations.

During most of the Titoist period there was a slow and steady rise in nationalism, marked by isolated outbursts of nationalistic fervor, such as the Stanković case, or the earlier incident involving the journal *Svedo-*

---

guaranteed under the constitution. In the event that the Chamber of Nationalities could not agree with the legislation under debate in the National Assembly, the matter would be resolved in a committee of the two houses. See Articles 190 and 191 of the constitution.

[83] At the Fourth Plenum of the Central Committee of the League of Communists in July, 1966. See *Komunist,* July 7, 1966.

[84] *Borba,* Sept. 18, 1966, pp. 1–2.

[85] *Vjesnik,* Sept. 17, 1966, p. 2.

čanstvo. Following the rise in economic nationalism, the split within the Party over the direction and tempo of the Titoist reforms, and the promulgation of the new constitution, something like a "national revival" was witnessed in many parts of the country. In Croatia it was evident in outbursts of nationalism that accompanied the performance of previously banned nationalistic theatrical works and the appearance of nationalistically minded student groups in the University of Zagreb.[86] The Ranković case, Party officials admitted, was interpreted from a chauvinistic position among Croatians, both students and workers.[87]

The repudiation of the Novi Sad agreement on the Serbo-Croatian language also testified to the strength of nationalism in Croatian intellectual circles. Ironically, the statement was only made possible by the greater freedom encouraged by the Party following the defeat of Ranković and his conservative following within the Serbian Party. While Party organs strongly criticized the resolution, Serbian intellectuals responded with a "Proposition for Discussion" in which with heavy irony they declared "the Vienna and Novi Sad agreements as no longer valid," while insisting that Serbs in Croatia be educated in their own language; they also urged that Radio-Television Belgrade stop its "unauthorized game in the role of a central Yugolsav studio and have Cyrillic in local programs" and "that common emissions to all Yugoslavia use both scripts." [88] Under Party pressure many of the Serbian writers concerned dissociated themselves from the "Proposition." The Croatian institutions responsible for the uproar stood behind their original statement, however, when replying to Party criticism.[89]

In Serbia, the struggle of the Ranković faction against the Party leadership gave a sharp stimulus to national feeling during the period between the Eighth Congress of the League of Communists (in the fall of 1964) and the Fourth Plenum of the Central Committee (July, 1966) at which Ranković was removed from his positions of power. During this period, the Party press began to single out Serbian nationalism for attack and to revive the demand, not heard since the mid-1930s, that the Serbs as the largest nationality had the greatest responsibility for curbing manifesta-

[86] New York *Times,* Feb. 20, 1966.
[87] *Vjesnik,* Sept. 27, p. 3.
[88] *Borba,* April 2, 1967, p. 5.
[89] *Ibid.,* March 26, 1967, p. 2.

tions of nationalism within their own ranks.[90] In Serbia, old national military hymns and patriotic songs, banned since the war, made their reappearance, as did the habit of discussing and "settling" issues in the informal and often emotional atmosphere of the local café. (This habit was strongly attacked on the front page of the Party press in the spring of 1966 as a return to the "café-nationalism" of the prewar period.) [91] Especially after the decisive steps taken in the summer of 1965 to free the economy from administration controls, national sentiment over economic issues became intense within the Serbian Party.

Among a number of the smaller national groups and minorities the trend toward nationalism was equally pronounced. One of the most interesting cases was that of the Slav Moslems of Bosnia-Hercegovina, whom the Party had consistently treated as a religious community rather than as a national group during and after World War II. The first change in this position could be detected in 1961, when the census of that year provided a category for "ethnic Moslems." The republic constitution for Bosnia-Hercegovina promulgated in 1963 made further concessions to the thesis that the Moslems were a distinct ethnic group.[92] It only remained to argue that the Moslems were a distinct nationality. This was hinted at in an article which appeared in the Sarajevo journal *Pregled* in 1964, arguing in strong terms that "the overwhelming majority of the Bosnian-Hercegovinian Moslems have made clear their feeling of belonging to the Moslem community as an ethnic, and not religious, group." [93]

In Kossovo-Metohija the problem of national feeling reached acute proportions in the mid-1950s, creating immensely difficult problems for the Yugoslav Communist Party leadership.

In the Albanian case, the problem stemmed in a large part from the distrust which the Communists instinctively felt toward the Albanians

[90] See the interesting account of an investigation on national relations in Belgrade carried out by the Belgrade City Committee of the League of Communists and published, in part, in *Komunist,* May 26, 1966, p. 6.

[91] *Komunist,* Jan. 13, 1966, p. 1.

[92] See the section of the republic constitution of Bosnia-Hercegovina dealing with "basic principles," in *Ustav Socijalističke Federativne Republike Jugoslavije,* p. 95.

[93] Purivatra, "Prilog proučavanju koncepcije o nacionalnom 'opredjeljivanju,' " *Pregled,* XVI (Oct. 1964), 331.

on the grounds of political unreliability. Following the ouster of Ranković it was revealed that, since the end of the war, the Albanians had
felt the full force of the brutal methods of the secret police.[94] At the
Sixth Plenum of the Central Committee of the League of Communists of
Serbia in September, 1966, at which these facts were made known, the
training manual of the security services was quoted to the effect that "nationalist feelings among national minorities are strong; because of this
the minorities are very often ready to work for the intelligence agencies
of their mother countries.[95] In 1955 and 1956—perhaps in connection
with the Party plan to integrate the minorities more fully into the life
of the Yugoslav nationalities—the security forces declared Kossovo-
Metohija in a state of emergency and carried out what was described at
the Sixth Plenum of the Serbian Party as a "bloody collection of arms"
from the inhabitants.[96]

In 1959 the whole question of relations with the minorities was reviewed in the Executive Committee (Politburo) of the Yugoslav League
of Communists; [97] as a result, plans were made to improve the status of
the minorities and to begin a program of economic development in
Kossovo-Metohija.[98] Financial aid initiated a period of economic growth
in the region, but also spurred the local party to demand greater amounts
of financial assistance than the federal government in Belgrade was in a
position to supply. Relations with the Albanian minority also became
more difficult when, after 1960, the Albanian government in Tirana incited the Albanian minority in Kossovo-Metohija against the Yugoslav
government. Arrests among the Albanians of Kossovo-Metohija in the
early 1960s for spying rose to an alarming level.[99] In 1964, when it
appeared that the economic demands of the region could not be satisfied

94 *Politika,* Sept. 18, 1966.
95 *Vjesnik u Srijedu,* Oct. 5, 1966, p. 5.
96 *Ibid.*
97 The resolution of the meeting was published three years after it was held in
Komunist, June 28, 1962, p. 8.
98 This program of economic aid is described in more detail in the chapter to
follow.
99 For trials of Albanian agents during this period, see *Borba,* March 3, 4, and
5, 1961; *Politika,* April 5 and 6, 1961; *Borba,* June 1, 1961. It was announced in
1961 that from 1948 to 1960, 675 agents had been smuggled into Kossovo-Metohija
from Albania, and that from 1957 to 1961, 115 Albanian agents had been tried in
Yugoslav courts. *Borba,* April 8, 1961.

by Belgrade, a group in Kossovo-Metohija engaged in an abortive conspiracy against the authorities, apparently with the aim of pressuring Belgrade into some form of autonomy for the region. What brief mention there was of the incident in the regional (Serbo-Croatian) press suggested that the group was not organized or supported by the Albanian government but was made up of Communists, or Party sympathizers.[100]

The possibility that federal-republic relations would develop in accordance with a polycentric model began to receive serious consideration in the 1960s, especially after the dismissal of Ranković. A polycentric system of planning was proposed during this period by a Croatian economist,[101] and the Croatian Party secretary, Vladimir Bakarić, felt compelled to defend the proposals for Party reorganization in 1966 as a step which would lead not to polycentrism but to "polyinitiative" in Yugoslavia.[102]

The amount of formal autonomy enjoyed by the republics through 1966 was not great, however. The mainstay of what was a fundamentally unitary system of government was the unified system of administration maintained during the Titoist period, which prevailed despite initial efforts to carry out sweeping decentralization in the bureaucracy as well as in the economic realm. The constitutional law of 1953, after abolishing the Union-Republic, All-Union, and Republic ministries, had established a system of administration in which the federal government had very few ways of checking on the execution of its acts at the republic and local levels. This led to considerable confusion and a breakdown in administrative efficiency, and in 1956 a comprehensive law on state ad-

---

[100] The author was assured by Yugoslav officials that no such plot against the authorities was organized. But stories of an incident of this kind were common in Yugoslavia at the time. *Jedinstvo,* Sept. 14, 1964, reported the arrest and trial in the latter half of August of a number of Albanians (Adem Demači, Ramadan Šalja, and Venhari Mustafa) for "unfriendly actions." Instead of being accused as Albanian agents, those arrested were labeled as "adventurists" and "demoralized individuals" who engaged in propaganda, first and foremost against brotherhood and unity. According to the report, the ideas of the group met with sharp resistance "in the circles of all nationalities." Such language would seem applicable only to a group which was not of the old (*Balista*) stripe, nor organized by Albanians, but of local persons, probably Party members, with some idea of autonomy for Kossovo-Metohija.

[101] Rudolf Bićanić, "O monocentričnom i policentričnom planiranju," *Ekonomski Pregled,* XIV (No. 6–7), 469–527.

[102] *Vjesnik,* Sept. 17, 1966.

ministration was promulgated which provided that in matters of exclusive federal competence, or in questions of "general" interest (the term was not to be confused with "general legislation" provided for in the constitution), the federal administrative organs had special rights to issue "binding instructions" on lower organs, to carry through programs of systematization of administration, and to carry out the acts of a subordinate administrative level if the organ in question failed to do so.[103] What areas were to be of "exclusive," and which of "general," interest for the purposes of administrative supervision was to be determined by federal law. The basic elements of this system of administrative control were contained in Article 127 of the 1963 constitution, which also provided that in matters of exclusive interest to the federation, the federal government might found its own organs, parellel to those of the republics and local governments.

In the field of lawmaking, the federal government enjoyed marked predominance over the republics. Both in 1952 and in 1962, in connection with constitutional reform, there was discussion of the need to increase republic responsibilities for legislation. But in practice, the complexities of economic and social reform, and the existence of a desire to standardize certain practices in the educational and cultural fields which had gone unregulated in the immediate postwar years, led to a great outpouring of federal legislation during the Titoist period.[104] Most of these laws were of a very detailed character which left very little to the discretion of the republics even in the field of "general" legislation.

The republics did not publicly challenge the dominant position of the federal government in the field of lawmaking. Prior to 1963, clashes between federal and republic laws, or between republic laws and the constitution, were to be resolved by the National Assembly in Belgrade; the same type of power was lodged in the federal government in respect to the acts of the republic governments. Never during the period 1953–63 did the federal government or the National Assembly find it necessary to employ these powers, although there were occasions when the threat to do so was invoked. (Thus, the federal government was forced in the course of 1955–56 to warn the Croatian Executive Council, or govern-

[103] "Zakon o državnoj upravi," *Službeni List,* No. 13 (1956), p. 185.
[104] For a recent complaint concerning this problem, see "Odnos izmedju država ili izmedju država i samoupravljanja," *Ekonomska Politika,* Oct. 22, 1966, p. 1346.

ment, that unless a Croatian law on maintenance of village roads was amended the law would be brought before the National Assembly to test its constitutionality; the law was subsequently modified by the Croatian Assembly and this step was averted.) The innovation of a constitutional court in 1963 did not immediately lead to an abandonment of the informal methods used to keep republic legislation in line with federal laws and the constitution. The place of consultation shifted, however, from government and Party bodies to the constitutional court itself, which on several occasions between 1963 and 1966 held informal meetings with representatives of the republics in order to determine areas in which the republics might legislate without coming into conflict wih federal laws, or violating the federal constitution.[105] The constitutionality of federal law was not tested during the first several years of the court's existence; the first case of a republic law being brought through the constitutional courts of the republics to the federal constitutional court took place in December, 1965.[106]

Finally, the Party apparatus and the centrally organized secret police provided strong instruments of control over the republics if used energetically and with the support of the Party leadership. The way in which Party organizations fell in line behind the decision of the Fourth Plenum, held at Brioni, to relieve Ranković of his positions in the government and Party was an impressive display of the power at the disposal of the Party leaders once they decided to take vigorous action against obstructions to their policies originating in the republics.

On the other hand, there were many ways in which the powers of the republics were significantly enlarged in the Titoist period. A number of them have been mentioned or will be discussed in connection with the economic aspect of the national question: the practice of securing republic representation in federal administrative bodies and organs of the League of Communists, a practice which was broadened in the proposed reforms of the Party in 1966 to include the Party's leading decision-making

[105] One such case involved the social insurance of agricultural workers in Croatia. See *Borba,* Nov. 19, 1964, p. 4. Another report of such a meeting was contained in *Ekonomska Politika,* Oct. 22, 1966, p. 1346.

[106] The case involved a Montengrin law permitting an increase of peasant holdings over the ten-hectare limit set in the federal constitution. For various aspects of the case, see *Borba,* Dec. 15, 1965.

bodies; [107] the recognition of a role in the economy which led to a marked increase in the role of republic planning.[108] An indication of the existence of a trend toward lodging the ultimate source of authority for Party matters in the republics was the fact that the Slovenian Central Committee in the fall of 1966 took it upon itself to choose candidates for the Executive Committee (Politburo) and Presidium of the Yugoslav League of Communists.[109]

In addition, the ability of republic parties to sabotage federal policy was a problem during this period. The problem was demonstrated by the success with which the Serbian Communist Party (and also the Montenegrin Party organization) prevented the execution of the liberal economic reforms introduced in the summer of 1965. Some hint of the ability of even the republic Ministries of the Interior to exercise autonomy against the wishes of Belgrade was evident in the revelations made in connection with the Ranković case. In Croatia, for example, the security service followed its own procedures in determining who was to be investigated, ignoring directives issued by Belgrade.[110] The Croatian secret police also refused to turn in reports to Belgrade on the views taken by members of the Croatian Central Committee on the national question.[111] With the breakup of the Ranković forces in the secret police, it seemed almost certain that control over this vital instrument of power would come to rest largely in the republics.

Efforts were also made, following the defeat of the Ranković faction, to give the Chamber of Nationalities a larger role in the Yugoslav parliament. For the first time since the constitutional law of 1953 had limited its powers, the Chamber was called into session in January, 1967, to hear the complaints of the deputies from Bosnia-Hercegovina and Kossovo-

[107] *Komunist,* Sept. 15, 1966.

[108] See the following chapter for further details.

[109] According to published reports, the Central Committee of the Slovenian Party chose individuals who would be "proposed" to the Central Committee of the League of Communists. It is doubtful that these names would have been published if their approval was not a foregone conclusion, however. *Borba,* Oct. 2, 1966, p. 1.

[110] *Komunist,* Sept. 22, 1966.

[111] *Vjesnik,* July 27, 1966. The Slovenians also claimed that the "Slovenian UDBa [secret police] regularly had conflicts with the group in Belgrade." *Borba,* Oct. 1, 1966, p. 3.

Metohija concerning the distribution of grants-in-aid and financial assistance from the fund for aid to less developed areas.[112] Not long afterward a leading Party spokesman was quoted to the effect that the Chamber of Nationalities should be transformed into a body enjoying equality with the popularly elected Union Chamber, and that "later developments would lead to the transformation of the Union Chamber into the Chamber of Nationalities." [113] Nevertheless, proposed amendments to the constitution publicized at the time as a response to the call for strengthening the Chamber of Nationalities did not add greatly to the limited existing powers of the Chamber set down in the constitution of 1963.[114]

These developments alone would not have been enough to warrant discussion of republic autonomy, or "polycentrism," if it was not for several other considerations. Notwithstanding the unitary character of the administration, the stress on the republics as nations had a deep influence on the Yugoslavs. This factor, and the reality of underlying national differences and sensitivities, made it impossible to treat the republics as just another type of provincial administrative unit, or for the republics to limit themselves to such a role. An indication of this was the agreements between the central committees of the Serbian and Montenegrin parties and the central committees of the Serbian and Macedonian parties for economic and cultural cooperation which were signed between 1964 and 1966.[115] This unusual development in republic relations was born of the split within the CPY over economic issues, but was nevertheless a striking example of how the republics on occasion bargained among themselves almost as sovereign states. In the complex political maneuvering that accompanied liberalization of the economy in the 1960s, Vladimir Bakarić found it necessary on several occasions to speak of the need for greater representation of his republic in the formulation of foreign affairs,[116] a position which betrayed an attitude toward republic rights at variance with even liberal Western concepts of federalism, not to speak of the rights usually accorded provincial authorities in a unitary system.

[112] *Borba*, Jan. 29, 1967, p. 5.

[113] *Ibid.*, March 10, 1967.

[114] *Ibid.*, March 16, 1967, p. 4. Under the new proposals, five instead of ten deputies could call the Chamber into session.

[115] Details on these agreements will be found in the following chapter.

[116] *NIN*, March 8, 1964, pp. 2–3; *Vjesnik*, Dec. 24, 1965.

The Macedonians also revealed that they considered the Macedonian republic to enjoy special rights, for in the resolution of the Macedonian National Assembly accompanying the promulgation of the republic constitution in 1963, reference was made to the "Macedonian state" and the realization of the rights of the Macedonian people to national independence and "state self-development" (*državna samostojnost*).[117] In the discussion of national relations following the political upheaval of 1966, it was confirmed in a television interview with a Slovenian Party official that the demand for "secession" had been raised in that republic in the course of the struggle with the Ranković faction.

The third development by which national relations in the Titoist period could be characterized (in addition to growing manifestations of nationalism and a trend toward a new concept of the republics' role in the federation) was the loss of a clear-cut sense of purpose and direction in policy devised to deal with the national question. In the Stalinist period, the principles of republic sovereignty and self-determination, voluntarily limited by the revolutionary unity of the Party, were given credibility by the unanimous support they received from the Party membership and the expectation that in this way a totally new solution to the national question was in the process of realization. By contrast, the concessions made to the republics after 1958 appear to have been forced on the Party leadership as a result of powerful republic pressures and considerations of expediency. In the retreat that followed, the Yugoslav idea was either abandoned or hopelessly enmeshed in intellectual, political, and economic rivalries.

Policy toward the minorities did seem to retain some sense of a larger purpose in adapting to the forces of liberalism and recognition of national rights in the late 1950s. Following the review of the minority question by the Executive Committee of the Party in the spring of 1959 and the efforts to improve the participation of minorities in administration, the status of minorities was officially upgraded by referring to them as "nationalities" instead of minorities. In the 1960s, dual-language administration (Serbo-Croatian and Hungarian) was introduced in Subotica in Vojvodina,[118] and

---

[117] *Ustav Socijalističke Federativne Republike Jugoslavije*, p. 341.

[118] *Borba*, Dec. 3, 1964. According to the new arrangements, special monetary allowances would be granted to officials who knew both Hungarian and Serbo-Croatian. Not only was there to be a bilingual administration, but in certain

following this, efforts were made to correct some of the shortcomings which existed in the bilingual system of administration already in effect in Kossovo-Metohija. Most remarkable of all, perhaps, was the effort to introduce the teaching of *minority* languages to students of Slavic nationality in the integrated schools in regions of mixed populations. In the spirit of these policies, it became the Yugoslav position that minorities could serve as a "bridge" between countries, rather than being the cause of international conflicts, as had been the case in the past.[119]

Meanwhile, the great unanswered question in respect to national policy concerned the switch that had led to the abandonment after 1958 of the campaign for "Yugoslavianism." Tito himself had for years opposed the attempts of the republics to impose their nationality on persons who wished to be known as Yugoslavs, and he continued to do so. This pro-Yugoslav note was struck by Tito in 1963, almost pleadingly, in remarks to a gathering of newspaper editors. "There are even individuals who simply don't dare call themselves Yugoslavs," said Tito on this occasion, continuing as follows:

I have received these days quite a few letters just in connection with this [question of nationality]. And mostly from children. Children understand what I am talking about. One little girl from Macedonia, a student in the fourth or fifth grade, whose father is a Slovenian and mother a Macedonian, has written me saying that she is happy that she can now be called a Yugoslav. Look, Comrades, a little girl wrote that in her own hand. That shows better than anything how absurd it is to force someone to belong to a nationality, Serb, Croat [or] Slovene.[120]

Shortly thereafter Tito felt compelled to remark to a congress of the youth organizations that "there are not a small number of people in particular republics, and among them some Communists, who find it difficult to speak the word 'Yugoslav.' "[121]

Because Kardelj had spoken up for the economic role of the republics at the Eighth Party Congress in 1964, he was in the anomalous position

---

instances, lectures in primary schools, and in vocational schools, would be delivered both in Serbo-Croatian and in Hungarian. According to the same source, 40 percent of all office employees in Subotica were Hungarian.

119 This new approach is described in Jončić, *passim.*

120 *Komunist,* Jan. 14, 1963, p. 3.

121 *Borba,* Jan. 24, 1963, p. 1.

of lending credence to the belief that the republics were "nations" in the sense in which he had developed this term in the introduction to his work *The Development of the Slovenian National Question.* From this it was easy to conclude that Kardelj had introduced important new theories justifying the national existence of the republics on economic grounds, quite the reverse of his original intent.

Why had this retreat taken place? One can only speculate that unexpected resistance to the policy of Yugoslavianism, and the necessity of relying on the more independent-minded republics—Slovenia and Croatia —in order to overcome the opposition to economic reform, made Tito and Kardelj drop their campaign to create a broader national consciousness among the Yugoslav peoples. It is possible, in the case of Kardelj, that the tendency to defend republic rights in the economic field was also motivated by a genuine fear that the Ranković faction might at one point gain control of the Party and attempt to turn back the clock of reform in Croatia and Slovenia, as well as in Serbia.

But the motives of Tito, Kardelj, and those in sympathy with them in grudgingly bowing to pressures for recognition of republic rights were closely tied to the position of Ranković on the national issue. Of all aspects of national policy, the attitude of Ranković and those who supported him in the Serbian Party was for years one of the most difficult to decipher. The events of the summer of 1966, however, produced dramatic revelations. Ranković was accused of organizing a bid for power and of exploiting Serbian nationalism to this end.[122] In the light of this challenge, it would hardly have been surprising if the Party leaders around Tito had felt compelled to divorce themselves from the policy of Yugoslavianism, with its suggestions of support for Serbian hegemonistic ambitions. But was Ranković guilty of encouraging nationalistic forces in Serbia? At the Third Plenum of the Central Committee held in March, 1966, at the height of the struggle over the issue of economic reform, Ranković had spoken unequivocally on the national issue, castigating nationalistic manifestations in Serbia. Apart from Ranković's actions in defense of what he conceived to be Serbian national interests in refusing to carry out the reforms aimed at liberalizing the economy in the summer of 1966, there was no concrete proof forthcoming that he had acted contrary to the spirit of the Party's national policy prior to his disgrace.

[122] *Komunist,* Sept. 22, 1966, p. 1.

The mystery surrounding Ranković and his Serbian supporters was therefore not entirely dispelled by the revelations following the Fourth Plenum. The old specter of Serbian hegemony which had obviously been influencing the opposition of other republics to the policy of Yugoslavianism was brought out into the open at last. But the party Leadership was still reluctant to give a full account of the scope of the threat to national relations posed by the activities of Ranković and his followers. On several occasions prior to 1966 Tito, as well as Kardelj, had alluded to the existence of bureaucratic forces in Yugoslavia who wished to see the immediate elimination of the republics as a solution to the national question. If this reference *was* to Ranković, no mention was made of the fact after Ranković's disgrace. If it was not, one is forced to conclude that some group, such as the army, continued to carry on the spirit of Serbian unitary rule even after Ranković's power was broken.[123]

The complexities of the national question in the Titoist period were also a product of the intrusion of the economic issue into national relations, and the reverse. But this problem requires extended comment, beginning with the origins of the Yugoslav Communists' efforts to use economics to bring about a solution of the national question following World War II. In the course of the discussion of the economic issue, the circumstances surrounding the struggle within the Party, and the role of the Ranković group in the national question, will receive closer scrutiny.

123 For example, see the remarks of Kardelj in *Razvoj,* p. 41.

6

Economics and the National Question

IN THE DEVELOPMENT of the national question in Yugoslavia, economics played a significant role, both before and after World War II. In the prewar period, every section of the country nourished some grievance against the central government in Belgrade, either because local economic needs were not being met, or because of real or imagined discrimination by the central government in the allocation of financial assistance and investment funds. In the postwar period the Communists themselves linked the national question to economic issues by asserting that the national question would still be a problem as long as inequalities in levels of economic development persisted in Yugoslavia.

There were differences in the impact of economic problems on the national question in the two periods, however. Despite the excited atmosphere bred by charges and countercharges over economic discrimination in the pre-World War II period, the economic question was only a part of the broader struggle for national rights, and not the most important part at that. In contrast, economic rivalry among national regions was perhaps *the* single most important factor contributing to the rise of nationalism in the Titoist era. In fact the tendency for each republic or region to pursue narrow economic interests without regard for the welfare of the country as a whole was more in evidence under Titoism than at any time in the prewar years, with the possible exception of the period of Croatian autonomy from 1939 to 1941.

The growth of economic nationalism (or what Ćosić called that "accursed dinar nationalism") in the Titoist period greatly distressed the Yugoslav Communists. Not surprisingly, there was a tendency to place the blame for this phenomenon on narrow-minded bureaucrats or to lash out at so-called remnants of bourgeois nationalism. While the responsibility of such elements for many outbreaks of nationalism was real enough, the need of the Party to find a scapegoat tended to obscure the fact that broader forces were at work in the rise of "dinar nationalism." These were forces, furthermore, which were not necessarily to be found in Yugoslavia alone.

On the one hand, the difficulties which the Yugoslav Communists began to experience with nationalism in the economic realm were common to all countries experiencing rapid economic growth but still not at an advanced stage of industrialization. The immense needs of these countries for development funds, especially the more backward regions, gave rise in many cases to intense regional rivalries, especially in multinational states. Yugoslavia in the 1950s and early 1960s was no exception to this rule.

On the other hand, the difficulties which the Yugoslavs began to encounter with nationally charged economic rivalries indicated rather clearly that a Communist political system could not expect immunity from economic pressures any more than other forms of government. The Yugoslav case indicated, on the contrary, that under certain conditions Communist states might be very susceptible to just such pressures.

In Communist Yugoslavia, economic problems became involved in the national question in numerous and subtle ways, but the tendency for economic disputes to assume a national character was particularly evident in two respects: first, in efforts to deal with the great contrast between the developed and underdeveloped regions of Yugoslavia; second, in competition between territorial units, either local or regional, which came to be known as particularism, but very often took the form of national rivalries as well.

In the course of liberalization of the economy, a third dimension to economic nationalism emerged, one which was closely associated with the other two, but which posed a unique, and for a time a very serious, threat to the Titoist system. This was the dispute which developed within the Party in the late 1950s over the pace of economic reform. The controversy was associated with the Ranković faction in the party, but also involved the interests of the republics in the economic field. Before this debate was resolved, national feeling among the republics had reached dangerous levels, and much of the work of the preceding years aimed at cementing relations among the nationalities of Yugoslavia was placed in jeopardy.

The presence of great contrasts in levels of economic development among regions (and often among districts within regions) was a fundamental problem of Yugoslavia since the time of the country's formation. These differences were not only apparent in variations among levels of income but reflected a profound gulf between primitive, traditional cultures on the one hand, ill-suited to the demands of a modern economy, and technically oriented, productive societies on the other. Although the existence of cultural differences among sections of the country was often overemphasized by the Yugoslavs themselves, the persistence of traditional folkways made it extremely difficult for the poorer regions, generally in the south, to take even the first steps toward economic development. Needless to say, the problems of these underdeveloped areas were compounded by illiteracy, poverty, and, in most cases, a lack of natural resources.

Before World War II the problem of aiding the passive regions was often discussed in Yugoslavia, but the issue did not assume great importance when the economic aspects of the national question were debated, perhaps because the controversies of the period tended to focus on the needs of Serbs, Croats, and Slovenes, all peoples from developed (or relatively developed) areas. When the Yugoslav Communists came to power, on the other hand, there were a number of compelling reasons for giving close attention to the problems of the underdeveloped regions. The Partisan army was drawn largely from the poorer sections of the country, giving these districts an influence in public life which they had not enjoyed earlier. In their attacks on the bourgeois system of government, the Communists had repeatedly focused on the issue of underdevelopment as evidence of exploitation of the poorer regions of Yugoslavia by the financial interests of the dominant nationalities. There is no doubt that the Communists were genuinely convinced that, under socialism, economic differences between regions (as well as between classes) would become a thing of the past.

Two methods were employed by the Yugoslav Communists to ease the plight of the economically underdeveloped regions. One, which was to become the center of controversy among the republics, was the allocation of investment funds to the poorer areas for the development of industry. The other was the practice of providing grants-in-aid, or their equivalent, to the republics to meet immediate financial needs. This important but often overlooked aspect of the question of aiding underdeveloped regions should be examined briefly prior to taking up the question of investment policies.

The policy of providing grants-in-aid to the republics was begun soon after the war with the aim of equalizing the position of the republics in the period before the economic development of the underdeveloped areas had been achieved. Regardless of wealth, every republic was in theory to enjoy the same educational facilities, provide the same public services, and disperse the same amount of pensions and other benefits. The financial means required to realize this ambitious goal were obtained in the early years by permitting the poorer republics to retain a large portion of the federal turnover tax collected on their territory; after 1949, the same effect was achieved by awarding grants-in-aid from the federal budget to the underdeveloped republics. Montenegro, in particular, was highly dependent on federal assistance, and in the 1950s regularly received over 50 percent of her revenue from this source. The minorities were also important beneficiaries of state aid, receiving funds from the republics to finance their educational and cultural activities.

This aid was especially effective in stimulating local programs in education, culture, and public health, activities in which the prewar regime had been notably lax in the depressed regions of the country. Also, differences between regions tended to become less important because the administrative system of centralized planning made it possible to set prices and wages at uniform levels throughout the entire country. The effect was a striking alteration after the war in the position of the poorer regions vis-à-vis the more wealthy and culturally advanced parts of the country. Although the more backward regions were in no sense transformed into modern and productive societies, there prevailed a sort of drab uniformity in living conditions which made differences among the more-advanced and less-developed republics seem less important, and perhaps convinced some persons that the economic problems of underdeveloped regions were not really so formidable after all.

This leveling process was not in itself an answer to the economic problems of the underdeveloped regions, however. The system also worked to conceal the arbitrary way in which grants-in-aid were dispensed: not only were they generous to a fault, but it was apparent that grants (or tax relief) were being awarded without reference to any objectively predetermined standards. The results of this policy could be seen during the 1940s and 1950s, when Montenegro, the poorest of the Yugoslav republics, recorded the highest per capita budgetary expenses (excluding investments) of any republic,[1] almost twice as high as that of Serbia or Bosnia-Hercegovina. The only possible explanation of this anomaly lay in the success with which the Montenegrins used political influence within the Party to obtain federal aid.[2] To complicate the problem still further, the poorer republics were often guilty of wasting federal assistance, or of directing it to purposes for which it was not intended. Some controls were finally instituted, but federal grants in the 1950s and early 1960s were for the most part used to make up republic budgetary deficits, while the American system of conditional grants-in-aid, in which the government sets certain standards governing the activities or projects to be financed, was practically unknown.[3]

These shortcomings in the program of federal aid were largely overlooked until the 1950s, when it became apparent that the poorer republics would not reach the level of economic development of the more advanced regions for a considerable period of time. This made the federal government reluctant to continue providing large sums for grants which did not serve any productive purpose, and at the Seventh Congress of the League of Communists in 1958, the Party leadership made

[1] Derived from republic expenditures given in *Statistički Godišnjak*, 1954, p. 264, and 1957, p. 290. Both local and republic expenses are included. For each republic, the average annual expenditure per capita in thousands of dinars, 1947–56, was as follows: Serbia, 4.56; Croatia, 6.18; Slovenia, 7.94; Bosnia-Hercegovina, 4.59; Macedonia, 5.53; Montenegro, 8.69. It is possible that republic expenditures reflect investment policies, especially investment aid to poorer republics. Calculating per capita expenditures without republic investment gives the same kinds of results as those just cited, however.

[2] A thorough study of public finances in Yugoslavia concluded, on the basis of figures similar to those cited above, that "it is obvious that the amount of this grant [to Montenegro] was determined under the influence of political and not economic considerations." Radovanović, p. 166.

[3] Certain grants-in-aid (for the development of roads and water resources) were marked for specific purposes. There existed, in addition, a small grant for improving conditions of annual vacations in the republics which required matching funds, and the building of highways was finally placed on this basis.

known its desire to find some alternative to the grants-in-aid program.[4] This did not prove possible. Either as a result of political pressures, or because the poorer republics were completely incapable of supporting themselves, grants continued to flow to the republics in great quantities. The problem of establishing some criteria for dividing the aid among the republics was not attacked until 1964, when the basic law on financing social-political communities set down a criterion for receiving subsidies based on the per capita income of the "average" Yugoslav republic;[5] even this law did not set an upper limit to aid (per capita) to any one republic.

Grants to the republics were a political headache and an economic burden, but unavoidable as long as backward republics remained without their own sources of income. The only long-term solution to the problem of meeting the needs of these areas lay in economic development or, more precisely, in realizing higher rates of economic growth in the underdeveloped areas than in the more advanced regions. This was a challenge which the Yugoslav Communists eagerly accepted after the war, pledging themselves to a program of economic assistance to the poorer republics which would make it possible to bring the economies of these regions up to the national average in a relatively short period of time.

When the Yugoslav Communists embarked on this program of aid, the goal of eliminating economic inequalities in Yugoslavia seemed, if not easy, well within reach. The idea of developing the poorer regions was deeply interwoven with the mystique of rapid industrial development along the Soviet pattern which would quickly transform Yugoslavia from a predominantly peasant country into a completely modern industrial

---

[4] In the Party program adopted at the congress it was stated that "material contributions in this area [less developed regions] must first of all go toward developing forces of production which will create an independent material basis for these areas, and only secondarily, and only in the case of unavoidable necessity, can that [material contribution] be grants-in-aid from the budget for ensuring a determinate uniform level of social services and social policies."

[5] See "Osnovni zakon o finansiranju društveno političke zajednice," *Službeni List SFRJ,* No. 31 (July 22, 1964), pp. 605–17. The law states: "The federation assures supplementary funds (*dopunska sredstva*) to the republics . . . in which the income which falls to the republics and opštinas by the provisions of this law is lower per capita than the per capita income in the republic in which these [sources of income] are at the Yugoslav average or approach the Yugoslav average."

nation. Where industry was located, to many at least, did not really matter, and there was no reason to think that the poorer republics, especially Macedonia and Montenegro, would not share equally, and more than equally, in the transformation of the country into a modern industrial power. The confidence in the ability of a Communist-directed economy to score quick successes even in the backward areas was reflected in the First Five-Year Plan, adopted in 1947. The more rapid development of the underdeveloped areas was made a central goal of the plan. It was foreseen that the value of industrial production in Macedonia in 1951 would be greater than in Croatia in 1939. Measured in terms of investment per capita, Montenegro would be the most "advanced" republic in Yugoslavia in 1951 (and Serbia the least so).[6]

In practice, it proved impossible to realize these goals. In order to meet the over-all targets of the plan, investments were allocated to those regions where they would give a maximum return, that is, to the developed republics. The need to maximize the profitability of investment became especially urgent after the dispute with the Soviet Union led to the termination of all aid from the Communist bloc in 1949. Another factor which worked against Macedonia and parts of Serbia after 1949 was the need to develop defense industries; for reasons of security, these were located chiefly in Bosnia-Hercegovina and parts of Croatia.

In theory, the policy of rapid industrial development in the underdeveloped republics remained in effect after the decentralization of the economy in 1952, but in practice the poorer republics found it increasingly difficult to obtain investment funds. In a period when the Yugoslav economy was orienting itself toward the West and still feeling the ill-effects of the overambitious First Five-Year Plan, the emphasis of the economic planners was on placing investments where they would do the most good, and this meant development of the more advanced areas. At the end of the period of adjustment, in 1956, the poorer republics had not appreciably improved their position relative to the more advanced

[6] See the figures for the value of industrial production and the value of investments for each republic given for 1939 and 1951 in 1947 prices, Article 8 of the five-year plan. It should be noted that the over-all value of investments—all investments, not merely those for industrial purposes—is unfavorable to agricultural regions such as Serbia because of the artificially low level of agricultural prices prevalent at the time.

republics. Only Bosnia-Hercegovina had surpassed the level of production of any of the advanced republics in 1947. Montenegro had received, after Slovenia, the most investment per capita, but remained the least developed republic in Yugoslavia. Macedonia gained the least, showing the lowest rate of growth of the three underdeveloped republics.[7]

It was inevitable that such results should prove disappointing to the underdeveloped regions, and evidence that a debate was going on among the republics appeared in 1953 when Vukmanović-Tempo referred to discussions of the question of investments which, in his words, had "lost any kind of principle." [8] Tempo promised that investment policy would not neglect the underdeveloped areas, as had been the case up to that time, but continued to insist on the principle that investments be channeled to the areas where they would give maximum returns. A year later the problem was taken up by a special conference of the Coordination Committee of the Federal Executive Committee, which met in September, 1954, and was attended by the presidents of the six republics. Although several methods of gathering funds for the underdeveloped areas were proposed, the committee was unable to agree on a formula which would satisfy both the advanced and the underdeveloped regions.[9] The matter was again widely debated in 1955, and also in 1956, when a special committee of the Federal Executive Committee was formed on the order of the Central Committee of the League of Communists to prepare a program of aid for the underdeveloped areas in connection with the new five-year plan, which was to run from 1957 to 1961.

[7] Macedonia had the lowest rate of growth, the lowest level of total capital goods per capita, and the second lowest level of investment per capita of the republics up to 1956. For comparative figures on Macedonia and the other republics, see Savezni zavod za privredno planiranje, "Uporedni pregled privrednog razvitka narodnih republika 1947–1955."

[8] *Komunist*, No. 7 (July, 1953), pp. 466–67.

[9] Representatives of the less developed republics proposed that either sums be earmarked from the federal investment fund for use in the development of underdeveloped areas, or that the distribution of enterprise income be regulated in such a way as to put industry in the underdeveloped areas in a better competitive position. The latter proposal was rejected by Vukmanović-Tempo (speaking for the government) because it would violate the principle of uniform taxation. Instead, Tempo proposed that a fund be established for the underdeveloped areas which would be supported by means of levies on the more advanced republics. For a discussion of the meeting, see "Doprinos nerazvijenim oblastima," *Ekonomska Politika*, Oct. 7, 1954, pp. 801–4.

The difficulty in hammering out a policy of aid for the underdeveloped republics was a continuing source of embarrassment to the Yugoslav Party leadership. The feeling of frustration which was growing over the issue came to the surface at the Seventh Congress of the League of Communists when Boris Krajger, speaking on the necessity of aiding the underdeveloped regions without endangering the economic growth of the country as a whole, pleaded for a solution "in principle,"

a solution which will not represent a compromise between the interests on one [side] or another, but the best path for satisfying the socialist interest of one and the other, and such a path exists, must exist, and must be found." [10]

The prospective social plan for 1957–61 did not provide an answer in principle, as the Seventh Congress had sought; it did supply greatly increased investment funds, in the form of guaranteed credits, to Macedonia and Kossovo-Metohija, the two regions most neglected in earlier years. Macedonia was to receive 20 billion dinars per annum, four times the level of investment she had been receiving in the preceding several years; Kossovo-Metohija was promised 10 billion dinars annually (the *total* invested in the region between 1952 and 1956 had been only 4 billion).[11]

The second development plan was the crucial test for the underdeveloped republics. Actual investments in the period 1957–61 came close to, or exceeded, the amounts foreseen in the plan.[12] In addition, Macedonia, Montenegro, and Kossovo-Metohija were relieved of the obligation of returning the principle on the credits they had received.

The underdeveloped republics were not in a position to utilize the aid effectively, however. There were long delays in finishing projects, many of which were still being financed from the federal budget in 1962, 1963, and even 1964. Investments were squandered in prestige projects, while inadequate attention was devoted to the location of markets, raw materials, and other factors which would determine the profitability of new

[10] *VII kongres*, p. 462.

[11] See *Društveni plan privrednog razvoja Jugoslavije, 1957–1961*, p. 53, and for Kossovo-Metohija, *Zajednica*, July 3, 1958, p. 3 (*Zajednica* was a supplement to the weekly *Komunist*).

[12] "Posleratni razvoj privredno nedovoljno razvijenih republika i krajeva," *Jugoslovenski Pregled*, IX, No. 2–3 (Feb.-March, 1965), 46, n. 13.

enterprises.[13] These problems were not confined to the underdeveloped republics, but the mistakes committed by these regions into which massive aid was being pumped were a source of acute irritation to the developed republics, which felt that their resources were being wasted, and the failure of new industries to prove their profitability placed in doubt the whole program of aiding underdeveloped regions. With the exception of the years 1961–63, when many of the projects of the Second Five-Year Plan were being completed, the rate of economic growth of the more advanced regions continued higher than in the underdeveloped areas, rather than the reverse, as had been foreseen in the prospective plan.[14] The position of the underdeveloped areas grew more difficult as funds became harder to obtain. The general investment fund, the chief source of assistance to the underdeveloped republics, was abolished at the end of 1963, while the social plans for the years 1961–65 cut back assistance to the underdeveloped areas, limiting federal aid largely to investments needed to complete projects begun under the Second Five-Year Plan.

As it became evident that injections of investment from the general investment fund were not having the desired effect in the underdeveloped republics, support grew for the establishment of a fund through which long-term programs of aid could be developed and through which, it is

[13] The 1964 social plan contained the warning to the less developed republics that "the social-political community and working organizations in the less developed regions should in 1964 undertake indispensable measures for creating favorable conditions for projects which have already been put into operation or whose construction is completed, create ever greater effectiveness in respect to production, profitability of investment, and other results in connection with the program of construction." "Društveni plan Jugoslavije za 1964 godinu," *Službeni List SFRJ*, No. 52 (Dec. 31, 1963), p. 953. For a frank criticism of the failure of the new industries set up in Bosnia-Hercegovina, see the report of the Eighth Plenum of the Central Committee of the League of Communists of Bosnia-Hercegovina published in *Borba*, Oct. 19, 1963. A highly critical article which gives many useful insights into the program of aiding underdeveloped areas in Serbia is Borislav Srebrić, "Problem metoda privrednog razvoja nerazvijenih krajeva Jugoslavije," *Ekonomist*, XVII (1964), 311–27.

[14] *Jugoslovenski Pregled*, IX, No. 2–3 (Feb.-March, 1965), p. 11. The index of growth of national income in the period 1956–63 in advanced regions was 195.1; for less developed areas, 184.5. Only Montenegro, among the less developed republics, showed a rise in income which exceeded that of the advanced republics, her index increasing to 197.3.

reasonable to surmise, the issue of aid could be taken out of the realm of politics. The creation of a fund was supported in principle at the time the prospective social plan for 1961–65 was presented,[15] and from that time on intensive discussions were held concerning the character of the fund and, most important, the method of its financing. The federal government promised that a law setting up the fund would be introduced in 1962, and made the same promise again in 1963,[16] but the problem of reconciling republic interests proved so delicate that nothing could be done until 1965. A law of February of that year established the fund at last. Under the provisions of the law, the Fund for Crediting the Economic Development of Economically Lesser Developed Republics and Regions was to have its own governing board made up of a president and twelve members, plus a director of the fund. The fund would work autonomously in deciding on plans for aid to the less developed areas. Assistance would be dispersed in the form of credits provided under more favorable conditions than those available to enterprises from the regular banking system. The fund was also to provide technical assistance to the less developed republics and had the right to raise loans within the country and abroad for its aid programs.[17]

The difficulty facing the economic planners lay in the demonstrable need to eliminate the burden placed on the country as a result of the necessity of maintaining the standard of living in the poorer republics. But the equally inescapable fact, proved by the experience of the five-year plans, was that scarce investment funds gave better results if used in the

[15] Kardelj proposed the fund in the spring of 1961 in the Federal Executive Committee report to the National Assembly.

[16] See the speech of Avdo Humo, *Borba,* Dec. 28, 1961, p. 4, and the remarks by Miloš Minić on the fund at the end of 1962, *Borba,* Dec. 30, p. 3. The role of the fund is confused in Yugoslav economic policy because the prospective social plan for 1961–65 provided for a fund for the development of less developed regions. The plan foresaw 169 billion dinars being paid out in the five-year period to less developed regions from this source. The "fund" in this plan was simply a new way of presenting an old practice, for the amount set aside was drawn from the general investment fund, and no separate body was set up to administer the program. Some of the annual social plans between 1961 and 1965 made no mention of this fund whatsoever, while others did. A separate law designated which areas were to be considered "less developed" and eligible for aid from the fund: Macedonia, Montenegro, and Kossovo-Metohija.

[17] See *Službeni List SFRJ,* No. 35 (Feb. 24, 1965), p. 181.

advanced republics. This dilemma was of course common to all developing countries. On the other hand, it was arguable that a Communist state was better equipped, through methods of economic planning, to deal with underdeveloped areas. That this was not necessarily the case—that in fact the reverse might be true under certain conditions—requires brief consideration.

The great advantage enjoyed by a Communist government in dealing with the challenge of underdeveloped regions is its ability to concentrate investment in the affected regions and, more important still, to shift personnel to backward areas to ensure that the necessary technical skills will be available for the proper utilization of the investment funds. The technique of ordering persons to underdeveloped areas was employed in Yugoslavia during the First Five-Year Plan.[18] However, such a policy could lead to national antagonisms between the local population and the technicians and skilled labor imported into the region; this occurred in the Soviet Union, and Yugoslavia did not entirely escape problems of this kind, even in the short time that the centralized planning system was in effect.[19]

The disadvantages of a Communist system of planning in allocating investments effectively lie in its disregard of standards of profitability. The Yugoslavs were well aware of this difficulty, but could never bring themselves to deal with the underdeveloped areas in a strictly businesslike manner. Once the factories were built they were required to show a profit, but it was always possible to subsidize faltering enterprises, while by law

[18] The number of those involved is not known, but it certainly ran into the thousands, and was the subject of a considerable number of directives. The 1946 law on state functionaries provided that personnel could be transferred by the President of the Federal government from the republics to the Union, from the Union to the republics, and between republics with the consent of the Presidents of the republics concerned. In 1948 this provision was modified by delegating the right to make such decisions to the Secretary of the Federal Government for Personnel and by adding that there was no right of appeal from the decision for transfer. In 1949 the necessity for approval by the Presidents of the republics for transfers was eliminated. The power to transfer personnel was given to the Federal Executive Council in 1953 and abolished only in 1957, when the new law on state functionaries of that year contained no provisions on the subject.

[19] Crvenkovski, "Treba se upornije i sistematskije boriti za sprovodjenje pisma CK SKJ u delo," *Komunist,* No. 9 (Sept., 1953), gave the example of Macedonian factories firing Slovenes in order to hire local personnel.

the establishment of *new* industry was forbidden to those who had a real interest in profitability—the established enterprises—and remained in the hands of the state, that is, the local or regional authorities.

After the introduction of economic decentralization in the Titoist period, investments continued to flow into underdeveloped areas (in fact, they increased substantially), but badly needed personnel could not be ordered around the country at will; while because of the peculiar constitutional limitations governing the establishment of new enterprises, the process of spontaneous business expansion into the underdeveloped regions by firms seeking profit, such as might have taken place in a nonsocialist economy, did not occur. Thus large sums of money were suddenly made available, but there was no one in the underdeveloped republics who was trained for the task of placing these funds in profitable sectors of the economy, nor was the technical skill available to operate the new plants effectively, with the unfortunate results described earlier.

As the Yugoslavs gained experience in the problems of aiding underdeveloped areas, a greater awareness emerged of some of the built-in dangers of the programs of aid adopted during the Second Five-Year Plan. Special provision was made in the law of 1965 establishing the development fund that the governing body of the Fund for Crediting the Economic Development of Economically Lesser Developed Republics and Regions would organize technical assistance for the less developed republics. An effort was made to get experienced enterprises from the advanced regions to cooperate with industry in the south, helping the new plants to organize production efficiently and operate at a profit.[20]

The spread of these new ideas, however, faced obstacles created by the political and ideological prejudices of Party members. Control by the local or regional authorities over plans for the expansion and development of industry was practically absolute. As already noted, the profitable enterprise from the north could not form plants in the less developed republics under its own management, but had to resort to more indirect, and less profitable, arrangements involving agreements with already established (and often economically shaky) enterprises. Any effort to introduce more flexibility into this system had to cope with the ingrained

[20] See the discussion of integration of enterprises below.

habit of local officials of thinking in Marxist terminology of the "exploitation" of the poorer regions by the advanced republics, or of the "imperialist" relationship which would be the result of the more advanced areas drawing off profit from the underdeveloped regions.[21]

The frustration that was felt on all sides over the failure of the program to aid the underdeveloped areas was reflected, almost from the start, in an intense controversy between the more developed and the less developed republics over the allocation of investment funds. Much of the dissatisfaction generated in the struggle came to be focused on the federal government for allegedly discriminating in favor of one side or the other in the dispute.

In the light of the efforts of the federal government to be fair to all parties, it was not always easy to see what grounds there were for these beliefs. This was particularly true in respect to the attitude of the developed republics—Slovenia and Croatia—which had clearly benefited most from the industrialization program. These republics felt, nevertheless, that they had not gained as much as might appear on the basis of official data. They argued, for example, that investment figures, when given in gross terms, made no distinction between the large sums spent for replacing existing plant and equipment in the developed areas, and the investments for expanding production, which were going in sizable quantities to the poorer republics.[22] The advanced republics also felt that they were the principal victim of the practice of diverting amortization funds into investment through the central amortization fund.[23]

[21] This type of argument was seldom used openly, but could be met with in private conversations, and influenced much of the thinking in the underdeveloped areas. For an attack on the theme of "exploitation," see Vukmirica, pp. 108–9.

[22] These arguments did not appear in print, but were usually referred to indirectly in discussions of the problem of underdeveloped regions. However, a Slovenian economist in 1955 did publish some statistics which were obviously meant to back up the claims of the more advanced republics in respect to investment figures. He calculated the percentage of net investment contained in gross investments for each republic. In the case of Slovenia he found that only one third of the investment went into plant and equipment for expanding production (net investment), while in Montenegro over three quarters of investment was utilized for this purpose. Evgen Lovšin, "Poročilo o delu medfakultetne konference ekonomskih fakultet," Ekonomske Revije (Ljubljana), No. 4 (1955), p. 330.

[23] Figures were calculated by a Slovene to show the per capita loss of amortization funds in each republic in the period up to 1955. With the average loss for the

The practices of giving investment in gross terms and of using amortization funds for investment purposes were abandoned after the First Five-Year Plan. The developed republics were convinced, nevertheless, that investments which were created from the profits of efficient industry in the developed regions were simply being thrown away in the underdeveloped republics.[24] This opposition to the federal government's policies grew especially strong in the early 1960s, when investments in the underdeveloped republics were greatest and were showing far less results than investments in developed regions.

The underdeveloped republics, for their part, argued that they were disadvantaged by the program for Yugoslavia's industrial development because of their position as producers of raw material for the industry of the developed regions.[25] The growing gap in income between the two types of regions, cited by the Slovenes and Croats as proof of the wasteful character of investment in the poorer regions, was used by the underdeveloped republics as an argument for the imperative need of even larger amounts of aid.[26]

---

entire country serving as an index of 100, it was claimed that Macedonia lost 42.5 of her amortization fund to investment per capita, while Slovenia lost 255.2. *Ibid.*

[24] Tito conceded this point, in part, in a speech to newsmen reprinted in *Komunist*, Jan. 4, 1963, in which he stated: "I agree that means created on the soil of Slovenia, Croatia, . . . were not always used for that for which they were intended. . . . It should not have been allowed for them to build various monumental buildings and other [things] which are now not necessary; rather they should have built industry and other [things] which must be built. For we can't demand, for example, from Slovenia, to wait and not raise its standard and its pay while in other areas the standard is not raised."

[25] The argument is not published, but reference to its use by the underdeveloped republics can be found in the speeches of Vladimir Bakarić on the national question. See especially *Vjesnik u Srijedu,* December 2, 1964, pp. 4–5.

[26] See, in particular, Panče Kirovski, *Teritorijalnata razmestenost na proizvodstvoto i regionalniot razvoj na Jugoslavija.* Kirovski cited figures showing that the growth of social product per capita in the regions north of the Sava and Danube (including Belgrade) was approximately 109,000 dinars, and south of the Sava and Danube, only 49,000 per capita. Figures on the growing differences between per capita incomes in the developed and underdeveloped regions were cited in Selimović, p. 239. Thus, income per capita in Macedonia in 1947 was 31 percent below the national average; in 1963 it was 36 percent below. Per capita income in Slovenia rose in the same period from 62 percent to a level of 95 percent above the national average. Selimović estimated that the needs of Bosnia-Hercegovina in housing, education, and social services simply to raise the republic up to the Yugo-

Attempts to limit the dispute were unsuccessful not only because of the insoluble economic problem but because the republics were caught up in a wave of particularism (the defense of local interests) which had become a prominent feature of the Titoist economic system.

This particularism was not simply a reflection of national rivalries. Nor could it be blamed on differences in levels of economic development among the republics or smaller territorial units in Yugoslavia. In the Titoist system, particularism was first and foremost the result of the fact that the reforms of the economy carried out in the early 1950s had decentralized control over large areas of planning and investment allocation without giving power to the enterprises to determine the flow of capital on the basis of profit considerations. As a result, the local "power elites" came to exercise great discretion in economic matters and invariably used their power to pursue the interests of their own region, which, as this practice was rather naïvely conceived, amounted to obtaining investments for the construction of industry and then protecting that industry at any cost.

This pattern of particularism was especially pronounced in rural areas seeking industry, and reflected the difficulty such areas were experiencing in adjusting to the impact of modernization and the free play of economic forces which the Titoist reforms were aimed at encouraging. Thus one critic of particularistic tendencies in the economy laid much of the blame for this phenomenon on the conviction of local officials in the predominantly rural areas that it was dangerous to specialize, leading to pressures on factories to produce a wide variety of products for local needs; when such methods tied down the factory and made it uncompetitive, pressures would develop to cut off competition, to give local industry favored treatment, and to integrate trade, industry, and agriculture within the boundaries of the local commune at the expense of normal market mechanisms.[27]

---

slav average would come to 2,000 billion dinars, in comparison to the 127 billion which was foreseen by the federal planners for the period 1964–70. The position of Kossovo-Metohija was most serious, and the regional Party committee took the position, in preparation for the prospective plan of 1964–70, that, as a minimum, industrial production there would have to grow at the rate of 17–20 percent, almost twice its previous rate. See interview with Dušan Mugoša in *Jedinstvo*, Jan. 6, 1964, p. 4.

27 "Integracija umesto autarkije," *Ekonomska Politika*, May 12, 1962, p. 571.

This particularism could take on unusual forms. Thus, a local government would find ways to prevent outside competition from entering the market reserved for the local factory; producers of raw materials were sometimes forbidden to sell their products outside the boundary of the commune, or factories to buy in other regions. Towns would set up rival bus lines, and then carry out reprisals against one another; there were instances of local officials closing down the ticket office of a rival bus line and of attempts to shut down the teletype connections of a large bus company that was threatening a local company with its competition.[28] Economic rivalry among the local governments was described in very unflattering terms by one critic as the ambition of local bureaucrats

to set up feudal barriers . . . within which they will be tutors over "their" enterprises, integrate them and "dis-integrate" them, manipulate the profits of labor, close the market, rap "disobedient" enterprises on the fingers, protect the extensive business of uneconomic enterprises, economic organizations, and so forth.[29]

Particularism was present at all levels of the economic system and was the inspiration for economic rivalry among republics as well as local government organs. There was a strong tendency to encourage economic autarchy within republic boundaries at the expense of free market forces and the interests of the country as a whole in large, efficient industry. Competition in the field of transportation, which sometimes took on such extreme forms at the local level, also appeared among the republics. Slovenia formed her own airline (Aviopromet) in competition with the Yugoslav national airways, and bus services among the republics suffered from duplication and lack of coordination.[30] The republics also tended to form boundaries for markets; at the instigation of local officials, enterprises not in the republic would be forbidden to open outlets or even to compete for contracts. One incident of this type recounted in the press in 1963 concerned the members of the workers' council and administrative committee of an enterprise who were transferred ten days

[28] For these and other examples, see *Ekonomska Politika*, March 31, 1962, p. 395; *Vjesnik u Srijedu*, March 24, 1965; *Borba*, March 11, 1963, p. 5; March 13, 1963, p. 4; Nov. 18, 1963, p. 5.

[29] *Vjesnik u Srijedu*, March 24, 1965.

[30] See *Borba*, Oct. 20, 1964, p. 6, for report on a conference of bus lines of Yugoslavia which attempted, without much success, to eliminate some of the anomalies which had grown up as a result of competition among the republics.

after accepting an offer for a large purchase of materials from an enterprise located in another republic rather than being guided by the rule of buying in "one's own republic." [31]

Above all, the effects of particularistic tendencies made themselves evident at the republic level in the construction of large plants which duplicated existing capacities in other republics. For a relatively small and far from wealthy country attempting to utilize her limited resources to a maximum, this procedure was difficult to justify. Each republic had built, or had plans for building, a steel mill. In the late 1950s, when duplication reached its peak, there were several plants manufacturing automobiles, a number of large electronic concerns in Serbia, Croatia, and Slovenia producing television sets, and duplication of facilities in other key industries of nation-wide importance.

Jack C. Fisher, in his work on regional differences in Yugoslavia, gives an excellent example of this process in the construction of plants for producing refrigerators:

Before the war not a single factory for the production of refrigerators existed in Yugoslavia. The first one was established at Maribor, a major industrial city in the North, in the Republic of Slovenia. The location was within the potential market area and in direct proximity to a well-developed transportation network. The quality of the labor force was high and the final product was therefore of a standardized quality. Under political pressure another factory was built at Cetinje in Montenegro and yet another at Bitola in southern Macedonia. The quality of the Bitola product has continued, at least by reputation, to be very poor, while the cost of shipping the products of both these southern factories to market is extremely high. For example, the Cetinje factory, which operates under an Italian license, imports raw materials which reach the coast by ship and then must be transported by truck over mountainous terrain and unpaved roads. Cetinje has no rail connection. The final product must be sent to the coast by truck, then shipped to a northern port which has rail connections to Zagreb or Sarajevo.[32]

In 1962, a strenuous effort was begun to "integrate" duplicate facilities, especially when unproductive firms were finding it difficult to survive except with local protection and subsidies. But the campaign for integration, except for a few widely publicized examples, seldom succeeded in

31 *Ekonomska Politika,* July 27, 1963, pp. 883–84.
32 Fisher, p. 11.

merging plants across republic boundaries [33] and the phenomenon of duplication and republic-oriented economies seemed destined to become a permanent feature of the Titoist system.

Competition among the republics was not restricted to industry alone, although this was the area where duplication was greatest and the struggle to obtain investments most widespread. Projects which had been the subject of controversy before the war, such as railroads and ports, were revived by the republics and federal aid was sought to ensure their construction. Serbia and Montenegro were enthusiastic supporters of the plan for a railway link between Belgrade and the sea at Bar. This project was begun in the early 1950s and continued for over a dozen years before the general squeeze on investments forced a halt to construction. Rijeka, Yugoslavia's main port, was enlarged and improved, and federal funds were made available to assist in the construction of a port at Kopar, for the Slovenes, and an outlet for Bosnia-Hercegovina at Ploče. In this way everybody got something, but hardly anyone felt he had received enough, and investments were too widely scattered to be of maximum effectiveness. The Croats were especially critical of the way funds were divided among the republics, instead of being used to improve port facilities at Rijeka.[34] Serbia and Montenegro defended the Belgrade-Bar railway line publicly, on the occasion of the declaration

[33] The most frequently cited example was the integration between Rade Končar, the large manufacturer of electrical equipment in Zagreb, and "Jug" in Skoplje. For an account of this merger, see *Vjesnik* (Zagreb), Feb. 11, 1963, p. 4. Other examples were the merger of "Jastreb" in Novi Sad with the Maribor enterprise TAM. See *Politika*, Jan. 23, 1963, p. 8. For the cooperation and merger of tobacco enterprises in Serbia and Montenegro, see *Borba*, Jan. 31, 1963, p. 5. The Communist parties of Serbia and Montenegro agreed on extensive cooperation in the economic field; the terms of this agreement are described below. For the integration of producers of leather in Croatia, Vojvodina, and Slovenia, see *Borba*, Dec. 21, 1963, p. 5. Numerous sources have admitted that integration across republic lines was the exception rather than the rule. See Tito's speech to newsmen reprinted in *Komunist*, Jan. 14, 1963, p. 1; *Borba*, March 20, 1963, p. 1; and *Vjesnik u Srijedu*, March 24, 1965. Plants which integrated also "dis-integrated" later.

[34] When the problem of ports was being discussed in the early 1950s, the Croats are said to have objected to a plan worked out by several federal ministries for the distribution of trade among Yugoslav ports. The plan foresaw a decline in over-all as well as relative volume of trade that would pass through Rijeka. For mention of the report and a criticism of its findings, see Biro za organizaciju uprave i privrede, *Dokumentacija iz stručnih časopisa i dnevne štampe*, No. 5 (1954), p.

issued in 1964 by the parties of the two regions on cooperation between their republics.[35]

The joint statement of the Montenegrin and Serbian Communist parties was unusual in putting the argument for the Belgrade-Bar railway openly before the public. In most cases, the specific grievances of the republics engaged in an economic dispute of this kind were not allowed to appear in print, nor, indeed, were the names of the republics ever mentioned. This saved the Communists from embarrassment, but made it difficult to determine the kinds of arguments, economic, nationalistic, or both, which were being put forth to justify republic claims.

For this reason it was not always easy for the outside observer to determine how far nationalism was coloring the economic disputes. But it was often difficult for the Party leadership itself to decide where economics ended and nationalism began. Tito, while favoring the view that economic interests were the prime cause of rivalry among republics and other territorial units, admitted that nationalism and economic particularism were often hard to tell apart.[36] Milovan Djilas, in his critique of Yugoslav society and politics, *The New Class,* strongly attacked the notion that rivalry among the territorial units in Yugoslavia had a national basis. Djilas's experience as a former leader of the Party turned anti-Communist makes his views especially significant. In his words:

National feelings and national interests, however, do not lie at the basis of the conflict between the communist national bureaucracies. The motive is quite different: it is supremacy in one's own administration. The struggle over the reputation and power of one's own republic does not go much further than a desire to strengthen one's own power. . . . The communist bureaucrats are vehement local patriots on behalf of their own administra-

---

70. A book published in 1953, which took a point of view similar to that of the federal planners, was also the subject of criticism in Croatia. See Slavko Suvadžić, *Razvitak saobraćaja i njegov privredni značaj* (Belgrade, Rad, 1953).

[35] The contents of the declaration are cited below.

[36] At the Second Plenum of the Central Committee of November, 1959, Tito remarked: "People often ask whether in such instances localism is in question, or whether it already becomes a question of national chauvinism." In Tito's opinion, "It is more localism, that is, that narrow outlook toward the interests of that which one administers directly." *Drugi plenum Centralnog komiteta Saveza komunista Jugoslavije,* p. 12.

tive units, even though they have not been trained for the part on either a linguistic or national basis. In some purely administrative units in Yugoslavia (the regional councils), chauvinism has been greater than in the national republic governments.[37]

Party declarations, on the other hand, frequently referred to the importance of nationalism in these controversies. The letter of the Executive Committee of the League of Communists of February, 1958, spoke of "powerful particularistic tendencies which are appearing [and] frequently assume a nationalistic, even chauvinistic, form." The most outspoken criticisms of nationalism originated with the leader of the Croatian Party, Vladimir Bakarić. His description of the manner in which the Communists sought to defend local interests bore a very close resemblance to accounts of national controversies over the economic question in the period between the two world wars:

Here there appear, among other things, examples of antagonism, of unscrupulous nationalistically tinged struggles for investments; there exists the tendency to shut oneself up in narrow administrative territorial boundaries, which makes normal economic development more difficult; cases occur of distorted presentation of conditions and the use of inexact indices in order to prove how in fact "our nation" is "plundered," that it is "threatened," how "everyone gets more and passes better than we," and similar [arguments]. In the race for funds, which must be gotten from somebody, arguments behind people's backs quickly become nationalistic. Thus "fear" and unfounded "concern," most frequently because of our falling behind, and "threatened position" become some kind of obsession and a fixed idea, in some hands even a political platform of a certain circle of persons.[38]

Description of Serbian economic nationalism in the mid-1960s was couched in similar terms; bureaucratic interests were accused of wishing

to create their monopoly in defense of national interests in many concrete questions of economic life still not settled at the level of the federation, giving nationalistic explanations "who is against whom," "who got what and who lost." They created national myths concerning a number of major (*krupnih*) economic projects, questions of "national honor" and "national equality." Uninterested in the position of the working man, the direct pro-

[37] *The New Class,* p. 101.
[38] *Komunist,* Nov. 5, 1964, p. 3.

ducer, or the development of self-managment, certain leading individuals, obsessed with investment grandomania, were very active and inflammatory with nationalistic explanations of political and economic events in our social life.[89]

In the light of the provincial outlook and the highly developed national sensitivities of so many Party members, it was to be expected that what may have begun as a clash of economic interests quickly became dominated by questions of national honor. At the same time, the appeal of nationalistic slogans was not apt to be overlooked by those with economic interests to defend. As the Party was fond of repeating, it was those persons with a personal stake in protecting local economic interests who were the most persistent in appealing to nationalistic sentiments. Unfortunately for the Communists, however, the ill effects of raising economic differences to the level of questions of national honor were not mitigated by the fact that the original impulse to the national controversy may have lain in the selfish or narrow concerns of certain individuals or groups in the republics.

These observations are particularly relevant in understanding the factional struggle against the Ranković group which played such a crucial role in the rise of economic nationalism in the mid-1960s. While there is still much that is obscure in connection with this dispute, remarks by Tito and others indicate that the split between the conservative group led by Ranković and the liberal wing of the Party began to develop in the late 1950s. The opposition of Ranković to the rest of the Party leadership could not initially be attributed solely to selfish interests of an economic character: the Second Five-Year Plan of the period 1957–61 was built on the type of transitional economic system which Ranković was later to defend; also, the role of Serbia in the Yugoslav economy was neither that of an advanced *nor* that of an underdeveloped republic, but combined elements of both. From the point of view of pure self-interest, Serbia in the 1950s had every reason to support increased aid to the agricultural sector over industry, for Serbia was an area in which agricultural production was of great importance to republic income. In the postwar period, Serbia's rate of economic growth was lower than that of most of the other republics as a consequence of low agricultural prices

[89] *Ibid.*, Sept. 15, 1966, p. 2.

and the flow of investments into the industrial sector at the expense of agriculture.

The position of Ranković was one of broad resistance to liberalization, a view in keeping with his background as head of the secret police and Party secretary in charge of cadres. As a group, the Serbian Communists did not give evidence of concern over the fact that industry was being given priority over agriculture at the expense of Serbia's economic interests. Undoubtedly, like all Communists, they felt that the only "real" source of wealth and economic power lay in industry. Whether Serbia's industrialization would be favored by a more liberal economy in which investments would flow in the direction of productive enterprises, or by a controlled economy in which initially nonproductive enterprises in underdeveloped areas would stand a better chance of receiving funds, was debatable. Most likely it was a primitive economic reasoning which put great value on conspicuous projects requiring large amounts of investment, rather than any clear-cut concept of the economic interests of Serbia, which led so many Serbian Communists to lend their support to Ranković and his opposition to economic reform.

This opposition began to crystallize in the early 1960s when a series of steps were taken to cut back investments, reduce duplication of industries, and liberalize regulations governing foreign trade and convertibility of the dinar. These measures were accompanied by a marked slowdown in the rapid growth of Yugoslav industrial production that had been characteristic of the period of the Second Five-Year Plan. The Serbian Communists became increasingly concerned with the fate of projects in Serbia whose completion was jeopardized by the cutback in investments. Decisions in the Central Committee of the League of Communists, it was later revealed, were taken by a majority vote and often not implemented if they were considered contrary to republic interests. While a number of republics, in particular Montenegro and Macedonia, may have been guilty of breaking Party discipline in this way,[40] it seems likely that Serbian Communists were the chief offenders in resisting the economic reforms initiated in the early 1960s.

The split between Ranković and his supporters on the one hand, and the remainder of the Party on the other, deepened in the spring of 1962

[40] See Chapter 5.

after a sharp clash of views at a Party plenum held in March.[41] The meeting also marked a deterioration in national relations among the republics. Although no admission was ever made that national animosities flared during the plenum, it seems reasonable to assume that, in what were acknowledged to be heated exchanges among Party leaders, national feelings became aroused; lurid accounts which later circulated about the meeting spoke of Serbs and Macedonians facing each other at pistol point and of threats by the Slovenians to secede from the federation. As noted in an earlier chapter, the rumor of Slovenian threats to secede was not entirely unfounded, although the origins of this demand in the events of the March, 1962, plenum cannot be taken as proven. An indication that what passed among the Party leaders nevertheless went beyond the bounds of propriety and respect for Party unity was provided in 1966 when it was revealed that Ranković had taped the proceedings of the plenum to use later, it was charged, in any succession crisis that might arise.[42]

The decisions of the March, 1962, plenum were never made public. The Ranković faction found itself in a minority but refused to recognize the need to push ahead with further liberalization measures. For the sake of Party unity a full-scale reform of the economy was delayed. In its place, a series of halfway measures followed, while a campaign was begun to democratize the power structure in Yugoslavia by placing greater reliance on workers' self-management, introducing a new and more democratic constitution, and curtailing the powers of local bureaucratic elements opposing change.

Between 1962 and 1966 this struggle continued unabated. Its effects on the policy of the League of Communists on the national question— especially in respect to the idea of Yugoslavianism—have already been described. The problems facing the economy continued to grow; excess investment encouraged inflation, the balance of payments situation deteriorated, and, although industrial output in Yugoslavia continued to

[41] No documents were published at the time of this meeting, which Tito later referred to as a broadened sitting of the Executive Committee, not a meeting of the Central Committee. A Central Committee meeting held at the same time discussed cadre questions but did not deal with any of the vital issues of economic reform and discrimination against various republics which were the subject of the March "plenum" under discussion here.

[42] *Vjesnik u Srijedu,* Sept. 7, 1966.

rise, it was clear that more drastic steps would have to be taken to curb public spending and encourage greater rationality and efficiency in production. In the struggle of economic interests, the Serbian Party began to seek allies among the underdeveloped republics whose economic progress was endangered by further cutbacks in investments. The notion of a "progressive northwest" and a "conservative southeast," which had little relevance as long as Serbia was neutral in the disputes between the developed and underdeveloped regions, now began to gain currency.[43]

The most striking evidence at this time that the Serbian Communists had committed themselves to a policy of independent action in order to protect Serbia's economic interests and gain allies in the fight against reducing investments came with the announcement of the agreement reached between the central committees of Serbia and Montenegro in December, 1963, for cooperation in the fields of culture, education, and economics.[44] Of these three forms of cooperation, the economic was the most comprehensive, encompassing the integration of industries in the two republics, cooperation in the development of communications, foreign trade and marketing, and long-term joint planning.

The statement issued by the two central committees sought to defend the propriety of the agreement by reference to that part of the constitution which foresaw the possibility of agreements between republics in order to further collaboration in the cultural sphere and in other related activities. The real intent of the pact was revealed, however, in the statement on the Belgrade-Bar railway, which took the position that

the documentation and analyses prepared up to this time convincingly confirm the economic justification of building the Belgrade-Bar line. They show that this is not only a matter of helping Montenegro and the inadequately developed regions of Serbia, but concerns the construction of a communications link which has great economic significance for the country as a whole. . . . It has been proven that this line should be finished without delay in the course of the Second Five-Year Plan.[45]

The impression that this agreement was meant to serve as leverage for bringing economic pressure against the Party leaders and economic planners was strengthened by reference in the statement of the need of the

[43] See the remarks of Krste Crvenkovski in *Komunist,* March 17, 1966, p. 8.
[44] *Komunist,* Feb. 6, 1964, p. 1.
[45] *Ibid.*

two republics "to reach a common position on the most significant problems which faced both areas in connection with the drawing up of the Yugoslav Seven-Year Plan for 1965–70." The conclusion was inescapable that the agreement between the parties was a political act dictated both by economic considerations and by the traditional ties of sentiment between the two republics—a step which could only encourage the growth of regional combinations and inject the national question more directly than ever before into economic disputes among the republics.

The action of the Serbian and Montenegrin Communists took on added significance in the light of the discussion, originating in the more advanced republics, of the benefits of a "polycentric" system of planning,[46] and demands, originating within the Party organization in Kossovo-Metohija during this period, that unless the economic development needs of the region could be met, Kossovo-Metohija should press for autonomy.[47] The recognition in the constitution of even a limited role for the republic in the organization of the economy strengthened the impression that the deep rift in the Party over how to solve Yugoslavia's economic difficulties was encouraging each republic or region to seek its own solutions to its economic problems.

The idea of a "polycentric" economy was rejected by Party leaders; Vladimir Bakarić condemned the idea of "republicanism" in the economy in an interview with a Belgrade paper in March, 1964.[48] Practically speaking, the ability of the republics to initiate changes in the economic system remained small. Beyond obstructing the execution of decisions of the federal government, the republics could only hope to develop independent economic mechanisms by replacing federal laws and regulations

[46] Rudolf Bičanić, "O monocentričnom i policentričnom planiranju," *Ekonomski Pregled,* XIV, No. 6–7, 469–527.

[47] See the speech by Dušan Mugoša to the Eighth Regional Plenum of the regional committee for Kossovo-Metohija. Said Mugoša, in part: "The difficult inheritance of the past still today presents very fruitful ground for the activity of hostile elements. Even among people with good intentions, and some [Communist] cadre, the economic position of the *oblast* is explained in a mistaken fashion, and [they] make comparisons with other regions which have not had such a past. Examples are quoted and discussions carried out about how much income per capita there is, the number employed, total production, and so on in our region, and how much in other areas. Such discussions encourage incorrect views, resentment, and theories of autonomy (*autonomizam*)." *Jedinstvo,* Jan. 21, 1963, pp. 4–5.

[48] *NIN,* March 8, 1964, pp. 2–3.

by republic legislation, a step no area was willing to take. On the other hand, the difficulties that could result from giving the republics even a limited initiative in the planning field were revealed on the occasion of the preparation of the economic development plan for the years 1965–70. Disregarding the inflationary crisis which had overtaken the country, the republics and autonomous regions went ahead with ambitious plans for economic development. The Autonomous Region of Kossovo-Metohija, after lengthy discussions among local and republic Party figures in the fall of 1964, announced a set of goals which called for the rise of industrial production of 18–19 percent a year.[49] Serbia announced an investment plan of 331 billion dinars for the seven-year period, and called for completion of the railway to Bar.[50] Despite the Croatian position in support of deflation for the Yugoslav economy, the Croatian Assembly approved proposals that included the construction of a steel mill at Zadar. This initiative on the part of the republics and national regions left the federal planners with the unpleasant task of drawing up a national plan which would scale down the economic goals to which the regional Party leaders had publicly committed themselves.

The solution to the problems of economic nationalism and republic rivalry came more and more, as time passed, to depend on the carrying out of economic reforms. If determined steps could be taken to free the enterprises and banks from political control and dry up the sources of investment in public works and "political factories," the poorer republics would suffer, but many of the particularistic forces born of the transitional, partially market-oriented, partially controlled economy of Yugoslavia would be destroyed, and the obstructionism of the Ranković forces defeated. Unfortunately for those favoring liberal reforms, prolonged delay in taking decisive action increased inflationary pressures and the balance of payments problem, making it more and more difficult to carry out the transition to a fully market-oriented economy in which investments would be allocated purely in accord with criteria of economic profitability. At the Eighth Congress of the League of Communists held in December, 1964, an attempt was made to line up the entire Party behind the policy of liberalization of the economy, the strengthening of

[49] *Jedinstvo,* Oct. 19 and 26, 1964.
[50] *Politika,* supplement, Feb. 13, 1965.

workers' self-management, and the reduction of bureaucratic interference in the operation of economic enterprises. The resolution of the congress embodying these points was accepted without opposition.[51] In their public pronouncements, the Party leaders stood together in support of the goals laid down by the Eighth Congress, but in practice the old splits between conservative and liberal elements grew deeper and the economic situation remained unchanged.

Finally, in July, 1965, decisive action was taken to end the uncertainty and overhaul the Yugoslav economy. A drastic restructuring of the system of taxation eliminated burdensome obligations of the enterprises to the government and gave them the freedom to accumulate and allocate investment funds without outside controls. This change was backed up by currency reform and emergency controls over prices to control inflation.

The reforms of July immediately faced heavy going. The complicated economic problems produced by inflation and the balance of payments crisis made it necessary for the government to maintain controls over prices and led to delays in introducing measures designed to bring about full convertibility of the dinar and reform of the banking system. Resistance in those regions opposed to the new economic measures manifested itself in a refusal to carry out the reforms. These problems were accompanied by new displays of nationalism.

Between November, 1965, and February, 1966, the Executive Committee of the League of Communists held several meetings at which the problem of implementing the economic reforms and dealing with rising national feeling were examined.[52] After the last of these meetings, held in early February, the press revealed what was by then common knowledge, that the center of resistance to reforms lay in Serbia, and that nationalistic manifestations in the republic had been going on for some time unchecked.[53] It was made known that it was the intention of the Executive Committee to set up an extraordinary commission, made up of members of the Executive Committee, the Central Committee, and "political activists" to look further into the national question.[54] Such a

[51] *Osmi kongres,* pp. 195–210.
[52] *Komunist,* March 3, 1966, p. 7.
[53] *Ibid.,* Feb. 3, 1966, p. 2.
[54] *Ibid.*

body, it would not be unreasonable to assume, could be used to gather incriminating evidence against the opposition on the basis of its attitude toward the national question.

Instead a final effort was made to force recalcitrant elements in the Party into line and end the split within the leadership without resorting to the application of Party sanctions. In early March the Third Plenum of the Central Committee took up the question of reform once more.[55] Divisions in the Party leadership were openly admitted, and the delay in carrying out the reforms severely castigated by Tito. Ranković, in a speech to the plenum which dealt extensively with the national question, voiced support for Party policy and attacked nationalistic manifestations in Serbia. But the continued resistance of the Serbian Party was revealed when the plenum, in a remarkable move, adjourned to allow the Executive Committee of the Serbian Party an opportunity to meet and debate its position on reform and the national question. For the moment the Serbian Executive Committee chose to follow the lead of the Central Committee of the Yugoslav Party, and attacked its own Party leadership (without naming names) for obstructing reform.[56] The final resolution of the third Plenum of the Yugoslav Central Committee contained an unusually blunt directive, obligating Party members in leading positions to carry out the tasks of reducing investment, permitting freedom of enterprises to invest throughout all of Yugoslavia, struggling against chauvinistic manifestations, and supporting other aspects of the policy of the Eighth Party Congress and the July, 1965, reforms.[57]

The Third Party Plenum of March was the most severely divided of any that had met since the prewar period. It revealed that the price of maintaining a veneer of unity in Party matters would be a deep and lasting internal division of the League of Communists; judging from all that had taken place up to that time, and by the intense concern being displayed by the Party leadership over nationalism, this split would be sure to break up the Party along national and regional lines.

The impossibility of compromise was in any case made clear in the weeks that followed. Reports of meetings of the Central Committee in Bosnia-Hercegovina and the Executive Committee of the Party in

[55] *Ibid.*, March 3, 1966, pp. 3–4.
[56] *Ibid.*, March 10, 1966, p. 2.
[57] *Ibid.*, March 17, 1966, p. 4.

Montenegro held after the Third Plenum indicated that opposition, especially in Montenegro, was still strong.[58] The answer of the Serbian Party to the Third Plenum was defiantly swift. On March 10, several days after the plenum adjourned, the Central Committee of the Serbian Party convened with representatives of its Executive Committee and representatives of the Executive Committee of the Central Committee of the Macedonian Party for the purpose of establishing broad areas of co-operation between the two republics.[59] The Third Plenum had seen expression of cautious approval of what was referred to as growing contacts among the central committees of the republics,[60] and Ranković, in his address to the plenum, had spoken more concretely of the positive contribution of the leadership in the republics in making agreements concerning joint cooperation in various fields.[61] Still the meeting of the two parties so soon after the plenum of the Central Committee of the Yugoslav Party could only be interpreted as a repudiation of the general Party line (and indeed, not a word was said at the meeting of the parties of the tasks set out at the Third Plenum).

The discussion between the Serbs and the Macedonians, it was reported, had a "distinct political character." [62] Like the agreements reached between Serbia and Montenegro two years earlier, the stress in these negotiations was on developing economic cooperation between enterprises of the two republics. (Not convincingly, it was stated that this did not imply the intrusion of "political factors" into the process of reaching agreement in concrete cases, but was limited simply to an exploration of the conditions for cooperation.) A report on the meeting went on to say that "the other area in which talks were carried out was that which might be placed under the general notion of culture." In this connection, the report continued,

it was emphasized in the talks that the past had made Macedonians rather sensitive about Serbian chauvinism, and that the public in Macedonia especially appreciates the battle being waged against all manifestations of the recrudescence of great Serbian nationalism.[63]

58 *Ibid.*, March 22, 1966, p. 5.
59 *Ibid.*, March 24, 1966, p. 2.
60 *Ibid.*, March 3, 1966, p. 7.
61 *Ibid.*, p. 4.
62 *Ibid.*, March 24, 1966, p. 2.
63 *Ibid.*

With the conclusion of this agreement, the forces of Ranković had apparently succeeded in turning their ideological opposition to the course of reform in Yugoslavia into an economic struggle between the "conservative southeast" and the "progressive northwest," largely because of the fear of the underdeveloped republics over the consequences of economic reform for their future development. The extent of the Serbian and Macedonian opposition to the position of the Third Plenum became clearer still as a result of Party meetings held in Serbia and Macedonia in March and April. The meeting of the Serbian Executive Committee, attended by Ranković, was subjected to an unprecedented criticism in the Yugoslav Party journal *Komunist* for its failure to take action against growing nationalism in Serbia and misguided investment policies.[64] Under public pressure from the Party press to take decisive steps in implementing the reforms,[65] the Macedonian Central Committee, at its meeting in April, failed after lengthy debate to reach any conclusion and adjourned without issuing a resolution.[66] This action was all the more significant in the light of the fact that the secretary of the Macedonian Party, Krste Crvenkovski, was a liberal in economic policy strongly in favor of reform.

By May it appeared that a stalemate had been reached and that all remedies short of disciplinary action had been exhausted. At a session of the Executive Committee of the Yugoslav League of Communists on June 16, the decision was made to take decisive action against the Ranković group. The tactic chosen to destroy Ranković was political, aimed at attacking Ranković at his weakest point—responsibility for the actions of the secret police. A commission made up of representatives of the six republics was appointed to investigate the state security apparatus. In less than two weeks it had completed its report. At the Fourth Plenum of the Central Committee of the Yugoslav Party, held early in July at Tito's retreat on the island of Brioni, Ranković was charged with responsibility for abuses perpetrated by the security apparatus.[67] Now the secret police themselves were blamed for blocking implementation of the economic reforms and were accused of wire-

[64] *Ibid.,* March 31, 1966, p. 5.
[65] See *Ibid.,* April 21, 1966, p. 2.
[66] *Ibid.,* April 28, 1966, p. 2.
[67] *Ibid.,* July 7, 1966, pp. 5–9.

tapping, intimidation, and various other forms of interference in the work of economic units. Ranković and several of his closest associates were expelled from their Party and government posts. Ranković himself was permitted to retain his membership in the Party. But it was Tito who made it clear there could be no compromise: the struggle against Ranković was no longer one of individuals, said Tito, but a "factional struggle, a struggle for power." [68]

In September, after the decisions of the Brioni plenum were widely publicized, the central committees of the republics were convened to take action against opposition elements. The Serbian Central Committee, in a dramatic meeting in which the abuses of the security services against minorities played a prominent role, dismissed Party secretary Vojin Lukić from his post and expelled him from the Party along with several others.[69] A week later the Central Committee of the Montenegrin Party met; its stand was somewhat difficult to determine in the evasive reports appearing in the Party press. Although not openly defying the Party, the Montenegrins seemed less ready to admit their faults and expel the Ranković adherents from their ranks than the Serbian Party.[70]

The events of the summer of 1966 marked a climax in the struggle over the future course of Yugoslavia's economic development, a struggle in which nationalism and republic rivalries had come to play a vital role. There could be no doubt that national relations had suffered a major setback, and that the scars of intra-Party strife would be a long time in healing.

The hopeful side of the outcome of this struggle, from the point of view of the Party leaders, was the final victory of the liberal reforms. What this implied was suggested by Kardelj in a speech in November, 1965, when he argued that

if what we now call the republican or communal economy could be inspired only by the logic of economic laws, if it could be influenced only by stimulation based on labor productivity, then the road toward de-territorialization would be open and the real process of economic integration would be put into motion. There is no other way than to merge the national, republican,

[68] *Ibid.*, p. 5.
[69] *Ibid.*, Sept. 15 and 22, 1966.
[70] *Ibid.*, Sept. 22, 1966, p. 3.

and communal interests into the interests of every individual working man and each collective. At least, I do not see any other way.[71]

In essence, Kardelj was rephrasing the original Titoist argument concerning the importance of economic and social forces in overcoming regional and national loyalties. Only now the Yugoslav Communists had come to see the problem not in terms of introducing socialist principles of behavior but rather as a struggle to remove politics from the economy and press forward with modernization guided by rigid standards of productivity and efficiency. It was perhaps symptomatic of the new era into which Yugoslavia was moving that in the struggle against the Ranković group Tito and those who approved of economic reform were able to win considerable support from modernizing forces in Serbia, such as the Serbian national assembly and the specialized professional journals who spoke for the management group in the republic. Important figures in the Serbian Party—chief among them Mihailo Todorović, responsible for guiding economic policy in the Yugoslav Party leadership—favored reform. The reliance of Ranković on the Executive Committee of the Serbian League of Communists rather than on the Central Committee during the period of divided Party leadership could well have been a sign of weakness, reflecting a lack of support for Ranković in the latter body where, although Party functionaries were well represented, a broader cross section of the new Communist professional and enterpreneurial elites existed than in the small hand-picked Executive Committee.[72]

In 1966, however, it was not clear whether the reforms would be successful in divorcing politics from economics and putting the Yugoslav economy back on its feet. Nor was it certain that the Yugoslavs had really found a way in which to make investments flow freely across republic boundaries. The existence of workers' self-management, by making it impossible for one enterprise to draw profit off from another, was one obstacle to this flow. It was also true that there were very few economic incentives for cooperation among enterprises, especially between those in advanced areas and those in less favored regions. In their

[71] *Borba,* Nov. 27, 1965.

[72] The Executive Committee of the Serbian Party met during the Third Plenum of March and again on March 19. In other republics the central committees were convened to discuss the conclusions of the Third Plenum, with the exception of Montenegro, where the Executive Committee met March 22.

struggle with Ranković, the liberals talked about the fact that political agreements aimed at overcoming localistic tendencies were not in themselves enough, and that economic instruments would have to be devised to do the job. But it was also admitted that loaning at 5 percent was, under conditions of capital scarcity, simply "not interesting" to profitable enterprises, which would rather invest in their own plant.[73] Given the fact that interrepublic migration in Yugoslavia was low, and that lower labor costs in poorer areas could not play a role in attracting industry because of the profit-sharing arrangement embodied in workers' self-management, the integration of the economy and the elimination of differences in economic levels of development among the republics might be a long time in coming.

[73] *Komunist,* March 24, 1966, p. 1.

Conclusion

WHEN the Communists came to power in Yugoslavia after World War II, they faced what was, by any standard, a problem of staggering dimensions in dealing with the national question. Although the record of the Party prior to World War II was not such as to inspire confidence in the ability of the Communists to cope with this situation, the experience of the Partisan struggle and the development of a broadly based, multinational Party organization during the war set the stage for a determined effort to solve the national question that was remarkable for its combination of firmness and flexibility in seeking to redress many long-standing national grievances.

It is not necessary to examine once more those areas in which Party policy on the national question made contributions to the goal of the unity of the Yugoslav peoples. That the Communists did make such contributions at a time when Yugoslavia was on the verge of disintegration as a result of nationality conflicts is beyond any serious doubt. It is also true that Communism in Yugoslavia owes its existence to the Yugoslav state, for, without it, the political and military factors conducive to the victory of the partisans in the civil war between 1941 and 1945 simply would not have existed. Thus Communism and the Yugoslav state have found their destinies intertwined.

Nevertheless the Yugoslav Communists, after a decade and a half of experimentation with a liberal form of Communism, seem to be succumbing to the sterile pattern of national conflict which so weakened the interwar regime. Why this has come to pass remains difficult to comprehend, even in the light of evidence which demonstrates the deeply rooted character of the national question and the fact that the Communist solution to the long-standing disputes of the Yugoslav nationalities was far from perfect, even when seemingly most successful.

One explanation of the difficulties which the Yugoslav Communists have encountered concerns the national sensitivities of the Yugoslav peoples themselves. Like all national groups with a history of protracted struggle for national rights behind them, the Yugoslavs are sensitive, romantic, and at times aggressive in giving expression to their national feelings. They are quick to take offense and slow to forget a grievance, while the sympathy they expect to arouse in others over their problems is not always reciprocated by a willingness to understand a point of view different from their own. To people with this kind of temperament, it has been difficult to be practical and view Yugoslavia as a mutually convenient arrangement in which diverse peoples cooperate out of a realization that it would be far worse not to do so. Even under Communist rule, the tendency to interpet the Yugoslav union in terms of purely local needs and traditional national aspirations has remained fundamentally unchanged. Indeed, as the previous account has sought to show, the Communist Party has done much to contribute to the continuance of such attitudes.

There was a time when the Communists would have considered such nationalism as a largely political problem, best attacked by means of ideological indoctrination and the elimination of conservative elements in Yugoslav society. But the thesis that the spread of Communist ideology would result in a rapid transformation of national attitudes was always of doubtful validity, and in any case was never applied in such a way as to obliterate regional national loyalties. And it is extremely unlikely that such methods can be employed to attack the national question in the future.

Still, one can grant the existence of deeply felt national beliefs in Yugoslavia without necessarily accepting the conclusion that they are to blame for the reemergence of the national question. Changes in national attitudes are difficult to measure, and cannot be gauged simply in terms of the intensity of the political or economic disputes carried on by a small percentage of the population. This was true in the interwar period, and remains the case today.

In this connection it must be pointed out that the feeling of being a Yugoslav has spread, perhaps to a degree not admitted by many Yugoslavs themselves, in the postwar period. Although it may appear paradoxical to talk of the growth of Yugoslav loyalties at a time of increasing friction among the nationalities, the average Yugoslav has grown accustomed to cultivating two national personalities. Abroad he is apt to forget his local pride and identify himself as a Yugoslav, while at home he is more likely to behave as a national of his own republic.

Under the Communists pro-Yugoslav feeling has been encouraged by the pride the Yugoslavs take in the important role their country plays in international affairs and the widespread respect which foreigners show toward the economic achievements and liberal experiments of the Titoist regime. Notwithstanding the presence of strong currents of alienation and frustration in Yugoslav society, the experience of living under Communism has revolutionized the Yugoslav mentality by making people accustomed to look to the future with hope for a better life, and by imparting to the Yugoslav peoples a sense of their own contribution to the shaping of the modern world, a feeling which was largely absent in earlier generations. Thus a foundation has been created for building deeper attachments to Yugoslavia among her peoples, although, in the period here under consideration, the Yugoslav Communists have been largely unable to capitalize on this development.

Thus, the dilemma of Communism and the national question in Yugoslavia has been one, in a sense, of nation-building: utilizing existing pro-Yugoslav sentiment in support of economic, cultural, and social policies aimed at slowly breaking down national barriers and creating new loyalties. Especially among the younger generation of Yugoslavs it would seem that such policies should have been highly effective.

If the nation-building process has broken down (and it is premature to conclude that the difficulties which face the Party represent such an extreme situation), the immediate cause lies in the severe centrifugal forces springing from rapid industrial development and economic reorganization in the Titoist period. But there were other equally important reasons. It is impossible to understand the recent history of the national question without grasping the fact that the politics of the Titoist period led to a leadership crisis which in turn posed a grave test of the ability of the Party to preserve its multinational image. True to its traditions under Tito's leadership, the Party fought to preserve this image against the real and imagined threats of Serbian dominance in Party affairs. By sacrificing the Yugoslav idea for the sake of maintaining its multinational character, the Party has repeated the strategy pursued in the early years of the Partisan campaigns.

It is evident, however, that the spirit of that earlier time has passed. The Party is not only suffering from the clashes of interest which eventually overtake revolutionary movements after they come to power but is experiencing a period of difficult readjustment in which it seeks once again to establish itself as a force for leadership and progress. That this latter question should even arise after over a decade of Titoist reforms is perhaps odd, but it is an extremely important factor in understanding the difficulties the Party has experienced in recent years in dealing effectively with the national question.

The source of this problem of leadership lies deep in the origins of the postwar party in the resistance movement of World War II. The growth of the Partisan army, without doubt, helped stimulate a powerful current of revolutionary change in Yugoslavia. But the recruitment of the Party from the resistance fighters also helped to create a new bureaucracy, especially at the local level, which was parochial in outlook and resistant to policies not cast in the Stalinist mold. This group has not found it easy to accept the flexible national attitudes of more modern elements of the population, and has on occasion tolerated the activities of nationalist elements. Here again one can see parallels in the situation that existed during the Partisan campaigns, when the Party leadership fought against the national outlooks of the liberation movements in various parts of the country. Today, however, this struggle goes on under quite altered conditions, without the unity at the highest levels that characterized the Partisan period, and with important liberal elements, out of fear of central control of the government in Belgrade over the economy, associated with the campaign to gain greater freedom of action for the republics.

There is a final factor which may help explain the inability of the Communists to tap pro-Yugoslav sentiment. This is the failure of the Party to generate a new pattern of social attitudes and relationships on which to anchor its rule. To make the point more directly, expressions of nationalism among the youth and the intellectuals, while they have many causes, have reflected a deep-seated feeling of frustration over the quality of life in Communist society. The maintenance of Party privileges has been a particularly sensitive and explosive issue which has worked to produce alienation from the regime at all levels of society. The Titoist period has also given rise to widespread impatience and irritation resulting from frequent and often unsuccessful economic and administrative experiments, many of which have had to be scrapped entirely after proving unworkable.

One wonders whether any simple and direct way can be found to cope with the negativistic attitudes prevalent in such a society. Perhaps it is not idle to suggest that only through a wide range of accomplishments in other fields, especially in lessening some of the anxiety, weariness, and even disillusionment which have overtaken large segments of Yugoslav life, can the Communists hope to overcome deeply entrenched national attitudes and break out of the vicious cycle of national rivalries and controversies which have plagued Yugoslavia since her creation.

Viewed in this light the national problem, notwithstanding its deep roots in Yugoslav history, is a symptom of the presently unsettled state of Yugoslav society and politics. Yugoslav Communism, however, is still in a state of transition, seeking a new identity and a new basis on which to build a viable political system and a healthy set of social and economic relationships. In these conditions, and keeping in mind the probable imminence of a succession crisis, one can only dimly foresee the course of national relations in the future. It is clear that one transitional phase, at least, has come to an end with the breakdown of the effort to create a new type of nationalism based on the quasi-Communist, quasi-democratic institutions of Titoist Communism.

Appendix A
Yugoslav Nationalities
1948, 1953, and 1961

TABLE 1. 1948

	Total	Serbia	Croatia	Slovenia	Bosnia-Hercegovina	Macedonia	Montenegro
Serbs	6,547,117	4,823,730	543,795	7,048	1,136,116	29,721	6,707
Croats	3,784,353	169,864	2,975,399	16,069	614,123	2,090	6,808
Slovenes	1,415,432	20,998	38,734	1,350,149	4,338	729	484
Montenegrins	425,703	74,860	2,871	521	3,094	2,348	342,009
Moslems	808,921	17,315	1,077	179	788,403	1,560	387
Albanians	750,431	532,011	635	216	755	197,389	19,425
Bulgarians	61,140	59,472	637	35	94	889	13
Czechs	39,015	6,760	28,991	1,063	1,978	130	93
Germans	55,337	41,460	10,144	1,824	1,174	360	375
Gypsies	72,736	52,181	405	46	442	19,500	162
Hungarians	496,492	433,701	51,399	10,579	532	219	62
Italians	79,575	863	76,093	1,458	964	56	141
Macedonians	810,126	17,917	1,387	366	675	789,648	133
Rumanians	64,095	63,130	743	71	71	77	3
Russians	20,069	13,329	3,210	796	1,316	1,141	277
Russini	37,140	22,667	6,397	170	7,883		23
Slovaks	83,626	73,140	10,097	82	274	29	44
Turks	97,954	1,914	13	5	80	95,940	2
Vlachs	102,953	93,440	1		1	9,511	
Remaining and unknown	19,883	9,214	4,779	1,196	2,964	1,649	81
Total	15,772,098	6,527,966	3,756,807	1,391,873	2,565,277	1,152,986	377,189

Source: Federativna Narodna Republika Jugoslavije, Savezni Zavod za Statistiku, *Konačni resultati popisa stanovništva od 15 marta 1948 godine*, Vol. IX: *Stanovništvo po narodnosti*, p. xiv.

TABLE 2. 1953

	Total	Serbia	Croatia	Slovenia	Bosnia-Hercegovina	Macedonia	Montenegro
Serbs	7,065,923	5,152,939	588,411	11,225	1,264,372	35,112	13,864
Croats	3,975,550	173,246	3,117,513	17,978	654,229	2,770	9,814
Slovenes	1,487,100	20,717	43,010	1,415,448	6,300	983	642
Macedonians	893,247	27,277	2,385	640	1,884	860,699	362
Montenegrins	466,093	86,061	5,128	1,356	7,336	2,526	363,686
Yugoslavs, undetermined	998,698	81,081	16,185	1,617	891,800	1,591	6,424
Albanians	754,245	565,513	1,001	169	1,578	162,524	23,460
Austrians	1,459	295	749	289	87	24	15
Bulgarians	61,708	60,146	464	49	108	920	21
Czechs	34,517	5,948	25,954	807	1,638	114	56
Slovaks	84,999	75,027	9,570	60	314	20	8
Greeks	2,304	1,279	105	24	26	848	22
Italians	35,874	636	33,316	854	909	41	118
Jews-Israelites	2,307	1,504	413	15	310	55	10
Hungarians	502,175	441,907	47,711	11,019	1,140	207	191
Germans	60,536	46,228	11,242	1,617	1,111	136	202
Poles	4,440	1,398	1,575	275	1,161	24	7
Vlachs	36,728	28,047	2	9	2	8,668	
Rumanians	60,364	59,705	418	41	91	103	6
Russini	37,353	23,720	5,980	46	7,473	127	7
Turks	259,535	54,526	276	68	435	203,938	292
Gypsies	84,713	58,800	1,261	1,663	2,297	20,462	230
Remaining Slavs	549	157	187	54	126	11	14
Remaining non-Slavs	2,791	1,837	546	100	90	187	31
Russians	12,426	7,829	2,183	593	951	672	198
Undetermined	4,550	1,337	826	198	660	1,383	146
Total	16,936,573	6,979,154	3,918,817	1,466,425	2,847,790	1,304,514	419,873

Source: Savezni Zavod za Statistiku, "Stanovnistvo po starosti, polu i narodnosti" (unpublished results of the census of 1953).

Appendix A

TABLE 3. 1961

Serbs	7,806,213
Croats	4,293,860
Slovenes	1,589,192
Montenegrins	513,833
Macedonians	1,045,530
Ethnic Moslems	972,954
Yugoslavs, undetermined	317,125
Albanians	914,760
Hungarians	504,368
Turks	182,964
Slovaks	86,433
Rumanians	60,862
Bulgarians	62,624
Italians	25,615
Czechs	30,331
Remaining and unknown	142,627
Total	18,549,291

Source: *Statisticki godišnjak SFRJ, 1964,* p. 84.

Appendix B
National Composition of the Yugoslav Communist Party

TABLE 1. COMMUNIST PARTY MEMBERS: NUMBER AND PERCENT OF POPULATION IN THE YUGOSLAV REPUBLICS[a]

	Serbia		Croatia		Slovenia		Bosnia-Hercegovina		Macedonia		Montenegro	
	Number	Percent	Number	Percent	Number	Percent	Number	Percent	Number	Percent	Number	Percent
At liberation	11,719	.18[b]	15,000	.4[b]	4,582	.33[b]	5,901	.23[b]	1,450	.13[b]	3,582	.95[b]
1949–1950	167,025	2.6[b]	85,748	2.3[b]	37,959	2.7[b]	54,150	2.1[b]	27,029	2.3[b]	16,245	4.3[b]
1959	351,378	5.0[c]	176,017	4.0[c]	61,000+	4.2[c]	113,117	3.4[c]	51,909	3.9[c]	28,000+	6.7[c]
1963	416,248	5.3[d]	215,586	5.1[d]	70,084	4.3[d]	126,537	3.7[d]	67,020	4.6[d]	33,289	6.7[d]

[a] All figures exclude Party members in the army. In 1952 there were 140,193 such members.
[b] On the basis of republic population in 1948.
[c] On the basis of republic population in 1953.
[d] On the basis of republic population in 1963.

TABLE 2. NATIONAL COMPOSITION OF THE LEAGUE OF
COMMUNISTS OF YUGOSLAVIA, 1957 AND 1964

	1957		Percent in Population (1953)	1964		Percent in Population (1961)
	Number	Percent		Number	Percent	
Total	686,387	100.0	100.0	1,030,041	100.0	100.0
Serbs	374,329	54.5	41.7	530,119	51.5	42.8
Croats	130,662	19.0	23.5	191,500	18.6	23.1
Slovenes	53,730	7.7	8.7	73,105	7.1	8.5
Macedonians	43,206	6.4	5.2	68,042	6.6	5.6
Montenegrins	46,108	6.7	2.1	63,876	6.1	2.8
Moslems (ethnic)				36,470	3.5	5.2
Yugoslavs			5.9	12,984	1.3	1.7
Albanians	16,727	2.4	4.5	28,460	2.8	4.9
Hungarians	7,469	1.1	3.0	12,865	1.2	2.7
Bulgarians	2,062	0.3	.4	3,283	0.3	.3
Italians	672	0.1	.2	712	0.1	.1
Czechs and Slovaks	1,346	0.2	.7	3,035	0.3	.6
Rumanians	934	0.1	.4	1,584	0.1	.3
Remaining nationalities	10,142	1.5	.7	4,996	0.5	.8

Source: *Jugoslovenski Pregled,* July–Aug., 1964, p. 294.

TABLE 3. NATIONAL COMPOSITION OF THE REPUBLIC PARTIES OF
SERBIA, CROATIA, AND MACEDONIA AND THE REGIONAL
PARTIES OF VOJVODINA AND KOSSOVO-METOHIJA

SERBIAN PARTY

	1953		1958		Percent of Nationality in Republic Population[a]
	Number	Percent of Party	Number	Percent of Party	
Serbs	221,675	81.9	270,972	80.5	74.0
Croats	7,586	2.8	9,801	2.9	2.5
Slovenes	1,475	.5	1,585	.5	.3
Macedonians	2,493	.9	2,920	.9	.4
Montenegrins	11,284	4.2	16,802	5.0	1.2
Albanians	13,605	5.0	19,049	5.7	8.1
Hungarians	5,530	2.0	8,148	2.4	6.3
Bulgarians	1,525	.6	2,042	.6	.9
Remaining	5,473	2.1	5,110	1.5	6.3
Total	270,646	100.0	336,429	100.0	100.0

Source: *Statistički podaci organizacije Saveza komunista Srbije od III do IV kongresa,* p. 9.

[a] Derived from 1953 census.

CROATIAN PARTY

	1953		1958		Percent of Nationality in Republic Population[a]
	Number	Percent of Party	Number	Percent of Party	
Croats	96,734	69.9	120,732	68.6	79.6
Serbs	36,028	26.0	48,794	27.7	15.0
Slovenes	2,164	1.6	2,354	1.3	1.1
Macedonians	257	.2	467	.3	0.1
Montenegrins	683	.5	1,132	.6	0.2
Czechs	509	.4	450	.3	0.7
Slovaks	113	.1	36	0	0.2
Italians	687	.5	478	.3	0.9
Hungarians	624	.5	536	.3	1.1
Remaining	449	.3	1,038	.6	1.1
Total	138,248	100.0	176,017	100.0	100.0

Source: *Statistički podaci organizacije Saveza komunista u NR Hrvatskoj za razdoblje od III do IV kongresa SKH*, p. 19.

MACEDONIAN PARTY

	1948 (Nov.)		1954 (April)		1958 (end)	Percent of Nationality in Republic Population[a]
	Number	Percent of Party	Number	Percent of Party	Percent of Party	
Macedonians	23,267	86.0	36,747	84.2	84.63	66.0
Serbs	599	2.2				2.7
Albanians	1,519	5.6	2,559	5.9	6.28	12.5
Turks	932	3.5	2,128	4.9	2.29	15.6
Vlachs	233	.9				.7
Others	489	1.8	2,161	5.0	6.8	2.5
Total	27,039	100.0	43,595	100.0	100.00	100.0

Sources: For number and percent of nationalities in the Macedonian Party in 1948, see *Informativni priručnik*, Book I (Nov.–Dec., 1948), p. 54. For the number of each nationality in the Party in 1954, see *Vtori kongres na Sojuzot na komunistite na Makedonija*, p. 68. For percentage of nationalities in Party in 1958, see *III kongres na Sojuzot na komunistite na Makedonija*, p. 119.

[a] Derived from 1953 census.

VOJVODINA

	1953		1958		Percent of Nationality in Region's Population[a]
	Number	*Percent of Party*	*Number*	*Percent of Party*	
Serbs	53,896	74.6	67,282	73.5	51.1
Croats	4,072	5.6	5,396	5.9	7.5
Slovenes	347	.5	395	.4	.4
Macedonians	1,043	1.4	1,124	1.2	.7
Montenegrins	4,403	6.1	5,847	6.4	1.8
Hungarians	5,318	7.4	7,688	8.4	25.4
Albanians	95	.1	121	.1	0
Bulgarians	77	.1	116	.1	.2
Remaining	2,971	4.1	3,674	4.0	12.9
Total	72,222	100.0	91,643	100.0	100.0

Source: *Statistički podaci organizacije Saveza komunista Srbije od III do IV kongres*, p. 10.

KOSSOVO-METOHIJA

	1953		1958		Percent of Nationality in Region's Population[a]
	Number	*Percent of Party*	*Number*	*Percent of Party*	
Serbs	10,052	38.5	13,439	37.0	23.5
Croats	147	.6	196	.6	0
Slovenes	18	0	31	0	0
Macedonians	53	.2	66	.2	1.0
Montenegrins	3,044	11.6	4,572	12.6	3.9
Hungarians	4	0	147	.3	0
Albanians	12,226	46.8	17,305	48.0	64.9
Bulgarians	6	0	50	.1	0
Others	588	2.3	448	1.2	6.7
Total	26,138	100.0	36,254	100.0	100.0

Source: *Statistički podaci organizacije Saveza komunista Srbije od III do IV kongres*, p. 10.

[a] Derived from 1953 census.

Appendix C
Opinions Concerning Relations Among Nationalities in Yugoslavia
(in percent)

Relations among Nationalities	Total	Bosnia and Hercegovina	Montenegro	Croatia	Macedonia	Slovenia	Narrow Serbia	Kossovo-Metohija	Vojvodina
Good	73.0	78.7	72.1	73.8	87.0	56.6	67.3	74.4	75.9
Satisfactory	8.0	8.0	6.0	8.8	1.8	18.7	9.5	3.6	6.9
Poor (Loši)	5.3	4.1	3.8	6.7	2.6	12.6	3.7	1.8	8.0
Unknown	13.7	9.2	18.1	10.7	8.6	12.3	19.5	20.2	9.2

Source: Jugoslovensko javno mnijenje, A-3 (1964), p. 66. Sample size: 2,527.

Appendix D
Nationality of Persons Occupying
Leading Government and Party Posts
in the Federal People's Republic of Yugoslavia
and the Republics of Serbia, Croatia,
Bosnia-Hercegovina, and Macedonia (1945–1963)

FPRY

I. Governments
Temporary Government

of March 7, 1945	Serbs	7	"Precani"	3
	Croats[a]	6	Montenegrins	1
	Slovenes	3	Macedonians	1
	Dalmations	1	Unknown	2
	Bosnia-Hercegovina[b]	4		
Government of Feb. 1, 1946	Serbs	8	Montenegrins	1
	Croats	4	Macedonians	1
	Slovenes	2	Unknown	4
	"Yugoslavs"[c]	1		
Government of Oct. 22, 1949	Serbs	11	Macedonians	2
	Croats	4	"Yugoslavs"	2
	Slovenes	3	Unknown	1
	Montenegrins	2		
Federal Executive Committee of Jan. 31, 1954	Serbs	9	Macedonians	3
	Croats	4	"Yugoslavs"	1
	Slovenes	6	Unknown	1
Federal Executive Committee, spring, 1958	Serbs	16	Macedonians	3
	Croats	5	Montenegrins	4
	Slovenes	6		
Federal Executive Committee, 1963	Serbs	10	Macedonians	6
	Croats	8	Montenegrins	3
	Slovenes	5	Unknown	6

[a] Tito included here and in subsequent references to Croats.
[b] Nationality not known.
[c] "Yugoslavs" are probably Moslems, but may be of other nationality as well (for example, Serbs from Croatia).

II. Party Central Committee

Central Committee, 1948	Serbs	25	Macedonians	5
	Croats	12	"Yugoslavs"	1
	Slovenes	8	Unknown	2
	Montenegrins	10		
Central Committee, 1953	Serbs	38	Hungarians	1
	Croats	23	"Yugoslavs"	3
	Slovenes	17	Albanians	1
	Montenegrins	12	Bulgarians	1
	Macedonians	10	Unknown	3
Central Committee, 1958	Serbs	43	"Yugoslavs"	5
	Croats	30	Albanians	2
	Slovenes	21	Hungarians	1
	Montenegrins	14	Bulgarians	1
	Macedonians	14	Unknown	4
Central Committee, 1963	Serbs	44	"Yugoslavs"	2
	Croats	19	Albanians	1
	Slovenes	19	Hungarians	1
	Montenegrins	14	Turks	1
	Macedonians	12	Unknown	40

III. Party Politburo (Executive Committee)

Politburo, 1948	Serbs	3	Slovenes	2
	Croats	2	Montenegrins	2
Party Executive Committee, 1953	Serbs	3	Montenegrins	2
	Croats	4	Macedonians	1
	Slovenes	3		
Party Executive Committee, spring, 1958	Serbs	4	Montenegrins	3
	Croats	4	Macedonians	1
	Slovenes	3		
Party Executive Committee, 1963	Serbs	5	Montenegrins	4
	Croats	5	Macedonians	3
	Slovenes	3		

SERBIA

I. Governments

Government of Oct. 22, 1949	Serbs	21	Albanians	1
	Croats	1	Unknown	1
Executive Committee of Feb. 6, 1953	Serbs	16	Hungarians	1
	Croats	1	Albanians	1
	Montenegrins	1	Unknown	7

Executive Committee,
spring, 1958

Serbs	21	Hungarians	1
Croats	1	Unknown	1
Montenegrins	1		

Executive Committee, 1963

Serbs	6	Hungarians	1
Albanians	1	Unknown	2

II. Party Central Committees

Central Committee, 1949

Serbs	48	"Yugoslavs"	2
Croats	2	Hungarians	1
Montenegrins	2	Unknown	6
Albanians	2		

Central Committee, 1954

Serbs	53	"Yugoslavs"	2
Croats	2	Hungarians	3
Montenegrins	5	Unknown	3
Albanians	3		

Central Committee, 1958

Serbs	87	"Yugoslavs"	3
Croats	1	Hungarians	5
Montenegrins	7	Unknown	21
Albanians	5		

Central Committee, 1963

Serbs	82	"Yugoslavs"	3
Croats	1	Hungarians	4
Montenegrins	6	Unknown	19
Albanians	8		

III. Serbian Politburos (Executive Committees)

Politburo, 1949 — Only Serbs

Party Executive Committee,
1954 — Only Serbs

Party Executive Committee,
1958

Serbs	10	Montenegrins	2

Party Executive Committee,
1963

Serbs	9	Albanians	1
Montenegrins	1		

CROATIA

I. Governments

Government of April 14, 1945

Croats	5	Unknown	8
Serbs	1		

Government of Oct. 22, 1949

Croats	13	"Yugoslavs"	1
Serbs	3	Unknown	7

Executive Committee
of Feb. 7, 1953

Croats	18	Unknown	3
Serbs	3		

Executive Committee,
spring, 1958

Croats	16	Unknown	6
Serbs	2		

Executive Committee, 1963

Croats	5	Unknown	6

II. Party Central Committees

Central Committee, 1948	Croats	42	Serbs	15
Central Committee, 1954	Croats	41	"Yugoslavs"	1
	Serbs	10	Unknown	9
Central Committee, 1957	Croats	67	Unknown	4
	Serbs	15		
Central Committee, 1963	Croats	55	"Yugoslavs"	1
	Serbs	13	Unknown	27
	Slovenes	1		

III. Politburos (Executive Committees)

Politburo, 1948	Croats	7	Serbs	5
Party Executive Committee, 1954	Croats	11	Unknown	1
	Serbs	3		
Party Executive Committee, 1959	Croats	12	Serbs	3
Party Executive Committee, 1963	Croats	10	Unknown	3

BOSNIA-HERCEGOVINA

I. Governments

Government of Feb. 20, 1946	Serbs	8	"Yugoslavs" [d]	0
	Croats	5	Unknown	2
Government of Oct. 22, 1949	Serbs	12	"Yugoslavs" [e]	2
	Croats	5	Unknown	2
Executive Committee of Jan. 31, 1953	Serbs	13	"Yugoslavs" [f]	3
	Croats	4	Unknown	1
Executive Committee, spring, 1958	Serbs	13	"Yugoslavs"	5
	Croats	1	Unknown	9
Executive Committee, 1963	Serbs	4	Unknown	4
	Croats	2		

II. Party Central Committees

Central Committee, 1948	Serbs	31	"Yugoslavs" [g]	5
	Croats	3	Unknown	9
Central Committee, 1954	Serbs	46	Montenegrins	1
	Croats	5	Unknown	1
	"Yugoslavs" [h]	6		

[d] "Yugoslavs" are Moslems. Moslems who gave Serbian nationality, 2; those who gave Croatian nationality, 2.

[e] Moslems who gave Serbian nationality, 1; those who gave Croatian nationality, 1.

[f] Moslems who gave Serbian nationality, 3.

[g] Moslems who gave Serbian nationality, 6; those who gave Croatian nationality, 1.

[h] Moslems who gave Serbian nationality, 8; those who gave Croatian nationality, 1.

Central Committee, 1959	Serbs	49	"Yugoslavs"	7
	Croats	12	Montenegrins	1
			Unknown	10
Central Committee, 1963	Serbs	52	Montenegrins	1
	Croats	12	Unknown	22
	"Yugoslavs"	5		

III. Politburos (Executive Committees)

Politburo, 1948	Serbs	6	"Yugoslavs" [i]	2
	Croats	2		
Party Executive Committee, 1954	Serbs	9	"Yugoslavs" [j]	2
	Croats	1		
Party Executive Committee, 1959	Serbs	9	"Yugoslavs"	3
	Croats	1	Unknown	1
Party Executive Committee, 1963	Serbs	7	"Yugoslavs"	1
	Croats	2	Unknown	1

MACEDONIA

I. Governments

Government of April 16, 1946	Macedonians	5	Unknown	7
Government of Oct. 22, 1949	Macedonians	16	Turks	1
	Albanians	1	Unknown	1
Executive Committee, Feb. 4, 1953	Macedonians	18	Turks	1
	Albanians	1	Unknown	1
Executive Committee, 1958	Macedonians	11	"Yugoslavs"	1
	Albanians	1	Unknown	2
Executive Committee, 1963	Macedonians	9	"Yugoslavs"	1
	Turks	1		

II. Party Central Committees

Central Committee, 1948	Macedonians	34	Albanians	1
	Turks	1	Unknown	8
	Montenegrins	1		
Central Committee, 1954	Macedonians	31	"Yugoslavs"	1
	Albanians	1	Jews	1
	Turks	1	Unknown	14
Central Committee, 1959	Macedonians	58	Turks	1
	Albanians	1	Unknown	2

[i] Moslems who gave Serbian nationality, 2; those who gave Croatian nationality, 1.
[j] Moslems who gave Serbian nationality, 2.

Central Committee, 1963	Macedonians	86	Turks	2
	Albanians	1	Unknown	8
	Jewish	1	"Yugoslavs"	1

III. Politburos (Executive Committees)

Politburo, 1948	Macedonians	8	Unknown	1
Party Executive Committee, 1954	All Macedonians			
Party Executive Committee, 1959	All Macedonians			
Party Executive Committee, 1963	All Macedonians			

Explanatory Note: Nationality is that given by the individual in *Ko je Ko u Jugoslaviji* (*Who's Who in Yugoslavia*) except in the following instances: (1) where source gives national composition of body in question; (2) when individual is known beyond any doubt to be of a certain nationality but is not given in *Ko je Ko;* (3) in the case of Moslems identified in the footnotes, names have been used; (4) in the case of the temporary government of March 7, 1945, nationality has been determined by place of birth.

Bibliography

I. CONGRESSES, PLENUMS, AND REPORTS

A. THE COMMUNIST INTERNATIONAL

Fourth Congress of the Communist International. London, Communist Party of Great Britain, n.d.

5th Congress of the Communist International: Abridged Report of Meetings Held at Moscow June 17th to July 18th. London, Communist Party of Great Britain, n.d.

B. THE YUGOSLAV COMMUNIST PARTY AND LEAGUE OF COMMUNISTS (REPUBLICS EXCLUDED)

V kongres Komunističke partije Jugoslavije: 18–21 jula 1948: Stenografske beleške. Belgrade, Kultura, 1949.

VI kongres Komunističke partije Jugoslavije (Saveza komunista Jugoslavije): 2–7 novembra 1952: Stenografske beleške. Belgrade, Kultura, n.d.

VII kongres Saveza komunista Jugoslavije: Stenografske beleske. Belgrade, Kultura, [1958].

Drugi plenum Centralnog komiteta Saveza komunista Jugoslavije. Belgrade, Kultura, 1960.

Osmi kongres Saveza komunista Jugoslavije. Belgrade, Komunist, 1964.

C. THE REPUBLICS

Osnivački kongres Komunističke partije Hrvatske. Zagreb, Naprijed, 1958.

I kongres na Komunističkata partija na Makedonija. Skoplje, Kultura, 1949.

Drugi kongres Komunističke partije Hrvatske. Zagreb, Ognjen Prica, 1949.

II kongres Komunističke partije Srbije. Belgrade, Prosveta, 1949.

Osnivački kongres Komunističke partije Bosne i Hercegovine. Sarajevo, Oslobodjenje, 1950.

III kongres Saveza komunista Srbije. Belgrade, Rad, 1954.

III kongres Zveze komunistov Slovenije. Ljubljana, Cankarjeva Založba, 1954.

Treći kongres Saveza komunista Hrvatske: 26–28 V 1954. Zagreb, Kultura, 1956.

Vtori kongres na Sojuzot na Komunistita na Makedonija. Skoplje, Kultura, 1954.

Izveštaj Centralnog komiteta Saveza komunista Bosne i Hercegovine. Sarajevo, Veselin Masleša, 1954.

Izveštaj Revizione komisije Saveza komunista Crne Gore za drugi kongres Saveza komunista Crne Gore. Titograd, 1954.

Izveštaj Zemaljske revizione komisije Saveza komunista Bosne i Hercegovine. Sarajevo, Veselin Masleša, 1954.

Sedma konferencija Saveza komunista Srbije za Kosovo i Metohiju. Priština, "Miladin Popović," 1956.

III kongres na Sojuzot na komunistita na Makedonija. Skoplje, Kultura, 1959.

Treći kongres Saveza komunista Bosne i Hercegovine. Belgrade, Kultura, 1959.

Četvrti kongres Saveza komunista Srbije; Četvrti kongres Saveza komunista Slovenije; Treći kongres Saveza komunista Crne Gore. Belgrade, Kultura, 1959.

Četvrti kongres Saveza komunista Bosne i Hercegovine. Sarajevo, Oslobodjenje, March, 1965.

Peti kongres SKS [Saveza komunista Srbije]. Belgrade, Kultura, 1965.

II. OTHER WORKS

Akcioni program Komunističke partije Jugoslavije: Referat Živka Topalovića na ll kongresu partije u Vukovaru. Belgrade, Štamparija Mirotović, 1920.

"Die Albanische Minderheit in Jugoslawien," *Wissenschaftlicher Dienst Südosteuropa,* VI (Sept.–Oct., 1957), 163–69.

Ammende, Ewald, ed. *Die Nationalitaten in den Staaten Europas.* Vienna, 1932.

Andrejev, Bane. *Znacenieto na manifest i nekoji prigovori na nego.* N.p., Goce Delčev, 1944.

Antonijević, Trajko S. *Hrvatski ustavni program u državi Srba, Hrvata i Slovenaca.* Belgrade, Published Ph.D. dissertation for the University of Belgrade, defended Nov. 28, 1939.

Apostolski, Mihailo. *Završnite operacii na N.O.B. za osloboduvanjeto na Makedonija.* Skoplje, Koco Racin, 1953.

Apostolski, Mihailo, Aleksandar Hristov, and Ratislav Terzioski. "Položaj okupirane Makedonije u Drugom svetskom ratu," *Jugoslovenski Istorijski Časopis,* No. 3 (1963), pp. 43–71.

Armstrong, Hamilton Fish. *Tito and Goliath.* New York, Macmillan, 1951.

"Autonomne pokrajine," *Jugoslovenski Pregled,* VIII (Nov., 1964), 425–34.
Avakumović, Ivan. *History of the Communist Party of Yugoslavia.* Aberdeen, Aberdeen University Press, 1964.
Babić, M. "Problem statističkog ispitavanja narodnosne pripadnosti stanovništva," *Statistička Revija,* IV (1954), 385–89.
Baerlein, Henry. *The Birth of Yugoslavia.* 2 vols. London, Leonard Parsons, 1922.
Bakarić, Vladimir. "Hrvatska u Jugoslaviji," *NIN,* March 8, 1964, pp. 2–3.
—— "Nešto o nacionalnoj vitalnosti Hrvata u ovom ratu," *Nova Jugoslavia,* No. 2 (March 15, 1944), pp. 17–19.
Barker, Elisabeth. *Macedonia: Its Place in Balkan Politics.* London, Royal Institute of International Affairs, 1950.
Barker, Thomas M. *The Slovenes of Carinthia: A National Minority Problem.* Washington, D.C., Studia Slovenica, 1960.
—— "The Croatian Minority of Burgenland," *Journal of Central European Affairs,* XIX (April, 1959), 32–56.
Bauer, Otto. *Die Nationalitatenfrage und die Sozialdemokratie.* 2d ed. Vienna, Verlag der Wiener Volksbuchhandlung, 1924.
Beard, Charles, and George Radin. *The Balkan Pivot: Yugoslavia.* New York, Macmillan, 1929.
Bićanić, Rudolf. "Ekonomska podloga hrvatskog pitanja." Zagreb, mimeographed, 1938.
—— "O monocentričnom i policentričnom planiranju," *Ekonomski Pregled,* XIV, No. 6–7, 469–527.
Bogdanov, Vaso. *Historijska uloga društvenih klasa u rješavanju južno-slovenskog nacionalnog pitanja.* Subotica, Minerva, 1956.
—— *Porijeklo i ciljevi šovinističkih teza o držanju Hrvata 1941.* Zagreb, Historijski institut Jugoslovenske akademije, 1961.
Boshkovich, B. [Filip Filipović]. *Krestianskoe dvizhenie i natsionalni vopros v Jugoslavii.* Moscow, Mezhdunarodni Agrarni Institut, 1929.
—— "Natsionalni vopros i raboche-krestianskii soiuz v Jugoslavii," *Krestianskii Internatsional,* No. 7–9 (Sept.–Oct., 1924), pp. 43–53.
Brailsford, H. N. *Macedonia: Its Races and Their Future.* London, Methuen and Co., 1906.
Brajović, Petar, ed. *Hercegovina u NOB.* Belgrade, Vojno delo, 1961.
Brashich, Branko. *Land Reform and Ownership in Yugoslavia, 1919–1953.* New York, Mid-European Studies Center, 1954.
Brkić, Husein,. "Ispravka jednog dokumenta u knjizi 'Magnem krimen' od V. Novaka," *Glasnik Vrhovnog Islamskog Starješinstva,* I, No. 4–6 (April–June, 1960), 126–33.
Bučar, Vekoslav. *Politička istorija Slovenačke.* Belgrade, Politika, 1939.
"Bugarska okupacija Makedonije i kratak pregled razvoja Nardnooslobodi-

lačke borbe u Makedoniji do novembra 1943 godina," *Vojno-istoriski Glasnik,* I (April, 1950), 7–49.

Bulgarskata Komunisticheska Partiia v rezoliutsii i resheniia. Vol. IV: *1944–1955.* Sofia, Bulgarskata Komunisticheska Partiia, 1957.

Burks, R. V. *The Dynamics of Communism in Eastern Europe.* Princeton, Princeton University Press, 1961.

Četrdeset godina: Zbornik sećanja aktivista jugoslovenskog revolucionarnog radničkog pokreta. 4 vols. Belgrade, Kultura, 1960.

Chmelar, Josef. *Die nationalen Minderheiten in Mitteleuropa.* Prague, 1937.

Christides, Christopher J. *The Macedonian Camouflage in the Light of Facts and Figures.* Athens, Hellenic Publishing House, 1949.

Ciliga, Anton. *The Russian Enigma.* London, Butler and Tanner, 1940.

—— "Nacionalizam i komunizam u hrvatskosrpskom sporu," *Hrvatska Revija,* IV (Dec., 1951), 365–96.

—— "O Rusiji i Južnim Slovenima," *Nova Evropa,* XXXIII (May 26, 1940), 140–44.

Clissold, Stephen. *Whirlwind: An Account of Marshal Tito's Rise to Power.* New York, Philosophical Library, 1949.

Čolaković, Rodoljub. "Rešenje nacionalnog pitanja u Jugoslaviji," *Komunist,* No. 4–5 (July–Sept., 1950), pp. 48–87.

Ćorović, Vladimir. *Istorija Jugoslavije.* Zagreb, Narodno delo, 1933.

—— *Političke prilike u Bosni i Hercegovini.* Belgrade, Politika, 1939.

Crvenkovski, Krste. "Treba se upornije i sistematskije boriti za sprovodjenje pisma CK SKJ u delo," *Komunist,* No. 9 (Sept., 1953), pp. 653–59.

Ćuković, Mirko. *Srbija u Narodnooslobodilačkoj borbi: Sandžak.* Belgrade, Nolit, 1964.

Čulinović, Ferdo. *Nacionalno pitanje u jugoslovenskim zemljama.* Zagreb, Novi list, 1955.

—— *Razvitak jugoslovenskog federalizma.* Zagreb, Školska Knjiga, 1952.

—— *Stvaranje nove Jugoslavenske države.* Zagreb, Grafički Zavod Hrvatske, 1959.

—— "Problemi o višedržavnosti jugoslovenske federacije," *Zbornik Pravnog Fakulteta u Zagrebu,* V, No. 3–4 (1955), 119–33.

—— "Srbi u Hrvatskoj," *Naprijed,* No. 35 (Aug. 22, 1952), p. 3.

Cvijić, Jovan. *Balkansko poluostrvo i južnoslovenske zemlje.* Vol. II: *Psihičke osobine Južnih Slovena.* Belgrade, Državna Štamparija, 1922.

Davičo, Oskar. "Levantinstvo; recidiv zla," *Svedočanstvo,* May 6, 1952, p. 8.

Dedijer, Vladimir. *Jugoslovensko-Albanski odnosi (1939–1948).* Belgrade, Borba, 1949.

—— *Tito.* New York, Simon and Schuster, 1953.

—— "Organizacije 'Ujedinjenje ili smrt' u svetlosti istoriske istine," *Nova Misao,* I, No. 7 (July, 1953), 115–23.

Demokratska Federativna Jugoslavija. Državna komisija za utvrdjivanje zločina okupatora i njihovih pomagača. *Saopštenja o zločinima okupatora i njihovih pomagača.* Nos. 1–93. Belgrade, Državna Štamparija, 1944–46.

Dimitrije Ljotić u revoluciji i ratu. Munich, Iskra, 1961.

Dimitrijević, Sergije, *et al.* eds. *Iz istorije Jugoslavije: 1918–1945.* Belgrade, Nolit, 1958.

Dimitrov, Evgeni. "Karakter federativnih odnosa u našoj zemlji," *Anali Pravnog Fakulteta u Beogradu,* I, No. 3–4 (1953), 277-86.

Dimitrov, Georgi. *Political Report: V Congress of the Bulgarian Communist Party.* Sofia, Press Department of the Ministry of Foreign Affairs, 1949.

Djilas, Milovan. *Članci, 1941–1946.* 1st ed. Belgrade, Kultura, 1947.

—— *Conversations with Stalin.* New York, Harcourt, Brace, and World, 1962.

—— *The New Class: An Analysis of the Communist System.* New York, F. A. Praeger, 1957.

—— "O nacionalnoj istoriji kao vaspitnom predmetu," *Komunist,* No. 1 (Jan., 1949), pp. 57–82.

Djordjević, Jovan. *Političko i državno uredjenje Federativne Narodne Republike Jugoslavije.* Belgrade, Udruženje pravnika Jugoslavije, 1954.

—— *Ustavno pravo,* 1st ed. Belgrade, 1947. 2d ed. Belgrade, Izdavačko preduzeće PIT, 1953.

—— *Ustavno pravo: Drugo dopunjeno izdanje.* Belgrade, Savremena Administracija, 1958.

—— "Federativna Jugoslavija i njen značaj," *Arhiv,* No. 1–2 (May-June, 1945), pp. 18–30.

Djordjevic, Tihomir. *Macedonia.* London, G. Allen and Unwin, 1918.

Djurdjević, Čedomir. *Komunistička partija Jugoslavije, 1937–1941.* Belgrade, Rad, 1959.

Djurić, Vladimir P. "Geografski raspored novog kolonizovanog stanovništva u Vojvodini," *Glasnik Etnografskog instituta Srpske akademije nauka,* Book II–III (1953–54), pp. 737–47.

Dokumenti od sozdavenjeto i razvitokot na N. R. Makedonija (1941–1946). Skoplje, Državno knigoizdatelstvo na NR Makedonija, 1949.

Domazetović, B. *Revolucija u Crnoj Gori.* Belgrade, 1944.

"Doprinos nerazvijenim oblastima," *Ekonomska Politika,* Oct. 7, 1954, pp. 801–4.

Dragnich, Alex N. *Tito's Promised Land, Yugoslavia.* New Brunswick, N.J., Rutgers University Press, 1954.

Drusković, Drago. "Društvena uloga nacije," *Danas,* March 28, 1962, p. 7.

Društveni plan privrednog razvoja Jugoslavije, 1957–1961. Belgrade, Kultura, 1957.

Društveni plan privrednog razvoja Jugoslavije, 1961–1965. Belgrade, Kultura, 1961.

Ekonomska Politika. Belgrade, 1951– .

La Fédération Balkanique. Vienna, 1924–31.

Federativna Narodna Republika Jugoslavije. Savezni Zavod za Statistiku. *Konačni resultati popisa stanovništva od 15 marta 1948 godine.* Vol. IX: *Stanovništvo po narodnosti.* Belgrade, Savezni Zavod za Statistiku, 1954.

Filipović, Filip. *Izabrani Spisi.* 2 vols. Belgrade, Kultura, 1962.

—— *See also* B. Boshkovich.

Fisher, Jack C. *Yugoslavia: A Multi-National State.* San Francisco, Chandler Publishing Co., 1966.

Fotitch, Constantine. *The War We Lost: Yugoslavia's Tragedy and the Failure of the West.* New York, Viking Press, 1948.

Frankel, Joseph. "Communism and the National Question in Yugoslavia," *Journal of Central European Affairs,* XV, (April, 1955), 49–65.

—— "Federalism in Yugoslavia," *American Political Science Review,* XLIX, No. 2 (June, 1955), 416–30.

Gavrić, Milan. "O nacionalnom pitanju i Sovjetskom revizionizmu," *Medjunarodni Problemi,* II, No. 6 (Nov.–Dec., 1950), 3–29.

Geršković, Leon. *Državna uprava Jugoslavije.* Belgrade, Izdavačko preduzeće PTT, 1956.

—— *Historija narodne vlasti.* Belgrade, Savremena Administracija, 1957.

—— "Neki problemi organizacije saveznih i republikanskih organa državne uprave," *Narodna Država,* II, No. 8–9 (Aug.–Sept., 1958), 18–34.

—— "O takozvanoj vertikalnoj povezanosti," *Nova Administracija,* III, No. 6 (Nov., 1955), 537–77.

—— ed. *Dokumenti o razvoju narodne vlasti.* Belgrade, Prosveta, 1948.

Gjankovic, Dan. "O federativnom karakteru naše države," *Zbornik Pravnog Fakulteta u Zagrebu,* IV (1954), 230–34.

Glasnik Vrhovnog Islamskog Starještinstva u Federativnoj Narodnoj Republici Jugoslavije. Sarajevo, 1950– .

Glavna politička uprava Jugoslovenke armije. *O Sofiskom procesu.* Belgrade, JNA Glavna politička uprava, 1950.

——*Stvaranje i razvoj Jugoslovenske armije.* Belgrade, JNA Glavna politička uprava, 1951.

Hadžić, Milos, ed. *Vojvodina, 1944–1954.* Novi Sad. Matica Srpska, 1954.

Hasanagić, Edib, ed. *Komunistička partija Jugoslavije, 1919–1941: Izabrani dokumenti.* Zagreb, Školska Knjiga, 1959.

Historijsko odeljenje Centralnog komiteta KPH. *Dokumenti historije Komunističke partije Hrvatske: "Naprijed" 1943.* Zagreb, Štamparski zavod Ognjen Prica, 1951.

Hoptner, J. B. *Yugoslavia in Crisis, 1934–1941.* New York, Columbia University Press, 1962.

Horvat, J., and Z. Stambuk, eds. *Dokumenti o protivnarodnom radu jednog dijela katoličkog klera.* Zagreb, Štamparija Rozankowski, 1946.

Horvat, Josip. *Politička povijest Hrvatske: 1918–1929.* Zagreb, Tipografija, 1938.

Industrijata vo NR Makedonija. Skoplje, Ekonomski institut, 1961.

Informativni Priručnik o Jugoslaviji. Belgrade, 1948–50.

Institut za nacionalna istorija. *Zbornik na dokumenti od Anti-fašističkoto sobranie na narodnoto osloboduvanje na Makedonija—ASNOM.* Skoplje, Institut za nacionalna istorija, 1964.

"Investment in Economic Development in Yugoslavia," *Vesnik Jugoslovenske banke—Special Supplement.* Belgrade, March, 1958.

Istina o ekonomskoj podlozi hrvatskog pitanja. Belgrade, Sloboda, 1940.

Istorijsko odelenje Centralnog komiteta KPJ. *Istorijski arhiv Komunističke partije Jugoslavije.* Vol. I, Book 1: *"Borba," 1941;* Book 2: *"Borba," 1942–1943.* Belgrade, Kultura, 1949.

—— *Istorijski arhiv Komunističke partije Jugoslavije.* Vol. II: *Kongresi i zemaljske konferencije KPJ 1919–1937.* Belgrade, Kultura, 1949.

—— *Istorijski arhiv Komunističke partije Jugoslavije.* Vol. III: *Socialistički pokret u Srbiji: 1900–1919.* Belgrade, Kultura, 1950.

—— *Istorijski arhiv Komunističke partije Jugoslavije.* Vol. IV: *Socijalistički pokret u Hrvatskoj i Slavoniji Dalmaciji i Istri 1892–1919.* Belgrade, Kultura, 1950.

—— *Istorijski arhiv Komunističke partije Jugoslavije.* Vol. V: *Socialistično gibanje v Sloveniji 1869–1920.* Belgrade, Kultura, 1951.

—— *Istorijski arhiv Komunističke partije Jugoslavije.* Vol. VI: *Socijalistički pokret u Bosnii, Vojvodini i Makedoniji,* Belgrade, Kultura, 1951.

Istorisko odelenie pri Centralniot Komitet na KPM. *Istoriski arhiv na Komunističkata partija na Makedonija.* Vol. I: *Odbrani materijali od "Socijalistička Zora" za 1920.* Skoplje, Kultura, 1951.

Istorisko odelenje Centralnog komiteta Komunističke partije Bosne i Hercegovine. *Arhiv Komunističke partije Bosne i Hercegovine.* Vol. II, Book 1: *Rad Komunističke partije u Bosni i Hercegovini 1941 godina.* Sarajevo, Veselin Masleša, 1951.

Istra i slovensko primorje. Belgrade, Rad, 1952.

Izdajnik i ratni zločinac Draža Mihailović pred sudom: Stenografske beleške i dokumenti sa sudjenja Dragoljubu Draži Mihailoviću. Belgrade, Državna Štamparija, 1946.

"Izjava Komunistične Stranke Jugoslavije, Komunistične Stranke Italije i Komunistične Stranke Austrije k Slovenskemu vprašanju," *Delo* (Ljubljana), XVII (July, 1948), 66.

Jackson, George D., Jr. *Comintern and Peasant in East Europe, 1919–1930.* New York, Columbia University Press, 1966.

Jareb, Jere. *Pola stoljeća Hrvatske politike: Povodom Mačekove autobiografije.* Buenos Aires, Knjižnica Hrvatske Revije, 1960.

Jedinstvo. Priština, 1945– .

Jelavich, Charles. "Serbian Nationalism and the Question of Union with Croatia in the Nineteenth Century," *Balkan Studies,* V (1962), 29–42.

Johnson, Chalmers A. *Peasant Nationalism and Communist Power: The Emergence of Revolutionary China, 1937–1945.* Stanford, Stanford University Press, 1962.

Jončić, Koča. *Nacionalne manjine u Jugoslaviji.* Belgrade, Savremena Administracija, 1962.

Jovanovič, Aleksa, ed. *Spomenica dvadesetpetogodišnice oslobodjenja Južne Srbije: 1912–1937.* Skoplje, "Južna Srbija," 1937.

Jovanović, Batrić. *Komunistička partija Jugoslavije u Crnoj Gori, 1919–1941.* Belgrade, Vojno Delo, 1959.

Jovanović, Blažo. *Izveštaj o političkom radu Pokrajinskog komiteta Komunističke partije Jugoslavije za Crnu Goru.* Cetinje, Pobjeda, 1948.

Jovanović, Slobodan. *Sabrana dela.* Vol. III, Book 2: *Političke i pravne rasprave.* Belgrade, Gece Kona, 1932.

—— *Ustavno pravo Kraljevine Srba Hrvata i Slovenaca.* Belgrade, Gece Kona, 1924.

Jugoslovenski Pregled. Belgrade, 1957– .

Jugowitsch, Pawao. "Sozialismus und Kommunismus in Jugoslawien," *Die Neue Zeit,* XXXVIII (1920), 559–66.

Kabakchiev, Kh. "Kompartiia Bolgarii i natsionalnyi vopros na Balkanakh," *Kommunisticheskii Internatsional,* No. 13 (May, 1934), pp. 44–50.

Kann, R. A. *The Multi-national Empire.* 2 vols. New York, Columbia University Press, 1950.

Karapandžić, Boris M. *Gradjanski rat u Srbiji, 1941–1945.* Munich, Buchdrückerei Dr. Peter Belej, 1958.

—— *Kočevje, Titov najkrvaviji zločin.* Cleveland, 1959.

Kardelj, Edvard. *O osnovama društvenog i političkog uredjenja FNRJ-a.* Belgrade, Kultura, 1953.

—— *Put nove Jugoslavije.* Belgrade, Kultura, 1946.

—— [Sperans]. *Razvoj Slovenačkog nacionalnog pitanja.* 2d ed. Belgrade, Kultura, 1958.

—— "O nekim nedostacima u radu Komunista," *Komunist,* No. 4 (1955), pp. 155–70.

—— "Naša državna uprava u novim uslovima," *Nova Administracija,* III, No. 2 (March-April, 1955), 129–33.

Kerner, Robert J., ed. *Yugoslavia.* Berkeley, University of California Press, 1949.

Kirovski, Pančе. *Teritorijalnata razmestenost na proizvodstvoto i regionalniot razvoj na Jugoslavija.* Skoplje, 1964.

Knežević, Radoje, ed. *Knjiga o Draži.* Vol. I: 1941–1943. Windsor, Canada, Avala Printing and Publishing Co., 1956.

Kofos, Evangelos. *Nationalism and Communism in Macedonia.* Thessalonica, Institute for Balkan Studies, 1964.

—— "The Making of Yugoslavia's Peoples Republic of Macedonia," *Balkan Studies,* III (1962), 375–96.

Kohn, Hans. *Nationalism: A Study in Its Origins and Background.* New York, Macmillan, 1944.

Ko je ko u Jugoslaviji. 1st ed. Belgrade, Sedme Sile, 1957.

Koliševski, Lazar. *Istorija, stvarnost, aspiracii.* Skoplje, Kultura, 1959.

—— *Macedonian National Question.* Belgrade, "Jugoslavija," 1959.

Kommunisticheskii Internatsional. Moscow, 1919–43.

Komunist. Belgrade. (*Komunist* appeared irregularly during World War II. Between 1946 and May, 1957, it appeared as a journal. After May, 1957, it appeared as a bimonthly newspaper. Between 1949 and 1953 it was issued at the same time as *Partiska Izgradnja,* which was also known as *Komunist.*)

Koneski, Blaže. *Gramatika na makedonskiot literaturen jazik.* Skoplje, Državno knigoizdatelstvo na NR Makedonija, 1952.

—— *Po povod najnoviot napad na našiot jazik.* Skoplje, Zemskiot odbor na Nar. front na Makedonija, 1948.

Korać, Vitomir. *Povjest radničkog pokreta u Hrvatskoj i Slavoniji od prvih početaka do ukidanja ovih pokrajina 1922 godine.* 3 vols. Zagreb, Radnička Komora za Hrvatsku, 1929–33.

Korbel, Josef. *Tito's Communism.* Denver, University of Denver Press, 1951.

K'osev, Dino G. *Borbite na Makedonskiia narod na osvobozhdenie.* Sofia, Narodna prosveta, 1950.

—— *Makedonskiiat vupros i Titovata klika.* Sofia, Tsentralen komitet na Makedonskite kulturnoprosvetni druzhestva v Bulgariia, August, 1949.

Kostić, Lazo M. *Sporni predeli Srba i Hrvata.* Chicago, American Institute for Balkan Affairs, 1957.

Kousoulas, Dimitrios. *The Price of Freedom: Greece in World Affairs.* Syracuse, Syracuse University Press, 1953.

—— *Revolution and Defeat: The Story of the Greek Communist Party.* London, Oxford University Press, 1965.

Kovač, Pavel. *O razvitku organizacije upravljanja privredom u FNRJ.* Belgrade, Rad, 1951.

KPJ i makedonskoto nacionalno prašanje. Skoplje, Kultura, 1949.

Krajger, Boris. "O nesoglasjih ob slovenskem narodnem vprašanju," *Delo* (Ljubljana), XVII (Oct., 1948), 11–42.

Krbek, Ivo. *Narodna Republika Hrvatska u Federativnoj Narodnoj Republici Jugoslaviji.* Zagreb, 1948.

Krizman, Bogdan. "Stvaranje jugoslavenske države," *Pregled,* X, No. 11–12 (Nov.-Dec., 1958), 333–54.

Krleža, Miroslav. *Deset krvavih godina i drugi politički eseji.* Zagreb, Zora, 1957.

—— "Na grobu Petra Dobrivoica," *Svedočanstvo*, No. 1 (March 22, 1952), pp. 1–2.

Krstić, Djordjo. *Kolonizacija u Južnoj Srbiji.* Sarajevo, Bosanka Pošta, 1928.

Kubović, Branko. *Regionalni aspekt privrednog razvitka Jugoslavije.* Zagreb, Časopis Ekonomski Pregled, 1961.

Lapčević, Dragiša. *Istorija socijalizma u Srbiji.* Belgrade, Gece Kona, 1922.

—— *Rat i srpska socijalna demokratija.* Belgrade, Štampa "Tucović," 1925.

The Law on the Five Year Plan for the Development of the National Economy of the Federal Peoples Republic of Yugoslavia in the Period from 1947 to 1951. Belgrade, Office of Information, 1947.

Lazić, Branko. *Tito et la Révolution Yougoslave.* Paris, Fasquelles, 1957.

Lekić, Radovan. *Andrijevički srez 1941–1944.* Cetinje, Obod, 1961.

Livadić, Stjepan. *Politički eseji.* Zagreb, Grafika, 1937.

Lizac, Andrija-Ljubomir. "Deportacija Srba iz Hrvatske, 1941," *Historijski Zbornik*, IX, No. 1–4 (1956), 125–45.

Lowenthal, Zdenko, ed. *The Crimes of the Fascist Occupants and Their Collaborators Against the Jews in Yugoslavia.* Belgrade, Federation of Jewish Communities of the Federative Peoples Republics of Yugoslavia, 1957.

Lukić, Radomir. "O nekim pitanjima iz oblasti teorije države i prava," *Anali Pravnog Fakulteta u Beogradu,* III (1955), 57–60.

Lunt, Horace G. *Grammar of the Macedonian Literary Language.* Skoplje, Državno knigoizdatelstvo na NR Makedonija, 1952.

—— "A Survey of Macedonian Literature," *Harvard Slavic Studies,* I (1953), 363–96.

Maček, Vladko. *In the Struggle for Freedom.* New York, Robert Speller, 1957.

Maclean, Fitzroy. *Eastern Approaches.* London, Jonathan Cape, 1949.

McVicker, Charles P. *Titoism: Pattern for International Communism.* New York, St. Martins, 1957.

Marinko, Miha. *Politički izveštaj CK KPS na II kongresu Komunističke Partije Slovenije.* Zagreb, Kultura, 1950.

Marjanović, Jovan. *Nastanak i razvitak radničkog pokreta u Jugoslovenskim zemljama do prvog svetskog rata.* Belgrade, Rad, 1954.

—— *Potsetnik iz istorije Komunističke partije Jugoslavije (1919–1941).* Belgrade, Rad, 1953.

—— *Srbija u Narodnooslobodilačkoj borbi.* Belgrade, Nolit-Prosveta, 1964.

—— "Politika KPJ u nacionalnom pitanju," *Komunist,* April 16, 1959, p. 6.

—— "Prilog uzučavanju jugoslovenstva u ustanku 1941," *Jugoslovenski Istorijski Časopis,* I, No. 1 (1962), 33–45.

Markert, Werner, ed. *Osteuropa Handbuch Jugoslawien.* Cologne-Graz, Bohlau Verlag, 1954.

Markham, R. H. *Tito's Imperial Communism.* Chapel Hill, University of North Carolina Press, 1947.

Marković, Lazar. *Jugoslovenska država i hrvatsko pitanje.* Belgrade, Gece Kona, 1935.

Marković, Moma, and Ivan Lača, *Organizacioni razvitak Komunističke partije Jugoslavije (SKJ).* Belgrade, Kultura, 1960.

Marković, Sima, *Der Kommunismus in Jugoslawien.* Hamburg, Verlag der Kommunistischen Internationale, 1922.

—— *Nacionalno pitanje u svetlosti Marksizma.* Belgrade, Narodna Misao, 1923.

—— *Ustavno pitanje i radnička klasa Jugoslavije.* Belgrade, Narodna Misao, 1923.

—— *See also* M. Semić.

Martin, David. *Ally Betrayed: The Uncensored Story of Tito and Mihailović.* New York, Prentice-Hall, 1946.

Martulkov, Alekso. *Moeto učestvo vo revolutsionarnite borbi na Makedonija.* Skoplje, Institut za nacionalna istorija, 1954.

"Materijali CK KPJ iz predratnog perioda," *Komunist,* No. 2 (Jan., 1947), pp. 70–100.

"Materijali pete konferencije KPJ održane novembra 1940 u Zagrebu," *Komunist,* No. 1 (Oct., 1946), pp. 59–122.

Mauer, Gilbert in der. *Die Jugoslawen Einst and Jetzt.* Vol. III: *Der Weg zur Nation.* Berlin, Payer and Co., 1938.

Mihailov, V. [Macedonius]. *Stalin and the Macedonian Question.* St. Louis, Pearlstone Publishing Co., 1948.

Mikuž, Metod. *Pregled razvoja NOB u Sloveniji.* Belgrade, Vojnoizdavački zavod JNA, 1956.

Milatović, Mile. *Slučaj Andrije Hebranga.* Belgrade, Kultura, 1952.

Miljovski, Kiro. *Za nekon prašanje od rabota nad našata nacionalna istorija.* Skoplje, Kultura, 1950.

Milković, Mita. "O položaju nacionalnih manjina u Narodnoj Republici Srbiji," *Crvena Zastava* (Belgrade), I (Oct., 1948), 29-42.

Milosavljević, J. Z. *Srpsko-Hrvatski spor i neimari Jugoslavije.* Belgrade, 1938.

Ministry of Foreign Affairs of the Federal People's Republic of Yugoslavia. *White Book on Aggressive Activities by the Governments of the USSR, Poland, Czechoslovakia, Hungary, Rumania, Bulgaria and Albania Towards Yugoslavia.* Belgrade, Ministry of Foreign Affairs, 1951.

Mirchev, K. *Za Makedonskiia literaturan ezik.* Sofia, 1952.

Mitrev, Dimitar. *BKP i Pirinska Makedonija.* Skoplje, Kultura, 1960.

Mittleman, Earl Neal. "The Nationality Problem in Yugoslavia: A Survey of Developments, 1921–1953." Unpublished Ph.D. dissertation, New York University, 1954.

Mojsov, Lazar. *Bugarska Radnička Partija (Komunista) i makedonsko nacionalno pitanje.* Belgrade, Borba, 1948.

—— "O južnoslovenskoj federaciji," *Komunist,* No. 4–5 (July-Sept., 1950), pp. 183–218.

Mosely, Philip. *The Kremlin and World Politics.* New York, Vintage Books, 1960.

Mugoša, Andrija. *Izveštaj o organizacionom radu Pokrajinskog komiteta Komunističke partije Jugoslavije za Crnu Goru.* Cetinje, Pobjeda, 1948.

Narodna Skupština FNRJ. *Ustavotvorni odbori Savezne skupštine i skupštine naroda.* Belgrade, n.d.

Narodna Skupština Narodne Republike Srbije. *Zasedanje Velike antifašističke narodnooslobodilačke skupštine Srbije (9–12 novembra 1944).* Belgrade, n.d.

—— *Zasedanja antifašističke skupštine narodnog oslobodjenja Srbije i Narodne skupštine Srbije (7–9 aprila 1945 i 26–27 juli 1946).* Belgrade, n.d.

Narodna vlada Hrvatske formirana u gradu Splitu dana 14 travnja 1945. Zagreb, 1945.

Naša Stvarnost. Belgrade, 1946– .

Neal, Fred Warner. *Titoism in Action: The Reforms in Yugoslavia.* Berkeley, University of California Press, 1958.

—— "The Communist Party of Yugoslavia," *American Political Science Review,* LI, No. 1 (March, 1957), 88–111.

Nikitović, Časlav. "Komunistička partija Jugoslavije." New York, typewritten, 1954.

Nikolić, Miodrag. *Kosovo i Metohija: Pregled društvenog ekonomskog razvitka.* Belgrade, "Sedma Sila," 1963.

Nikolov, Kiril. *Za Makedonskata nacija.* Skoplje, Zemski odbor na Narodniot front na Makedonija, 1948.

Nova Doba. Sarajevo, 1945–46.

Nova Makedonija. Skoplje, 1944– .

Novak, Antun. *I Served Tito.* Prague, Orbis, 1951.

Novak, Viktor. *Antologija jugoslovenske misli i narodnog jedinstva.* Belgrade, Državna Štamparija, 1930.

—— *Magnem krimen.* Zagreb, Nakladni Zavod, 1948.

Novi ustav: Ustavni zakon od 13-1-1953 i ustav od 31-1-1946 (delovi koji nisu ukinuti). Belgrade, Službeni List, 1953.

O kontrarevolucionarnoj i klevetničkoj kampanji protiv socialističke Jugoslavije. Belgrade, Borba, 1949.

"O narednim zadacima Saveza komunista u borbi za otklanjanje negativnih pojava u političkom, privednom i drustvenom životu, kao i za otklanjanje slabosti u radu Saveza komunista," *Komunist,* Feb. 28, 1958, pp. 1–2.

Organdžieva, Cveta. "Po povod statijata od M. Djilas 'Dvostruka uloga Prof. Nedelković-a,' " *Sovremenost* [Skoplje], IV, No. 6 (1954), 449–61.

Oslobodjenje. Sarajevo, 1943– .

Ostović, P. D. *The Truth about Yugoslavia.* New York, Roy Publishers, 1952.

Pattee, Richard. *The Case of Cardinal Aloysius Stepinac.* Milwaukee, Bruce Publishing Co., 1953.

Paris, Edmond. *Genocide in Satellite Croatia, 1941–1945.* Chicago, American Institute for Balkan Affairs, n.d.

Pavelić, Ante. *Die Kroatische Frage.* Berlin, Des Instituts für Grenz und Auslandstudien, 1941.

Pejanović, Djordje. *Stanovništvo Bosne i Hercegovine.* Belgrade, Naučna Kniga, 1955.

Pejov, Naum. *Prilozi za odnosot na rakovoditelite na KPG po Makedonskoto nacionalno prašanje.* Skoplje, Glaven odbor na Makedoncite od Egejska Makedonija, 1953.

Petrović, Vojislav. *Razvitak privrednog sistema FNRJ posmatran kroz pravne propise.* 4 vols. Belgrade, Ekonomski institut FNRJ, 1954–57.

Pijade, Moša. *Balanced Representation in a Multi-National State.* London, 1950.

—— *Izabrani govori i članci, 1941–1947.* 1st ed. Belgrade, Kultura, 1948.

Pilar, Ivo. *Južno-slovensko pitanje.* Zagreb, Matica Hrvatska, 1944.

Pirinsko Delo. Blagoevgrad, 1946–49 (?).

Plenča, Dušan. *Medjunarodni odnosi Jugoslavije u toku drugog svetskog rata.* Belgrade, Institut Društvenih Nauka, 1962.

Politika. Belgrade, 1904– .

Popović, Milentije. *Jedinstvo privrednog sistema samoupravlenje planiranje.* Belgrade, Komunist, 1963.

Popović, Stevo. "Nekoliko podataka o razvoju i delovanju NOO u Istočnoj Bosni u toku NO rata," *Godišnjak Istoriskog Društva Bosne-Hercegovine* (1951), pp. 181–209.

Popovski, Blagoj. *Špiuni vo odbrana na linijata na informbiroto i na BKP.* Skoplje, Združeneto na Novinarite od NR Makedonija, 1949.

Poulakos, Dimitrios. "The Balkan Communist Federation and the Macedonian Question." Unpublished Master's thesis, Columbia University, 1954.

Pravopis hrvatsko-srpskog književnog jezika s pravopisnim rječnikom. Zagreb, Novi Sad, Matica Hrvatska and Matica Srpska, 1960.

Pregled. Sarajevo, 1948——.

Pregled istorije Saveza komunista Jugoslavije. Belgrade, Institut za izučavanje radničkog pokreta, 1963.

Prezidium Narodne skupštine FNRJ. *Prvo i drugo zasedanje Antifašističkog veća narodnog oslobodjenja Jugoslavije.* Belgrade, Prezidium Narodne skupštine, n.d.

—— *Zakonodavni rad pretsedništva Antifašističkog veća narodnog oslobodjenja Jugoslavije i pretsedništva Privremene Narodne Skupštine DFJ (19 novembra 1944–27 oktobra 1945).* Belgrade, Prezidium Narodne skupštine, n.d.

Pribićević, Svetozar. *Diktatura kralja Aleksandra.* Belgrade, Prosveta, 1952.

—— "Narodno i državno jedinstvo," *Budućnost,* I No. 6 (March 15, 1922), 245–53.

Prica, Bogdan. *Hrvatsko pitanje i brojke.* Belgrade, 1937.

Privremena narodna skupština DFJ. *Rad zakonodavnih odbora pretsedništva Antifašističkog Veća Narodnog Oslobodjenja Jugoslavije i Privremene Narodne Skupštine DFJ (3 aprila–25 oktobra 1945).* Belgrade, n.d.

—— *Treće zasedanje Antifašističkog Veća Narodnog Oslobodjenja Jugo-—slavije i zasedanje Privremene Narodne Skupštine: Stenografske beleške (7–26 avgusta 1945).* Belgrade, n.d.

Problemi regionalnog privrednog razvoja: Zbornik radova. Belgrade, Savez Ekonomista Jugoslavije, 1962.

Protić, Stojan M. *O Makedoniji i Makedoncima.* 2d ed. Belgrade, "Skerlić," 1928.

Purivatra, Atif. "Prilog proučavanju koncepcije o nacionalnom 'opredjeljivanju' Bosanko-Hercegovačkih musimana," *Pregled,* XVI (Oct., 1964), 323–32.

Putevi sporazuma Srba i Hrvata. Belgrade, 1939.

Radošević, Mijo. *Marksizam, Panslavism i Jugoslovenstvo.* Zagreb, 1921.

Radovanović, Radomir. "Finansijski odnosi izmedju državnih organa." Unpublished Ph.D. dissertation, University of Belgrade, 1958.

Radulović, Monty. *Tito's Republic.* London, Coldharbour Press, 1948.

Ranković, Aleksander. *Izabrani govori i članci, 1941–1945.* Belgrade, Kultura, 1951.

—— "Problemi iz rada Saveza komunista," *Komunist,* No. 3–4 (1956), pp. 166–84.

Redžić, Enver. *Prilozi o nacionalnom pitanju.* Sarajevo, Svjetlost, 1963.

—— "Jedna teorija o nacionalnom razvitku Jugoslavije," *Pregled,* IX, No. 4 (April, 1957), 227–32.

— "Jedan prilog marksističkoj teoriji nacije," *Pregled,* X, No. 11–12 (Nov.-Dec., 1958), 355–66.

Referat druga Hasana Brkića održan na trećem sastanku plenuma Glavnog odbora muslimana 9–IX–1946. Sarajevo, Oslobedjenje, n.d.

Ribar, Ivan. *Politički zapisi.* Belgrade, Prosveta, 1948.

Ristić, Marko. "Da mržnje više ne bude," *Svedočanstvo,* April 19, 1952, p. 5.

Rothschild, Joseph. *The Communist Party of Bulgaria.* New York, Columbia University Press, 1959.

Royal Institute of International Affairs. *Chronology of International Events and Documents.* London, Royal Institute of International Affairs, June, 1945–Dec., 1955.

—— *Documents on International Affairs, 1947–1948.* London, Royal Institute of International affairs, 1952.

—— *The Soviet-Yugoslav Dispute*. London, Royal Institute of International affairs, 1948.

Saikowski, Charlotte. "Albania in Soviet Satellite Policy." Unpublished Master's thesis, Columbia University, 1954.

Savezni zavod za privredno planiranje. "Uporedni pregled privrednog razvitka narodnih republika 1947–1955." Belgrade, mimeographed, July 26, 1957.

"Schulwesen, Erwachsenbildung und Wissenschaftliche Einrichtung der Volksrepublic Mazedonien in Zahlen," *Wissenschaftlicher Dienst Südosteuropa*, III (1954), 242–44.

Selimović, Hilmo. "O nekim momentima iz politike razvoja privredno nedovoljno razvijenih područja," *Pregled*, XVI (Sept., 1964,) 239–43.

Semić, M. [Sima Markovic], "K natsionalnomu voprosu v Jugoslavii," *Bolshevik*, No. 11–12 (June 30, 1925), pp. 20–22.

Serbian Eastern Orthodox Diocese for the United States of America and Canada. *Martyrdom of the Serbs: Persecutions of the Serbian Orthodox Church and Massacre of the Serbian People*. Chicago, Palandech's Press, n.d.

Seton-Watson, Hugh. *The East European Revolution*. New York, Praeger, 1951.

Seton-Watson, R. W. *The Rise of Nationality in the Balkans*. London, Constable and Co., 1917.

—— *The Southern Slav Question and the Hapsburg Monarchy*. London, Constable and Co., 1917.

Shoup, Paul. "Problems of Party Reform in Yugoslavia," *American Slavic and East European Review*, XVIII, No. 3 (Oct., 1959), 334–50.

Sinadinovski, Jokim. "Sociološka istraživanja participacije i integracije šiptarske nacionalne manjine u Makedoniji," *Sociologija*, III (1961), 120–31.

Skendi, Stavro, ed. *Albania*, New York, F. A. Praeger, 1956.

Slijepčević, Djoko. *The Macedonian Question: The Struggle for South Serbia*. Munich, Buchdrükerei Dr. Peter Belej, 1958.

Službeni glasnik na Narodna Republika Makedonija, Skoplje, 1945– .

Službeni glasnik Narodne Republike Srbije. Belgrade, 1945– .

Službeni list Autonomne Kosovske Metohijske Oblasti. Pristina. 1948— .

Službeni list Demokratske Federativne Jugoslavije. Belgrade, 1945– .

Službeni list Federativne Narodne Republike Jugoslavije. Belgrade, 1946– .

Službeni list Narodne Republike Bosne i Hercegovine. Sarajevo, 1945– .

Smilevski, Vedeo. "Osvrt na razvoj Makedonskog nacionalnog pitanja," *Komunist*, No. 1 (Jan., 1950), pp. 81–116.

Šnuderlj, Maks. "O državnosti Narodne Republike Jugoslavije," *Anali Pravnog Fakulteta u Beogradu*, I, No. 3–4 (1953), 277–86.

Socijalizm. Belgrade, 1958– .

Srebrić, Borislav. "Problem metoda privrednog razvoja nerazvijenih krajeva Jugoslavije," *Ekonomist*, XVII (1964), 311–27.

Srpska Riječ. Zagreb, 1945– .

Stalin, Joseph. *Marxism and the National and Colonial Question.* Moscow, Co-operative Publishing Society of Foreign Workers in the USSR, 1935.

—— "Eshche raz k nacionalnomu voprosu," *Bolshevik,* No. 11–12 (June 30, 1925), pp. 23–29.

—— "K natsionalnomu voprosu v Jugoslavii," *Bolshevik,* No. 7 (April 15, 1925), pp. 20–23.

Statistički podaci organizacije Saveza komunista u NR Hrvatskoj za razdoblje od III do IV kongresa SKH. Zagreb, Vjesnik, Feb. 27, 1959.

Statistički podaci organizacije Saveza komunista Srbije od III do IV kongresa. Belgrade, Kultura, May, 1959.

Statut Autonomne Pokrajine Vojvodine u Narodnoj Republici Srbiji. Novi Sad, 1948.

Štedimlija, S. M. *Crna Gora u Jugoslaviji.* Zagreb, Politička Biblioteka, 1936.

Stefanović, Jovan. *Ustavno pravo FNR Jugoslavije i komparativno.* 1st ed. Zagreb, Nakladni Zavod Hrvatske, 1950. 2nd ed. 2 vols. Zagreb, Školska Knjiga, 1956.

—— "Primjena federativnog načela u saveznom ustavnom zakonu," *Anali Pravnog Fakulteta u Beogradu,* I, No. 3–4 (1953), 257–70.

Stojković, Ljubiša, and Miloš Martić. *Nacionalne manjine u Jugoslaviji.* Belgrade, Rad, 1953.

—— National Minorities in Yugoslavia. Belgrade, "Jugoslavia," 1952.

Strugar, Vlado. *Socijalna demokratija o nacionalnom pitanju Jugoslovenskih naroda.* Belgrade, Rad, 1956.

Sudjenje članovima političkog i vojnog rukovodstva organizacije Draže Mihailovića: Stenografske beleške. Belgrade, Prosveta, 1945.

Sudland, L. V. *Die Süd-Slawische Frage.* Vienna, Manzsche K.U.K. Hof-, Verlags—U. Universitats—Buchhandlung, 1918.

Supilo, Fran. *Politika u Hrvatskoj.* Zagreb, Kultura, 1953.

Svedočanstvo. Belgrade, 1953.

"Svim organizacijama Saveza komunista Jugoslavije," *Komunist,* No. 7 (July, 1953), pp. 430–31.

Swire, Joseph. *Bulgarian Conspiracy.* London, Robert Hale Ltd., 1939.

Tadić, Jorjo, ed. *Ten Years of Yugoslav Historiography.* National Committee for Historical Studies. Belgrade, "Yugoslavia," 1955.

Taylor, A. H. E. *The Future of the Southern Slavs.* London, T. F. Unwin, 1917.

Terzić, Velimir. *Jugoslavija u aprilskom ratu 1941.* Titograd, Grafički zavod, 1962.

Tito, Josip Broz. *Borba za oslobodjenje Jugoslavije 1941–1944.* 2d ed. Belgrade, Državni Izdavački Zavod Jugoslavije, 1945.

—— *Izgradnja nove Jugoslavije.* 4 vols. Belgrade, Kultura, 1946–52.

—— "Zur Lage in Jugoslawien," *Die Welt,* I (Nov. 30, 1939), 241–42.

Todorović, Mihailo, ed. *Srpski socijalistički pokret za vreme prvog svetskog rata.* Belgrade, Rad. 1958.

Tomasevich, Jozo. *Peasants, Politics and Economic Change in Yugoslavia.* Stanford, Stanford University Press, 1955.

Tomasič, D. A. *National Communism and Soviet Strategy.* Washington, D.C., Public Affairs Press, 1957.

—— *Politički razvitak Hrvata.* Zagreb, Hrvatske književne naklade, 1938.

—— "Nationality Problems and Partisan Yugoslavia," *Journal of Central European Affairs,* VI (July, 1946), 111–25.

—— "The New Class and Nationalism," *Journal of Croatian Studies,* I (1960), 53–74.

Topalović, Živko. *Pokreti narodnog otpora u Jugoslaviji, 1941–1945.* Paris, Jugoslavenskih Sindikalista, 1958.

Tosev, Drum. "Die mazedonische Schriftsprache," *Südost Forschungen,* XV (1956), 491–503.

Traikov, Peco. *Nationalizmut na skopskite rukovoditelie.* Sofia, 1949.

The Trial of Traïcho Kostov and His Group. Sofia, 1949.

Tucović, Dimitrije. *Izabrani Spisi.* Belgrade, Prosveta, 1949.

—— *Srbija i Arbanija: Jedan prilog kritici zavojevacke politike srpske buržoazije.* Belgrade, Kultura, 1946.

Tudjman, Franjo. *Stvaranje socijalističke Jugoslavije.* Zagreb, Naprijed, 1960.

—— *Uvod u historiju socijalističke Jugoslavije.* Zagreb. Privately bound, 1963. See also *Forum* (Zagreb), Nos. 2, 3, 4, 5, 6, 7, and 8, 1963, and No. 1–2, 1964.

Ulam, Adam. B. *Titoism and the Cominform.* Cambridge, Mass., Harvard University Press, 1952.

Uradni list Ljudske Republike Slovenije. Ljubljana, 1945– .

U.S. Department of State. "Macedonian Nationalism and the Communist Party of Yugoslavia." Washington, D.C., mimeographed, October 11, 1954.

Ustav FNRJ i ustavi narodnih republika. Belgrade, Službeni List, 1950.

Ustav Kraljevine Jugoslavije od 3 septembra 1931 god. Belgrade, Državna Štamparija, 1931.

Ustav Kraljevine Srba Hrvata i Slovenaca. Belgrade, Državna Štamparija, 1921.

Ustavotvorne skupstine, statistički pogled izbora narodnih poslanika. Belgrade, 1921.

Ustav Socijalističke Federativne Republike Jugoslavije sa ustavima socialističkih republike i statutima autonomnih pokrajina. Belgrade, Službeni List, 1963.

Uzunovski, Cvetko. "UDB-moken organ na našeta narodna revolucija," *Socialistička Zora,* I, No. 2 (March-April), 1–17.

Vasilev, Mitro H. *Majska Manifest i deklaracijata na UMRO (obedinena)*. Skoplje, 1948.

Vinsko, Ivo. "Regionalna procjena rasta fiksnih fondova Jugoslavije od 1946 do 1960," *Ekonomski Pregled*, XV (1964), 417–46.

Vjesnik. Zagreb. 1940– .

Vlahov, Dimitar. *Kroz historiju Makedonskog naroda: Zbirka članaka*. Zagreb, Slavenski Komitet, 1949.

Vojno-istoriski institut Jugoslovenske armije. *Oslobodilački rat naroda Jugoslavije: 1941–1945*. Vol. I. Belgrade, Vojnoistoriski Institut JNA, 1950.

—— *Pregled narodnooslobodilačkog rata u Makedoniji: 1941–1945*. Belgrade, Vojno-istoriski Institut JNA, 1950.

—— *Zbornik dokumenata i podataka o narodno-oslobodilačkom ratu jugoslovenskih naroda*. 7 vols. Belgrade, Vojno-istoriski institut JNA, 1949– .

Vukmanović-Tempo, Svetozar. "Aktuelnı privredno-politički problemi," *Komunist*, No. 7 (July, 1953), pp. 466–67.

—— "Komunistička partija Grčke i narodnooslobodilačka borba," *Komunist*, No. 6 (Nov., 1949), pp. 1–82.

Vukmirica, Vujo. "Savremena tehnika i razvoj nerazvijenih područja u našoj zemlji," *Naša Stvarnost*, VI (1963), 99–121.

Walling, William English. *The Socialists and the War*. New York, Henry Holt, 1915.

Wendel, Hermann. *Aus der Welt der Südslawen*. Berlin, J.H.W. Dietz, 1926.

—— *Der Kampf der Südslawen um Freiheit und Einheit*. Frankfurt, Frankfurter Societats-Druckerei GMBH, 1925.

—— "Marxism and the Southern Slav Question," *Slavonic Review*, II (Dec., 1923), 289–307.

Wilkinson, H. R. *Maps and Politics: A Review of Ethnographic Cartography of Macedonia*. Liverpool, University Press, 1951.

—— "Yugoslav Macedonia in Transition," *Geographical Journal*, CXVIII (Dec., 1952), 389–405.

Williams, Suzanne Somes. "The Communist Party of Yugoslavia and the Nationality Problem." Unpublished Master's thesis, Columbia University, 1955.

Wolff, Robert Lee. *The Balkans in Our Time*. 1st ed. Cambridge, Mass., Harvard University Press, 1956.

La Yougoslavie sous la terreur de la Clique Tito. Paris, SEDIO, SARL, Oct. 10, 1949.

"Zaključci Izvršnog komiteta CK SKJ o pitanjima nacionalnih manjina," *Komunist*, June 28, 1962, p. 8.

Zakon o državnoj upravi (sa uredbom o organizaciji i radu Saveznog izvršnog veća). Belgrade, Nova administracija, 1956.

Zakon o organima unutrašnjih poslova. Belgrade, Službeni List, 1956.

Zbornik na dokumenti ASNOM 1944–1946. Skoplje, Institut za nacionalna istorija, 1964.

Zdravkovski, P. "Nacionalnite malcinstva vo Narodna Republika Makedonija," *Socialisticka Zora,* I (Nov.-Dec., 1949), 49–53.

Zemski odbor na Narodniot front na Makedonija. *Procesot protiv Špionskoterorističkata organizacija "Judžel."* Skoplje, Zemski odbor na Narodniot front na Makedonija, 1948.

Ziherl, Boris. *Članci i rasprave.* Belgrade, Kultura, 1948.

—— *Komunizam i otadžbina.* Belgrade, Kultura, 1950.

Živančević, Mihailo. *Jugoslavija i federacija.* Belgrade, 1938.

Značenje drugog zasjedanja AVNOJa za socijalističku revoluciju u Jugoslaviji. Zagreb, Informator, 1963.

Zografski, D. *et. al. Egejska Makedonija vo našata istorija.* Skoplje, Ilinden, 1951.

—— *Za rabotničkoto dviženje vo Makedonija do balkanskata vojna.* Skoplje, Institut za nacionalna istorija na Makedonskiot narod, 1950.

Zotiades, George B. *The Macedonian Controversy.* Thessalonica, Society of Macedonian Studies, 1954.

Žujović, Sreten. *Članci o nacionalnom pitanju.* Požarevac, 1945.

Index